Early Film Culture in Hong Kong, Taiwan, and Republican China

Early Film Culture in Hong Kong, Taiwan, and Republican China

KALEIDOSCOPIC HISTORIES

Emilie Yueh-yu Yeh, editor

University of Michigan Press
Ann Arbor

Published in the United States of America by the
University of Michigan Press
Manufactured in the United States of America
♾ Printed on acid-free paper

2021 2020 2019 2018 4 3 2 1

A CIP catalog record for this book is available from the British Library.

Library of Congress Cataloging-in-Publication data has been applied for.

978-0-472-07372-6 (Hardcover : alk paper)
978-0-472-05372-8 (Paperback : alk paper)
978-0-472-12344-5 (ebook)

Acknowledgments

Many people were supportive of this publication and did their utmost to direct it toward completion. I would like to thank the twelve contributors for their trust and support. Without them, our knowledge of the early film culture would remain impoverished. Among outside supporters, I thank Nicole Huang for her valuable advice. Thanks also to Markus Nornes and Matthew Solomon for putting their hats into the ring. Mary Francis, the Editorial Director at the University of Michigan Press, guided this project from the beginning, and her editorial nous was essential for this work to get in shape. The anonymous readers' comments were incisive in refining individual chapters and reframing the book as a whole. Zhang Zhen's pioneering work in Shanghai cinema injected theoretical rigor to the studies of early film culture in East Asia. Poshek Fu's vision in reshaping Chinese film historiography opened many gates for new studies, including this one. Xiaocai Feng showed us how to craft exemplary historical research. David Bordwell, Michael Curtin, Melissa Curtin, Dudley Andrew, David Der-wei Wang, Chris Berry, Wenchi Lin, Isabelle Pei-tzu Wu, Sheldon Lu, Weihong Bao, Song-Yong Sing, Michael Berry, Shi Chuan, and Paul Katz offered their help, encouragement, and fellowship at various stages. I thank the Chiang Ching-kuo Foundation for International Scholarly Exchange, the Research Grants Council of Hong Kong Government, and Hong Kong Baptist University for their research support. I also want to thank my colleagues at the School of Communication for their friendship and help over the years. My research assistant Wai Ka Yan deserves special mention. Without her backing, this book would not be published on time. Four chapters in this volume were previously published in a special issue of the *Journal of Chinese Cinemas*. I thank the then-editor, Song Hwee Lim, for the opportunity. I thank Jenny Geyer and Mary Hashman at the University of Michigan Press for their care and help throughout the entire production. Most of all, I am indebted to my family in Taiwan, Hong Kong, and the United States. Their unfailing support has given me much-needed stamina and faith in my embarkation on early screen histories in this part of the world.

Emilie Yueh-yu Yeh
February 2017
Hong Kong

Contents

A Note on Transliteration and Translation ix

Introduction 1
Emilie Yueh-yu Yeh

Part I. Revising Historiography: Early Film Culture in Hong Kong, Taiwan, and Guangzhou

CHAPTER 1. Translating *Yingxi*: Chinese Film Genealogy and Early Cinema in Hong Kong 19
Emilie Yueh-yu Yeh

CHAPTER 2. Magic Lantern Shows and Screen Modernity in Colonial Taiwan 51
Laura Jo-Han Wen

CHAPTER 3. From an Imported Novelty to an Indigenized Practice: Hong Kong Cinema in the 1920s 71
Ting-yan Cheung and Pablo Sze-pang Tsoi

CHAPTER 4. Enlightenment, Propaganda, and Image Creation: A Descriptive Analysis of the Usage of Film by the Taiwan Education Society and the Colonial Government Before 1937 101
Daw-Ming Lee

CHAPTER 5. "Guangzhou Film" and Guangzhou Urban Culture: An Overview 134
Hui Liu, Shi-Yan Chao, and Richard Xiaying Xu

CHAPTER 6. The Way of *The Platinum Dragon*: Xue Juexian and the Sound of Politics in 1930s Cantonese Cinema 156
Kenny K. K. Ng

Part II. Intermediaries, Cinephiles, and Film Literati

CHAPTER 7. Toward the Opposite Side of "Vulgarity": The Birth of Cinema as a "Healthful Entertainment" and the Shanghai YMCA 179
Yoshino Sugawara

CHAPTER 8. Movie Matchmakers: The Intermediaries between Hollywood and China in the Early Twentieth Century 202
Yongchun Fu

CHAPTER 9. The Silver Star Group: A First Attempt at Theorizing *Wenyi* in the 1920s 223
Enoch Yee-lok Tam

CHAPTER 10. Forming the Movie Field: Film Literati in Republican China 244
Emilie Yueh-yu Yeh and Enoch Yee-lok Tam

CHAPTER 11. Rhythmic Movement, Metaphoric Sound, and Transcultural Transmediality: Liu Na'ou and *The Man Who Has a Camera* (1933) 277
Ling Zhang

Chinese and Japanese Glossary 303

Contributors 309

Bibliography 313

Index 345

A Note on Transliteration and Translation

Romanization of Chinese characters has become simpler in recent decades. For the most part, essays in this volume use the pinyin system to transliterate and render Chinese names, titles, places, and people. In some cases the authors provide additional Cantonese pronunciation for further specification. When filmmakers or authors refer to English renditions of their work, we usually follow that convention in subsequent references. This was a common convention during the Republican period, with many companies and political bodies adopting official English names. Several essays also use loanwords from Japanese, which are romanized in the usual Hepburn system.

Introduction

Emilie Yueh-yu Yeh

Studies on Chinese early cinema and its extended history in the Republican period (1911–1949) have trod a rocky path.[1] After the founding of the People's Republic in 1949, film historiography developed into a guarded field, even until today. In the immediate postwar time the term "Republican" was tainted by its attachment to the defeated Nationalist Party and its associated autocratic capitalism, corrupt bureaucracy, and dependence on foreign imperialist powers. Because of these negative associations, the notion of Republican cinema became suspect and was subject to monitoring and constraint, in the 1950s and after. The formerly "infamous" epoch was acknowledged as pivotal to the development of Chinese modernity when the censorious treatment of the Republican period relaxed in the twenty-first century. Subsequently, Republican history was reconstructed by many scholars as Shanghai history, given the city's unrivaled position (so-called Paris of the Orient) in early twentieth-century China. "Shanghai cinema" was then upheld as a synecdoche for cinema of the entire era as the city was then the country's center of film production, distribution, and exhibition. The term "Shanghai," despite its mythology (*qipao*, jazz, dance halls, intrigues, department stores, hippodrome, canidrome, dandies, motor cars, Ruan Lingyu, sultry Mandarin pop), risks reducing the scope of Republican history into a "looking glass" containing the most alluring facets. "Shanghai cinema," too, when used as the overarching Republican cinema or Chinese cinema before 1949, entails a limited, partial approach to the vast terrains of cinema practices in many parts of China and colonies like Hong Kong, Taiwan, Macao, and the Chinese diaspora generally.

Granted, Shanghai is central in the development of China's modernity before 1949, including not just cinema, but other cultural formations. To quote Wen-hsin Yeh in her pioneering article: "Shanghai in the first half of the 20th century emerged to become China's largest metropolis for trade, finance, manufacturing, publishing, higher education, journalism and many other important functions, performed by a growing population increasingly diversified into multiple classes of different incomes and interests."[2] Major publications by Leo Ou-fan Lee (1999), Zhang Yingjin (ed., 1999), Andrew Jones (2001), Barbara Mittler (2004), Zhang Zhen (2005), Nicole Huang (2005), Wen-hsin Yeh (2008),[3] and many others fasten on Shanghai as the wellspring of modern China in consumer and media culture.[4] Through the concerted efforts of two generations of scholars, Shanghai was decisively crowned as the jewel of Chinese modernity and cosmopolitanism; film and media culture associated with the city—celebrities, advertising, magazines, popular fiction, theaters, and the urban space—also emerged to typify Chinese cinema in general. Hence the currency of "Shanghai cinema." Further, in the course of rewriting Chinese film history, the cinema of Shanghai was useful in presenting alternatives to party-inflected hagiography of the national cinema, including those claimed by the Communist and Nationalist parties. Since the beginning of the new millennium, "Shanghai cinema" has returned with a vengeance with its voluptuous endowment. Resonance with historic sounds and sights of the International Settlement, recollections of China's cosmopolitan glamour of the early twentieth century, and archival resources hidden in old magazines, diaries, and warehouses have turned Shanghai into a centerpiece, the one and only film capital in contemporary Chinese film studies.

"Shanghai cinema" may deserve its reputation for luminous glamour, but it may also obscure roads not taken. It is fair to say that the talisman of "Shanghai cinema" has eclipsed other sites and activities important to the makeup of an inclusive history. There are gaping holes and omissions when we pigeonhole Shanghai as the sole repository of Republican movie experience. To address this issue, we must adjust the existing binary of Communist-orthodox versus Shanghai-modern historiography by probing the cinema histories of less familiar sites located in different sociopolitical institutions. Republican China is too large, too diverse to be shackled to just one city, no matter Shanghai's enchantment. In this book we focus on cities in addition to Shanghai—Hong Kong, Taipei, and Guangzhou—by identifying lesser-known practices beyond the dizzying and colliding reflections of early cinema as defined by Shanghai *moderne*. We present the notion of *yin-*

ghua (photo pictures), a common term for motion pictures used in Southern China, to critique *yingxi*, the Shanghai term for cinema, and its English translation, shadow play. The shadow play *yingxi* has been used as a protocol in defining early Chinese cinema against Western counterparts. This protocol needs to be exposed, revisited and revised. We delineate the long process of indigenizing cinema into a sustainable sociocultural institution in Hong Kong throughout the teens to the 1920s. Hong Kong was not just at the receiving end of showcasing Western musicals and motion pictures. The city developed a base of cinephilia culture before local production took off. In Taipei, we include magic lantern projection in the Japanese occupied areas to expand the frontier of early film historiography beyond the "first" screening events that took place in Xu Garden and other amusement venues in Shanghai. We cover the early film history of Taiwan by focusing on Japanese utilization of cinema for colonial governance. As hard as the Japanese administration tried to use film to propagate colonial policy, the effect was ambiguous. We introduce "Guangzhou film" and Cantophone cinema to complement and balance the overbearing resonance of "Shanghai cinema."

Our attraction to early film practices in the treaty port of Guangzhou and colonial cities like Hong Kong and Taipei does not foreclose uncovering overlooked film histories of Shanghai. Several articles in this volume stay close to the orbit of Shanghai, offering fascinating historiographies on practices and institutions caught in historians' peripheral vision. For instance, an extensive study on the Shanghai YMCA's film program widens our scope in considering early film exhibition and shows us that film screening in early twentieth-century Shanghai was not exclusively a commercial transaction, available only in Western theaters located in the French concession. The investigation of the activities of foreign businessmen and itinerant cameramen illuminates the faded international veneers of the Shanghai filmscape. A treatment of "film literati" (traditional writers cum filmmakers) and cine-fiction (fiction adapted from screen stories) unveils the multilayered crossover between film and literature in Republican cinema.

The idea of probing alternative film histories beyond Shanghai was first introduced by Poshek Fu, whose pioneering work in the bilateral relations between Shanghai and Hong Kong has led studies on Chinese-language film into not only "extra" but also critical dimensions.[5] Fu considered the liminality between art and politics, and his work on Shanghai cinema during wartime was the earliest work in resuscitating Shanghai filmmakers and writers who collaborated with the Japanese occupiers in maintaining the life of Chinese cinema during the second Sino-Japanese War.[6] His take on the intertwined histories between Shanghai and Hong Kong reverses the Shanghai-centric view, situating Hong Kong as a comparable film capital of Chinese cinema. As historian, Fu wished to extend Chinese film research to cover different locales and to excavate new primary materials. In 2009 he initiated the research idea of "Beyond Shanghai" with me and mainland-based scholars Hui Liu and Xiaocai Feng. Together we began a research project entitled "Chinese Film Industry Beyond Shanghai: 1900–1950." Given the rapid growth of Chinese film scholarship, we felt there was a need to look beyond Shanghai in order to come to a comprehensive, in-depth knowledge of the film industry as a whole, before it was nationalized under the People's Republic of China in 1950. To fill the immense gap in the existing scholarship, our project set out to collect film advertisements, news items, and articles from early newspapers in Hong Kong, Guangzhou, Hangzhou, and Tianjin. From 2010 to 2013, our team read through eight newspapers from late Qing to the Republican era in the four cities and collected over twenty thousand useful items relating to our research objectives. Next, we categorized and summarized the collected data. In early 2015 we built an online database in collaboration with the Hong Kong Baptist University Library. This database made available a keyword index to allow easy search. Our hope is that the database will be of help for future research on regional film history.[7]

The importance of the local and (trans)regional histories against the grand narrative of the national cinema was previously advocated in Stephen Teo's *Hong Kong Cinema: The Extra Dimension* (1997), Sheldon Lu's *Transnational Chinese Cinemas: Identity, Nationhood, Gender* (1997), and Zhang Yingjin's *Screening China: Critical Interventions, Cinematic Reconfigurations, and the Transnational Imaginary in Contemporary Chinese Cinema* (2002).[8] Jeremy Taylor's book-length study on Amoy-dialect film is a valuable addition, while Weihong Bao's *Fiery Cinema* offers challenging theoretical discussion on Chongqing cinema.[9] These are extraordinary milestones in the studies of Chinese cinema, but few have covered the early periods, between 1896 and the 1920s. This is where our present volume seeks to intervene. Our fieldwork, especially the data collected in Hong Kong and Guangzhou, uncovered eye-opening information in relation to the initial practices of exhibition, censorship, and reception of film. With these new materials, we have begun to form an alternative vision of the past. Meanwhile, there was a growing interest in early film culture in colonial Taiwan and in institutions and figures that were historically viewed as marginal and problematic.[10] Seizing on the momentum and research energy on old colonial cities and on early moving image culture, the eleven articles here present a new historiography of Chinese-language cinema. These eleven chapters traverse a wide territory, from Shanghai to Guangzhou, connecting Hong Kong and Taipei, bringing topics specific to early cinema practices such as magic lantern shows, colonial film policy, missionary film, itinerant cameramen, and cine-fiction. Taken together, they recall a kaleidoscope, a proto-cinematic visual toy of optical seduction and pleasure. A kaleidoscopic view arises from the array of institutional and historiographic turns that produce intriguing patterns. These patterns shift and mutate; they converge and diverge according to the adjustments made by the historical agent. These adjustments eventuate in multiple and intertwined views out toward the cinematic histories of the sites the chapters of this volume navigate.

The first two turns of our kaleidoscopic survey are Hong Kong and Taipei, two Chinese colonial cities grown out of nineteenth-century imperialism. In these two cases, a newly arrived cinema is a colonial tool and technology par excellence. Motion pictures come from the West, from capitals like Paris, London, and New York; they carry novelty, a marvel that combines virtues of photography and projected imagery, of which we can choose phantasmagoria or magic lantern slides as prime examples. It prompts amazement and wonder, due to accurately reproduced motion of the subjects captured, and multiplied by the reaction of many others sitting nearby in the hall. Cinema, with a sensitive operator, could be a powerful collective reinscription of the senses for a new century. To fin de siècle colonial audiences in Hong Kong and Taipei, cinema was also a means of forging an imagined cosmopolitan identity for colonized subjects. To recipients in the colonies, cinema carried from the imperial centers news and views of technological advances; cinematic absorption was cast wide, along with incipient show business models purveyed by travelers from abroad. This was an important colonial function—affiliation via mechanical reproduction—also deployed, unevenly, in dynastic and Republican China. Cinema could function as a "civilizing" mission, a means to propagate metropolitan ideas (from West and East alike), and demonstrate leading-edge machines. It was sometimes hortatory, mixing ethical, modernizing and "wholesome" messages to young people in appropriate gatherings, like the YMCA. For Christian missionaries, motion pictures were important source material from the field, taken to advertise conversions and church planting, a way of raising funds at home.[11]

In Taiwan, there were government bodies circulating educational films for children and the public, but they also showed propaganda films to cultivate national spirit and promote the all-important concept of loyalty, identifying with the Japanese empire and nationalism. Evangelism and education were key functions of the new technology of motion pictures. But this was not all.

From the first, movies were commercialized by making them cognate with other popular art forms, such as musicals, comic repartee, illustrated lectures, and news announcements. The flickering pictures were staples of variety halls, sing-alongs, and comedy revues. Just as cinema could be mobilized on behalf of the church, school, and public health, it was most visible on the stage, where cinema inclined toward feature film entertainment. But this took quite some time, as full-length features did not become institutionalized until the teens. Even then they had overtures and live musical accompaniment to enhance the pictures. Until then, pictures shared the bill of fare with other kinds of live entertainment, which often followed well-established patterns. These patterns had roots in the nineteenth century, and many scholars have traced motion pictures' imbrications in stage, musical, and performance traditions.[12] In Hong Kong, there is clear evidence for the common settings of screen entertainment with vaudeville, cabaret, and musical revues. This followed British practices of live amusement, but given the locale, links with teahouse, opera, and Chinese entertainment venues were evident. Hong Kong was a British colony set in a Chinese community, so cinema moved on dual cultural tracks, while also progressing toward greater autonomy of exhibition and economic sustenance. Cosmopolitans like Spaniard Antonio Ramos helped propel cinema exhibition toward more opulent surroundings in Shanghai, Hong Kong, and Macao, as well as treaty ports like Guangzhou.[13]

Entitled "Revising Historiography: Early Film Culture in Hong Kong, Taiwan and Guangzhou," the first part of this book features six chapters, and it begins with my "Translating *Yingxi*: Chinese Film Genealogy and Early Cinema in Hong Kong." This chapter targets concepts of *yingxi*, "shadow play," in prevailing histories of Chinese cinema and argues that the presumed links forged between early cinema and traditional art forms like opera or shadow play resulted from a problematic English rendition of the Chinese term *yingxi*. As a predominant term used to refer to motion pictures in the Republican period, we found little evidence supporting *yingxi* as a neologism, linking such art forms as shadow play or opera to motion pictures. Following this line of correction, I argue that *yingxi* should be understood as the Chinese term for "photoplay," instead of, "shadow play." In addition, based on the primary sources we recovered on early film exhibition in Hong Kong (1900–1916), we found an alternative term—*yinghua* (photo pictures)—was used more widely than *yingxi*, indicating the early reception of cinema was more fluid than that assumed by the *yingxi*, "shadow play" designation. Following the footsteps of *yinghua*, we traced the history of early film exhibition in Hong Kong and discovered that prior to 1924, cinema exhibition in Hong Kong was often held alongside other forms of amusements, including magic lantern shows, lectures, live performances, facilities, and services. In light of this manifold exhibition culture, movies were not the only attraction and screenings were not always commercially oriented. More often, audiences in the colonial Hong Kong of the 1910s and 1920s experienced a screening event of multiple stimuli, from visual attraction to religious indoctrination, from social reform to community building. Cinema's multifaceted practices were fully embedded in colonial Hong Kong.

Following my revisiting of prevailing concepts of Chinese film historiography are three chapters that focus on the relationship between colonialism and cinema, including indigenous practice against the odds of colonial suppression. The colonial utilization of motion pictures was a salient feature in early film practices.[14] In Japanese-ruled Taiwan, the introduction of visual technology was managed to facilitate, if not fulfill, colonial mission building. Laura Jo-Han Wen's "Magic Lantern Shows and Screen Modernity in Colonial Taiwan" investigates the "one and multiple" modernity mediated by the magic lantern shows in colonial Taiwan in the context of early cinema, media archaeology, modes of colonial edification, and the projection of empires. The magic lantern show (*gentō-kai*) appeared in Japanese textbooks in colonial Taiwan as early as 1897. By the 1910s, the show was among the frequent public events to project Japan's ideas of news, hygiene, charity, and modern knowledge on the *benshi*-voiced, theatrical screen. In the 1940s, due to the pressing necessity of wartime propaganda, Japanese authorities restored magic lanterns as substitutes for the cinema in rural villages. The magic lantern might have been indeed an extension of colonial power; nonetheless, Wen argues the process of its projection and mediation also revealed the different stages of development between the colony and the imperial screen. To what extent did these shows do the magic for the colonial subjects? Did the Japanese screen truly function as a one-way mirror projecting the idealized empire? Wen's chapter opens an important string of issues deserving our close attention.

In "From an Imported Novelty to an Indigenized Practice: Hong Kong Cinema in the 1920s," Ting-yan Cheung and Pablo Sze-pang Tsoi unveil a key milestone in Hong Kong film history, arguing that the emergence of Hong Kong cinema was rooted in a specific economic and cultural context of the 1920s. In the prevailing film history, early cinema in Hong Kong (1897–1925) is considered uneventful and ineffectual. Within this historiographical framework, individual film pioneers and the activities they carried out were often marginalized, leading to an impression that the early film-related events mobilized by local filmmakers were of little significance. This chapter corrects this view and explores the early filmscape of Hong Kong in three evolutionary stages: first, the cinema as imported novelty and its popularization among local Chinese; second, the cinema as profitable investment and emergence of Chinese proprietors; third, the cinema as cultural text and the subsequent critical reception within Chinese communities. This evolution saw a growing variety of film-related activities that inadvertently nourished the growth of Hong Kong cinema in the decades to follow. Returning to colonial Taiwan, Daw-Ming Lee covers the dynamics between colonial machinery and cinema practice. His "Enlightenment, Propaganda, and Image Creation: A Descriptive Analysis of the Usage of Film by the Taiwan Education Society and the Colonial Government Before 1937" documents the use of motion pictures in the colony before the breakout of the second Sino-Japanese war in 1937, when heightened imperial indoctrination permeated every corner of the Japanese empire. Lee's research shows that from very early on the colonial administration had seized on the novelty of motion pictures to propel its colonial rule and legitimacy. To achieve this, film was not used only as a pure propaganda machine but took on other functions such as "enlightenment," (seeing the world), education, healthcare and so on. Lee also focuses on government organizations, such as the Taiwan Education Society and Taiwan Patriotic Women's Association, to delineate the early stage of colonial film practice in Taiwan, its activities, agencies, audiences, and receptions. Lee's chapter makes an important contribution to understanding the complexity of cinema's place in empire building and colonial development.

Following Hong Kong and Taiwan, we travel to Republican-era Guangzhou (Canton) and examine the nexus between the city's development and the flourishing movie business. The Republican era is a major transition in modern China, marked by extremes. This was the first republic in Chinese history, followed by optimism in anticipation of sovereignty and democracy. But such hopes brought despair because of incessant civil wars that tore the country apart for decades. Warfare, internal rivalries, ideological rifts, and intensified contact with the outside world made the Republican a highly conflicted time in modern China. Guangzhou is the birthplace of the 1911 revolution and military capital of the Republican administration. And given its importance as staging ground for Qing dynasty trade with the West, Guangzhou is elder or even avuncular to the upstart Hong Kong. The city of Guangzhou, even more than Shanghai, may signify the Republican ethos and its centrifugal forces of disunity, contradiction, and ambivalence. Film activities in Guangzhou can be traced through advertisements and stories published in local newspapers; these outline the features of a distinct Guangzhou cinema mode, which has close ties to its colonial cousin across the Pearl River Delta.

The distinct Guangzhou cinema is illustrated in "'Guangzhou Film' and Guangzhou Urban Culture: An Overview," co-written by Hui Liu, Shi-Yan Chao, and Richard Xiaying Xu. The chapter identifies "Guangzhou film" as a term of departure from the Shanghai-centered historiography that dominated the writing of cinema history in China. Based on news materials collected from the *Guangzhou Republican Daily* (*Guangzhou minguo ribao*) and secondary sources on the urban development of Guangzhou, the historical overview of "Guangzhou film" provides an alternative history of urban cinema. By aligning local film consumption and production with the development of Guangzhou's urban space, the chapter allows the identity of the city and specificities of local practices to surface. The authors caution against a narrow view of Guangzhou as a city of enclosed, unique boundaries. Guangzhou's historical tie with Hong Kong was key to the formation of the Cantonese cinema as a sphere of linguistic and cultural convergence. The term "Guangzhou film" cannot operate independently outside Hong Kong and its colonial dimension. Tracking "Guangzhou film," Kenny K. K. Ng presents a compelling study on Cantophone cinema as a site of cultural and linguistic struggle. Ng's "The Way of *The Platinum Dragon*: Xue Juexian and the Sound of Politics in 1930s Cantonese Cinema" argues that the advent of sound film technology in the 1930s facilitated the formation of the Hong Kong–Guangdong region as the largest production center of Cantonese talkies, or Cantophone cinema, servicing not only Cantonese-speaking communities in South China, but also the Chinese diaspora in Southeast Asia, Australia, and North America. Ng's analysis illuminates two important methods of Chinese film studies: national identity and craftsmanship. The struggle for a place in national cinema has been an issue to non-Mandarin, or so-called dialect, films. In this context, Cantonese film is similar to Shanghainese, Taiwanese/Amoy, and Teochew films in terms of their historical marginality, and tenacity in demanding their voices be heard, instead of being dubbed, on screen. Cantonese filmmakers' negotiation and efforts in carving a space of "national belonging" has always been a trying journey in the centennial development of Chinese-language cinema. Ng's examination of the production history of *The Platinum Dragon* pinpoints an inherent cultural politics in regional cinema. Occupying the center of the struggle is craftsmanship at its best—resources of traditional performing arts, including its flexible creativity and transformative energy in alignment with modern media like cinema. Ng's article offers readers a riveting account on the dissonant Cantophone film history and how individual talents played pivotal roles in balancing market need, national politics, and a regional identity in need of reinforcement.

Following Guangzhou cinema and specifically Cantonese talkies, we extend our historiographical expedition to Republican Shanghai. The return journey to Shanghai begins with new pages on filmmakers and institutions germane to the making of early Chinese cinema. Part II focuses on filmmakers and writers who were hitherto marginalized in the standard history of Chinese cinema. We call these overlooked practitioners "intermediaries, cinephiles, and film literati," addressing the heterogeneous kaleidoscope of culture and practice in the Republican period. Here we introduce lesser-known figures that mediated cinema as a new invention from abroad and facilitated its local practice, forecasting its eventual Chinese indigenization. A rare study on the Shanghai YMCA's film programs adds an extra dimension to cinema's complicity with evangelism, along with its promotion of an enlightened, hygienic, modern entertainment. Yoshino Sugawara's "Toward the Opposite of 'Vulgarity': The Birth of Cinema as a 'Healthful Entertainment' and the Shanghai YMCA" explores alternative, Christian movie activities, exemplified by the movie shows held at the Shanghai YMCA. Sugawara suggests that among the prevailing modes of exhibition, the noncommercial shows organized by the Shanghai YMCA in the teens contributed to the improvement of cinema's social standing. She argues that Christian uses of cinema not only helped forge the cinema's institutional structure, but also had an impact on changing the public perception of motion pictures. The YMCA's movie program, with its state-of-the-art facilities and equipment and its uplifting repertoires, was the benchmark for Shanghai's exhibition industry in the next decades. YMCA members He Tingran and Bao Qingjia were crucial in building the thriving film history in Shanghai. He and Bao were groomed at the YMCA via its various physical education and language programs as exemplary young Chinese Christians. He Tingran then emerged as a film mogul in late 1920s Shanghai: he controlled Shanghai United Amusements and later Asia Theaters, two foreign-registered companies whose major business was film exhibition and distribution.[15] He's business philosophy was not merely commercial, but aimed to "modernize" film exhibition and showcase "noble," affordable movies for Shanghai audiences.[16] He's vision of using cinema for social reform was inherited from the YMCA's film mission, although all of his theaters showed Hollywood pictures, leading to the dominance of Hollywood on China's screens before the outbreak of the Pacific War.[17] He's fellow Christian Bao Qingjia was also a key player in early Shanghai film industry. Bao set up one of the initial motion picture production units of what was then the city's largest publishing firm, the Commercial Press.

Following the investigation on foreign power in shaping Shanghai film industry, Yongchun Fu's chapter, "Movie Matchmakers: The Intermediaries between Hollywood and China in the Early Twentieth Century," examines the interchange between China and Hollywood in the formation of the Chinese film industry in its early years. Fu calls the foreign filmmakers and go-betweens in Shanghai "intermediaries" in crediting their contribution. He looks into the role these go-betweens played between Hollywood and China, against the background of the ethnocentric writing of Chinese film history of the 1920s and 1930s, which tended to, understandably, only privilege Chinese players. Fu's two major representatives are the American cinematographer William H. Lynch from Los Angeles and Hong Kong–based movie mogul Lo Kan (Lo Gun, Lu Gen). Lynch was the cameraman for the first narrative pictures made by the film forerunners Zhang Shichuan and Zheng Zhengqiu in 1913, while Lo Kan branched out of his exhibition empire to production, anxious to get ahead in the emerging market in talkies. These figures and their ambition, though previously neglected, were instrumental in shaping China's national cinema in the decades to come.

Cinema's connection to other arts and media has been a major concern in film historiography. In my chapter, I raise the problem of an ethnocentric tendency in aligning cinema with such vernacular performing arts as shadow play and opera. But in literature, astoundingly, we see a keen interest in engaging cinema and vice versa. Using the keyword *wenyi* (letters and art) and the unique "fields" of film and literature, two chapters study the film activities of leading authors of the popular Mandarin Ducks and Butterflies fiction. These authors crossed over to the emergent film field by writing scripts, handbills, and advertisements, translating title cards, and crafting a new genre called cine-fiction. Their activities and their versatility qualify them as the earliest generation of cinephiles. Their enthusiasm for the new medium and its mode of storytelling set the stage for film criticism to flourish in the subsequent decade. Enoch Yee-lok Tam's "The Silver Star Group: A First Attempt at Theorizing *Wenyi* in the 1920s" analyzes the generic concept of *wenyi*, "literature and art," as it relates to Chinese cinema. Building on my previous work on *wenyi*,[18] Tam offers a discourse analysis of the evolution of *wenyi*, focusing on the midpoint in its development, from 1926 to 1928. In presenting the work of the journal *Silver Screen*, he locates evidence of foreign literary criticism in *wenyi*'s formation, from France (Romain Rolland) and Japan (Kuriyagawa Hakuson, by way of Lu Xun). Well before the advertising copy of the 1930s that utilized the *wenyi* label to sell certain kinds of pictures (literary adaptation, romance and art film), *wenyi* was discussed and debated as a cognate for artistic prestige and edifying screen works. My coauthored chapter with Tam, "Forming the Movie Field: Film Literati in Republican China" identifies several key Mandarin Ducks and Butterflies authors instrumental in making the film industry in Republican China. We call these writers "film literati," focusing on their negotiation between traditional and emergent forms of narrative, and their crossover from the literary to the cinematic field. We also examine closely the term *yingxi xiaoshuo*—"cine-fiction"—a common practice among the film literati for their adaptation of foreign films into fiction. The investigation of the dual career of the film literati permits a more finessed account of the synergy between letters and images and the dynamics between film and literary fields.

Liu Na'ou, the controversial, tragic figure among modern film literati, is the ultimate cinephile of the late Republican era. Given the films he made and debates he sparked on cinema's autonomy and its future, it is no wonder that Liu was a marked man, and was assassinated in a darkening Shanghai in 1938. Yet his contributions were prescient, and a thorough study of his work and thought illuminates the plurality of both Shanghai and Republican cinema. While Liu slips easily into clichés about Shanghai cinema (effete, sensual, decadent, "yellow"), his work has a richness that indicates the complexity of Republican cinematic culture. Ling Zhang's chapter is an important addition to the growing literature on Liu. In her "Rhythmic Movement, Metaphoric Sound, and Transcultural Transmediality: Liu Na'ou and *The Man Who Has a Camera* (1933)," Zhang reappraises Liu's works, including his documentary and writing, in the context of transcultural and transmedial practices. Through a close analysis of Liu's famous travelogue, Zhang reconnects Liu's film practice with the international avant-garde, both in cinema (à la Soviet montage) and literature (Japanese neosensationalism). Zhang's rigorous reading warrants a new understanding of the cinema culture in the Republican period that moves beyond the normative model of the national cinema characterized by the usual directors, studios, stars, and genres.

Peeping through a kaleidoscope, we exercise our vision in motion, mobilizing our voyeur curiosity. Astonishing sights of moving images from the past appear as a result. This volume introduces three new cities besides Shanghai, resuscitating the missing pieces from historiography informed by national cinema and the precepts of modernity. Here we try to broaden the scope of film development beyond the regulated geographic, ideological, and conceptual bounds. We foreground the cinema's relationships with imperialism and colonialism and emphasize the potency of cinema as a sociocultural institution. We look deeply into the activities, agents, and events beyond the Shanghai silver screens. These vectors intersect in productive ways, with colonial, ideological, and technological dimensions working in tandem, and sometimes off balance. As with most fields, Chinese film history is overdetermined with unexpected, surprising findings and discoveries, like turning and adjusting views from inside of a kaleidoscope. It is high time to embark on the expedition into new movie horizons, and to scope out the opulent reflections, distortions, and refractions of early film culture.

Notes

1. The idea for this volume grew from a special issue published in *Journal of Chinese Cinemas* I guest-edited. The current introduction is an expanded version of the introduction to the special issue. See Emilie Yueh-yu Yeh, "New Takes on Film Historiography: Republican Cinema Redux, an Introduction," *Journal of Cinema Cinemas* 9, no. 1 (2015): 1–7. Four chapters from this special issue were revised and included in this current volume. They include Yongchun Fu, "Movie Matchmakers: The Intermediaries between Hollywood and China in the Early Twentieth Century" (8–22); Ling Zhang, "Rhythmic Movement: The City Symphony and Transcultural Transmediality:

Liu Na'ou and *The Man Who Has a Camera* (1933)" (42–61); Enoch Yee-lok Tam, "The Silver Star Group: A First Attempt at Theorizing Wenyi in the 1920s" (62–75); and Emilie Yueh-yu Yeh, "Translating *Yingxi*: Chinese Film Genealogy and Early Cinema in Hong Kong" (76–107).

2. Wen-hsin Yeh, "Shanghai Modernity: Commerce and Culture in a Republican City," *China Quarterly* 150 (1997): 378.

3. See, for example, Leo Ou-fan Lee, *Shanghai Modern: The Flowering of a New Urban Culture in China, 1930–1945* (Cambridge, MA: Harvard University Press, 1999); Yingjin Zhang, ed., *Cinema and Urban Culture in Shanghai, 1922–1943* (Stanford, CA: Stanford University Press, 1999); Andrew F. Jones, *Yellow Music: Media Culture and Colonial Modernity in Chinese Jazz Age* (Durham, NC: Duke University Press, 2001); Barbara Mittler, *A Newspaper for China: Power, Identity, and Change in Shanghai's News Media, 1872–1912* (Cambridge, MA: Harvard University Asia Center, 2004); Zhang Zhen, *An Amorous History of the Silver Screen: Shanghai Cinema, 1896–1937* (Chicago: University of Chicago Press, 2005); Nicole Huang, *Women, War, Domesticity: Shanghai Literature and Popular Culture of the 1940s* (Leiden: Brill, 2005); and Wen-hsin Yeh, *Shanghai Splendor: A Cultural History, 1843–1949* (Berkeley: University of California Press, 2008).

4. See, for instance, Jason C. Kuo, ed., *Visual Culture in Shanghai, 1850s–1930s* (Washington, DC: New Academic Publishing, 2007); Christopher A. Reed, *Gutenberg in Shanghai: Chinese Print Capitalism, 1876–1937* (Vancouver: UBC Press, 2004); Paul Pickowicz, Kuiyi Shen, and Yingjin Zhang, eds., *Liangyou: Kaleidoscopic Modernity and the Shanghai Global Metropolis, 1926–1945* (Leiden: Brill, 2013). For a long list of publications on Shanghai as the birthplace of Chinese modernity, please see Pickowicz, Shen, and Zhang, "Introduction: *Liangyou*, Popular Print Media, and Visual Culture in Republican Shanghai", in *Liangyou*, 12 nn. 5–11.

5. Poshek Fu, *Between Shanghai and Hong Kong: The Politics of Chinese Cinemas* (Stanford, CA: Stanford University Press, 2003). See also Emilie Yueh-yu Yeh, "Between Shanghai and Hong Kong: The Politics of Chinese Cinemas," review of *Between Shanghai and Hong Kong: The Politics of Chinese Cinemas*, by Poshek Fu, *Film Quarterly* 59, no. 3 (2006): 64–65.

6. Poshek Fu, *Passivity, Resistance, and Collaboration: Intellectual Choices in Occupied Shanghai, 1937–1945* (Stanford, CA: Stanford University Press, 1993).

7. Emilie Yueh-yu Yeh, Feng Xiaocai, Liu Hui, and Poshek Fu, eds., *Early Chinese Film Database*, Hong Kong: Hong Kong Baptist University Library, 2015. http://digital.lib.hkbu.edu.hk/chinesefilms/

8. Stephen Teo, *Hong Kong Cinema: The Extra Dimension* (London: BFI Publishing, 1997); Sheldon Hsiao-peng Lu, ed., *Transnational Chinese Cinemas: Identity, Nationhood, Gender* (Honolulu: University of Hawai'i Press, 1997); Yingjin Zhang, *Screening China: Critical Interventions, Cinematic Reconfigurations and the Transnational Imaginary in Contemporary Chinese Cinema* (Ann Arbor, MI: Center for Chinese Studies, 2002).

9. Jeremy E. Taylor, *Rethinking Transnational Chinese Cinemas: The Amoy-Dialect Film Industry in Cold War Asia* (London: Routledge, 2011); Weihong Bao, *Fiery Cinema: The Emergence of an Affective Medium in China, 1915–1945* (Minneapolis: University of Minnesota Press, 2015).

10. Misawa Mamie, *Zai "diguo" yu "zuguo" de jiafeng jian: Rizhi shiqi Taiwan dianyingren de jiaoshe yu kuajing* [Sandwiched between the "Empire" and the "Motherland": Taiwan Film Workers' Negotiation and Border-Crossing during Japanese Occupation], trans. Li Wenqing and Hsu Shijia (Taipei: National Taiwan University Press, 2012).

11. For an excellent overview of missionary evangelism and early cinema, please see Terry Lindvall, introduction to *Sanctuary Cinema: Origins of Christian Film Industry* (New York: New York University Press, 2007), 1–12. See also Manthia Diawara, *African Cinema: Politics and Culture* (Bloomington: Indiana University of Press, 1992), 1–12; and Maria Francesca Piredda, "Cinema and Popular Preaching: The Italian Missionary Film and *Fiamm*," in *Italian Popular Cinema*, ed. Louis Bayman and Sergio Rigoletto (London: Palgrave Macmillan, 2013), 214–225.

12. See, for example, Rick Altman, *Silent Film Sound* (New York: Columbia University Press, 2007); Aaron Gerow, *Visions of Japanese Modernity: Articulations of Cinema, Nation, and Spectatorship, 1895–1925* (Berkeley: University of California Press, 2010); Charles Musser, *The Emergence of Cinema: The American Screen to 1907* (Berkeley: University of California Press, 1990); Zhang, *Amorous History*; Hideaki Fujiki, *Making Personas: Transnational Film Stardom in Modern Japan* (Cambridge, MA: Harvard University Asian Center, 2013); and Daisuke Miyao, *Sessue Hayakawa: Silent Cinema and Transnational Stardom* (Durham, NC: Duke University Press, 2007).

13. Antonio Ramos began as a Spanish solider based in Manila, and was said to have shot the first shorts in the Philippines, using a Lumière Cinematograph. He was a key film exhibitor in Shanghai, Macao, Hong Kong, and Manila in the early twentieth century. Ramos built some of the earliest formal film theaters in the region, such as Victoria Cinematograph in Hong Kong (1907) and Hongkew Cinema in Shanghai (1908). By the teens, he had set up a transnational network of film distribution and exhibition across cities like Shanghai, Macao, Tianjin, Hong Kong, and Manila. In Shanghai alone, Ramos owned seven major theaters: Hongkew, Victoria, Olympic, Embassy, Empire, National, and Carter. Historians have yet to uncover a thorough account of Ramos's film enterprises in China, South China, and Southeast Asia, but there are some useful references available in English and Spanish. See Nick Deocampo, *Cine: Spanish Influences on Early Cinema in the Philippines* (Manila: National Commission for Culture and the Arts, 2003), 45–72; and Juan Ignacio Toro Escudero, "España y los españoles en el Shanghai de entreguerras (1918–1939)" [Spain and Spaniards in Shanghai between the Wars] (master's thesis, East China Normal University, 2012). I thank Yongchun Fu for providing me a copy of the thesis.

14. Nadine Chan illustrates a compelling study of how the mobile film exhibition in rural Malaya was carefully managed, programmed, and controlled by the colonial state;

see Nadine Chan, "Making 'Ahmad Problem Conscious': Educational Film and the Rural Lecture Caravan in 1930s British Malaya," *Cinema Journal* 55, no. 4 (2016): 84–107.

15. Yoshino Sugawara, "Beyond the Boundary between China and the West: Changing Identities of Foreign-Registered Film Theatre Companies in Republican Shanghai," *Journal of Chinese Cinemas* 9, no. 1 (2015): 23–41.

16. Sugawara, "Beyond the Boundary," 34–35.

17. Sugawara, "Beyond the Boundary," 28.

18. Emilie Yueh-yu Yeh, "Pitfalls of Cross-Cultural Analysis: Chinese *Wenyi* Film and Melodrama," *Asian Journal of Communication* 19, no. 4 (2009): 438–452; Emilie Yueh-yu Yeh, "*Wenyi* and the Branding of Early Chinese Film," *Journal of Chinese Cinemas* 6, no. 1 (2012): 65–94; Emilie Yueh-yu Yeh, "A Small History of *Wenyi*," in *The Oxford Handbook of Chinese Cinemas*, ed. Carlos Rojas and Eileen Chow (New York: Oxford University Press, 2013), 225–249.

PART I

Revising Historiography

Early Film Culture in Hong Kong, Taiwan, and Guangzhou

CHAPTER I

Translating Yingxi

Chinese Film Genealogy and Early Cinema in Hong Kong

Emilie Yueh-yu Yeh

INTRODUCTION: TEAHOUSE, GARDEN, AND EARLY FILM SCHOLARSHIP

The probable earliest film screenings in China, according to Law and Bren, took place between April and July 1897, in a variety of venues, from the City Hall in Hong Kong to the Astor House (Pujiang Hotel) in Shanghai and foreign-owned theaters in Tianjin (Lyceum) and Beijing (Legation).[1] The date Law and Bren identify as the "first" screening was almost a year later than the date of August 1896 asserted by Cheng Jihua, Li Shaobai, and Xing Zuwen, in their seminal volumes on Chinese cinema.[2] Immediately after the debut in Hong Kong in April 1897, subsequent screenings were held at a number of tea gardens and amusement parks in Shanghai, Tianjin, and Beijing. These new dates and venues proposed by Law and Bren are supported by another historian, Huang Dequan, in his studies on the arrival of cinema in China.[3] Based on the research by Law and Bren and the subsequent endorsement by Huang, it is safe to say that our prior knowledge of early film exhibitions in China is equivocal, specifically, the dates and venues of the first screenings. Instead of traditional places like the tea garden or teahouse (*chayuan*)[4] as venues for film's debut to Chinese audiences, generic Western portals like public halls, a hotel ballroom, and theater stage were more likely to have housed the first film shows. A corollary arises from these findings: we need to revisit the existing scholarship of early Chinese film culture that has repeatedly asserted the teahouse and the garden[5] as the inaugural sites of film exhibition and germination of movie spectatorship in China. The methods that scholars have employed in examining early Chinese film history, be they archival[6] or sociocultural,[7] require adjustment and a thorough reexamination. Furthermore, the conceptualizations of a native spectatorship hovering between the vernacular[8] and the elite[9] during the late Qing dynasty (circa 1900) may also need new calibration. With recent findings that alert us to gaps and flaws in early film scholarship, I intend to revisit some prevailing concepts and terms by presenting additional new evidence.

Central to these dominant historiographical discourses lies the *yingxi* concept and its literal English translation, "shadow play." Scholars of Chinese film history, in both China and the West, have adopted the ideas of *yingxi* and its translated twin, "shadow play," to frame the reception of cinema in late Qing and early Republican years. Almost without exception, they write that, given *yingxi* as the earliest Chinese term for motion pictures, there exists a tie between shadow puppetry, opera, and early cinema. This "umbilical cord," in Zhang Zhen's image, found its historical backup in the tea garden setting, where traditional performances were held for centuries in China. "*Yingxi* in the teahouse" thus depicts an early cinema scene as a synecdoche: viewing of moving pictures is better understood when we align it with the enjoyment of puppetry or opera within the teahouse backdrop. Does this picture help explain early film exhibition and reception? Is there an alternative to the *yingxi*-teahouse couplet? Considering the disparate nature of film projection and live performance, is *yingxi* (shadow play) an appropriate entry to the understanding of early cinema in Chinese communities? With the support of new research, I suggest we look at *yinghua*, the photo pictures, a term referring to motion pictures used in Hong Kong and Guangzhou, as an alternative genealogy of cinema in China.[10] By superimposing the core image of early cinema—*yingxi*—with *yinghua*, I make note of the import of film experiences in lesser-known locales, such as Hong Kong and Guangzhou. Let me begin my itinerary with two sites—a teahouse and a Chinese garden, known as the first cinema locations in Shanghai. I wish to question the historiographic fitness of these places for an accurate understanding of movies' Chinese root, and route.

THE TEAHOUSE

In her "Teahouse, Shadowplay, Bricolage: *Laborer's Love* and the Question of Early Chinese Cinema" (1999) and *An Amorous History of the Silver Screen* (2005), Zhang Zhen seizes on the account by Cheng, Li, and Xing on the initial film screening in Shanghai's Xu Garden (Xu Yuan) to set the stage for the application of vernacular modernism in early Republican China: "In a broad context, [the cinematic vernacular] stems from the fertile ground of a vibrant vernacular culture—including the teahouses, the theaters, storytelling, popular fiction, music, dance, painting, photography, and discourses of modern wonders and magic."[11] The teahouse setting, according to Zhang, represents a cogent "spatial trope"[12] to encapsulate Chinese urbanites' immersion in the emerging cinematic vernacular, conjuring a colloquial setting equipped with a modern form of mass entertainment:

> Because the film experience is public and requires an architectural infrastructure, a history of film culture would be inadequate without considerations of the physical forms, geographical distributions, and social and aesthetic function of exhibition venues. Thus the vernacular also encompasses the urban architectural environment essential to the film experiences—the theaters, the amusement halls, teahouses, parks.[13]

The everydayness of the teahouse setting coupled with the projection of electric images transforms a traditional entertainment site into a "tension-driven"[14] sight fraught with frictions and uncertainties, that is, the vernacular modern.

Guided by the vernacular modern, one may picture film viewing within the teahouse as an oscillating experience. Movie shows were interspersed with regular activities of the teahouse, such as music, opera, acrobats, gossip, loitering, and food and drink.[15] Meanwhile, as Goldstein suggests, late-Qing teahouses offered more than just an array of entertainments; they were also a marketplace where other attractions besides opera were on sale, including the actors themselves.[16] Precisely because of the interchangeability between the teahouse environment and an open market, the boundary between the stage and the audience space was more fluid and permeable.[17] The relatively free and spontaneous ambience inside the teahouse, imaginably, was not entirely compatible with a movie show wherein the audience's vision had to focus on the screen. I believe this is the basis for Zhang Zheng's depiction of the "tension-driven" movie shows in the early period. However, that tension embodied in the movie shows was somewhat alleviated, thanks to the teahouse setting. Charles Musser has made a key remark on the way cinema managed its foray into the public's entertainment sphere:

> During cinema's first year of success, motion pictures enjoyed the status of a novelty. This very concept or category served to address the problem of managing change within a rapidly industrializing society: novelties typically introduced the public to important technological innovations within a reassuring context that permitted spectators to take pleasure in the discontinuities and dislocations. While technological change created uncertainty and anxiety, "novelty" always embodied significant elements of familiarity, including the very genre of novelty itself. In the case of cinema, greater verisimilitude was initially emphasized at the expense of narrative.[18]

Early movie shows brought a bizarre, yet exhilarating visual stimulus to audiences accustomed to the cozy, boisterous milieu of the teahouse opera. Illuminated by electricity, the screen projected a series of black-and-white events that were not just rare because of distance (e.g., *Street Scenes in Madrid*) and novelty (e.g., *Lynching Scene in the Far West*), but astonishing due to the verisimilitude and animation of the images (e.g., *Passing of Cavalry*).[19] And the life on the screen vanished once the electricity was turned off: "All of a sudden, lights on, all images turned to ashes" ("Notes on Viewing American Cinema," 1897). Imagine the patrons' reaction—the exhilaration and thrill—when they witnessed these lifelike images in motion. As a viewer noted: "Watching the newly arrived motion picture show was fascinating—from small things like ducklings floating on water, rats jumping over the beam to shipwreck and houses on fire." ("On a Movie Show at the Weichun Theater," 1897). Perhaps the initial shock was somewhat mitigated by the immediate restitution (lights back on) of the raucous teahouse setting.

Using the marketplace-like teahouse as a trope to construct early film spectatorship was crucial to implementing the theory of vernacular modernism in China. Miriam Hansen proposes that cinema carries a "sensorium" of urban stimulation in the new twentieth century, allegedly narrowing the gap between First World cosmopolitan sensation and regional, provincial, and foreign horizons.[20] That this was "mass mediated" by cinema[21] and other modern apparatuses meant that the new technology not only pictured faraway people and places, but also introduced Chinese viewers to novel pleasures, coeval with those of modern capitals such as New York or Paris. Cinema thus brought distant peoples into view, while also bringing them into configurations of modernity.[22] First screenings, or the primordial scenes of Chinese movies, were embedded in the context of traditional, "reassuring" Chinese amusements. This is a thesis arising from the economy of vernacular modernism in the case of China. Subsequently the vernacular teahouse trope was linked with the *yingxi* concept already propagated by native historians:

> Until the early 1930s, cinema in Chinese was called "shadowplay" (*yingxi*) before the term gradually changed to "electric shadows" (*dianying*), indicating its umbilical tie to the puppet show and other . . . theatrical arts. The emphasis on "play" rather than "shadow"—in other words, the "play" as the end and "shadow" as means—has, according to the film historian Zhong Dafeng, been the kernel of Chinese cinematic experience.[23]

Here suffice it to say that vernacular modernism provides a rationale for the organic connection ("umbilical") between cinema and endogenous Chinese art forms. Film historians located *yingxi* in constructing a film historiography nicely laced by vernacular modernism—vernacular because of the affiliations with shadow play and the teahouse; modernist because of the medium specificities. The connection between cinema and shadow play, however, begs support from empirical research. Does the *xi* (drama or play) in *yingxi* theory share the same provenance of the traditional theaters with puppet shadow play and opera? Furthermore, can the term *yingxi* be understood and translated as other than its literal Chinese meaning, "shadow play"? I will return to these questions later.

THE GARDEN

Following the previous literature on the teahouse as the primary locale initiating a brand-new visual experience, Pang Laikwan calls attention to what she considers a more precise account of early film spectatorship. Pang is interested in exploring "questions of film reception."[24] She avers that the new visual apparatus of cinema interacted with "the spaces designated for screening movies," and so film spectatorship "connected to the overall modern visual culture" and "the social class of the viewers."[25] Putting aside the substance of "modern visual culture" in this context, Pang's revision has to do with her reservation toward the teahouse as the very *first* film scene where the earliest film spectatorship might have taken shape. Pang argues that though the first screening was staged in the Youyicun (Another Village) playhouse inside Xu Garden, historians have largely neglected the setting that encircled that playhouse—Xu Garden itself, a private garden converted to a public amusement venue.

The Chinese garden in early twentieth-century Shanghai, Pang says, allowed a unique viewing experience for its patrons, unique because the visitor's engagement with the space inside the amusement arena could be both "public" and "private," in that the visitor's movement was guided between a regulated program (where to go and what to see) and spontaneous motion (at your leisure and at your own pace):

> The new public garden was a venue simultaneously incorporating many different visual entertainments. This plurality of activities taking place within and around the screening sites renders the relationship between subject and spectacle more complex, and reveals the limitations of focusing solely on the teahouse to study early film reception in China. This "publicness" can be analysed by focusing on two aspects of the new garden culture: the connections between different forms of visual experience in the garden, and the mutual transformation of the viewer and the viewed.[26]

Taking cues from Zhang's invocation of the built environment as a context to theorize early film culture, Pang urges us to move beyond the teahouse and look into the visual economy of the public garden within which film reception was conditioned. The visitor's attention was easily diffused by many simultaneous displays, and that, Pang suggests, was key to forming early spectatorship.

Two problems arise from Pang's argument. According to Law and Bren, there is no "hard evidence" to indicate that Xu Garden staged the earliest film screenings in China.[27] Huang Dequan, who consulted new Chinese-language materials, also arrives at the same conclusion. And Huang goes further; he shows that the alleged "first" screenings held in Xu Garden in

August 1896 were most likely magic lantern shows, not motion pictures.[28] Huang is not alone in his view. According to our survey, during the years between 1900 and 1903, concurrent with cinema's entry to East Asia, magic lantern shows continued to dominate local screens in Hong Kong (see below). Based on the new evidence, it may not be correct to name Another Village and Xu Garden as the earliest film scene, rendering the garden viewership untenable.

The reason that historians confuse the lantern slide show with the first film screening, Huang argues, is the overlapping use of the term *yingxi* for both magic lantern and motion pictures between 1890 and the early 1920s. Magic lantern shows were called *xiyang yingxi* (Western shadow play) in Shanghai or *qiqiao yanghua* (marvelous and exquisite Western pictures) in Hong Kong (figure 1.1). They were regularly programmed in public amusements beginning in the 1870s.[29] As *yingxi* was already a popular Western show known to Chinese audiences, when film exhibition arrived, exhibitors borrowed the existing term, *yingxi*, and coupled it with "electric light" (*dian guang*), or "moving" (*huodong*), to label motion pictures. Without taking stock of the overlap between magic lanterns and motion pictures, earlier historians such as Cheng Jihua and his colleagues came to an unverified date of film's initial entry into Shanghai, announcing the premature beginning of film screening cinema in China. So, for more than half a century, historians believed that movies arrived in China just a few months after their Paris debut, dutifully following the trail blazed by Cheng and coauthors. In reality, however, cinema's trip to China was more likely a slower journey, embarked from Hong Kong, at the margin of the country, instead of the film capital, Shanghai. This puts the focus on the Shanghai garden in doubt, making the subsequent claim of the garden as "primal scene" shaky.

To Pang, to behold the garden as a central location of early film is tactical. She attempts to distinguish early Chinese film spectatorship from its Western counterparts as detailed by the prevailing literature[30] and argues that, unlike working-class audiences dazzled by "the cinema of attractions," Chinese elites accustomed to garden pleasures would accept film images with equanimity.[31] Pang concludes that Chinese viewers could literally walk the garden and move in and out of the cinematic spectacle as the garden path provided them immunity to screen illusions, and made them unlikely to be hoodwinked by the reality effects of motion pictures.[32] This presumes that film exhibition is integral to the garden landscape and ignores the mechanism of projection as an attraction in itself. Mary Ann Doane writes

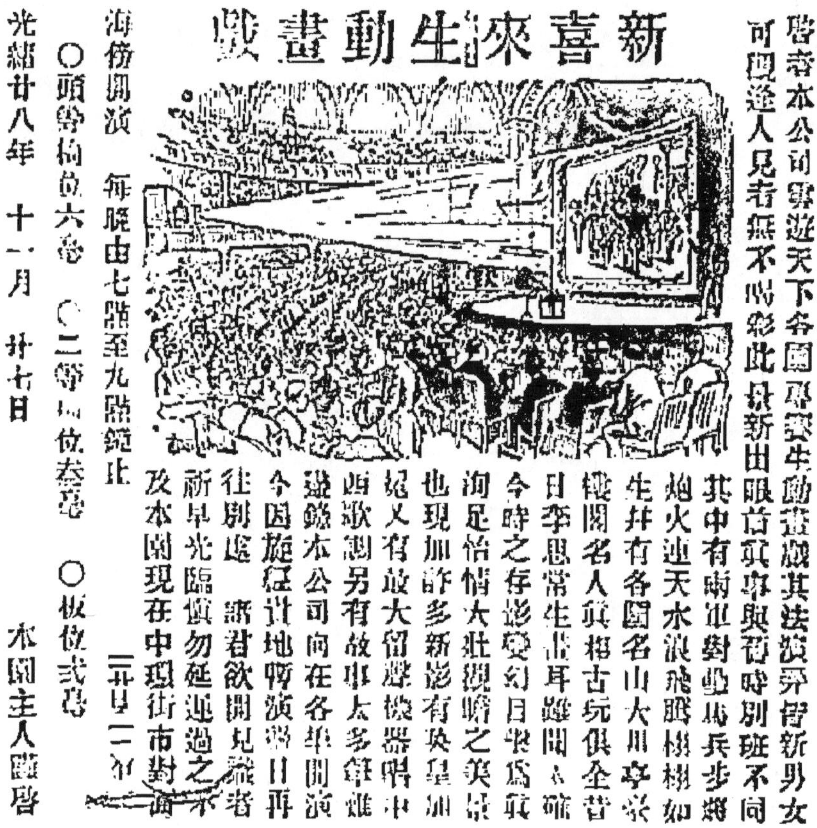

Figure 1.1. A film ad on a magic lantern show at a Hong Kong theater circa 1900: "Lively Photoplay Show at the New Hei Loi Theatre" (Jan. 9, 1903, *Chinese Mail*).

about the location of images and argues that the place to locate the image begins with where projection takes place. Projection hence transforms image to spectacle and activates spectatorship:

> Projection of the illusion of motion collapses representation and exhibition and calls up the notion of *spectacle*. It magnifies the image whose scale is no longer dominated by the scale of a body but by that of an architecture, of the abstract authority of spectacle and a collective, public life.[33]

Here a film event is enabled by the act of projection, which throws the image on the screen and turns it into a larger-than-life illusion, whose magic is enlarged by the enclosed, darkened space and the crowd inside that space. Doane's analysis of film projection and its by-product—the spectacle—calls our attention to the construction of film spectacle and its collective spectatorship in early cinematic exhibition. This is *jouissance*, a unique sensation not to be conflated with garden viewing routines. Early film shows indeed shared the space with other types of entertainments—acrobats, fireworks, live shows, lectures, and so on. However, the specific realm mapped by film projection superseded those constructed by preexisting forms of exhibition, such as magic lanterns and optical toys. Interchange of the exhibition space (venue sharing) was thus unlikely to lead to a transferrable spectatorship or crossover from garden viewing to cinema viewing. A film spectatorship rooted in the garden tends toward a romantic depiction of Chinese spectators. It projects a sophisticated ethnic spectatorship, distinct from Western counterparts. By suggesting an alternative to the cinema of attractions and vernacular modernism, Pang presents another fantasy of cinema origins in China.

Called electric-light photoplay (*dianguan yingxi*) at the time by exhibitors, film was an electrifying visual experience, departing significantly from the magic lantern and optical toys such as zoetrope and thaumatrope, comprised of painted sequences or still photos. Those film shows held in a hotel ballroom, the hall of an amusement park (which was unlikely to be a traditional garden, as indicated in Pang's essay), and their subsequent reruns in the playhouses were not to be confused with entertainments available in standard venues. Advertisements of these events used sensational copy like "don't make any mistake!!! see the cinematograph!!!"[34] and "Special engagement"[35] to promote motion pictures as powerful new attractions. This is quite different from the bland advertisements for magic lantern shows, which by the advent of the twentieth century had run out of novelty value. By the late 1890s slide shows had become routine in program schedules, along with other popular amusements like fireworks and opera performance. Some shows would provide detailed contents (e.g., floods in San Francisco), but most would not. We can safely assume that after motion pictures arrived, slide shows disappeared bit by bit.

From the teahouse to the amusement park, historians have been writing early history based on incomplete historical records. Subsequent postulations have been made about the genealogy of Chinese cinema, including the various "origins" concerning exhibition, audience, reception and production. Next, I will focus on the *yingxi* concept, a commonly accepted provenance of Chinese film genealogy and its ubiquitous English translation "shadow play," which links cinema with traditional art forms. My purpose in revisiting *yingxi* and its English translation is to call attention to the gap between empirical study and dominant theoretical models on early Chinese cinema. The discovery made by Law and Bren opens a new page in the study of Chinese film history, but they have not moved toward a renewed, compelling conceptual framework. Meanwhile, theory-driven historiography without primary research runs the risk of repeating erroneous claims and inferences. In revisiting *yingxi*, I am also concerned with the operative modes and politics in our cross-lingual practice. What discourse has driven our habitual use of "shadow play" in our practice as bilingual film scholars? Which context did we lean on in choosing the best term to unveil history? Do we need to pay more attention to the interstices between tradition and invention, between indigenous and the foreign in our historical excavation? This is where my second story begins.

YINGXI, SHADOW PLAY: CHINESE FILM GENEALOGY AND TRANSLATION

As we know, before the term *dianying* became the definitive name for movies, *yingxi* was circulating in the teens and 1920s, mostly in Shanghai newspapers and film magazines. In the 1930s, the term *yingxi* gave way to a supposedly more modern term, *dianying*, motion pictures. Ever since then, *yingxi* has receded to the background, risking becoming obsolete as a designator. It did not reappear in film studies until the 1980s, when historians revived it to build the genealogy of Chinese cinema. Zhong Dafeng and Chen Xihe used *yingxi* to reconstruct a film theory with a distinctly Chinese character and ownership. With the exception of Zhang Yingjin, who questioned the validity of the "shadowplay theory,"[36], the *yingxi* proposition soon led scholars to connect the "origin" with traditional performing arts like puppet shadow play (*piyingxi*) and Peking opera (*jing ju*).

Zhong and Chen identify *yingxi* as the root of indigenous Chinese film theory. In the first essay on *yingxi*, Zhong Dafeng writes:

> As a film concept, "yingxi" reflected the basic view toward cinema among filmmakers at the time. "What is cinema?" This has been a major issue for filmmakers and theorists and has an effect on the aspects of film production. To early [Chinese] filmmakers, cinema was not a simple depiction of nature, nor was it a pure play irrespective of contents. To them, cinema is a kind of drama.[37]

By evoking *yingxi* as China's take on motion pictures, Zhong suggests that cinema in China from its inception had a specific mission, which in many ways determined the pattern of its reception in China and the ethos of domestic production. By defining *yingxi* exclusively as drama, thus excluding cinema's other properties, such as photography and movement, Zhong argues that storytelling is core to Chinese film practice and criticism.

Following Zhong's introduction of *yingxi* as drama, Chen Xihe went on to elaborate on *yingxi* as a Chinese response to cinema: "Just as montage and long takes are core to Westerners' understanding of cinema, I want to establish *yingxi,* a concept that emerged in early Chinese cinema, as central to the Chinese understanding of cinema."[38] To Zhong and Chen, Chinese cinema does not organize itself around the profilmic, an objective presence open to perception. Instead of privileging *ying* as photographic image, Chinese filmmakers focused on *xi*—fabrication, performance, narrative—and valorized cinema's dramatic effects and their attending ethos.[39] Emphasis on *xi* positions Chinese cinema as a plot-driven medium, mindful of its sociopolitical promise. This quality, according to Zhong and Chen, is the bedrock of Chinese film practice and criticism.[40]

With the compelling presentation made by Zhong and Chen, *yingxi* became a leitmotif and guiding light in Chinese film historiography. One very early record on the term *yingxi* appeared on *Shiwu jiyuan* (On the origin of things), published circa the eleventh century.[41] There, *yingxi* referred to *piyingxi*—Chinese shadow puppetry—a type of folk performance prevalent in many parts of China. Note that Zhong and Chen never identify Peking opera and/or puppet shadow play as sources of the concept *xi,* the dramatic propensity of Chinese cinema, in their view. Though Zhong acknowledges the term is indeed related to the folk art,[42] he avoids linking *yingxi* as *motion pictures* to any given traditional performing art. Apparently Zhong and Chen resurrect the term *yingxi* in order to invent a new theory for Chinese cinema, and therefore their use of *yingxi* was never meant to suggest there existed a shared history between puppet shadow play and motion pictures. *Yingxi* in this context is intended as a Chinese *theory*, not history, of cinema. Hence we clearly see, in Chen Xihe's subsequent article on *yingxi*, his emphatic distinction between Western and Chinese cinema in terms of their disparate orientations: "Chinese filmmakers took 'drama' as the fundamental of cinema; Westerners thought of 'image' as the fundamental of cinema."[43] Following Chen, Chinese cinema that aligned itself with the ethos of moviemaking was divided from its Western counterpart, as the latter focused on the specificity of the film medium, such as movement and photographic verisimilitude.

It is difficult to verify the *yingxi* theory proposed by Zhong and Chen. We have yet to see strong evidence to show that Chinese cinema has a unique expression inherently different from any other cinema. The subsequent development of the *yingxi* theory has, however, codified *yingxi* as definitive, ethnic historiography. *Yingxi* as theory took a different turn when it was used in writing Chinese film history. Scholars began to assimilate *yingxi* with historiography, habitually associated the theoretical term *yingxi* (for cinema) with such generic fields as opera and puppet shadow play, without a rigorous examination of their historical (dis)connections. For instance, Hu Jubin repeats the information recorded in Cheng et al.'s statement on film's arrival in China: "The term 'shadow play' appeared in the first advertisement for a film screening and the earliest film review traceable today. This usage clearly indicates that film was to a certain degree conceptually connected with the traditional Chinese artform of shadow play."[44] In a different passage, Hu reiterates the affinity between "shadow play" and opera, again based on questionable documentation of teahouses as the site of the initial screenings:

> In Beijing and Hong Kong, films were also first screened in teahouses. I believe that a single factor accounts for this phenomenon. Because film was called "shadow play," it was situated in a location appropriate for "play," that is, in teahouses, one of the most important places of recreation in Chinese society, and the site where traditional Chinese operas were performed.[45]

Granted, Hu's assertion was published in 2003, when the field had yet to produce new evidence to correct previous errors. Film screening in Hong Kong was very different from that in Beijing and Shanghai (more details to follow). And with new knowledge of *yingxi*'s multiple reference (ranging from puppetry to magic lantern shows and cinema), we need to move beyond the genealogical linkage between cinema and traditional arts and look at *yingxi* as motion pictures, instead of remnants of ancient puppetry or a continuation of Chinese opera.

Another problem is the constant use of *yingxi* as a pedigree of Chinese cinema. Zhong cautions against the use of the term *yingxi*. By *yingxi* he meant a "specific art field" in early Chinese film, rather than a term for cinema in general.[46] Despite the disclaimer, scholars have broadly taken *yingxi* to be a term for early Chinese cinema, as shown in recent publications.[47] Moreover, because of an affiliation presumed between cinema and China's standing traditional arts, the scholarly community translated *yingxi* (literally "shadow" and "play") as "shadow play" without taking stock of cinematic specificity, not to mention the incongruity between puppet shadow play and motion pictures. First there was Jay Leyda's 1972 book entitled *Dianying/Electric Shadows: An Account of Films and the Film Audience in China*.[48] Leyda wanted to emphasize cinema's reception in China and used the Chinese term *dianying* and its literal translation, "electric shadows," to title the first English volume on Chinese film. Thus begins the interpretation of *ying* as "shadows," as if China's cinematic past were filtered through a shadowy lens—beguiling, mysterious, exotic. The rendition of *ying* as shadow was almost intuitive and emphatically ethnic. Curiously scholars have not considered the possibility of rendering *ying* as "photograph," as both verb (to take a picture as *ying* in Cantonese dialect) and noun (an image as *yingxiang* in Chinese language generally). So this "shadowy" trope remains, into the new century, as seen in many works.[49] These renditions build bridges between cinema and shadow puppetry and opera; yet this assumed connection is seen as a given, not a hypothesis. Accordingly, in accounts of early film exhibition there is no discussion of cinema's synchronic exhibition with shadow puppets. Film in the teahouse seems like a picture painted from secondary sources; to have a better understanding, we must seek additional evidence. Farquhar and Berry apply the "cinema of attractions" to *yingxi* and propose a new translation of *yingxi* as "shadow opera."[50] Such a translation, according to Farquhar and Berry, pinpoints the exact locus of the *xi* as a form of theatrical attraction: "*Xi* and its synonym, *ju*, more commonly mean opera or performance to ordinary Chinese rather than the Western-style realistic theater familiar to educated, urban elites. Hence, one valid translation of *yingxi* is shadow opera."[51] Shadow opera, they argue, is an entry point to "a new archaeology of Chinese cinema" as it grounds the development of Chinese film production in the first half of the twentieth century. The basis for this idea of "shadow opera" comes from the source materials of two "first" native productions made in China proper, including *Dingjun Mountain* (*Dingjunshan*, dir. Ren Jingfeng, 1905) in Beijing, and *Zhuang Zi Tests His Wife* (*Zhuangzi shi qi*, dir. Li Beihai, 1913).

Dingjun Mountain is crucial in the "shadow opera" proposal, as it was believed to be the "first" Chinese motion picture, a film recording of an opera performance shot in a Beijing photo studio, Fengtai. The significance of the film is monumental in this historical narrative, for it not only inaugurated Chinese filmmaking, but also grounded Chinese cinema firmly in the national tradition. But research done by Huang Dequan (2008) suggests this legendary film may never have been made; it remains only a "legend" in film history and should be treated with great caution when commemorated as the inception of Chinese cinema. For decades historians relied on a photo of leading opera star Tan Xinpei dressed in the *Dingjun Mountain* costume as evidence for the production of the alleged first Chinese motion picture. According to Huang, there is no concrete evidence showing that Tan starred in a film around 1905. The only evidence Huang found that connected Tan to the Fengtai Studio was a commissioned audio recorded at Fengtai in 1913.[52] Tan was an acclaimed *laosheng* (older male character) actor and the "greatest star of his generation."[53] Known for his soaring voice and thrilling heroic performances, Tan was a high-profile actor in his time because of imperial patronage. He enjoyed unprecedented fame in the capital city, Beijing, and achieved a nationwide celebrity beyond the opera field. Thus Tan was instrumental in leading Peking opera into a new phase of stardom and commercialization. Tan would utilize modern technologies of sound recording, photography, and possibly movies to sustain his career as opera's "Big Boss" (*da laoguan*) in the new century.

Here I will not speculate on how and why an opera performance was linked to the beginning of indigenous filmmaking. One thing we are sure of is that the mystery surrounding the "first" picture(s) not only compels us to reconsider the entire shadow play proposition, including its spinoffs; it also reveals a problem in our study of film history—that there has not been enough primary research to corroborate claims made by a series of historians, including myself. In my own essay on the discourse of music in films of the 1930s, I argued that the Chinese early filmmakers were anxious to "sinify" cinema, and one way to do this was to adapt popular opera repertories to the screen. I too used the alleged "first" Chinese picture *Dingjun Mountain* to make my case.[54] But I was wrong, following the existing discourse instead of seeking evidence to verify the standard history. In retrospect, it is clear that we did not have enough material to show how early film arose and to see the possible gaps and loopholes in its genealogy. More importantly, we need to reexamine the prevailing discourse of Chinese film historiography by finding additional and reliable primary data. Translating *yingxi* as shadow play or other derivative of traditional performing arts is hasty, exposing our drift toward conformity and our lack of attention to details. The persistent literal translation of *yingxi* as shadow play reveals our unconscious anxiety, to salvage ethnic heritage in forging genealogy.[55] Foucault once defined genealogy as "gray, meticulous, and patiently documentary. It operates on a field of entangled and confused parchments, on documents that have been scratched over and recopied many times."[56] Foucault went on to explain that documentary of genealogy "requires patience, and a knowledge of details, and depends on a vast accumulation of source materials."[57]

Taking Foucault's cue on the difficult and slippery path in constructing genealogy, we ask just how motion pictures, as *yingxi,* inherited from or interacted or commingled with puppetry or opera. This remains an "entangled and confused parchment" of early cinema in China. While *yingxi* may explain the proclivity of film practice in China, as proposed by Zhong Dafeng and Chen Xihe, it has not been complete in telling us how films were screened, used, and received in the first few years after those initial screening events operated by foreign showmen. *Yingxi* leaves many shadowy, unrealized spots to which we need to attend. To know how early film was viewed, we need to move out of our comfort zone and begin to accumulate a vast source of historical materials. Only by a wider, deeper excavation of history can we arrive at a better definition of *yingxi* as a cogent genealogical term. And we must be open to jettisoning it if it is a stumbling block.

NEWS FROM HONG KONG

Zhang Zhen asserts that the cinema of attractions received by mass audiences in Shanghai of the 1910s was "distinctly concerned with contemporary subjects, ranging from current affairs, slapstick comedies, and scenic panoramas to educational materials."[58] She leaves this page of early film exhibition open for investigation. Given these holes in early film history, a research team headed by me embarked on a project to investigate film exhibition, promotion, and reception at the turn of the twentieth century in China.[59] Our team collected film advertisements and film news from newspapers in Hong Kong. We found that at the turn of the century, film exhibition in Hong Kong did not take place just in the tea/theater garden setting, nor did it fit the traditional *yingxi* cluster. Movie consumption in Hong Kong, as a British colony and Chinese-speaking territory, was highly varied. It was Janus-faced, embodying numerous roles and multiple functions. Movies were used as a promotional tool for Cantonese operas and a handy illustration for Christian deputation and, at the same time, served charitable and educational aims for the local community. More importantly, film in Hong Kong rapidly evolved as a commodity, a social institution and a business of the new century. As we shall see, the early film scene in Hong Kong was too rich to be subsumed under an enchanting shadow play or "shadow opera" image, housed in the local tea gardens or opera venues. As the editors of *Beyond the Screen: Institutions, Networks and Publics of Early Cinema* write, "Projecting mainstream moving pictures in churches, convincing educators of the benefits of using film in the classroom, and collaborating with charitable organizations . . . enlarged the role of cinema within the public sphere while also demonstrating its usefulness as a tool of instruction."[60] This collection of essays starkly shows the variety of social causes that early cinema served, before its eventual resolution into the show business of motion pictures.

MOTION PICTURES' ARRIVAL IN HONG KONG

As Law and Bren assert, the first report of public film screening in Hong Kong is dated April 27, 1897, about seventeen months after the first screening of moving pictures in Paris.[61] Indeed, in our survey we located the source cited by Law and Bren: a news report in the *China Mail* on April 24, 1897. The news announced: "Professor Maurice Charvet, who arrived today by the French mail steamer, has [come] to Hong Kong from Paris to exhibit 'Cinematograph' and the 'Kinetoscope,' the twin marvels of the age. These marvels have never been shown in Hongkong or the Far East before."[62] Two days afterward, a similar advertisement appeared in the *Hong Kong Daily Press*, promoting "the Cinematograph" as "the latest and greatest success of London and Paris."[63] Further coverage of the event was also reported in the *Hong Kong Daily Press* two days later: "Few people [were] privileged to witness the pictures"; "about a dozen scenes were shown on the screen and in each the movements were plainly visible."[64] The coverage described the contents of the screening: "[The] entry of the Czar into Paris and the march past of a regiment of French cavalry [was] so life-like"; it even mentioned the mechanical problem of the new invention from France: "an irritating quiver as the pictures are being displayed. . . . this fault is common with every cinematograph and a fortune awaits the man who will devise a means of escaping it."[65] An item in the *China Mail* provided details of cinematograph: "a long strip of film, containing very minute photographs, is wound from one cylinder to the photographs passing the lenses, at the rate of fifty per second. The photographs are projected on a screen by a very powerful electric lamp."[66]

Film was introduced to Hong Kong audiences with high expectations and curiosity, as evinced by this detailed coverage. Similar hype and enthusiasm were shown at every subsequent screening. At least six more exhibition events following the City Hall screening were announced in the *Hong Kong Daily Press*.[67] Each of the exhibitions was coupled with accounts of the content screened, information on the venue, the owner or operator of the property, and reports of its reception, or reviews.

Following these events, motion pictures gradually entered into local Chinese entertainments. To better understand the process, our team surveyed a leading Chinese newspaper, the *Chinese Mail* (*Wah Tsz Yat Po*, literally "Chinese-language daily") from 1896 to 1940 (figure 1.2). The *Chinese Mail*, along with *Universal Circulating Herald* (*Hsun Huan Jih Pao*, 1874–1963) were the earliest Chinese newspapers published in Hong Kong with a history of over seventy years.[68] The *Chinese Mail* began as the Chinese edition of the leading English newspaper, *China Mail*, but soon became an independent press. It started publishing in 1872 and closed down in 1946. Because the microfilm of *Universal Circulating Herald* was unavailable locally for the period we wished to search, we could only work on the *Chinese Mail*, which had nearly a complete collection (save 1899) in Hong Kong libraries.

We went over the papers to collect reports and advertisements related to film. Our assumption was that press coverage of movies would yield information on details of exhibition, venues, and reception among Chinese viewers. The reason to use newspapers as the primary source for our data collection is twofold. One is that newspapers contain the most wide-ranging record of both the formal and informal film trade and screening activities. *Chinese Mail* was published daily and covered the commercial sectors, as it

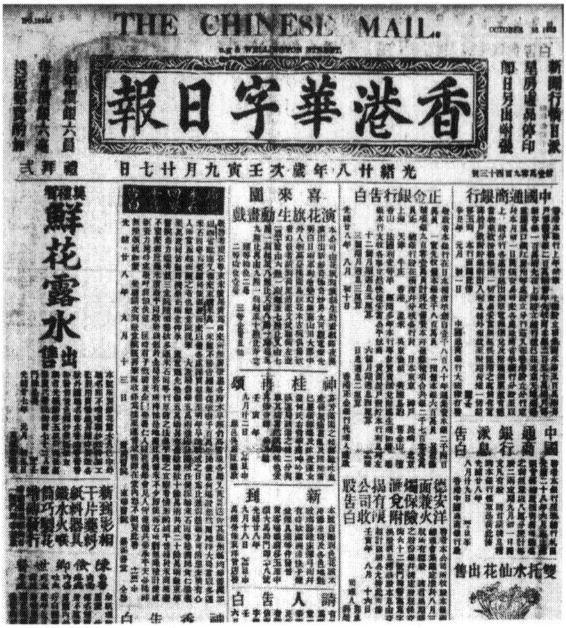

THE CHINESE MAIL.

香港華字日報

光緒廿八年歲次壬寅九月廿七日

鮮花露水

喜來園
演花旗生動畫戲

Figure 1.2. *Chinese Mail*, circa 1902. Center: "Hei Loi Theatre Playing Lively American Photoplay."

appeared in paid advertisements, and public screening announcements from the YMCA, for instance. The second reason is that we could not find any source materials that offered information on the period from 1895 to 1905, and that was as systematic and consistent as the news coverage of the local press. In order to fulfill our research objective, we had to rely on newspapers.

Facing a plenitude of information, we adopted a comprehensive search method, wishing to collect as many items as possible. We believed by conducting such a carpet search we might come closer to uncovering the early film scene in Hong Kong. We found no coverage on film before 1900. So for the period between 1900 to the end of 1940, when Hong Kong was seized by the Japanese, we collected, scanned, and transcribed a total of 11,786 entries, including 4,231 news items and 7,555 advertisements. For the purpose of this chapter, I will focus on the data collected from 1900, the year when film ads and news began to appear in the *Chinese Mail*, to 1924, the year when film exhibition became more organized and institutionalized. Below is a summary of our initial findings with respect to the *yingxi* thesis and Hong Kong's early film scene.

SURVEY SUMMARY: 1900–1924

1. Nearly a thousand entries were collected during the period between 1900 and 1924.
2. Different terms for motion pictures other than *yingxi* were used. They are *yinghua* (photo pictures) and *dianhua* (electric pictures), drawing our attention to *hua*, the "picture" quality of the shorts shown at the time. This concurs partly with the statement made by Zhou Chengren and Li Yizhuang in their *History of Early Hong Kong Film.*[69] *Yingxi* was not the only, or even dominant, term used in Hong Kong, indicating that early film exhibition was more heterogeneous than has been prescribed by the *yingxi* concept. I will tentatively translate *yinghua* and its equivalents as "photo pictures" in the following as a way to distinguish the term from its Shanghai cousin, *yingxi*, or "shadow play."
3. The data were sorted and classified into five categories, according to the venue and purpose of screening: (1) advertisements for opera theaters; (2) YMCA illustrated lectures; (3) philanthropy, charity, and fund-raising; (4) hygiene, science, and current affairs; (5) film exhibition as a new business and institution. These categories indicate that actualities, travelogues, newsreels, and documentaries featured more prominently on Hong Kong screens in the early Republican period, similar to early film exhibition in the United States[70] and Europe.[71] The seven categories listed in the book *Beyond the Screen*, for instance, find their correspondence on Hong Kong screens between 1900 and 1920. These categories are: charity/religion; government/civics; education/advocacy; science/magic; art/aesthetics; exhibition/showmanship; community / public sphere.[72] Based on the newspaper evidence, the early film scene was not at all drama centered. The period when the *yingxi* concept began to take hold was not until the late 1920s. Variety shows were displayed in theaters, and also in local Chinese playhouses, where movie shorts also found a place. Short films thus helped complete an assorted program of entertainment, information and inspiration. To some extent, cinema was marketed as a new commodity; further, it was utilized as a tool to advance social and religious agendas. Moving pictures carried the world to viewers, and were often mobilized to illustrate Christian doctrines.[73]

4. The discovery above raises questions about the *yingxi* genealogy in the existing literature.
5. Additional data collected from three Chinese newspapers in Guangzhou also indicates a more prevalent use of the term *yinghua* (photo pictures) than *yingxi* (shadow play). We have enough evidence to suggest that the *yingxi* discourse is too singular and simplistic to explain the multitude of film culture in late Qing and the early Republican periods.

In what follows, I will provide an account for each of the five categories previously listed. Many of the ads contain more than one piece of information, ranging from the number of films packaged in the program, screening conditions, special features of the venue, promotion, and so on. To place these multiple pieces of information in proper categories, we end up using some ads or news more than once. Hence the number of ads and news items cited below is not meant to reflect the sum of our data.

THE HONG KONG FILM SCENE, 1900–1924

The first category is advertisements for opera theaters. Between 1903 to 1909, eighty-two film ads were sponsored by opera theaters, forty of which advertised opera performance bundled with motion pictures. In addition to these forty ads, there were twenty or so ads (printed between February 1900 and October 1900) that could have been promoting either movies or magic lantern shows. Sponsored by Chung Hing (Chongqing) Theatre and Ko Shing (Gaosheng) Theatre, these ads used terms like *qiqiao yanghua*, "exquisite and marvelous Western pictures," to attract potential customers. These were most probably either magic lantern or slide shows, based on previous findings.[74]

Here films were named variously, including *yinghua* (photo pictures), which appeared sixty-one times; and *huatu yingxi* or *huaxi* (picture photoplay), which appeared nine times. *Yingxi* appeared only ten times. These ads show the concurrence of opera and motion pictures, revealing traditional theaters' intent to secure or to broaden their audience via film screenings. These ads also have something in common: they advertised a change of repertoire. With the new opening, a foreign picture would be added to the program as a bonus.

Before cinema houses like Victoria Cinematograph and Bijou Scenic Theatre began to operate around 1907, these opera theaters were the established venues for movie screening.[75] Then, starting from 1905, motion pictures gradually moved from the edge to the center, as sometimes the theater would only screen films. And from 1904 on, the opera theaters listed film screening as the main attraction in their ads, indicating film's increasing popularity and possibly dominance.

The second category is YMCA illustrated lectures. This category captures early film's function as community outreach. Sugawara Yoshino writes about the robust film exhibition at Shanghai's YMCA in the early twentieth century. Promoting "healthful entertainment," film shows at the Shanghai YMCA not only formed an alternative screening culture, they also helped nourish the first generation of Chinese film entrepreneurs with business ambition and aspirations to social reform (see Sugawara's chapter in this volume). Similarly, in the newspapers in Guangzhou and Hong Kong we found frequent reports on the YMCA's film activities in treaty ports like Guangzhou[76] and Xiamen ("Theaters in Xiamen," April 19, 1929, *Gongpingbao*), demonstrating the use of cinema to advance the cause of evangelism, by introducing sights and scenes from the world to local populations.

In Hong Kong, there were fourteen local news stories printed between 1908 to 1913 featuring talks held at the YMCA by missionaries or travelers on their tours in various places like the UK, the Canadian Rockies, Korea, Beijing, Manchuria, America (including the story of Columbus), the Philippines, Turkey, and so on. These talks informed Hong Kong audiences about the culture, scenery, customs, and history of foreign countries or cities. To enhance the interest and the credibility of the lectures, screening of motion pictures of such places was included. It is worth noting that the news items used the term "projecting" (*ying*) to highlight the accompanying visual presentations, implying that the events were not just talks, but had additional attractions, extras, and amusement by moving images. The films shown at the YMCA were called either *dianhua* (electric pictures) or *yinghua* (photo pictures). *Dianhua* appears five times, while *yinghua* appears four times. Here too use of *yingxi* is nowhere to be seen.

Based on the opera ads and the illustrated lectures, we can see that in Hong Kong between 1903 and 1913 cinema was mainly understood as *yinghua* (photo pictures),[77] not shadow play or some derivative of Chinese performing arts. *Yinghua* appear to be representations marketed as performance or show, mechanically mediated. They are not meant to be (mis)taken for traditional amusements. Movies were not indebted to or extensions of shadow play or opera; they were utilized to sell traditional amusements, just as they were mobilized to illustrate lectures with religious and colonial messages. The practices of early cinema in Hong Kong exceeded the cultural boundaries of "shadow opera" as formerly purported by scholars.

The service-oriented film events at the YMCA culminated between 1925 and 1927 when the general strike in Hong Kong and Kowloon brought temporary closure of theaters, leaving local audiences with very few film activities they could attend. During this period, the YMCA held regular film screenings, including Chinese and American feature films.[78]

"Philanthropy, charity, and fund-raising" is the third category in our list. Between 1908 and 1924, we identified eight ads and eight news stories on fund-raising for disaster relief in South China or secondary school fund-raisers where either commercial pictures or newsreels of the disaster sites were the main attraction, or "hook," to arouse audiences' sympathy.

"Hygiene, science, and current affairs" also testifies to cinema's social function. Films were used to promote scientific hygiene, and visualization of current affairs. Between 1904 and 1924, eleven news stories and ninety-five ads appeared. These movies projected ideals of public health, scientific and geographical knowledge, and views of public affairs, including the 1904–5 Russo-Japanese War, the coronation of King George V in 1911, military exploits of the warlords Zhang Zuoling and Wu Peifu in the North, and footage of floods and other natural disasters. A film about the Russo-Japanese War was particularly popular, showing consecutively for over six weeks (from June 21 to August 5, 1905) at a temporary outdoor space near the Central Market. Organized by a Japanese distribution company, this documentary short was possibly the longest-running film show in the decade. Among these news stories we found an advertisement printed in 1908 selling a phantom ride to famous sites in France. Phantom rides, like amusement park rides, mounted the camera on locomotives, trams, or boats shooting rapids. Like the Hales Tours (simulated railroad trips), these were virtual journeys through real space and sometimes, creative geography. Tom Gunning comments on these rides: "Such phantom rides substitute sensation for contemplation, overcoming effects of distance in a rush of visual motion."[79] The information on phantom rides in Hong Kong opens a new research link on the early visual experience of Hong Kong audiences.

"Film exhibition as a new business and institution" is the last and the largest cluster of film-related news and ads. Some of the bigger ads are about the "state of the art" theatrical experience. Film exhibition was noted as a novelty, with reports on theater fires, on public safety, and on film exhibition as a business and institution. There are five distinct subcategories within this one, given the huge amount of materials.

a. Screening conditions. We found at least nine news stories and thirty-one ads on movie-screening conditions between 1907 and 1924: stability of the pictures, crispness of the image, lighting, noise control, sound effects, and comforts of the viewing experience, such as seats, fans, air conditioners, fresh air, cleanliness.
b. Theater ads, with opening of new cinemas, opening of new pictures, financing, ownership, administration. Thirty-two news stories and 218 ads were printed on these matters between 1902 and 1924.
c. Public affairs at movie theaters. From 1905 to 1922, we found nineteen news stories on public safety, fire hazard, inspections, commotion, and the excitement of audiences incited by the images. An interesting one concerns a 1910 boxing film shown in the United States, with a white versus a black pugilist. The black fighter wins, and this caused a major ruckus. The British Parliament debated the pros and cons of allowing such incendiary screenings.
d. Film narrators and other guides to the programs. We found 270 ads between 1913 and 1924 featuring film narrators and 9 ads emphasizing the provision of a bilingual synopsis or handbill; one news item on film narrators; and one on the handbill. This subcategory collects the largest number of advertisements, indicating the importance of translation in receiving foreign silent pictures. As we can see, over 90 percent of the pictures screened in Hong Kong by the mid-1920s were foreign pictures. Despite being a British colony, the majority populations in Hong Kong were Chinese speakers. In order to boost attendance and ticket sales, it was necessary for the theaters to provide a bilingual synopsis of the pictures with English intertitles. The statement by historians Zhou Chengren and Li Yizhuan that in Hong Kong narrators (or interpreters) started to work in September 1916 is proven to be incorrect.[80] We found that narrators accompanying foreign pictures operated as early as February 1916. Judging from the number of ads, film narrators were an important side of film exhibition for at least six years. But their importance began to decline in late 1922 when printed handbills or synopses were gaining importance as movie guides, to

reduce distraction from the screening. This information may change the standard view of the decline of film narrators in the late 1920s. Historians sometimes claim that the advent of sound pictures killed off the accompanying narration.[81] But the stories we found in Hong Kong indicate that a handbill or a brochure made exclusively for the screening was more desirable to viewers than the interpreters. Note that this happened in the early 1920s, long before the introduction of sound films, calling our attention to possible apertures in the established historiography. Further investigation would be needed to see if indeed film narrators had already confronted competition from print publicity before the coming of the sound era.

e. Exhibition promotion and marketing. There were ways to add value with a ticket purchase: reimbursement of ferry fares between Hong Kong Island and Kowloon; extras such as Western musical performances and magic shows and acrobatics. Between 1905 and 1924, there are at least eight news stories and 246 ads on exhibition promotion and marketing, demonstrating the transformation of movie exhibition from erratic operations to an organized, capitalist enterprise competing for profits.

RETRANSLATING *YINGXI* AS PHOTOPLAY

Before 1924, most of the public information on movies concerned screening events, screening conditions, and their purposes. Movies were not just entertainment; they served multiple functions. Sometimes they might just be an adornment; other times they were tools for other aims, such as Christian deputation, as in illustrated lectures held in the YMCA, and fund-raising. Movie screenings facilitated social interactions and gathered people together to participate in a worthy cause.

Among these five categories, film exhibition as a new institution, commodity and business takes center stage from 1910 and onward.[82] Over six hundred ads and news stories combined can be found under this rubric, more than the other four categories combined. Magic lantern ads and cinematic and proto-cinematic exhibition as business pursuit constituted the majority of the collected data on cinema during this period. Stories on film production, on the other hand, were virtually nonexistent at this stage, with the exception of a call for shareholding by the China Sun Motion Picture Company (Minxin) managed by Lai Man-wai (Li Minwei), the forerunner of Hong Kong cinema.[83] Early film in Hong Kong thus is primarily an exhibitor's cinema, a novelty for visual pleasure and a new medium for socialization and cultural uplift. Furthermore, in the early 1920s screening motion pictures was harnessed as a capitalist activity, whose surplus value was enhanced by adding physical comfort and aesthetic decoration. After 1920 we see the domination of Hollywood pictures and the emergence of professional film criticism (see Cheung and Tsoi's chapter in this volume), which seems closely related to Hollywood's popularity. Stars, genres, business operation, and the technology of American cinema occupy the center of movie reviews. There is ample evidence to chart the growing influence and maturation of movie screenings, with technical, aesthetic, and economic improvements. In Hong Kong, journalism of the time indicates the institutionalization of cinema as a growing business and entertainment enterprise.

Tom Gunning's "cinema of attractions" includes a variety of moving pictures aimed at seizing viewers' attention, not absorbing them into a narrative experience. In the West, narrative structures of character, settings, goals, cause and effect, and wish fulfillment were yet to come, after the nickelodeon boom around 1905. Meanwhile, moving picture attractions boldly grabbed people's notice, with crashes, animal antics, contortionists, erotic views, biblical vignettes, trick shots, scenery, and famous events like coronations, funerals, and battles (often re-created). Charles Musser's study on American showman Lyman Hakes Howe (1856–1923) provides another insight. Howe is known for his phonographic exhibition and curatorship that provided middle-class patrons the pleasure of cinema without attendant anxieties over sensual indulgence. Musser used the term "cinema of reassurance"[84] for Howe's soothing film programming. Musser's idea allows a useful entry to tell the story of early film culture in Hong Kong. In Hong Kong and perhaps other cities in China, as evidenced in the YMCA's "wholesome" film entertainment, film screening remained eclectic, accommodating a variety of interests and incentives, ranging from a "cinema of attractions" that provided sensual stimuli to a "cinema of reassurance" that balanced pleasure with civility.

The two cinemas of different appeals were evident on Hong Kong's early screens, as there were plenty of news and ads on the visual presentation of warfare, current affairs, enlightenment, and instruction. For instance, the 1904–5 Russo-Japanese War, the coronation of George V in 1911, the exploits of northern warlords, and footage of floods and other natural disasters prove that movie exhibitions were not limited to *yingxi*—dramatic features with fine performances and well-crafted storytelling. Instead, the cinematic experiences were varied and multivalent. *Yinghua*, photo pictures, the Hong Kong term for cinema, testifies to the wider scope of movies' local meaning. Via the lenses of photo pictures, we may reconsider the ways and means of movie screening as functions, that is, events with specific social and educational aims. Screenings were often a means to some further end, such as education/evangelism as in the YMCA talks, fund-raising, or building business synergies with a cognate enterprise, such as opera. If the cinema of attractions was a prenarrative exhibitionist "come-on," similar to fairground barkers and ballyhoo, *yinghua* by way of its picture quality and visual appeal promoted community aims through illustration, showing, presentation. *Yinghua*, the idea of photo pictures, thus departs from the shadow play *yingxi* concept in its distance from a drama-based dogma that predefined the specific ethnic audience: Chinese audience's preference for *xi*, dramatic effect.

In the 1980s historians found *yingxi* an entry to formulating an indigenous film theory and aesthetics. *Yingxi*'s emphasis on script and literature differentiates Chinese cinema and is a strategic enunciation. However, translating *yingxi* as "shadow play" opened an unlikely link from motion pictures to puppetry and opera. This improbable connection has led scholars to continuously return to the same sites and sources to reinforce cinema's genealogy in China—the teahouse, traditional garden, shadow puppetry, and the opera. We have overlooked the materiality of *yingxi*—images, movements, projecting light beams—that might have transformed the theatrical experiences of the audience into a phantasmagoric adventure beyond a recurrence of live performance. Following *yingxi*'s earlier meaning as magic lantern, we could retranslate *yingxi* as photoplay, switching from our habitually literal translation of *ying* as shadow to *ying* as photography, image, or projection. Redirecting our attention to the first component of the *yingxi* pair, that is, the glow of *ying*, I suggest relocating *ying* in the cinema's apparatus—shooting, processing, and projection. And by reregistering the photographic quality of *ying* as moving images, instead of its ethnic connotation, we widen the understanding of how cinema was received by Chinese audiences. Imagining *yingxi* as photoplay, we might reconsider the early audience's view of the world, and further unleash its perceptual bonds in the first decade of cinema's settlement in China. It may be true that *yingxi* represents Chinese filmmakers' initial engagement with motion pictures in that the new medium's dramatic proclivity presided over any other renderings. But *yingxi*'s translation has misrepresented the multiplicities of film exhibition and the rich cinematic culture comprising attractions and reassurance on Chinese screens, once upon a time. It is time for us to reconsider *yingxi* as "photoplay," lighting up a more lively, diverse screen(ing) culture of early cinema in China.

ACKNOWLEDGMENT

This chapter is a partial fulfillment of the General Research Fund (GRF) project "Chinese Film History Beyond Shanghai: 1900–1950" funded by the Research Grants Council of Hong Kong SAR (grant number HKBU 245310).

Notes

1. Kar Law and Frank Bren, *Hong Kong Cinema: A Cross-Cultural View* (Lanham, MD: Scarecrow Press, 2004), 6–17.

2. Cheng Jihua, Li Shaobai, and Xing Zuwen, *Zhongguo dianying fazhanshi* [A History of the Development of Chinese Film] (Beijing: Zhongguo dianying chubanshe, 1980), 8.

3. Huang Dequan, "Dianying chudao Shanghai kao" [On the Arrival of Cinema in Shanghai], *Dianying yishu* 314 (2007): 102–109.

4. Cheng, Li, and Xing, *Zhongguo dianying fazhanshi*, 8; Li Suyuan and Hu Jubin, *Zhongguo wusheng dianyingshi* [A History of Chinese Silent Film] (Beijing: Zhongguo dianying chubanshe, 1996), 3–4; Jubin Hu, *Projecting a Nation: Chinese National Cinema before 1949* (Hong Kong: Hong Kong University Press, 2003), 30–31, 35; Zhen Zhang, "Teahouse, Shadowplay, Bricolage: *Laborer's Love* and the Question of Early Chinese Cinema," in *Cinema and Urban Culture in Shanghai, 1922–1943*, ed. Yingjin Zhang (Stanford, CA: Stanford University Press, 1999), 27–50.

5. Laikwan Pang, "Walking into and out of the Spectacle: China's Earliest Film Scene," *Screen* 47, no. 1 (2006): 66–80.

6. Cheng, Li, and Xing, *Zhongguo dianying fazhanshi*; Li and Hu, *Zhongguo wusheng dianyingshi*; Hu, *Projecting a Nation*, 30–31.

7. Zhen Zhang, *An Amorous History of the Silver Screen: Shanghai Cinema, 1896–1937* (Chicago: University of Chicago Press, 2005); Pang, "Walking."

8. Zhang, *Amorous History*.

9. Pang, "Walking."

10. Weihong Bao also wrote about the concept of "genealogy" in Chinese film history and media technology, though in terms very different from mine. See Weihong Bao, *Fiery Cinema: The Emergence of an Affective Medium in China, 1915–1945* (Minneapolis: University of Minnesota Press, 2015), 26–28.

11. Zhang, *Amorous History*, 3.

12. Zhang, "Teahouse, Shadowplay, Bricolage."

13. Zhang, *Amorous History*, 4.

14. Zhang, *Amorous History*, 89.

15. Zhang, "Teahouse, Shadowplay, Bricolage," 32; Di Wang, *The Teahouse: Small Business, Everyday Culture, and Public Politics in Chengdu, 1900–1950* (Stanford, CA: Stanford University Press, 2008), 155–156.

16. Joshua Goldstein, *Drama Kings: Players and Publics in the Re-creation of Peking Opera, 1970–1937* (Berkeley: University of California Press, 2007), 69–70.

17. Goldstein, *Drama Kings*, 73.

18. Charles Musser, *The Emergence of Cinema: The American Screen to 1907*, vol. 1 of *History of the American Cinema* (Berkeley: University of California Press, 1990), 187–188.

19. *Street Scenes in Madrid, Lynching Scene in the Far West*, and *Passing of Cavalry* are the shorts billed in the newspaper advertisement for the movie shows at Astor Hall. See Law and Bren, *Hong Kong Cinema*, 13–14.

20. Miriam Hansen, *Babel and Babylon: Spectatorship in American Silent Film* (Cambridge, MA: Harvard University Press, 1991).

21. Zhang, *Amorous History*, 43.

22. Miriam Hansen, "Fallen Women, Rising Stars, New Horizons: Shanghai Silent Film as Vernacular Modernism," *Film Quarterly* 54, no. 1 (2000): 10–22.

23. Zhang, "Teahouse, Shadowplay, Bricolage," 34.

24. Pang, "Walking," 67.

25. Pang, "Walking," 67.

26. Pang, "Walking," 74.

27. Law and Bren, *Hong Kong Cinema*, 11.

28. Huang, "Dianying chudao Shanghai kao," 102–104; Huang Dequan, "Dianying gujin ciyi kao" [The Meaning of Film in the Ancient Time and Now], *Contemporary Cinema* 6 (2009): 62–64.

29. Huang, "Dianying chudao Shanghai kao," 103.

30. Tom Gunning, "An Aesthetic of Astonishment: Early Film and the (In)Credulous Spectator," *Art and Text* 34 (1989): 114–133; Hansen, *Babel and Babylon*.

31. Pang, "Walking," 77–78.

32. Pang, "Walking," 76.

33. Mary Ann Doane, "The Location of the Image: Cinematic Projection and Scale in Modernity," in *Art of Projection*, ed. Stan Douglas and Christopher Eamon (Berlin: Verlag, 2009), 156; emphasis added.

34. "Lyceum Theatre," *Peking and Tientsin Times*, June 26, 1897, n.p.

35. "Zhang Garden," *Xinwenbao*, June 8–13, 1897, n.p.; "Tong Qing Tea Garden," *Xinwenbao*, October 3, 1897, n.p.

36. Yingjin Zhang, *Chinese National Cinema* (New York: Routledge, 2004), 55–56.

37. Zhong Dafeng, "Lun 'yingxi'" [On "Shadow Play"], *Beijing dianying xuebao* 2 (1985): 78; my translation.

38. Chen Xihe, "Zhongguo dianying meixue de zairengshi—ping yingxi jubeng zuofa" [Rethinking Chinese Film Aesthetics: On the Writing of Filmscripts], *Dangdai dianying* 1 (1986): 82; my translation.

39. Zhong Dafeng, "'Yingxi' lilun lishi suoyuan" [Tracing the History of the "Shadow Play" Theory], *Dangdai dianying* 3 (1986): 76–77; Chen, "Zhongguo dianying meixue de zairengshi," 85–87.

40. Zhong, "Lun 'yingxi,'" 63–70; Chen, "Zhongguo dianying meixue de zairengshi," 83.

41. Zhang Huiyu, "Yingxilun de xingcheng: chongti shangshiji bashi niandai de yici dianying shixue yanjiu" [The Formation of *Yingxi*: Reaffirming a Study on Cinematic History in the 1980s], *Dianying yishu* 350 (2013): 110.

42. Zhong, "Lun 'yingxi,'" 75.

43. Chen, "Zhongguo dianying meixue de zairengshi," 86.

44. Hu, *Projecting a Nation*, 30.

45. Hu, *Projecting a Nation*, 35.

46. Zhong, "Lun 'yingxi,'" 75.

47. For example, Weihong Bao, "Diary of a Homecoming: (Dis-)Inhabiting the Theatrical in Postwar Shanghai Cinema," in *The Blackwell Handbook on Chinese Cinema*, ed. Yingjin Zhang (London: Blackwell, 2012), 377–378; and Bao, *Fiery Cinema*, 29; Jason McGrath, "Acting Real: Cinema, Stage and the Modernity of Performance in Chinese Silent Film," in *The Oxford Handbook of Chinese Cinemas*, ed. Carlos Rojas and Eileen Cheng-ying Chow (New York: Oxford University Press, 2013), 401–402; Victor Fan, *Cinema Approaching Reality: Locating Chinese Film Theory* (Minneapolis: University of Minnesota Press, 2015). Note that Bao mentions the term *yingxihua* as one of several names for motion pictures in the early stage, but she translates *yingxihua* as "shadow picture play," indicating her emphasis on the interactivity of cinema and (stage) play, instead of the photographic property of the moving images; see Bao, *Fiery Cinema*, 29.

48. Jay Leyda, *Dianying/Electric Shadows: An Account of Films and the Film Audience in China* (Cambridge, MA: MIT Press, 1972).

49. Zhang, "Teahouse, Shadowplay, Bricolage"; Zhang, *Amorous History*; Mary Ann Farquhar and Chris Berry, "Shadow Opera: Toward a New Archaeology of the Chinese Cinema," *Post Script* 20, nos. 2–3 (2000): 27–42; Chris Berry and Mary Farquhar, *China on Screen: Cinema and Nation* (New York: Columbia University Press, 2006), 49–52; Hu, *Projecting a Nation*; Zhang, *Chinese National Cinema*; Pang, "Walking"; McGrath, "Acting Real"; Fan, *Cinema Approaching Reality*.

50. Farquhar and Berry, "Shadow Opera."

51. Farquhar and Berry, "Shadow Opera," 27.

52. Huang Dequan, "Xiqu dianying *Dingjunshan* zhi youlai yu yanbian" [The Origin and Development of *Dingjun Mountain*], *Dangdai dianying* 2 (2008): 110–111.

53. Goldstein, *Drama Kings*, 18.

54. Yueh-yu Yeh, "Historiography and Sinification: Music in Chinese Cinema of the 1930s," *Cinema Journal* 40, no. 3 (2002): 82–83.

55. Jason McGrath translates the "first" film magazine published in Shanghai as "Shadowplay Magazine," despite its English title, "The Motion Picture Review," printed on the cover. About this choice he explains: "I use the more literal translation of the journal title to underscore the connotations of the original" (McGrath, "Acting Real," 402). The question here is what does the author imply when he mentions the "connotations" of the original Chinese title? Shadow puppetry?

56. Michel Foucault, "Nietzsche, Genealogy, History," in *Language, Counter-Memory, Practice: Selected Essays and Interviews*, ed. Donald F. Bouchard (Ithaca, NY: Cornell University Press, 1977), 76.

57. Foucault, "Nietzsche, Genealogy, History," 76–77.

58. Zhang, *Amorous*, 66.

59. This is a three-year research project entitled "Chinese Film Industry beyond Shanghai: 1900–1950" funded by the Research Grant Council of Hong Kong, 2010. The research team comprises Emilie Yeh, Poshek Fu, Feng Xiaocai, Liu Hui, Elizabeth Cheung, Luo Juan, Jeff Lai, Yan Wai Ka, So Hui Ying, and Sun Qi.

60. Marta Braun, Charles Keil, Rob King, Paul Moore, and Louis Pelletier, eds., *Beyond the Screen: Institutions, Networks and Publics of Early Cinema* (New Barnet UK: John Libbey, 2012), 2.

61. Law and Bren, *Hong Kong Cinema*, 20.

62. "Local and General," *China Mail*, April 24, 1897, 3.

63. "City Hall–Music Room: For the First Time in Hongkong,"*Hong Kong Daily Press*, April 26, 1897, 1.

64. "Announcement," *Hong Kong Daily Press*, April 28, 1897, 2.

65. "Announcement," *Hong Kong Daily Press*, April 28, 1897, 2.

66. "Local and General," *China Mail*, April 27, 1897, 2.

67. "H. Wellby-Cook's Animatoscope," *Hong Kong Daily Press*, August 19, 1897; "Theatre Royal: City Hall," *Hong Kong Daily Press*, October 16, 1897, 1; "Edison's Latest: The Wonderful Animatoscope," *Hong Kong Daily Press*, January 20, 1898, 1; "Theatre Royal: City Hall," *Hong Kong Daily Press*, March 28, 1898, 1; "Xylophone & Kinematograph Entertainment," *Hong Kong Daily Press*, December 23, 1899, 1; "Theatre Royal," *Hong Kong Daily Press*, April 16, 1900, 1.

68. Li Gucheng, *Xianggang baoye bainian cangsang* [One Hundred Years of Hong Kong Newspapers] (Hong Kong: Ming Pao Publications, 2000), 65.

69. Zhou Chengren and Li Yizhuang, *Zaoqi Xianggang dianying shi, 1897–1945* [A History of Early Hong Kong Film, 1897–1945] (Hong Kong: Joint Publishing, 2005), 15.

70. Musser, *The Emergence of Cinema*, 193–224.

71. Braun et al., *Beyond the Screen*.

72. Braun et al., *Beyond the Screen*, v–vii.

73. Dean Rapp, "The British Salvation Army, the Early Film Industry and Urban

Working-Class Adolescents, 1897–1918," *Twentieth Century British History* 7, no. 2 (1996): 157–188.

74. Huang, "Dianying gujin ciyi kao"; Zhou and Li, *Zaoqi xianggang dianying shi*, 10.

75. It is widely accepted and cited in almost all existing studies that the first dedicated cinema in Hong Kong was the Bijou Theatre, according to the following sources: Yu Mo-wan, *Xianggang dianying shihua (juan yi)-mopian niandai: 1896–1929* [Notes on Hong Kong Film History I: The Silent Era, 1896–1929] (Hong Kong: Subculture Press, 1996), 37; Zhou and Li, *Zaoqi xianggang dianying shi*, 19; and Stephanie Po-yin Chung, *Xianggang yingshiye bainian* [One Hundred Years of Hong Kong Film and Television Industry] (Hong Kong: Joint Publishing, 2011), 47. Here "dedicated" means a venue specifically used for film exhibition. But our research shows that the Victoria Cinematograph was the earliest movie theater in Hong Kong; see "To-night: Grand Opening of the Victoria Cinematograph," *China Mail*, October 31, 1907, 8.

76. Between 1923 to 1947 research found twenty-eight news reports on film exhibitions held in Guangzhou's YMCA, from three local papers, *Guangzhou minguo ribao* (November 9, 18, 19, December 27, 1926; April, July 1927; February 2, 6, 9, 1928; March, October 1929; 1930; 1931; 1933; 1934), *Yuet Wa Po* (July, September 1933; 1947), and *Gongpingbao* (April, October, November 1929; 1930; 1947). See "Ping 'Xinren de jia ting'" [On *The Newlyweds*], *Guangzhou minguo ribao*, November 9, 1926, 4; "Wo ping 'Kong gu lan'" [On *Orchid of the Valley*], *Guangzhou minguo ribao*, November 18, 1926, 4; "Wo ping 'kong gu lan' xu" [Second Take on *Orchid of the Valley*], *Guangzhou minguo ribao*, November 19, 1926, 4; "Guochan yingpian zhi jianglai" [The Future of Domestic Film], *Guangzhou minguo ribao*, December 20, 1926, 4; "'Lou dong yuan' yuxi ji" [Site Visit of Lou dong yuan], *Guangzhou minguo ribao*, April 15, 1927, 11; "Yingxi chang zhi mao" [Hat Off in the Cinema], *Guangzhou minguo ribao*, July 12, 1927, 11; "Jinnian dianying tan" [On Films of the Year], *Guangzhou minguo ribao*, February 2, 1928, 8; "Kan le 'Huan jin ji' yihou" [On *Returning the Money*], *Guangzhou minguo ribao*, February 6, 1928, 8; "Qingnianhui guan ju ji" [On a Film Show at the YMCA], *Guangzhou minguo ribao*, February 9, 1928, 8; "Qingnianhui fayin dianying gongkai yanjiu" [A Public Talk on Sound Film at the YMCA], *Guangzhou minguo ribao*, March 4, 1929, 6; "Jiaoyu ju jin ying 'Wan wang zhi wang' qingnianhui qing reng zhunyu fangying jiao ju chi reng zun qian ling banli" [Education Bureau Banned *The King of Kings*; YMCA Pleaded; Education Bureau Overruled], *Guangzhou minguo ribao*, October 28, 1929, 6; "Jin ying ru guo huapian fang zhi wenhua qinlue" [Racist Films Banned to Thwart Cultural Invasion], *Guangzhou minguo ribao*, May 2, 1930, 2.2; "'Kong gu lan' yu ye zhi ji qita" [*Orchid of the Valley* and Other Films], *Guangzhou minguo ribao*, August 22, 1931, 4.1; "Meiguo dianying nuzi qingxin dianying de tongji" [Statistics on American Women's Interest in Film Acting], *Guangzhou minguo ribao*, May 28, 1933, 3.1; "Gudu yi tan xin zuzhi" [New Art Organization], *Guangzhou minguo ribao*, February 1, 1934, 4.4; "Qingnianhui sheng pian ying chang que xun" [An

Exact Account on Sound Films at the YMCA], *Yuet Wa Po*, July 16, 1933, 1; "Qingnianhui shen pian ying chang jin xun" [Latest Sound Films at the YMCA], *Yuet Wa Po*, September 18, 1933, 1; "Fang lao yanjiang dianyinghui canguan hou zhongzhong ganxiang" [Film Screening for Tuberculosis Prevention at the YMCA], *Yuet Wa Po*, November 25, 1947, 8; "Xiamen zhi dianyingyuan" [Theaters in Xiamen], *Gongpingbao*, April 19, 1929, 8; "Yousheng yingpian suo ji" [On Sound Film], *Gongpingbao*, April 20, 1929, 8; "You 'Fushide' shuo dao 'Wan wang zhi wang'" [Review of *Faust* and *The King of Kings*], *Gongpingbao*, October 26, 1929, 8; "Shi nian qian zhi yousheng dianying" [A Decade of Sound Films], *Gongpingbao*, November 26, 1929, 8; "Guan kexue yingpian hou" [On Science Film], *Gongpingbao*, October 14, 1930, 2.3; "'Xuanya zhi lian' jijiang shangyan" [Cliff Love Coming Soon], *Gongpingbao*, October 9, 1947, 6.

77. The ads sponsored by Ko Shing Theatre used *yinghua xi* (photo picture play) to promote the coronation of King Edward VII ("Queshenyuan yinghua" [Kok San Yun Screening], *Chinese Mail*, December 3, 1902, 3). Another frequently used term was *huatu yingxi* (picture photoplay), emphasizing the pictographic quality of motion pictures. For example, a 1902 ad sponsored by New Hei Loi Theatre, featuring "a life-like picture photoplay" ("Xinxilai shengdong huaxi" [New Hei Loi Theatre Life-like Photoplay], *Chinese Mail*, December 27, 1902).

78. "Qingnianhui yinghua" [YMCA Film Screening], *Chinese Mail*, February 2, 1925, 2.3; "Yanying Zhongguo minghua (haishi)" [Showing a Famous Chinese Film, *A Fisherman's Honor*], *Chinese Mail*, December 1, 1925, 2.3; "Yingmu xiaoxi" [Screen News], *Chinese Mail*, January 19, 1926, 2.3; "Yinghua xiaoxi" [Film News], *Chinese Mail*, May 16, 1927, 2.3.

79. Tom Gunning, "Landscape and the Fantasy of Moving Pictures: Early Cinema's Phantom Rides," in *Cinema and Landscape*, ed. Graeme Harper and Jonathan Rayner (Bristol: Intellect, 2010), 56.

80. Zhou and Li, *Zaoqi xianggang dianying shi*, 18.

81. Donald Richie, *A Hundred Years of Japanese Cinema* (Tokyo: Kodansha, 2001), 19; Hideaki Fujiki, "Benshi as Stars: The Irony of the Popularity and Respectability of Voice Performers in Japanese Cinema," *Cinema Journal* 40, no. 2 (2006): 79–80.

82. A similar claim was made concerning early Japanese cinema by Aaron Gerow, "The Subject of the Text: Benshi, Authors, and Industry," in *Visions of Japanese Modernity: Articulations of Cinema, Nation, and Spectatorship, 1895–1925* (Berkeley: University of California Press, 2010), 133–173. Matthew D. Johnson also queried the overarching definition of *yingxi* as "drama" in early film exhibition. See Matthew D. Johnson, "Journey to the Seat of War: The International Exhibition of China in Early Cinema," *Journal of Chinese Cinemas* 3, no. 2 (2009): 109.

83. "Xianggang min xin zhizao yinghua pian youxian gongsi" [Minxin Film Company], *Chinese Mail*, April 9, 1925, 2.3.

84. Charles Musser, *High-Class Moving Pictures: Lyman H. Howe and the Forgotten Era of Traveling Exhibition, 1880–1920* (Princeton, NJ: Princeton University Press, 1991).

CHAPTER 2

Magic Lantern Shows and Screen Modernity in Colonial Taiwan

Laura Jo-Han Wen

"ELECTRIC LANTERN PICTURES"

In 1899, a screening of foreign motion pictures made its way to Taiwan. The island was under Japanese colonial rule at that time. The *Taiwan Daily News* (*Taiwan nichinichi shimpō*), then the most widely circulated newspaper, reported this screening event in Chinese:

> A person from the Fushi Company, name unknown, purchased a "Western electric-lantern picture machine" from abroad and brought it to Taipei. It was exhibited and played at Luzhujiao District, Dadaocheng. Audiences from all over the place had to pay 0.15 Silver for a ticket to the show. The show ran for a month, and its earnings were not bad. Yesterday, the show relocated to a venue at Old District, Báng-kah. The ticket price was down to 0.1 Silver per visit; half price for children. Nevertheless, not many visitors came because the show had already played for quite a while at Dadaocheng; even people at Báng-kah had gone to see it. In addition, the show was similar to the magic lantern shows—the only difference was that the projected figures were movable, which was not that new or interesting.[1]

Entitled, "Electric Lantern Pictures" (*Diandeng yingxi*), this news account carries many vague messages that raise a number of questions on Taiwan's early film history. First of all, what exactly was the "Western electric-lantern picture machine" featured in this article, and what were the images that the screening showed to the public at that time? Who brought the machine—and from where—to Taiwan? Why did the person organize the public screenings mainly, if not merely, in Dadaocheng and Báng-kah—Taiwanese neighborhoods instead of Japanese districts—while the report of the event only appeared in the "Chinese section" of the colonial newspaper, the major language of which was Japanese? Finally, but not least of all, what might be implied from the last sentence of this piece of news, which compares the modernity of a film screening with magic lantern shows?

The news account "Electric Lantern Pictures" is frequently mentioned in contemporary research on Taiwan's colonial film history. Scholars consider this account a piece of evidence that potentially points to the earliest film screenings in colonial Taiwan (1895–1945) and have proposed several hypotheses on the details of the screening. For instance, film historian Huang Jen compared news accounts during the same period of time and found another screening event similar to the ones described in "Electric Lantern Pictures." The new material located by Huang was also from the *Taiwan Daily News*, entitled "Western Drama, Grand Magic Lantern," seen in the advertisement column of the Japanese section in mixed Chinese-Japanese style.[2] According to the ad, published approximately one month before the "Electric Lantern Pictures," the screening of "Western Drama" also took place in the Luzhujiao District, Dadaocheng. In other words, information from "Western Drama" seems to correspond with "Electric Lantern Pictures," as both accounts point to the screenings that featured Western moving images at Dadaocheng in August 1899. Huang thus infers that "Western Drama" (August 4, 1899) and "Electric Lantern Pictures" (September 5, 1899) described the same set of motion pictures, while the former only exhibited at Dadaocheng and the latter were seen at both Dadaocheng and Báng-kah. With this exciting find, Huang went on to excavate another screening record, "Motion Pictures at the Cross Theater," which featured Thomas Edison's *The Spanish-American War* and other films at the Cross Theater in Taipei on September 8, 1899. In Huang's opinion, the screenings in Dadaocheng, Báng-kah, and the Cross Theater could be of the same film materials, that is, the screening contents in "Electric Lantern Pictures" might include *The Spanish-American War*, and thus the "Western electric-lantern picture machine" mentioned in the news account might be the Vitascope made by the Edison Manufacturing Company. Huang's research sheds new light on

Taiwan's early film history. Yet, due to the lack of further evidence to confirm the connection between the events in Dadaocheng and the Cross Theater, it is difficult to prove Huang's theory.

Film scholar Lee Daw-Ming further discusses the three news accounts mentioned in Huang's research and proposes more hypotheses. Countering Huang's argument, Lee questions the connection between Edison's Vitascope and the "Western electric-lantern picture machine."[3] According to Lee, the audiences at the Cross Theater would be mainly Japanese, while Dadaocheng and Báng-kah were districts frequented by the Taiwanese people. The segregated culture in colonial Taiwan made it almost impossible to share the same screening materials between Dadaocheng, Báng-kah, and the Cross Theater. In addition, Lee considers it unlikely that the Taiwanese would have the chance to see new films earlier than Japanese audiences. Thus, in Lee's opinion, there seems to be no connection between the Cross Theater's Edison films and the "Electric Lantern Pictures," despite the fact that the *Taiwan Daily News* reported both screenings during September 1899. Nevertheless, Lee agrees that the machine introduced in Dadaocheng and Báng-kah was a type of film projector. In Lee's revision of Huang's theory, "Western Drama" and "Electric Lantern Pictures" concern the same materials in their screenings, which were different from the ones described in "Motion Pictures at the Cross Theater." With his new perspective on the materials, Lee follows a clue in "Western Drama," which notes "Zhang Boju (Cantonese)" as the projectionist of the screening event. Lee thereafter develops several hypotheses on the interactions of film activities between colonial Taiwan, Hong Kong, Japan, China, and Indochina during the late nineteenth century. Yet, as Lee states, more evidence to support his hypotheses is yet to be found. At this point, research on "Electric Lantern Pictures" and its relation to Taiwan's film history comes to an impasse.

To date, many questions concerning early cinema in colonial Taiwan—when, by whom, and how the first film screening took place—remain unresolved. Facts are limited and difficult to locate. The scarcity of film materials and historical evidence makes the subject a challenge to researchers, not to mention that remaining records might well be problematic, since collectable materials had to survive the strict censorship in colonial and postwar martial-law periods. For instance, the *Taiwan Daily News*, the venue that published "Electric Lantern Pictures," was primarily Japanese-sponsored and thus seen by many as the mouthpiece of the colonial administration. Yet since this newspaper received stable financial and governmental support at its time, it was also the most long-lived press in colonial Taiwan and one of the richest cultural archives for postcolonial research.

Besides the insufficiency of colonial archives, there is another challenge in configuring Taiwan's prewar film history, which concerns the dire circumstances under which the domestic film industry labored during the Japanese colonial period. A review of previous scholarship shows that, compared to works by Japanese filmmakers, records of locally made cinema in Taiwan are sporadic to nonexistent. Calling it the paradoxical condition in composing film history, Guo-Juin Hong, in his *Taiwan Cinema: A Contested Nation on Screen*, thus characterizes the history of cinema in colonial Taiwan as "film history without film." Nevertheless, Hong provides his keen observations:

> Three important aspects of Taiwan's cinema in the colonial period warrant further attention: the role of the *benzi* (commentators of silent films, the equivalent of Japanese cinema's *benshi*); traveling exhibitions; and imported films (from China, especially Shanghai, as well as from elsewhere around the globe).[4]

The culture of *benshi*, traveling exhibitions, and imported films are indeed significant aspects of Taiwan's colonial film culture. Building on Hong's observations, this chapter will further point out that these aspects, especially the culture of *benshi*, were not merely pertinent to film per se but also deeply connected to the magic lantern shows, the screen practice mentioned in "Electric Lantern Pictures" in the *Taiwan Daily News*.

All three of Hong's aspects of film culture in colonial Taiwan had connections with the practice of magic lantern shows. The *benshi*, the onsite narrator for projected images during public screenings, already existed in Japanese magic lantern shows before the emergence of cinema.[5] Traveling exhibition was a convention of magic lantern practice. Moreover, in terms of imported films, the transnational network that made possible the border-crossing distribution of cinema had taken shape since the circulation of magic lantern materials. Therefore, it is important to reconstruct the context of screen culture in colonial Taiwan that made possible the comment on modernity in "Electric Lantern Pictures," as the news account implied the existence of a contested screen practice between magic lantern shows and early film screenings at that time.

According to extant historical records, magic lantern shows and early film screenings developed in colonial Taiwan almost simultaneously, as their earliest records both appeared during the last five years of the nineteenth century. Japanese magic lantern shows became a frequent screen practice in Taiwan during the early years of colonization. The magic lantern show in colonial Taiwan was a public screen practice of modern education, science, and a new form of entertainment, but more fundamentally, it was an effective media of modern colonial power. Different from the magic lantern show in Europe, Japan, and China that had its own course of development before the emergence of cinema, the magic lantern show in Taiwan was an instrument of colonial assimilation, introduced by the Japanese administration soon after 1895 and thenceforth coexisting with the development of early, colonial film culture.

The Japanese-refashioned, colonial-redistributed magic lantern shows played an important role in the film culture of colonial Taiwan, not only preceding but also intervening in the culture of film screenings at that time. The history of magic lantern shows would help us understand more on the development of cinema in colonial Taiwan. Particularly in colonial Taiwan, the relationship between magic lantern shows and cinema was not causal and linear. It might not be the case that magic lantern shows "prepared the foundation for cinema" (as commonly understood in film historiography); instead, in colonial Taiwan the magic lanterns and motion pictures developed during nearly the same period of time, while each medium contested and refashioned the other. In colonial Taiwan, the magic lantern shows were not only "prefilmic" but also intersected film practice in both the periods of early cinema (1890s–1910s) and wartime cinema (mid-1930s–1940s).

The practice of magic lantern shows was a part of the establishment of modern screen culture in colonial Taiwan, as a complex result of the expansion of, and the competition between, Japanese and Western empires. By engaging magic lantern studies in the research of colonial film history, this chapter aims to, on one hand, propose new approach to the diverse context of Taiwan's colonial film history, and, on the other hand, contribute to the underexplored colonial legacies in the study of early cinema. In the following sections, I will discuss issues of screen modernity, cultural assimilation, colonial screen practice, and wartime discourses evoked by the magic lantern shows in Taiwan during the Japanese ruling period.

SCREEN MODERNITY

The study of magic lantern shows is currently most developed in Western and Japanese scholarship. In both contexts, the modern screen practice is considered a key connection between magic lantern shows and early film screenings. The screen modernity of magic lantern shows influenced how early cinema was then conceptualized and practiced, from the structure of the show, the role of showman or image narrator, to the modern contents on the public screen. What is more, the screen modernity inextricably intertwined with the development of imperial power during the same period of time and played a role in Japan's colonial control of Taiwan.

The magic lantern show establishes the modernity of screen culture after the "demystification of the screen" in Europe during the seventeenth century. Charles Musser, in his seminal article, "Toward a History of Screen Practice," identifies the magic lantern as an alternate beginning of cinema. Musser marks Athanasius Kircher's (1602–1680) "catoptric lamp" and his "militant stance toward the demystification of the projected image" as a decisive starting point for modern screen practice.[6] According to Musser, Kircher's idea of lantern projection eventually contributed to the cultivation of the modern spectator, the observer who would view the projected images as art instead of magic, "as life-like, not as life itself."[7] The modern screen practice in magic lantern shows prepares the foundation for later film screenings, in which the relationship between producer, image, and audience "has remained fundamentally unaltered."[8]

A strong similarity is found between the screen practice in magic lantern shows and early motion pictures, despite the difference of their technological models. In the same article, Musser points out that the moving picture machine is historically understood as a modified lantern device. For instance, in 1898, C. Francis Jenkins described the early film machine as "a lantern equipped with a mechanical slide changer."[9] Musser thus situates cinema "within a larger context of screen history," and notes, "A history of screen practice presents cinema as a continuation and transformation of magic lantern traditions in which showmen displayed images on screen, accompanying them with voice, music and sound effects."[10] It is imperative to mention here that the unaltered screen practice in magic lantern shows and early cinema is not only exclusively seen in the Western context but also in Japanese and East Asian visual culture.

The Meiji period is a significant historical moment for modern magic lantern practice in Japan. Iwamoto Kenji, in *Centuries of Magic Lantern in Japan: A History of Visual Culture on the Eve of Cinema,* parallels Western magic lantern history with the development of *gentō,* the Japanese magic lantern.[11] In the Western section of *Centuries of Magic Lantern in Japan,* Iwamoto traces the history of magic lanterns back to seventeenth-century Europe, where Athanasius Kircher and Christiaan Huygens (1629–1695) were among the early inventors of lantern projections. The magic lanterns gave rise to the popularity of phantasmagoria in Europe during the late eighteenth century, which involved projecting images such as ghosts and skeletons in a theatrical setting of entertainment. Then, in the Japanese section of the book, Iwamoto considers the exhibition of spine-chillers in *utsushi-e* (Japanese projection-image) during the late Edo period a practice similar to European phantasmagoria. Later, during the Meiji Restoration, an imported, advanced model of a Western magic lantern device was introduced to Japan. Different from *utsushi-e,* which featured Japanese phantasmagoria and uncanny optical attractions, the new magic lantern shows, called *gentō-kai,* were scientific, educational demonstrations of modern pictures. During the second half of the nineteenth century, the *gentō-kai,* as an instrument of the civilization and enlightenment movement (*bunmei kaika*) in Meiji Japan, played a significant role in the modernization of Japanese screen culture. The culture of *gentō-kai,* as a refashion of traditional *utsushi-e* with new technical models and ideas during the Meiji period, was not only modern but also popular nationwide. The popularity of *gentō-kai* became a "lantern fever," especially in the last two decades of the nineteenth century, widely available for education and entertainment in public spaces such as schoolyards, playhouses, temples, and shrines.[12]

Similar to Musser's observation on an unaltered screen practice in Western magic lanterns and early cinema, the *gentō-kai* and early silent films in Japan also shared a structure of practice that involved the showman's instruction and various forms of sound performance (such as voice and music) during screenings. The showman in *gentō-kai* is called the *benshi,* the image narrator who also played an active role in Japanese silent film era. The *benshi,* as an onsite image narrator, directs the audience's attention to important images and ideas during the magic lantern show. In many cases, the *benshi* also becomes the attraction of the show. For instance, Ryo Okubo describes the effective performance of *benshi* during a magic lantern show that featured Sino-Japanese War themes:

> The role of the *benshi* is not just a narrator in the show. His enthusiastic talk directly affects the spectators' emotions and makes them shed tears or get angry. Because of the integration of the *benshi*'s skillful voice performance and the visual stimulus aroused by the lantern images, spectators devoted themselves to the show and were involved in the spectacle.[13]

Serving an active and effective role during lantern fever, the *benshi* significantly contributed to the popularity and modernity of Japanese *gentō-kai*. As part of the visual (and audio) attraction that delivered new ideas of the time in modern image projections, the instruction and performance of the *benshi* helped popularize Japanese magic lantern shows, in the screenings of news, scientific demonstrations, education, entertainment, and even war-themed images to the common public.

In colonial Taiwan, the earliest reception of Japanese *gentō-kai* was also during the period of Meiji lantern fever, the peak of Japan's modern lantern practice. What is different, however, is that such screen modernity in Taiwan is less of a continuation of established visual traditions than a colonial transplantation. There seem to be no records of mechanical projection (such as Japanese *utsushi-e*) in the Taiwanese context before the introduction of Japanese *gentō-kai*. The demystification of the screen in Taiwan's magic lantern shows, as the following sections will demonstrate, is a screen practice complicated by modern colonialism. Many magic lantern shows in colonial Taiwan represented the Japanese administration as a modern educator of the colonized island, while the effective images, the *benshi*'s instruction, and sound performance in these shows altogether reinforced not-so-subtle colonial discourses.

COLONIAL CULTURAL ASSIMILATION

During the late nineteenth century to the early twentieth century, the magic lantern shows in Taiwan often appeared in venues of Japanese modern education. Serving for both knowledge dissemination and colonial governance, the magic lantern show carried not only new visual contents and attractions on the public screen but also missions of cultural assimilation for the Japanese empire. *Gentō-kai*, the Japanese term widely used for magic lantern show during Meiji lantern fever, is seen in a Japanese-language textbook: *Instruction for Writing Letters and Documents: Applicable to Taiwan*.[14] Found

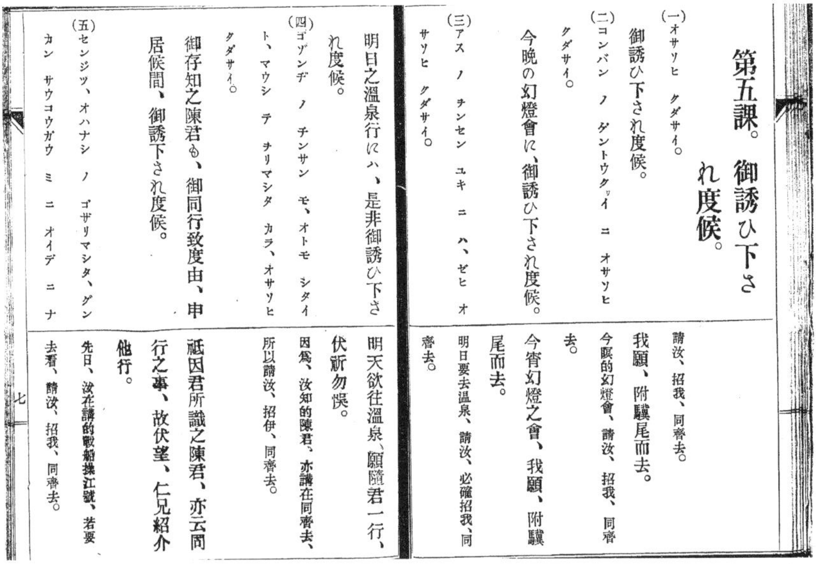

第五課。御誘ひ下され度候。

(一) オサソヒ　クダサイ。

請汝、招我、同齊去。

御誘ひ下され度候。

我願、附驥尾而去。

(二) コンバン　ノ　ゲントウクヮイ　ニ　オサソヒ　クダサイ。

今暝的幻燈會、請汝、招我、同齊去。

今晩の幻燈會に、御誘ひ下され度候。

今宵幻燈之會、我願、附驥尾而去。

(三) アス　ノ　オンセン　ユキ　ニ　ハ、ゼヒ　オサソヒ　クダサイ。

明日要去温泉、請汝、必確招我、同齊去。

明日之温泉行には、是非御誘ひ下され度候。

明天欲往温泉、願隨君一行、伏祈勿悞。

(四) ゴゾンヂ　ノ　チンサン　モ、オトモ　シタイ　ト、マウシテ　オリマシタ　カラ、オサソヒ　クダサイ。

因爲、汝知的陳君、亦講在同齊去、所以請汝、招伊、同齊去。

御存知之陳君も、御同行致度由、申居候間、御誘下され度候。

祇因君所識之陳君、亦云同行之事、故伏望、仁兄紹介他行。

(五) センジツ、オハナシ　ノ　ゴザリマシタ、ゲンカン　サウコウガウ　ミ　ニ　オイデ　ニ　ナ

先日、汝在講的戰船操江號、若要去看、請汝、招我、同齊去。

七

Figure 2.1. First page of "Lesson Five," *Instruction for Writing Letters and Documents: Applicable to Taiwan*, 1897. Courtesy of National Diet Library Digital Collections. Tokyo, Japan.

in lesson 5 of the textbook, *gentō-kai* appears in a sample sentence: "Konban no **gentō-kai** ni osasoi kudasai" (Please let me join you to the magic lantern show tonight). In the textbook, the Japanese sample sentence appears in the upper section of the page, while the section below presents two Han-Taiwanese translations, the first one in colloquial language and the second in written form (figure 2.1).

A *gentō-kai* is a social event to participate in with others, as suggested in the context of the sample sentence in *Instruction*. Besides the aforementioned sentence that demonstrated the proper expression of invitation and social activities, there are also other sample sentences in lesson 5 that feature culturally specific vocabulary in a similar grammar structure, for instance, "visiting *onsen* (hot springs)" in the third sentence, and in the fifth sentence, "seeing the *Sōkōgō* (a Chinese battleship used during the First Sino-Japanese War)." The selection of vocabulary and sample sentences shows that *Instruction* was a textbook not only for language learning but also for Japanese cultural assimilation. Visiting hot springs has long been a cultural tradition in Japanese life, and seeing the *Sōkōgō*—reminds readers of a victory in war in Japanese history, the result of which made Taiwan Japan's first overseas colony. According to historian Zhou Wan-Yao's research, *Instruction* was one of the several textbooks published by the Administration of Governor General of Taiwan (GGT) to supply an early modern model of education before the establishment of a formal public school system in 1898. Known as "National Language Learning Centers" across fourteen counties in Taiwan, these centers carried the goal of teaching Japanese language and culture to Taiwanese students, whom widely ranged in age, from eight to thirty years old at that time.[15] In such a context, *gentō-kai*, the new Japanese vocabulary, played a role in the empire's assimilation plan for colonial Taiwan.

In 1915, a magic lantern show, alongside a screening of motion pictures, was held at the "Exhibition of Educational Materials at the Twentieth Anniversary of Japanese Administration." Among the display of sample textbooks and student works from language centers, elementary schools, professional training organizations, and libraries in Taiwan and other Japanese territories (and from other countries' colonies), the show gathered onsite a large group of people. On July 30 of the same year, the *Journal of Taiwan Education* published a photo of this screening event. The photo was among the very few visual materials that have survived from the colonial period (figure 2.2). Captured from behind the spectators, whose facial expressions were invisible to the readers of the journal, this photo made the show's wide screen—the material destination of magic lantern and motion picture projections—the largest item in its frame. Located at the exhibition of colonial edification, the screen itself was also a trope of Japanese modern education. Regardless of projected images, the screen, as the focal point of the spectators' gaze, exhibited its power and attraction to subjects of the colonial island.

As a Japanese screen cultural practice (which began its course of development in Japan several decades before the colonization of Taiwan), the magic lantern show was often presented to colonial Taiwan in the light of education and modern science. In 1929, the *Journal of Taiwan Police Association*, a periodical issued by the GGT, published an article introducing some optical instruments under the title of "The Essential Knowledge of Physics." The author of the article, Hiroshi Nishimura, was a Japanese teacher at the Taipei First Girls' High School. In this article, "The Magic Lantern Device" was introduced first, among other optical devices. With an illustration, Nishimura explains the work of a magic lantern projection (figure 2.3):

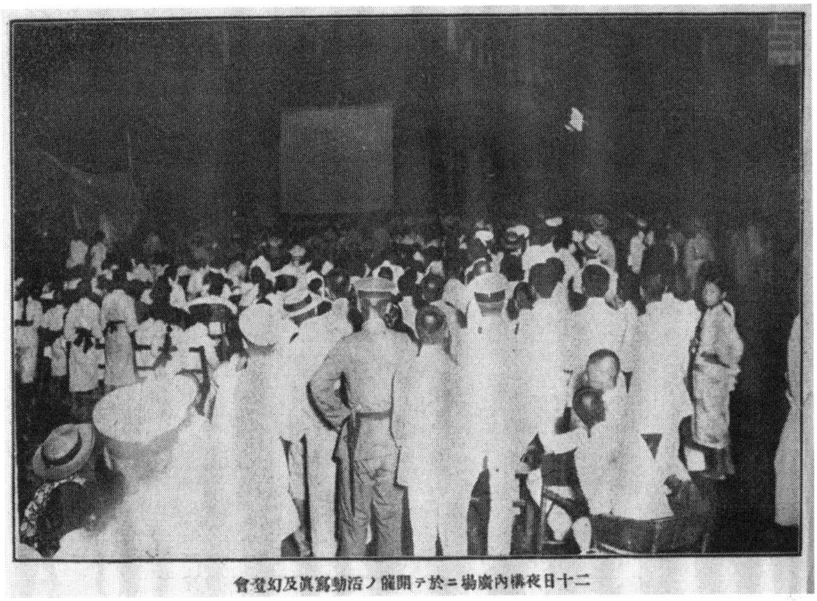

Figure 2.2. Screening event at the "Exhibition of Educational Materials at the Twentieth Anniversary of Japanese Administration," 1915. Courtesy of National Taiwan Library, New Taipei City, Taiwan.

> Coming from "S," the light source focuses on the first convex lens (L1) and illuminates on painted glass slide (AB). Then, through the second convex lens (L2), a real image of that on the glass slide is formed on the screen, enlarged.[16]

The magic lantern in this article serves as an introductory concept for science education. Published by GGT and its police system, the article was in line with the colonial authority's self image: an educator of modern knowledge.

EDUCATION, EXHIBITION, ENTERTAINMENT

The magic lantern shows in colonial Taiwan were mostly active during the first decade of the twentieth century. From 1900 to 1909, the *Taiwan Daily*

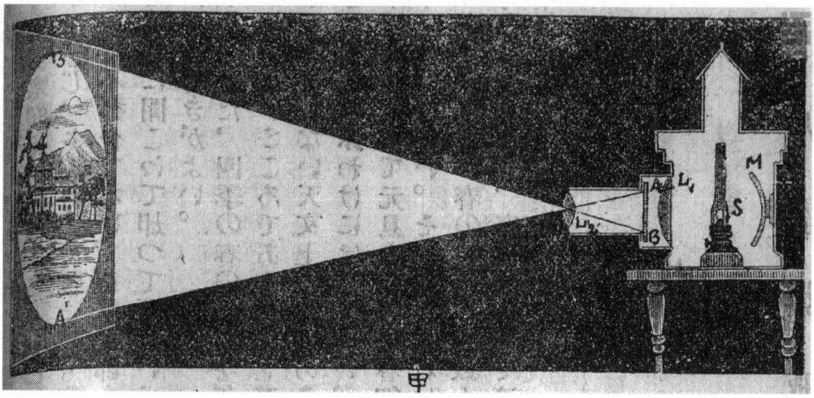

Figure 2.3. Illustration of the work of a magic lantern in *Journal of Taiwan Police Association*, 1929. Courtesy of National Taiwan Library, New Taipei City, Taiwan.

News published around 126 news coverage related to the *gentō-kai*, which was almost twice the number of its *gentō-kai* reports in the following decade and more than half of its total *gentō-kai* news throughout the Japanese colonial period.[17] Among them, many shows were held by the GGT and its affiliates, such as the Association of Patriotic Women, the Japanese Red Cross and its local chapters, and community leaders. These shows took place at Taiwanese public spaces, including elementary schools for Taiwanese children (*kō-gakkō*), temples, hospitals, and regional community centers. The target spectators of these shows were *hontō-jin*, the general Han inhabitants of the island, while many news reports of such shows featured the attendance of elementary school students, local farmers, laborers, and women. The number of attendees at the shows, according to newspaper records at that time, ranged from hundreds to thousands of people. Primarily seen in local Han Taiwanese neighborhoods, the shows often organized for the following purposes: common education, popularization of Japanese language, infection prevention and epidemic control (malaria in particular), earthquake information and disaster relief, knowledge about modern agriculture, religious gatherings, and wartime mobilization. From the late nineteenth century to the 1940s, these magic lantern shows, as a modern screen practice, a medium for knowledge and propaganda, and an extension of imperial governance, seemingly appeared in line with the authority's colonial construction and Japanization in Taiwan.

Besides a majority of public, educational events for Han Taiwanese population, there were also magic lantern shows for exclusive groups, which sometimes resembled the phenomenon of colonial segregation at that time. For instance, the *gentō-kai* specially held for indigenous Taiwanese, the native ethnic groups of people who were discriminatively classified as *banjin* (savages). In colonial Taiwan, the indigenous Taiwanese had to live in separate tribal districts with strict border control, and from time to time, the colonial administration arranged sightseeing tours for indigenous groups, transporting them from tribal areas to see other parts of Taiwan (and sometimes abroad). Considered by the GGT office an effective cultural policy to "civilize" indigenous groups, the sightseeing tours themselves were a strategic visual demonstration of colonial control. The magic lantern show, as a practice of Japanese visual modernity, was sometimes held exclusively for the attendance of indigenous people during their sightseeing tours. The magic lantern shows for indigenous tours, instead of being organized by cultural departments, were often arranged by the colonial police system at the Butokuden, a Japanese martial arts training center managed by the police administration in various locales of the colony. For instance, the *Taiwan Daily News* reported such a show on November 5, 1904: "Last night, a magic lantern show was held at the Butokuden for the Taidong savages who currently visited the Fuchū District. There were also gramophones and music for them to experience."[18] Although it is unclear what kinds of images were screened at that show, the title of the news account, "Mountain Savages and Magic Lantern Show," seems to address the contrast between the indigenous culture and Japanese culture, the colonized and the colonizer, and stereotypically, the primitive and the modern. During their viewing of the magic lantern show, the indigenous people were also exhibited to and viewed by their Others.[19] Such magic lantern shows exhibited multilayered power relations of seeing and being seen, while during the show, the desire and efficacy of colonial power was projected on the colonizer's "modern" screen.

In addition to the magic lantern shows for Taiwanese and indigenous people, there were also the ones *exclusively for* governmental and social elites. The shows often took place at theaters or high-class clubs, attended mainly by Japanese authorities and expatriates. For instance, in 1903, by presenting a series of photographic images of international cities, a magic lantern show in Taipei took its spectators on a virtual world tour:

> Held at the Tansui Hall on the 25th [of July], this magic lantern show took Taipei as its point of departure, from the Tansui Harbor to Amoy, Hong Kong, Singapore, and all around the world. It travelled back from the United States of America to Yokohama. Then, we sightsaw our long-missed, nostalgic Tokyo. The show, presented in photography with brief oral explanations, concluded by returning to Taipei. In only a bit more than two hours, the mind of the spectators took a trip around the globe. A new model of gramophone from the Hiruta Store was also presented as an additional entertainment in that evening. The show adjourned at ten o'clock at night.[20]

As entertainment for the elites, the show served to evoke new visual and audio experiences. Bringing together the real and the virtual, the visual and the acoustic, this magic lantern show effectively demonstrated the attraction of modern media. On the screen, real photographic images ranged widely from foreign novelties and distant hometowns to domestic neighborhoods, and it was the remediation of the show that enacted the immediacy of the images, making its local spectators transnational travelers at the very site of photo projection. The magic lantern show, as a modern screen practice, was thus a multimedia platform for new images, sound, and modes of presentation.

Despite the presentation in Taipei, the news account in *Taiwan Daily News* seemed to presume a Japanese spectatorship for the magic lantern show. As a matter of fact, the venue of the show, Tansui Hall, was itself a "new" space during the colonial period. Known as Dengying Academy before Japanese colonization, Tansui Hall was originally a classical Chinese academy, established in Taipei during the late Qing period. In colonial Taiwan, Governor General Kabayama Sukenori (1837–1922) renamed the place "Tansui Hall" and turned it into a club for colonial governmental officials, most of which were Japanese.[21] Tansui Hall thus became a new venue for the exercise of both colonial power and modern screen practice. In addition to magic lantern entertainment, some of the earliest film screenings took place at the Tansui Hall, including the presentation of the Lumières' works in 1900. Tansui Hall, seemingly reminiscent of and an extension of Japanese social circles in colonial Taiwan, held magic lantern shows regularly for charity, governmental entertainment, and the appreciation of photography and moving images—although in those events, Taiwanese participation was limited. The virtual world tour at Tansui Hall, featuring images and ideas such as "nostalgic Tokyo," was after all an exclusive entertaining program for Japanese expatriates in the colony.

WARS AND SHADOWS OF THE EMPIRE

In 1904, amid the Russo-Japanese War, a magic lantern show was held at the Fule Theater in Keelung, northern Taiwan. According to related news coverage, the show presented war-themed images, such as photography of sea battles and portraits of soldiers, arranged with "hundreds of new, fascinating images of other kinds."[22] Describing such images as "new and fascinating" was a common tactic in the advertisements of war-themed magic lantern shows. Through the mechanical projection of a combination of war images and other "interesting" pictures on the public screen, the magic lantern show presented news and propaganda in sensational spectacles with the *benshi*'s narrative and performance.

The Russo-Japanese War continued to be a theme in magic lantern shows after the end of the war. On September 12, 1905, a news account written in Chinese reported a magic lantern show at a Taiwanese elementary school in Hengchun, southern Taiwan. The reporter's introduction of the show, and the narrative of the *benshi* described in the news, altogether reinforced the deliberately projected "colonial others" during the screening. According to the news, Mr. Yamakawa, a Japanese man from mainland Japan (*naichi*), had organized a series of "enlightening" magic lantern shows in colonial Taiwan with the support of local authorities and social elites. The shows ran for a month at the time of the news coverage on a set schedule: beginning at 7:00 o'clock in the evening, ending at midnight, seven days a week. The news also reported the images, goals, and achievements of these shows:

> Despite the new, interesting, and diverse picture-projections—which were a visual pleasure to the audience—it was the images of Russo-Japanese War that indeed impressed the spectators. In Japan, everyone already knew about the war. Yet people in rural coastal Hengchun were like frogs living at the bottom of a well. Not to mention that the uneducated folks knew nothing about the war; there even were quite a few elites unaware of the news. This time, the magic lantern was able to project the real land and sea battles between Japan and Russia on the screen.

> The viewers felt as though they had personally visited the very battlefields and encountered situations through their own eyes and bodies. There was also an interpreter at the show, who courteously explained in clear order the reasons why Japan won the war and Russia lost, and what the war means to the people in our country. Enlightened by the show, people felt greatly excited.[23]

Through its deliberate description of the images, goals, and achievements of the Japanese man's magic lantern shows, the news report characterized the local spectators in Taiwan as ignorant folks who were "frogs living at the bottom of a well," imperial Japan as a stronger power than Russia and a necessary educator for colonial Taiwan, and the lantern images as effective materials to realize the "enlightenment" of the empire. The information on the Russo-Japanese War was described as something to shorten the intellectual distance between the empire and its colonial subjects. Without subtlety, the news account was not simply a report of the magic lantern show, but more essentially, a medium of propaganda to legitimize war and colonialism. Here the power of a magic lantern show had to be confirmed by its effectiveness in reinforcing the power of the empire in its colony. Through the projection of lifelike war images during the show, a powerful Japan appeared in its shadowed images, substantialized by the *benshi*'s courteous explanations. This was an evident moment when the modernity of screen culture and the imperial practice of colonialism converged, after the creation of an enlightened spectatorship—whether such a creation was historical, ideological, or phantasmagorical.

In 1925, Taiwanese intellectuals began to tour motion picture shows around the island. The films screened in these tours mainly concerned modern knowledge and social information. Often accompanied by the instruction and performance of Taiwanese *benshi*, the film tours were a means of local cultivation and a screening practice of counterculture against Japanese colonial ideologies. These tours were organized by members of Taiwanese Cultural Association, many of whom grew up as the first generation in colonial Taiwan to receive modern Japanese education. The screenings operated with a theme (education and enlightenment) and a structure (public screening, *benshi*, and music) similar to those of earlier Japanese magic lantern and motion picture shows, and yet developed toward the construction of a Taiwanese identity (instead of the identity of "Japanese subject"), which was potentially anticolonial. The emergence of locally organized film tours in the

1920s signifies a more developed phase in Taiwan's screen culture, when the cinema—Taiwanese-selected cinema in particular—continued and revised the screening tradition imposed by Japanese magic lantern shows and early motion pictures on the colonial island.

Yet wartime discourses facilitated a revival of magic lantern shows in colonial Taiwan, bringing the linear historiography of mechanical vision, as well as the presumptions about old and new media, into question. In the 1940s, magic lantern shows seemed to make a comeback—at least in governmental discourses with regard to the urgent need for, again, wartime propaganda at the dawn of the Pacific War. On March 12, 1941, the *Taiwan Daily News* reported a Japanese governmental plan to reenact magic lantern shows for sociopolitical campaigns, as a more convenient and cheaper substitute for the insufficient film equipment in rural farming and fishing villages in the Japanese empire and its extensive territories.[24] Although the language used in the news account was not directly war-related, as it claimed the purpose of reenacting magic lanterns was "to disseminate scientific education and culture edification," the shadow of the war was hard to ignore.

Two years later, "Magic Lantern Slides Campaign" was listed as an entry in the table of contents of an official report published in Taipei.[25] The report showed the plans and results of the Imperial People Public Service Association, a propagandistic organization of wartime militarism in colonial Taiwan, which was equivalent to the Imperial Rule Assistance Association in Japan during the same time period. Such a revival of magic lantern shows took place not only in Taiwan but also in Japan, as Hana Washitani notes: "*Gentō* experienced a full revival in the early 1940s for the purpose of the [Japanese] national mobilization propaganda during the total war against the Allied Forces."[26] Although the war pushed Taiwan to "become Japanese" in a rapid manner, the revival of the magic lantern may have had different meanings in the colony and have led to consequences distinct from those in Japan. Washitani's research shows that postwar Shōwa Japan continued magic lantern shows in education, entertainment, and social movements. Yet in postwar Taiwan, the culture was short-lived and gradually disappeared with the coming of another political regime led by the Chinese Nationalists, and thereafter the Taiwanese culture has undergone waves of identity reformation.

"Modernity is one and multiple." In his article "Magic Lantern, Dark Precursor of Animation," Thomas LaMarre makes this comment when discussing Gilles Deleuze's conception of the ruptures and successions evoked in modern scientific revolutions.[27] LaMarre's statement might find a new interpretation in the cinematic modernity manifested by the magic lantern shows in colonial Taiwan. Although frequently described as new and fascinating, the magic lantern shows were not merely an inspiring practice in screen culture or novel visual excitement; they were also a modern medium for the exercise of colonial power. The modernity evoked by magic lantern shows was both exciting and threatening in colonial Taiwan. Taiwan's magic lantern shows were all at once a continuation of Japanese and transnational screen tradition, a medium for modern knowledge, education, and scientific demonstration, and a practice of colonial propaganda. In pre-1945 Taiwan, the practice of magic lantern shows was a result of the convergence of screen modernity and colonial modernity. The projection of multilayered modernity and the shadows it left on the screen were the consequences of uneven power relations between the empires and their extensive territories.

A side account should be provided at this point. Reminiscent of colonial Taiwan's 1899 news report "Electric Lantern Pictures," in 1912, Japanese film essayist Terada Torahiko (1878–1935) stated in an article on his first film viewing experience: "[This is] the sort of experience of 'not believing until you see it, but once you see it, you are surprised yet at the same time think it's not out of the ordinary.' Anyway, it seems I was not as surprised as the first time I saw *gentō*."[28] The reason why colonial Taiwan and Japan made similar comments to compare the modernity of film screenings with magic lantern shows is curious, although it is difficult to find out who originally wrote the Chinese comment in colonial Taiwan. (Was this reporter familiar with Japanese magic lantern tradition, or did she or he experience magic lantern shows in other contexts?) In spite of the uncertainties noted above, "Electric Lantern Pictures" can be read not only as an account concerning cinema per se but also as a piece of historical evidence that reveals complicated forces and mediations of colonial screen modernity. Proposing a diverse screen culture, the study of magic lantern shows suggests a reconsideration of media historiography, which might help develop new approaches to the unresolved mysteries in the cinema of colonial Taiwan.

ACKNOWLEDGMENT

Grateful acknowledgment is given to National Taiwan Library for permission to use images from *Journal of Taiwan Education* and *Journal of Taiwan Police Association*.

Notes

1. "Diandeng yingxi" [Electric Lantern Pictures], *Taiwan nichinichi shimpō*, September 5, 1899, 4. For the interest of readability, here, I have translated the purchased site of the "Western electric-lantern picture machine" as "from abroad." The original text seems to indicate the location of purchase, but due to the unclear text on the extant copy of the news page, it is difficult to identify the message.

2. The mixed language, as stated in the advertisement, intended to attract both Japanese and Taiwanese readers. Huang Jen and Wang Wei, eds., *Taiwan dianying bainian shihua* [One Hundred Years of Taiwan Cinema], vol. 1 (Taipei: Zhonghua yingpingren xiehui, 2004).

3. Lee Daw-Ming, "Shijiu shiji mo dianyingren zai Taiwan, Xianggang, Riben, Zhongguo yu Zhongnanbandao jian de (keneng) liudong" [The (Possible) Circulation of Movie Industry Professionals between Taiwan, Hong Kong, Japan, China, and Indochina in the Late Nineteenth Century], in *Zhongguo dianying suyuan* [Chinese Cinema: Tracing the Origins], ed. Wong Ain-ling (Hong Kong: Hong Kong Film Archive, 2011), 126–143.

4. Guo-Juin Hong, *Taiwan Cinema: A Contested Nation on Screen* (New York: Palgrave Macmillan, 2011), 20.

5. Ryo Okubo, "The Magic Lantern Show and Its Spectators during Late Nineteenth-Century Japan: Control of Perception in Lantern Shows for Education and News Report of Sino-Japanese War," *Iconics* 11 (2014): 7–26.

6. Charles Musser, "Toward a History of Screen Practice," *Quarterly Review of Film Studies* 9, no. 1 (1984): 61. The original source discussed in Musser's article is Athanasius Kircher, *Ars Magna Lucis et umbrae* (Amsterdam: Joannem Janssonium à Waesbergem, 1646).

7. Musser, "Toward a History," 61.

8. Musser, "Toward a History," 63.

9. Musser, "Toward a History," 63. The original source discussed in Musser's article is C. Francis Jenkins, *Animated Pictures: An Exposition of the Historical Development of Chromophotography* (Washington, DC: Press of H. L. McQueen, 1898), 100. Here Musser also addresses Henry V. Hopwood, "A film for projecting a living picture is nothing more, after all, than a multiple lantern slide." The original source is Henry V. Hopwood, *Living Pictures: Their History, Photoduplication and Practical Working* (London: Optician and Photographic Trades Review, 1899).

10. Musser, "Toward a History," 59.

11. Iwamoto Kenji, *Gentō no seiki: eiga zenya no shikaku bunkashi* [Centuries of Magic Lantern in Japan: A History of Visual Culture on the Eve of Cinema] (Tokyo: Shinwasha, 2002).

12. Okubo, "Magic Lantern Show," 8.

13. Okubo, "Magic Lantern Show," 17.

14. "Dai go ka" [Lesson 5], in *Shotokubun kyōjusho: Taiwan tekiyō* [Instruction for Writing Letters and Documents: Applicable to Taiwan] (Tokyo: Taiwan Sōtokufu Minseikyoku Gakumubu, 1897).

15. Zhou Wan-yao, *Haiyang yu zhimindi Taiwan lunji* [Essays on Maritime and Colonial Taiwan] (Taipei: Lianjing chuban shiye gufen youxian gongsi, 2012).

16. Nishimura Hiroshi, "Jōshiki butsuri" [The Essential Knowledge of Physics], *Taiwan keisatsu kyōkai zasshi* (1929): 151–162.

17. The rough number of magic lantern news covered by the *Taiwan Daily News* (as sorted and counted by Laura Jo-han Wen through the digital database of the newspaper built by Tudor Tech Systems Co., Ltd): 1899: 5 accounts; 1900s: 126 accounts; 1910s: 66 accounts; 1920s: 13 accounts; 1930s: 1 account; 1940s: 2 accounts. Some magic lantern events appeared more than one time in the *Taiwan Daily News*, and some were published in both Japanese and Chinese sections of the newspaper.

18. "Nama-ban to gentō-kai" [Mountain Savages and Magic Lantern Show], *Taiwan nichinichi shimpō*, November 5, 1904, 5.

19. "Tansui-kan getsurei-kai" [Monthly Meeting at Tansui Hall], *Taiwan nichinichi shimpō*, July 28, 1903, 5; my translation.

20. Yeh Lung-yen, *Taipei Ximenting dianying shi, 1896–1997* [The Film History of *Ximenting* in Taipei, 1896–1997] (Taipei: Xingzhengyuan wenhua jianshe weiyuanhui: Guojia dianying ziliaoguan, 1997).

21. Zheng Zhengcheng, *Renshi tazhe de tiankong: Rizhi shiqi Taiwan yuanzhumin de guanguang xinglü* [The Sky of the Other: Indigenous People's Sightseeing Tours in Colonial Taiwan] (Taipei: Boyang wenhua shiye youxian gongsi, 2005).

22. "Nichirosensō gentō" [Magic Lantern Show on the Russo-Japanese War], *Taiwan nichinichi shimpō*, April 15, 1904, 5.

23. "Dakai huandenghui" [Grand Scale Magic Lantern Shows], *Kanbun Taiwan nichinichi shimpō*, September 12, 1905: 4; my translation.

24. "Gentō no riyō ga saigen" [Use of Magic Lantern Resurged], *Taiwan nichinichi shimpō*, March 12, 1941, 4.

25. *Dai ni nen ni okeru kōmin hōkō undō no jisseki* [Imperial People Public Service Movement: Second-Year Report] (Taipei: Imperial People Public Service Association, 1943).

26. Hana Washitani, "The Revival of '*Gentou*' (magic lantern, filmstrips, slides) in Showa Period Japan: Focusing on Its Developments in the Media of Post-war Social Movements," *Iconics* 11 (2014): 27–46.

27. Thomas LaMarre, "Magic Lantern, Dark Precursor of Animation," *Animation* 6, no. 2 (2011): 127–48.

28. Aaron Gerow, *Visions of Japanese Modernity: Articulations of Cinema, Nation, and Spectatorship, 1895–1925* (Berkeley: University of California Press, 2010): 27.

CHAPTER 3

From an Imported Novelty to an Indigenized Practice

Hong Kong Cinema in the 1920s

Ting-yan Cheung and Pablo Sze-pang Tsoi

Hong Kong film history[1] began in 1897 when two motion picture machines were brought in from the West for the island's first-ever public screening.[2] Then in 1925, a strike that lasted for sixteen months paralyzed almost all commercial activities in Hong Kong, including the early film industry. In between, there is not much written. These first three decades of Hong Kong film history are normally dismissed as uneventful and insignificant in general. In such views, focus is always given to a few individuals who conducted preliminary trials involving film productions, distribution, and exhibition. Doubtless, owing to these essential narratives, early film activities can be reconstructed, and the early filmscape of Hong Kong sketched out. However, these somewhat crude historical accounts may sometimes lead to an impression that the early participants in Hong Kong film industry as well as events they were associated with were separated from and unrelated to the social, cultural, and economic circumstances of Hong Kong in that era. The historical context of these early pioneers is lacking.

While acknowledging the existing film literature, the current chapter explores how the early Hong Kong film industry contributed to the development in the three areas specified above, arguing that the dramatic evolution of this particular industry was rooted in increase of both economic growth and cultural awareness. The chapter further reveals that such an evolution reached its watershed in the 1920s, a period that is now seen to have played a more significant role than some film critics may have believed. Indeed, this period indicates that film was transformed from an imported novelty into an indigenized commercial and cultural activity; and so the enormous growth of Hong Kong cinema in the subsequent decades can be seen as one of the important factors shaping the establishment of the local bourgeois public sphere.

The thesis of this chapter—indigenization of an imported novelty—will be presented through three sections. To set the scene, we give an overview of Hong Kong society at the time when film first arrived. Then the second section looks at how film became ever more popularized among local Chinese, resulting in the whole industry being widely seen as a profitable investment, leading soon to the emergence of Chinese proprietorship. Finally, the third section discusses the rise of an awareness of film being a cultural institution, which primarily generated a new kind of journalistic literature, prompting film to fulfill social and moral functions among Chinese communities. Drawing on materials from both the early Chinese and English newspapers, the goal of this chapter is to retouch the early Hong Kong filmscape, so as to restore and unveil its true and quite boisterous image.

EARLY HONG KONG: ONE ISLAND, TWO COMMUNITIES

The formation (and transformation) of the social structure in early Hong Kong was closely connected to its economic development since the Union Jack first flew over the island in 1841. The colony with its ideal geographical location was turned into a free port, which soon thrived on the transshipment trading industry. From the beginning, the British ruling class monopolized the political and financial sectors of Hong Kong in the capacity of officials, policymakers, capitalists, and bankers. Local Chinese, on the other hand, formed the laboring class comprising farmers, fishermen, and masons, and, as the economy gradually grew and diversified, became craftsmen, sedan-chair bearers, porters, coolies, servants, and hawkers. The colonial government implemented a segregation policy that restricted the local Chinese population to living apart from the Western community, which in addition to the British consisted mainly of Portuguese, Americans, French, German, and Spanish.[3]

Then in the 1850s, the influx of Chinese coming from the nearby Pearl River Delta and returning from overseas countries added a new dimension to the colony's polarized social structure.[4] These immigrants were no illiterate laborers—at the time common among the Chinese population in Hong Kong—but rich merchants and compradors. Having arrived at the entrepôt with considerable financial resources and substantial trading experience, this prominent group began to run businesses as import-export agents and by the 1870s had already emerged as an economic force to be reckoned with. These wealthy Chinese proprietors contributed significantly to the development of the local economy and hence grew into a particular social stratum for which the colonial authority had a high regard. The rise of the Chinese elites might have reconfigured the former social structure; still, with the colony's segregation practice and the majority of the local Chinese struggling to survive their poverty, inhabitants of early Hong Kong lived largely apart in two separated communities in terms of space, culture, and social status.

The two communities naturally differed in their favourite pastimes. For example, while all of the inhabitants, regardless of race and social class, evidently enjoyed stage shows, the exact forms of this universal entertainment were here obviously categorized by the islanders' different cultural backgrounds. Even before 1841, the local Chinese inhabitants had enjoyed Chinese operas, which were occasionally brought to the island by traveling troupes from the Mainland. Later, the colony with its economic development and population growth attracted more and more such troupes, which led eventually to the setting up of various opera theaters. The first one, Dai Loi (Dalai) Theatre, was built in 1865,[5] which was followed by others with increasing scale that would accommodate an audience of as many as six hundred to seven hundred people.[6] For the Western community, on the other hand, the first such activities took place as early as 1842, when a troupe of considerable scale from Australia brought a few lively and joyful nights to the Western inhabitants of this *undeveloped* island.[7] In the same year, Western theaters were being set up. The Western community in early Hong Kong favored performances in the forms of drama, opera, concerts, variety shows, acrobatics, boxing, and circuses—which were held at clubhouses, hotels, and outdoor venues. In 1869, the first City Hall opened in the Central District, in which both St. Andrew's Hall and Theatre Royal became immediate favorites among the upper classes and the cultured. At the turn of the twentieth century, the onetime fishing village in Southeast China emerged as a dynamic entrepôt where the population rose from 7,450[8] in 1841 to 368,987[9] in 1901. Of the total population, 95 percent were Chinese.[10]

This was the time when the "greatest marvel of the age" hit the town.

FILM IN EARLY HONG KONG: TWO COMMUNITIES, ONE ENTERTAINMENT

Whereas retrospectively we see that film as an enthralling entertainment later developed quickly and successfully over the territories, the first activities relating to film viewing were indeed rooted only in the small local Western community. But the exact information about these early activities has never been clear in view of the fact that scholarly study focusing on this part of history has been rare. Therefore, to unveil these early scenes we have to look for firsthand materials by resorting to a close scrutiny at early local English and Chinese newspapers.

On April 24, 1897, the local English newspaper *China Mail* announced that a certain "Professor Maurice Charvet" would introduce the "twin marvels of the age,"[11] called the "Cinématograph" and the "Kinetoscope," at the Music Room of City Hall (i.e., St. Andrew's Hall). Of course, it should be noted that neither machine can be ascertained to be those two genuine apparatuses invented respectively by the Lumière brothers and Thomas Edison. In fact, according to L'Institut Lumière, after its first screening in Paris on December 28, 1895, the "Cinématograph" touring the globe was supposed to be brought along by representatives of the Lumière brothers.[12] As for the "Kinetoscope," again, there is no evidence of whether Professor Charvet's machine was authorized by Thomas Edison. It can be certain, however, that the two marvels had never been shown before in Hong Kong or the Far East—according to the news coverage and advertisements in the *China Mail.*

Meanwhile, a private exhibition of the Cinématograph was held on April 26 for an invited few from the press, followed by a public screening to be conducted on the day after, only to be postponed to April 28 because, as revealed by an advertisement posted in the *China Mail,* "the delicate and intricate mechanical arrangements combined with the elaborate and most modern electrical appliances of the machine require such perfect adjustment and manipulation";[13] it was later also noted by the *Hong Kong Daily Press* that "a rather irritating quiver" was being observed during the private screening on April 26.[14] Such close and extensive reports from the press show how seminal the event was for the Western public at that moment, to such an extent that the machine itself was even given a meticulous technical introduction in a piece of news coverage:

> A long strip of photographic film, containing very minute photographs, is wound from one cylinder to the other, the photographs passing the lenses, at rate of fifty per second. The photographs are projected on a screen by a very powerful electric lamp. The rapidity with which the pictures are projected on the screen gives the impression of like picture [*sic*], every motion being portrayed.[15]

Following this thrilling introduction of the greatest marvel, a number of similar short-term film exhibitions took place before the turn of the twentieth century, presenting various kinds of machines to the audiences in Hong Kong. They included the Animatoscope, which was branded by the advertisement as "Edison's latest wonder,"[16] the Kinematograph,[17] and the Bioscope, claimed by the press to be "an improvement on the cinematograph."[18] None of these early film exhibitions, however, were mentioned in any local Chinese newspaper.

In 1900, in fact, there were indeed a number of "film advertisements" appearing in Chinese newspapers such as *Wah Tsz Yat Po* (or the *Chinese Mail*), the most commonly read local Chinese newspaper at the time. In February, June, and July, respectively, advertisements in that newspaper featured screenings of "amazing Western pictures" by various Chinese opera troupes. Later that year, in December, another advertisement showed that a screening of "imported scenery and amazing light magic" was presented by Hei Loi (Xilai) Theatre. However, although the above mentioned have been generally regarded by the existing literature as the "earliest" film advertisements in the local Chinese newspapers, there is no proof of whether these "pictures" and "light magic" were indeed film screenings. Rather, it may be more likely that they were magic lantern shows, that is, a form of slide show with pictures projected onto revolving screens.[19] In fact, a later advertisement in 1902, also featuring a Hei Loi Theatre screening, may reveal the first true film screening in the local Chinese community. Unlike the focus on "light magic" in Hei Loi Theatre's previous ad, the announcement this time emphasized "lively *moving* pictures from the United States," which also highlighted the use of powerful electric light.[20] Thus, it can be seen that Chinese newspapers in early Hong Kong, at least in the case of the *Chinese Mail*, advertised no film until 1902.

Indeed, early news coverage on film in local Chinese newspapers was usually brief and simple, focusing first merely on basic technological traits like the clarity of pictures and later on trivial story-related matters such as plot, setting, cast and acting, and so on. Other film industry concerns noticeably interesting to the English papers, such as the background, business nature, or simply the previous successes of those traveling film exhibitors, however, were not mentioned in either the news coverage or event advertisements in their Chinese counterpart. So like the Hong Kong communities themselves, there was some linguistic segregation in the newspaper coverage of the new import.

An Imported Novelty

Why is it that the English newspapers showed more interest in film as a commercial activity than their Chinese counterparts? The answer lies in the fact that these film enterprises were run by Westerners; to be precise, the early Hong Kong film scene was dominated by non-Chinese. Hence, before exploring how film industry eventually became indigenized in Hong Kong, it is important to further examine the role played by the non-Chinese agents in early Hong Kong film history. In doing so, clarification of some currently rooted problematic assumptions will be made.

Bijou and the First Cinemas in Hong Kong

The controversy over the question "Which was the first cinema in Hong Kong?" is perhaps a good example illustrating such shaky inferences concerning early film businesses. Using only the Chinese press as the source of information has led to some widely accepted "facts" about the early Hong Kong film industry that are not necessarily accurate and complete—because the information about the earliest film activities in Chinese newspapers is rather scant and partial. That is why in some existing study of Hong Kong film history, the "Bijou Theatre" is frequently claimed to be the first cinema in Hong Kong, and the cinema, which opened on September 4, 1907, on Wyndham Street, Central District, is believed to have been a joint venture by a Jewish proprietor named Ray and a local Chinese, Lo Gun (Lo Kan, Lo Gen).[21]

The commonly adopted evidence supporting this claim is an advertisement in the *Chinese Mail* on September 4, 1907, which announced a screening at Cafe Weismann.[22] The site was indeed on Wyndham Street, but there was no mention of the name "Bijou," let alone "cinema." As advertised in the English paper *China Mail,* the screening was in fact only a cinematograph show of Pathé pictures that took place in Weismann's large hall.[23] It was reported that "the company running the business hail from Paris and have five similar shows in Shanghai, two in Tientsin and others at Hankow and Peking and other places up north."[24] So instead of being the "first cinema in Hong Kong," the screening advertised by the Chinese press on September 4, 1907, was no more than a temporary film exhibition. Furthermore, the show had nothing to do with H. W. Ray and Lo Gun. The *China Mail* reported in 1908 that a certain "Mr. Dietrich," who was to become the new proprietor of Hong Kong Cinematograph, "previously controlled the cinematograph at Weismann's rooms."[25]

"Bijou" was actually the name of another cinema that did not exist until 1910. In October 1910, the *South China Morning Post* advertised that Bijou Scenic Theatre would open on the Flower Street (a nickname of Wyndham Street) under the direction of Robert Stephenson, "lately the Stage Manager of the Dallas' and Bandmann's Opera Companies."[26] Bijou later announced its official opening on November 16, at the previous site of Salon-Cinema,[27] and Stephenson was the "Lessee & Manager."[28] Another English newspaper, the *Hong Kong Telegraph*, confirmed the role of Stephenson in the Bijou: "Mr. R. H. Stephenson is sparing no efforts to make his new enterprise a success in every way."[29] Later, in 1913, it was noted in both the Chinese and English presses that the Bijou would be closed for renovation, but the latter told us more: "The Bijou will be re-opened shortly under new management," undersigned "R. F. Barrat, Manager."[30]

With "Bijou" clearly ruled out as the first cinema in Hong Kong, the Victoria Cinematograph, located at the intersection of Des Voeux Road Central and Pottinger Street (also in the Central District), is likely the earliest cinema in the territory. On November 1, 1907, the *China Mail* advertised the "Grand Opening" of the Victoria and introduced it as a "splendid and comfortable saloon."[31] Antonio Ramos, a Spanish showman who is now well known as one of the key pioneers in the early film industry in places like Shanghai, Hong Kong, and the Philippines, was the owner of the Victoria. Soon afterward, in 1910, Ramos also erected "a theatre worthy of the Colony [by securing] the site on which stood the old Hongkong Cinematograph, opposite the market."[32] That was the Empire Cinematograph, "designed by Messrs Palmer and Turner . . . a graceful hall capable of seating over 800 people," which was completed with six boxes, a dress circle, first-class and second-class stalls, and a spacious stage. Describing the interior decoration, the news report noted that the place was fireproof, with an "abundance of ventilation" provided by electric fans.[33] In the same year, the Victoria was torn down and rebuilt, reopening at the same spot in May 1911. Ramos again engaged Messrs. Palmer and Turner as the architects. The newly built Victoria could accommodate the same size audience, with chairs of the "tip-up style" and electric lights and fans, and again was fireproof: the "machine room for the cinematograph apparatus [is] entirely shut off from the public by a thick concrete wall" and "wood work has been reduced to a minimum."[34]

Although Ray is not the founder of the first Bijou, he was in fact the proprietor of a later cinema that was built on or, to be more precise, "transformed" from, the exact premises of that first Bijou. On December 28, 1918, the *Hong Kong Daily Press* reported,

> The old Bijou Theatre has been recently transformed in order to make it in every way a suitable hall for high class cinematograph entertainments. It has now blossomed out as the Coronet Theatre and under the personal management of Mr. Ray.[35]

The Coronet Theatre was named the "New Bijou"[36] in the Chinese press—a probable explanation of why Ray was mistakenly thought to be the founder of the original Bijou Scenic Theatre. There is also evidence proving that Lo Gun was at a certain point a proprietor of the "New Bijou"; this will be discussed in greater detail in the next sections.

Until at least the mid-1910s, the Victoria Cinematograph, Empire Theatre, Bijou Scenic Theatre, and Coronet Theatre (or "New Bijou") were the major cinemas in Hong Kong. And they were all founded by non-Chinese. But the indifference toward this marvellous new wizardry among the Chinese locals would not last for long.

First Film Screenings at the Chinese Opera Theaters

While introducing film to the colony and founding its earliest cinemas targeting only the local Western community as their patrons, those non-Chinese agents being seasoned businessmen also ventured into the local Chinese market. As previously mentioned, early film exhibitions that took place before the turn of the century were only held in the Westerner zones. But by 1903, this novelty was brought to the local Chinese's major entertainment site, the Chinese opera theaters.

In January 1903, the *Chinese Mail* told readers that Ko Shing (Gaosheng) Theatre, one of the oldest Chinese opera theaters in Hong Kong, showed "Stevenson's Pictures from London"[37] after an opera performance. It seems that these pictures enjoyed popularity; later that month the same newspaper revealed that the pictures were shown again at another Chinese opera theater, the Chung Hing (Chongqing) Theatre, and that this time the special screening sessions had no opera performances.[38] Furthermore, reruns were subsequently scheduled in February and March. As usual, however, the Chinese newspapers said rather little about "Stevenson's Pictures," leading to today's speculation whether, for example, Robert Stephenson (i.e., the proprietor of the Bijou Scenic Theatre) was involved,[39] given the same Chinese characters transcribing the two names "Stevenson" and "Stephenson." But if we also refer to the English newspapers, we can have a much clearer picture about the exact contents of these screenings. On January 9, 1903, the *Hong Kong Daily Press* revealed that at the time of the screenings at Ko Shing and Chung Hing, good shows were given at the Theatre Royal by the Imperial Bioscope and Animated Picture Co.:

> The instrument is a first-class one and the pictures which it threw on the screen were clear and distinct, while at the same time of a most interesting character. Specially appreciated were the scenes descriptive of the Coronation festivities . . . the Bioscope carried the spectators [on] a voyage across the Atlantic on the *Kronprinz Wilhelm,* and a ride on the St. Gothard express through the famous Wassen. The comic pictures, of which these was [in] abundance, kept the audience greatly amused.[40]

One special program consisted of "a number of local pictures illustrative of Chinese life" including "scenes in Canton and Hongkong" and "a view of a ride down the Peak Tramway."[41] The report highlighted that the proprietor of this successful venture was T. J. Stevenson, "a gentleman who has been associated with the business since its invention and who understands it from top to bottom," whose enterprise was well received in North China[42] and voted a great success in Shanghai.[43] A veteran like Stevenson would have had extensive experience in doing business with the Chinese, which resulted in the screenings at Ko Shing and Chung Hing. The above description of contents of the screenings offers a glimpse of what was being shown to the local Chinese moviegoers.

Just one year later, an account of Chinese participation in the local film industry appeared for the first time in the local press, which was almost seven years later than the first film screenings initiated by Westerners.

An Indigenized Practice

On March 8, 1904, an advertisement in the *Chinese Mail*, signed by Yu Fung-shun (Yu Fengshun), announced that new pictures and devices were available for rent: reels that measured up to fourteen to sixteen feet in diameter, devices that enabled smooth screenings of lively movements with no quivering or risk of fire.[44] It was suggested that, for best viewing quality, the ideal venues for screenings were theaters or halls in large mansions. Subsequently, in 1905 and 1908, Yu's pictures were shown at some of the major Chinese opera theaters, including the Ko Shing, Chung Hing, and Tai Ping, and some of these pictures were from the United States.[45] As Yu seems to be the first Chinese tradesman involved in film businesses that we can identify from the local press, he is arguably the first Chinese participant in the film industry in early Hong Kong.

The next Chinese players in the industry came onto the scene in the mid-1910s, and their activities were reported equally by both the English and the Chinese press. In 1914, a Chinese named Lan Sum-ng was identified as the proprietor of the Bijou Scenic Theatre in the *South China Morning Post*.[46] In 1915, the *Chinese Mail* reported that a Chinese businessman, who was then the new manager of the Victoria Cinematograph, became also the joint proprietor (another partner was a Filipino) of the Empire Cinematograph.[47] In 1916, the same newspaper advertised an outdoor film exhibition highlighting the enterprise as a venture by Chinese.[48] The *South China Morning Post* reported in 1918 that the owner of the "Hongkong Cinema," Mr. Lai Wing-kee, was fined for an overcrowded theater.[49]

If film-related activities involving Chinese were still not plentiful in the second decade of the twentieth century, the next five years saw a huge increase in such activities. Table 3.1 shows figures for advertisements and news coverage having appeared in the *Chinese Mail* during the first fifteen years

Table 3.1. Local Chinese Participation in the Hong Kong Film Industry, 1910–1925

Year	1910–19	1920–25
Advertisement	41	808
News coverage	4	169

of the twentieth century, related to local Chinese involvement in film businesses. Comparing the figures for the 1910s with those for the first half of the 1920s, we find a dramatic rise in the overall participation of the local Chinese in the film industry.

With such an overwhelming increase in participation in film businesses in general, it is significant to note that during this period, the *Chinese Mail* began to cover much more extensively local Chinese investments in the film industry in relation to three major areas, exhibition, distribution, and production. While in the domain of exhibition and distribution, such investments and business operations were always centered on two names, which are Lo Gun and the Lai brothers, notable people in the field of production also include Pang Nin (Peng Nian), Lo Kok-fei (Lu Juefei), and Chan Kwan-chiu (Chen Junchao).

Exhibition

Lo Gun, mistakenly thought to be the owner of the first Bijou Theatre, indeed played a significant role in the early development of the Hong Kong film industry, leading to his being called the "king of cinema owners." However, there was very little mention of Lo Gun's participation in either the Chinese or the English press from 1920 until 1924; in fact, over 90 percent of the *Chinese Mail*'s film advertisements and news coverage between 1920 and 1925 related only to two cinemas: the Coronet Theatre (or "New Bijou" in Chinese) and the World Theatre. The Coronet, which opened in December 1918, as mentioned previously, was under the management of Ray. In 1924, Lo Gun's name became also associated with the Coronet; it turned out that the Ming Tat (Mingda) Company, which was in charge of the management of the cinema, was owned by Lo Gun.[50] Lo, according to an account given by the *Chinese Mail*, was tycoon hosting a chain of cinemas in Hong Kong, Guangzhou, and Shanghai. He was hence quite appropriately branded the king of cinema owners in China.[51]

Also prominent figures contributing to the indigenization of the film industry were the Lai brothers, who owned the World Theatre, which, opening on July 12, 1921, was the earliest cinema founded and fully funded by local Chinese. Proudly branded the "World Theatre by Chinese Merchants" in the Chinese advertisements, the cinema was built on Des Voeux Road Central and west of Central Market by the Lai brothers—Lai Hoi-shan (Li Haishan), Lai Dong-hoi (Li Donghai), Lai Buk-hoi (Li Beihai), and Lai Man-wai (Li Minwei)—who had to raise a fund of HK$50,000 in opening this enterprise.[52] Descended from a local family of well-off merchants, Lai Hoi-shan, the eldest of the brothers, was the major shareholder with a share of HK$40,000. Lai Buk-hoi and Lai Man-wai, the fourth and the sixth sons, were probably the earliest among the brothers (and indeed among the local Chinese) to have had experience in film production, having worked as actors, scriptwriters, and directors in early adulthood. Lai Man-wai, in particular, had nurtured an immense interest in filmmaking. He bought books about cinematography from the United States and became absorbed in the art of motion picture photography, together with his friend, Law Wing-cheung (Luo Yongxiang), who was to become Hong Kong's first professional cinematographer.[53] Such enthusiasm would result not only in the first cinema but also the first film production company run by local Chinese.

The significance of the World was that, apart from being the first cinema founded by local Chinese, it was probably the "first theatre in the territory to regularly program Western *and* Chinese films."[54] As seen from the advertisements, there were pictures from Europe and Hollywood by Pathé, Warner Bros., and Paramount, alongside those latest productions from Shanghai, then known as the "Hollywood of the East," by studios including Great China Lilium (Dazhonghua baihe) Pictures Co. and Commercial Press. Apart from offering various selections and coming up with new programs once every three days, the World also paid attention to improvements of the film-viewing experience. For example, in-house film narrators were employed, and a well-crafted screen costing HK$3,000 was installed only one year after the cinema's opening.[55]

In addition to having always done its utmost to guarantee the quality of film screening and viewing, the World also made great efforts to initiate new business strategies, making the enterprise an all-round entertainment industry. For example, the cinema demonstrated two marketing strategies commonly used today: offering value-added experience and targeting festive consumers. Before or after the screenings, audiences at the World could enjoy acrobatic shows or musical performances. During Christmas, and alternatively the birthday of Confucius, patrons were offered gifts[56] or a lucky draw.[57] Management of the World also made efforts to expand its business. Three months after its opening, the World called for advertising, offering advertisement space on screen and in the handbills and brochures.[58] And the efforts paid off. Evidence shows that the World was indeed well regarded at the time. During its first two years in business, the World was selected twice by the Hong Kong government as the spot to entertain the visiting U.S. Navy.[59]

Such efforts, however, did not protect the Lai's from financial pressure and eventually the fatal blow from the general strike in 1925. The brothers tried hard to remain proprietors by selling off shares but finally had to relinquish the World to its creditor, Lo Gun's Ming Tat Company.[60]

Distribution

Founded by Lo Gun in the 1920s, the Ming Tat Company was the earliest film distributer in Hong Kong, which the World relied on for its supply of films. In 1924, the Coronet advertised in the *Chinese Mail* that the management, that is, Lo Gun, traveled to the United States to meet with Charlie Chaplin and secured the right to serve as China's exclusive agent for Chaplin's productions.[61] Ming Tat, the owner of the Coronet, as mentioned in the previous section, was also involved in the film exhibition business even before it took over the World.

The company's business kept soaring in the 1930s. For instance, in 1932 the representatives of Ming Tat traveled to the United States to purchase productions from two Hollywood majors, that is, First National Pictures and Warner Bros.[62] In addition to owning Coronet and the World, Ming Tat later took control of two more cinemas in Hong Kong: the Queen's Theatre and the Central Theatre. In 1935, Lo Gun also ventured into the film production business at a key moment, running the Chun Yip (Zhenye) Film Company.[63] The company's manager, Pang Nin, was one of Hong Kong's pioneers in film production.

Production

The Lai brothers, in particular Lai Man-wai, were celebrated as the pioneers of Hong Kong cinema. By setting up the China Sun (Minxin) Motion Picture Co. in 1923, the Lai's became the first in Hong Kong to have proprietorship over both film exhibition and production.

On December 13, 1922, Lai Man-wai, "a local entrepreneur," so called by the *Chinese Mail*, registered a film production company under the name "China Sun Motion Picture Co. Ltd." and raised capital of HK$500,000 at HK$5 per share.[64] The China Sun Co. was officially set up on July 14, 1923, and released its first production in March 1924 at Lai's own cinema, the World. China Sun started out shooting newsreels and documentaries of local events, such as dragon boat races, a U.S. aviator arriving in Hong Kong, the Hong Kong governor inspecting a military parade during the celebration ceremony of the birthday of King George V, and so on.[65] In addition to local news, there were also rare records of Sun Yat-sen's military campaigns taking place in China.

The year 1924 witnessed the emergence of a number of Hong Kong's earliest film production companies, all founded by local Chinese. These companies included Dai Hon (Dahan), Leung Yee (Liangyi), Kwong Ah (Guangya), and Sei Si (Sishi). Dai Hon was set up by Pang Nin, who later worked as the manager for Lo Gun's film company, Chun Yip—as mentioned earlier. Pang was a cinematographer educated in the United States. Unlike China Sun, Dai Hon was less an enterprise that made films than a service provider. The company provided shooting services on demand for family events, advertisements, and other production-related services. It even declared that requests for shooting of narrative film genres with scripts involving themes like "rewarding the good and punishing the bad" would be welcomed.[66] In the spring of 1924, Dai Hon was engaged by a local merchant, Mok Kon-sang (Mo Gansheng), to film at a school that Mok was sponsoring in his China hometown.[67] The company was also appointed by the Coronet to shoot a newsreel of the British comedian Harry Lauder when he visited Hong Kong.[68] According to Yu Mo-wan, a Hong Kong film historian, Dai Hon was commissioned to shoot some of the earliest short narrative films in Hong Kong, including Leung Yee's *The Calamity of Money* (*Jinqian nie*, dir. Lo Kok-fei, 1924), Kwong Ah's *A Thief Comes Unstuck* (*Zuozei bucheng*, 1924), and *Army Dream* (*Congjun meng*, dir. Chan Kwan-chiu, 1926).

Leung Yee was founded by Lo Kok-fei with partners. Lo was an all-round practitioner in the early film industry. In 1923, Lo Kok-fei, then the manager of Macau's Victoria Theatre, was invited by the Coronet to be a special film narrator.[69] Starting in April 1924, Lo wrote regularly for Hong Kong's first newspaper film page, "Ying Hei Ho (Yingxihao)," or "Film Corner," launched by the *Chinese Mail*. At the same time, he remained active in the Hong Kong film scene, assisting the management of the Coronet, translating synopses for the cinema's film handbills and brochures,[70] and founding at least two film production companies, while at the same time taking up directing and acting in film productions. *The Calamity of Money* (1924), the only production by Leung Yee, was well received when it was released in late 1924. The film was a "short comedy of moral values, filmed on the Kowloon side of Hong Kong."[71]

At about the same time, Dai Hon's founder, Pang Nin, together with Lo Kok-fei and Chan Kwan-chiu (the latter being the manager of the Coronet), set up yet another film production company, Kwong Ah. In November 1924, the *Chinese Mail* reported that a number of cinemas competed for the theatrical right of Kwong Ah's newly completed *Army Dream* (1926).[72] However, due to the general strike, the film was not released until 1926.

Sei Si, being contemporary with Dai Hon, Leung Yee, and Kwong Ah, advertised a public call for cast and script in September 1924,[73] supposedly for the production of a film to be entitled *One True Love* (*Shui shi zhenai*). Soon afterward, by November, the shooting of the film was taking place at various spots across Hong Kong, including the Castle Peak in the New Territories, the Western district, and North Point on Hong Kong island.[74] This production, however, was never released, and whether or not it was completed remains unknown. Like Dai Hon, Sei Si also provided shooting services on demand.[75]

These film production companies, while still taking shape, were already facing criticism from local movie lovers for their lack of accomplishment. The crowd was desperately eager to have a locally produced feature film, something that could measure up to two applauded Chinese productions, Shanghai Film Company's *Revival of an Old Well* (*Gujing chongbo ji*, dir. Dan Duyu, 1923) and Mingxing Film Company's *An Orphan Rescues His Grandpa* (*Gu'er jiuzu ji*, dir. Zhang Shichuan, 1923). Leung Yee's short comedy *The Calamity of Money* (1924) was literally too short to meet expectations. The anxious public did not have to wait long. For in February 1925, Hong Kong saw its first feature-length production (of eight reels), *Love Is Dangerous* (*Rouge, Yanzhi, dir. Lai Buk-hoi, 1925*),[76] by China Sun. The film was directed and written by Lai Buk-hoi, starring Lai Man-wai and Leung Siu-bo (Liang Shaopo). In the advertisements, *Love Is Dangerous* was recommended for its moral values, amusing plot, expressive acting, delicate setting, and lighting quality. Released at none other than the China Sun's own exhibition outlet, the World Theatre, the production was a huge success, attracting full houses and having its period of showing extended.

With growing involvement in the film industry, from exhibition, to distribution, to production, local Chinese gradually moved up front in the early Hong Kong film scene during the 1920s. They transformed the early filmscape of Hong Kong, changing the relationship between film, as a Western new marvel, and the local Hong Kong society: the meaning of film for the Hong Kong Chinese had changed from an imported novelty to an indigenized commercial activity, and this change laid a firm foundation for subsequent developments of the Hong Kong film industry. The determination to succeed in improving this new industry among Hong Kong locals had nourished a social tendency toward viewing film as a cultural institution.

Such changed perceptions toward film and the growing concerns over the development of film industry led directly to the emergence of Hong Kong's first film page appearing in the local Chinese newspapers.

CINEMA AS A CULTURAL INSTITUTION: FILM CULTURE IN EARLY HONG KONG

The Rise of Cultural Awareness

On February 19, 1924, the *Chinese Mail* launched a short film column, which marked the Chinese press's first attempt to give analytic and critical comments on film-related activities. Two months later, from April 19 onward, the column expanded into a weekly film page named "Ying Hei Ho" ("Film Corner"). It was published every Saturday until March 7, 1925, a total of thirty-eight issues. The launch of *Film Corner* in the 1920s was certainly no overnight sensation. Film had by that time become a regular form of entertainment and a more indigenous practice among the local Chinese.

First, we note that from the 1900s to 1920s, there was a dramatic increase in film exhibitions in Hong Kong (table 3.2) and a growing involvement of the local Chinese in the film industry.

Second, during this period the Chinese had evolved from passive receivers to active participants in the film industry. As observed in the *Chinese Mail*, the earliest films shown in Hong Kong were without exception imported productions with Western casts and crew. Starting in the mid-1910s, there were mentions of Chinese performances in Western productions. And 1920s saw a blooming industry where Chinese productions began to occupy more and more screen time locally. The Hong Kong film industry was becoming indigenous.

"Film Corner" occupied a full upper-half page of the newspaper, with articles about films produced both abroad and locally (table 3.3). Based on the different purposes they distinctively served, these articles can be categorized into four domains (table 3.4): film review, which introduced and commented on new movies; industry news, which covered new business and technological developments in the film entertainment industry; movie star news, which followed the public exposure and private lives of movie stars; and film appreciation, which provided a wide variety of educational resources aiming to enhance the general public's overall ability to appreciate film—being, after all, an innovative art and entertainment form.

The figures in tables 3.3 and 3.4 reveal a vibrant film culture in formation in the early 1920s, reflecting that Western films were well appraised and Chinese films were equally important, while the Hong Kong film industry was still taking shape. The predominant stance of "Film Corner" can be summed up in the following four tendencies:

1. The column focused on Western productions, and news about the movie stars proved to be the most popular among readers.
2. Coverage of movie heartthrobs ranged from fact to rumor and gossip about their latest activities, personal details, and private life.
3. The Chinese film industry was positioned at center stage, and everything about Chinese productions, from script to acting to cinema-

Table 3.2. Film Advertisements and News Coverage in the *Chinese Mail*, 1900–1920s

Year	1900s	1910s	1920s
Advertisement	111	366	2,342
News coverage	30	104	387

Note: Articles from special issues on films not included.

Table 3.3. Regions Mentioned in "Film Corner," 1924–1925

Region	Foreign countries	China	Hong Kong	Others
Number of appearances	151	87	32	21

Table 3.4. Types of Article in "Film Corner," 1924–1925

Region	Foreign countries	China	Hong Kong	Others
Film review	25	39	4	
Industry news	6	12	11	
Movie star news	83	8	0	
Film appreciation	28	36	11	21

tography, in particular technical and artistic aspects, attracted close attention.

4. The development of the Hong Kong film industry was under close scrutiny, and concerns were raised on how to improve local production values and the standard of appreciation within the local viewing community.

With these key orientations in mind, "Film Corner" can be seen to have closely witnessed and specifically evaluated the development of this new entertainment industry in the sense that it was clearly inclined to explore various kinds of cultural significance associated with film.

Such concerns, moreover, showed that the film page was also characterized by a new species of cultural awareness—as radically different from the traditional Chinese thinking—initiated by the cultured bourgeois elites. Through these endeavors undertaken by individual film critics, film industry was to become a culturally influential power for the local bourgeois public, instead of being just another supplementary business capitalizing on the rise of a new kind of entertainment. With the birth of film criticism (or film-related criticism—to be precise), indeed, the Hong Kong film industry developed into a quintessential element in what Jürgen Habermas calls the "bourgeois public sphere"—which is "conceived . . . as the sphere of private people come together as a public; they soon claimed the public sphere regulated from above against the public authorities themselves, *to engage them in a debate over the general rules governing relations in the basically privatized but publicly relevant sphere of commodity exchange and social labour*."[77] The role of film criticism, reflecting the transformation of private interests into public cultural concerns, can be further followed by looking at a set of rigorously institutionalized standards regulated by the film page.

Film Culture in Early Hong Kong and Its Emphases

In its first appearance, "Film Corner" made an outspoken statement, written by its chief contributor, Lo Kok-fei, declaring unequivocally the film page's social and cultural vision:

> Film is indisputably a classy form of entertainment with potential educational benefit and, in particular, moral values. It can be instrumental in supplementing the low educational and cultural level within the Chinese

> community. There have been attempts to see improvements in these areas, yet due to the high illiteracy rate, little has been accomplished. Film can achieve much in this capacity since, first, as an art form it impresses; and, second, as the product of Western civilization it cultivates. Yet film is still being perceived as mere entertainment by many due to the fact that little of its cultural value has been explored. It is with such an impetus that the editor launched the weekly "Film Corner" and invited me to be one of the contributors.[78]

Lo Kok-fei, as discussed previously, possessed extended experience in the film industry, ranging from cinema management, film production, and acting to film criticism. Among Hong Kong filmmakers at the time, there was no better spokesman than such an all-rounded practitioner to convey concerns and expectations regarding filmmaking. Lo's ideas can in fact be seen as reflecting four aesthetic inclinations. First, they show a deliberate gesture toward establishing a specialist field of film criticism. Second, they are concerned about the civic education function of film. Third, they are devoted to both film technologies and its artistic specialties. Last, they expect to establish a complete and consistent system of film theories and concepts. Characterized by these fundamentally teleological dispositions, "Film Corner" reflected film as a cultural institution in early Hong Kong, and its social and cultural concerns can be categorized into the following five domains: appreciation, education, art and science, concept and translation, and international aspiration.

Appreciation

The first domain was cinema etiquette. Critics made a list of practices that were considered inappropriate for any serious attempt at film appreciation. For example, they advised against reading through film handbills and brochures before the actual screening, since the practice would undermine the appreciation of the plot.[79] Also, since hawkers and noisy crowds greatly disturbed the viewing experience, sensible audiences were encouraged to attend well-managed cinemas with civilized patrons, comfortable seating, and good lighting.[80] As for choosing programs, cinemagoers were told to refrain from being casually won over by film advertisements. Instead, they should be adequately informed about, and be able to judge for themselves, the quality of particular productions based on, for example, directorship and performances,[81] and should frequently seek references from film reviews as well.[82]

Concerns were raised about the way film reviews were composed. Two major shortcomings among film critics were identified: some failed to display substantial understanding about the cinematic arts,[83] while others were being too harsh about Chinese and local productions.[84] It was advised that film critics should be knowledgeable about both the art and the scientific aspects of cinema. Also, it was stressed that the tendency in only using Western productions as the sole standard in film reviews should be avoided, and that film critics should always take into account the difference in levels of technological development, financial investment, and cultural preference between the Chinese and Western film industries.[85] Prejudiced accounts would be unproductive in furthering the development of Chinese film industry, and so more recognition should be given to its achievements so far.[86]

Education

In its inauguration, "Film Corner" emphasized cinema's role in education, making an argument that film should first and foremost be an educational tool, not just an entertainment. Some observers expressed relief on realizing that film was beginning to receive recognition from society solely because of its artistic and social functions, and it was this growing recognition that made critics optimistic about the prosperous future of the Chinese film industry, brought about by its functions of education.[87] Some columnists further pointed out that the Chinese film industry should produce more movies for moral education purposes, so as to replace prevailing genres of foreign movies, like the detective genre and romance, that were deemed to "hinder the development of civil education," merely due to differences between Chinese and Western culture.[88]

"Film Corner" provided detailed recommendations on how to incorporate moral education into film. First, in view of moneymaking as the widely expected objective in Chinese film industry, the film page summoned concern for a serious and thorough review of the industry as a whole, particularly scriptwriting, for the sake of pursuing a mission of moral betterment and popularization of education.[89] As a means of social education, filmmakers were asked to adopt the vernacular—which was commonly used by the general public—in subtitles, instead of the classical Chinese conventionally used only by the educated elites.[90] Some columnists analyzed how animated images as visual aids could assist children in more effectively understanding what they were learning. Furthermore, they reminded filmmakers that, in the process of film production, "the fundamental purpose of filmmaking cannot be forgotten and mistaken, the industry cannot go awry in terms of solely fulfilling entertainment purposes, [and] children should not be shaped to only enjoy the pleasure of visual satisfaction while neglecting intelligence building."[91]

Art and Science

"Film Corner" also devoted itself to the enhancement of knowledge in cinematic arts, with articles that covered film history, aesthetic appreciation, and technical understanding. "The Evolution of Film," a series of five articles written by Lo Kok-fei, for example, provided a comprehensive account of the principle of film and its evolution, dating from optical theories developed by the Greeks and Romans to the modern invention of the camera and its use in filmmaking, and introducing the different names of film in different countries.[92] Some other articles, furthermore, proposed the idea of "five basic domains in film studies," dividing film production into "scriptwriting, directing, performing, cinematography, and makeup," and each of these domains was given extensive discussion.[93] Such in-depth examination and enthusiastic pursuit of film knowledge and culture undertaken by these early film critics constituted the framework of film studies.

The most commonly explored topics in such articles were those related to the art and technique of performance and cinematography. The discussion of art and techniques of performing mainly focused on methodological issues such as cast training, practicing facial expressions, makeup, characterization, and so on. Some articles noted that, in order to enhance empathy in performing, filmmakers employed an orchestra to play live music to stimulate the actors' cultivation of sentiments;[94] others mentioned that detailed suggestions were made about how to perform fight scenes featuring kung fu;[95] some pointed out that costumes should not be created only to look lavish and grand but rather to fit particular film characters and plots.[96] Articles provided technological explorations of cinematography, introducing, for instance, technical issues like lighting, developing, retouching, coloring, and so on,[97] and they conducted detailed analyses of the popular tricks featured in the innovative special effects in Hollywood cinematography.[98] Substantial attention was also devoted to topics relating to mise-en-scène, encompassing concerns over the number of cameras and their arrangements, lighting and setting design, and so on.

Concept and Translation

The problem of translation also aroused enormous attention from contributors to "Film Corner." The chaotic and inconsistent translating of titles of foreign films and their actors' names led very commonly to, for example, the same movie or actor having many different Chinese translations. A typical example of these confusions is that "film" was given a variety of Chinese translations: the term *dianying* prevailed in the Beijing-Tianjin regions, *yingxi* in the Jiangxu-Zhejiang districts, and *yinghua* in the Canton–Hong Kong areas.[99] Showing their concern over such inconsistencies in translation, some articles provided a glossary to identify these cross-regional discrepancies.[100] Certain visionary columnists became aware that this translation problem could well hinder the development of film exhibition, resulting, in foreseeable ways, in distortion of the meaning of film as a whole. They hence suggested that matters relating to translation should be left to the film distributors who were bound to come up with a consistent set of terminology.

International Aspiration

"Film Corner" featured film developments in Hong Kong and the entire Chinese region, showing that even in the beginning the film industry already had ambitions of being an international player. The following anecdotes illustrate film practitioners' determination. In the winter of 1923, on knowing that the president of a motion picture association in the United States, a certain Mr. Wood, was paying a visit to Shanghai, the local Coronet Theatre immediately grasped the opportunity to send its staff as tour guides to accompany Wood in order to learn from him about new developments in areas like film theories and facilities management.[101] In the summer of 1924, some film scholars and journalists from Hong Kong and China visited Nikkatsu Production Company in Japan. They undertook a special journey to the company's Kansai Studio in Kyoto. "Film Corner" reported the visit with a meticulous description of Nikkatsu's facilities, the scale of its cast and studios, the leading movie stars of the studio, and so on.[102]

Local filmmakers' aspiration to be part of the global film market is indicated by the English titles that popular Chinese films at that time, like *Women Skeletons* (*Hongfen kulou*, dir. Guan Haifeng, 1922) and *An Orphan Rescues His Grandpa* (1923), carried. Such as endeavor reflected the filmmakers' ambition that Chinese films be produced not only "for satisfying our nation-wide need" but for "striving for the international status" as well as "financial successes" like those enjoyed by popular foreign productions.[103] Having such high expectations, of course, they were also aware that the standards of Chinese films still needed improvement. Doubting the effectiveness of certain superficial marketing gimmicks meant to attract the foreign market, such as bilingual subtitling, they raised the point that Chinese filmmakers should first and foremost pay attention to the artistic aspects in film production, arguing that artistic advancement was the crucial element needed for winning recognition abroad.

To sum up, through close monitoring of the development of the film industry in early Hong Kong, "Film Corner" revealed the local society's ever-growing awareness of cinema as one of the major cultural discourses in the bourgeois public sphere. In other words, a film page that was supposed to express the private utterances of individual cultured elites had been transformed into a site for public cultural discourse, which, to use Miriam Hansen's words, "the dominant public sphere leaves out, privatizes, or acknowledges only in an abstract and fragmented form."[104] In fact, this unique kind of cultural discourse, characterized by strong social and political concerns, echoed what Leo Lee calls the "business of Enlightenment"—which for him had permeated the cultural scenes of Chinese modernity as a whole. Actually, early Hong Kong film culture can be seen as a particular mode of cultural enterprise in Chinese *qimeng* (enlightenment), "a term taken from the traditional educational practice in which a child received his first lesson from a teacher or tutor."[105] Through this cultural enterprise, we can see that while social critics tended to endow what was supposed to be no more than a certain kind of entertainment with social and moral functions, film entrepreneurs were also aware of their role and responsibilities as social reformers with a nationalist undertone. Indeed, a geographically small and politically "forsaken" island, early Hong Kong did nourish a film culture whose nature was in line with a broader historical context featured by a Republican nationalism that, to borrow Emilie Yueh-yu Yeh's incisive commentary on the Republican cinema as a whole, "was founded with a vision and ambition to rebuild China as a modern nation-state . . . [whose] ethos was uplifting, forward-looking and resolutely 'virtuous.'"[106]

The early Hong Kong film development reached its summit in the 1920s, but at that prosperous moment it suffered an outrageous challenge. On May 30, 1925, demonstrators in Shanghai fighting for labor rights against Japanese textile factory owners were attacked by the British police force, suffering deaths and casualties. This event, known as the May Thirtieth Incident, directly led to the general strike, which first broke out in Shanghai, then quickly swept through almost all Chinese regions. In June, over 250,000 workers in Hong Kong went on strike,[107] 40 percent of the Hong Kong population, and they left Hong Kong to bolster strike actions. The strike paralyzed the entire social life and economy of Hong Kong. Most local newspapers, Chinese and English alike, ceased to publish because of the strike—the *Chinese Mail* only resumed operation in late 1925.[108] The Hong Kong government imposed curfews and banned all public gatherings. All entertainment spots, including the cinemas, were closed for more than a month.[109] It was not until October 1926 that the general strike in Hong Kong finally ended.

The sixteen-month strike paralyzed Hong Kong and dealt a heavy blow to the early Hong Kong film industry. The *Chinese Mail* reported that out of the seventeen Hong Kong film production companies, only a very few survived the strike.[110] Such an unproductive and poignant phase in Hong Kong history doubtlessly caused a destructive break, seriously hindering the once-anticipated growth of the film industry.

CONCLUSION

Aiming to trace the early development of Hong Kong film and to restore a currently incomplete and blurry image of the early Hong Kong filmscape, this chapter has scrutinized an array of personages and events by means of reading early Hong Kong English and Chinese newspaper coverage. This early period of evolution, or indeed grafting of the newly imported Western novelty onto an essentially Chinese cultural soil, was not without impediments due to a series of innate disadvantages, such as a "small local market, minimal capital, inadequate human resources, and sterile innovativeness."[111] But films soon became favorably and auspiciously indigenized because of the vast economic and cultural resources that this new industry was able to provide. Following such a successful indigenization, Hong Kong film development reached its first important climax in the mid-1920s.

The early Hong Kong film development that ended in the mid-1920s formed a quintessential foundation for the industry's eventual bursting into bloom in later decades, not only inaugurating the enormous commercial success of this particular entertainment industry, but also boosting a unique mode of cultural institution that fulfilled the local entrepreneurs' as well as cultural elites' social and ideological pursuits. This somewhat unexpected evolution led to a distinctively reciprocal relationship between film and society, revealing how the former constantly performed a variety of social functions while contributing greatly to the economic progress of the latter. Therefore, in a thorough account of the overall Hong Kong film development, the 1920s cannot be seen as a primitive period, but should rightly be regarded as a formative one that had far-reaching influences on the later, notable growth of the Hong Kong film industry, setting the stage for the golden age of Hong Kong cinema, that is, the 1930s.

Notes

1. Research for this chapter is supported by GRF, "Chinese Film History Beyond Shanghai: 1900–1950," funded by the Research Grants Council of Hong Kong (grant number HKBU 245310). This chapter is revised and rewritten from an earlier Chinese article, "Chengxian qihou de 1920 niandai: Xianggang zaoqi dianying cong wanyi, shiye dao wenhua" [Early Hong Kong Cinema in the 1920s: From an Imported Novelty to an Indigenized Commercial and Cultural Industry], in *Zouchu Shanghai: Zaoqi dianying de linglei jingguan* [Beyond Shanghai: New Perspectives on Early Chinese Cinema], eds. Emilie Yueh-yu Yeh, Feng Xiaocai, and Liu Hui (Beijing: Beijing University Press, 2016), 119–149.

2. Kar Law and Frank Bren, *Hong Kong Cinema: A Cross-Cultural View* (Lanham, MD: Scarecrow Press, 2004), 6–7.

3. Liu Shuyong, *Jianming xianggang shi* [A Brief History of Hong Kong] (Hong Kong: Joint Publishing, 2009), 91.

4. Liu, *Jianming xianggang shi*, 64, 94.

5. Cheng Po-hung, *Entertainment for the Chinese in Hong Kong over a Century* (Hong Kong: iGlobe Publishing, 2013), 8.

6. Kar Law and Frank Bren, *From Artform to Platform: Hong Kong Plays and Performances, 1900–1941* (Hong Kong: International Association of Theatre Critics, 1999), 15.

7. Law and Bren, *From Artform to Platform*, 4–5.

8. Yu Shengwu and Liu Cunkuan, *Shijiu shiji de xianggang* [Hong Kong in the Nineteenth Century] (Hong Kong: Qilun, 1994), 300.

9. Yu and Liu, *Shijiu shiji de xianggang*, 302.

10. Yu and Liu, *Shijiu shiji de xianggang*, 302.

11. "Local and General," *China Mail*, April 24, 1897, 3.

12. In the case of the "Hong Kong tour" of the Cinematograph—as confirmed by Law

Kar and Frank Bren after having verified it with L'Institut Lumière, there is no record of Professor Charvet being one of the representatives, nor is there any record of Professor Charvet having purchased a machine from the Lumière brothers. According to *Société Lumière*, the current owner of the brand, since 1896 there had been over six hundred copycat machines manufactured or patented in France alone. For more details, please refer to Law and Bren, *Hong Kong Cinema*, 5–6.

13. "Local and General," *China Mail*, April 27, 1897, 2.

14. "Announcement," *Hong Kong Daily Press*, April 28, 1897, 2.

15. "Local and General," *China Mail*, April 27, 1897, 2.

16. "H. Wellby-Cook's Animatoscope," *Hong Kong Daily Press*, August 19, 1897, 1.

17. "Xylophone & Kinematograph Entertainment," *Hong Kong Daily Press*, December 23, 1899, 1.

18. "Announcement," *Hong Kong Daily Press*, April 18, 1900, 2.

19. Emilie Yueh-yu Yeh, "Translating *Yingxi*: Chinese Film Genealogy and Early Cinema in Hong Kong," *Journal of Chinese Cinemas* 9, no. 1 (2015): 89–90.

20. "Xilai yuan yan huaqi shengdong huaxi" [Lively Moving Pictures from the United States at Hei Loi], Supplements of *Chinese Mail*, October 28, 1902, 1; emphasis added.

21. Yu Mo-wan, *Xianggang dianying shihua (juan yi)-mopian niandai: 1896–1929* [Notes on Hong Kong Film History I: The Silent Era, 1896–1929] (Hong Kong: Subculture Press, 1996), 37; Zhao Weifang, *Xianggang dianying shi (1897–2006)* [A History of Hong Kong Cinema (1897–2006)] (Beijing: China Broadcast Television Press, 2007), 15; Zhou Chengren and Li Yizhuang, *Zaoqi Xianggang dianying shi, 1897–1945* [A History of Early Hong Kong Cinema, 1897–1945] (Shanghai: Shanghai People's Publishing House, 2009), 20; Stephanie Po-yin Chung, *Xianggang yingshiye bainian* [One Hundred Years Hong Kong Cinema and Television Industry] (Hong Kong: Joint Publishing, 2011), 47.

22. "Qimiao yingxi" [Amazing Pictures], *Chinese Mail*, September 4, 1907, 3.

23. "The Triumph of Moving Pictures," *China Mail*, July 19, 1907, 5.

24. "Moving Picture Exhibition," *China Mail*, July 17, 1907, 6.

25. "Hongkong Cinematograph—under New Management," *China Mail*, April 13, 1908, 5.

26. "Look Out! Look Out!," *South China Morning Post*, October 24, 1910, 3.

27. "The Bijou Scenic Theatre," *South China Morning Post*, November 1, 1910, 10.

28. "Bijou Scenic Theatre," *South China Morning Post*, November 26, 1910, 10.

29. "Bijou Scenic Theatre," *Hong Kong Telegraph*, December 3, 1910, 16.

30. "Bijou," *Hong Kong Telegraph*, June 2, 1913, 11.

31. "To-night," *China Mail*, November 1, 1907, 1.

32. "The Empire—New Cinematograph Theatre," *South China Morning Post*, April 4, 1910, 11.

33. Ibid.

34. "The New Theatre—Opened Last Night," *South China Morning Post*, May 27, 1911, 8.

35. "Announcement," *Hong Kong Daily Press*, December 28, 1918, 6.

36. "Xin bizhao yinghua xiyuan" [Coronet Theatre], *Chinese Mail*, June 27, 1919, 3.

37. "Gaoxing yuan rongji yan hedingcai ban" [Performances by Ho Ting Choi Troupe at Ko Shing Theatre], Supplements of *Chinese Mail*, January 1, 1903, 1.

38. "Chongqing yuan huaji yan shidi fenchen yingxu" [Stevenson's Pictures at Chung Hing], Supplements of *Chinese Mail*, January 19, 1903, 1.

39. Wang Gang, *An Illustrated Story of Wyndham Street, Hong Kong 1840s–1960s* (Hong Kong: Chung Hwa Book Co., 2008), 254.

40. "The Imperial Bioscope Co.," *Hong Kong Daily Press*, January 9, 1903, 2.

41. "The Imperial Bioscope," *Hong Kong Daily Press*, January 8, 1903, 2.

42. "The Imperial Bioscope Co.," *Hong Kong Daily Press*, January 9, 1903, 2.

43. "The Imperial Bioscope Co.," *Hong Kong Daily Press*, January 7, 1903, 2.

44. "Huaxi chudai" [Pictures for Rent], *Chinese Mail*, March 8, 1904, 3.

45. "Taiping xiyuan yan yinghua xi" [Film Screening at Tai Ping Theatre], *Chinese Mail*, March 16, 1905, 1.

46. "Local News," *South China Morning Post*, October 10, 1914, 2.

47. "Yu duo li yingxi yuan teping yingyue chuanjia" [Music Talents at Victoria Cinematograph], *Chinese Mail*, November 1, 1915, 3.

48. "Huashang bu tai xi tebie tongtian yinghua chang" [Outdoor Film Screening by Chinese Merchants], *Chinese Mail*, August 25, 1916, 3.

49. "A Crowded Cinema: Proprietor Fined," *South China Morning Post*, April 6, 1918, 10.

50. "Zhenye zhipian chang canquan ji" [A Visit to the Chun Yip Studio], *Chinese Mail*, April 1, 1935, 2.

51. "Zhenye zhipian chang canquan ji," 2.

52. "Xin shijie yingxi yuan zhi jiu gudong" [Ex-Shareholders of the New World Theatre], *Chinese Mail*, August 3, 1927, 3.

53. Kar Law and Lai Shek, *Li Minwei: ren, shidai, dianying* [Lai Man-wai: The Man, the Time, and the Cinema] (Hong Kong: Mingchuang Publishing, 1999), 169.

54. Law and Bren, *Hong Kong Cinema*, 47.

55. "Xinshe yinghua zhang" [The New Film Screen], Supplements of *Chinese Mail*, May 15, 1922, 2.

56. "Guan yinghua you zengpin" [Gifts for Moviegoers], Supplements of *Chinese Mail*, December 24, 1921, 1.

57. "Xin shijie xiyuan shengdan ri teshe zengpin guanggao" [Advertisement by New World Theatre: Special Gifts on Birthday of Confucius], *Chinese Mail*, September 28, 1921, 3.

58. "Huashang Xin shijie yinghua xiyuan guangao" [Advertisement by Chinese Merchants' New World Theatre], Supplements of *Chinese Mail*, October 12, 1921, 3.

59. "Huashang Xin shijie yinghua xiyuan guangao"; "Ying haijun yan mei shuibing" [British Navy Receiving U.S. Navy], *Chinese Mail*, October 31, 1922, 2.

60. "Xin shijie yingxi yuan zhi jiu gudong," 3.

61. "Chalei minghua da jihui" [Famous Pictures of Charlie], *Chinese Mail*, November 20, 1924, 9.

62. "Mingda yingpian chuanyuan huigang" [Ming Tat Representatives Return to Hong Kong], *Chinese Mail*, July 12, 1932, 4.

63. "Zhenye zhipian chang canquan ji," 2.

64. "Jiangyou zhicao yingpian gongsi chuxian" [New Film Production Company], Supplements of *Chinese Mail*, December 13, 1922, 3.

65. "Zhongguo xin zhi yingpian da mingxing" [A New Star in Film Production], *Chinese Mail*, August 2, 1924, 1.

66. "Dahan yingye gongsi gaobai" [Advertisements by Dai Hon], *Chinese Mail*, February 20, 1924, 3.

67. "Xiangshan mofan xiang zhi yingpian" [A Film about Xiangshan], *Chinese Mail*, May 24, 1924, 9.

68. "Yingxi xiaoshi" [Film News], *Chinese Mail*, February 17, 1925, 2.

69. "Xin bizhao yingxi yuan guanggao" [Advertisement by Coronet Theatre], *Chinese Mail*, January 19, 1923, 3.

70. Taking into consideration the fact that film narrators might be the source of disturbance during screenings, the Coronet Theatre offered film brochures completed with synopsis to replace film narrators from May 1924 onward. "Xin bizhao yingxi yuan zhi ba da teshe" [Eight Highlights of the Coronet Theatre], *Chinese Mail*, May 31, 1924, 13.

71. "Yinghua xiaoshi" [Film News], *Chinese Mail*, September 27, 1924, 9.

72. "Zuixin yingpian jiang chushi" [Latest Films to Be Released], *Chinese Mail*, November 12, 1924, 9.

73. "Sishi huapian gongsi guanggao" [Advertisement by the Sei Si Film Company], *Chinese Mail*, September 12, 1924, 3.

74. "Sishi huapian gongsi shexi," [Sei Si Film Company Shooting], *Chinese Mail*, November 12, 1924, 9.

75. "Sishi huapian gongsi guanggao," 3.

76. "Yinghua xiaoshi" [Film News], *Chinese Mail*, February 23, 1925, 2.

77. Jürgen Habermas, *The Structural Transformation of Public Sphere: An Inquiry into a Category of Bourgeois Society*, trans. Thomas Burger (Cambridge, MA: MIT Press, 1989), 27.

78. Kok-fei, "Xiaoyan" [A Few Words], Film Corner, *Chinese Mail*, April 19, 1924, 13; our translation.

79. Yat-shi, "Yingmu tanpian" [About the Silver Screen], Film Corner, *Chinese Mail*, June 28, 1924, 13.

80. Jing-tsz, "Yingpian de guancha (xu)" [Film Observations (continued)], Film Corner, *Chinese Mail*, July 26, 1924, 13.

81. Wa, "Yingpian de timing" [The Naming of Films], Film Corner, *Chinese Mail*, November 15, 1924, 14.

82. Jing-tsz, "Yingpian de guancha (xu)" [Film Observations (continued)], Film Corner, *Chinese Mail*, July 19, 1924, 13.

83. Yat-shi, "Pingju zuidi xiandu zhi tiaojian" [The Least Quality That a Film Critic Should Possess], Film Corner, *Chinese Mail*, August 9, 1924, 14.

84. Tsz-suet, "Yingmu tanpian" [About the Silver Screen], Film Corner, *Chinese Mail*, August 23, 1924, 14.

85. Tsz-suet, "Yingmu tanpian," 14.

86. King-ming, "Wo de Zhongguo xiying tan" [My Views on Chinese Films], Film Corner, *Chinese Mail*, August 23, 1924, 14.

87. Jing-tsz, "Yingpian de guancha" [Film Observations], Film Corner, *Chinese Mail*, July 12, 1924, 13.

88. Tsing-po, "Yingpian wenti de taolun" [A Discussion on Film], Film Corner, *Chinese Mail*, May 31, 1924, 13.

89. King-ming, "Wei gangzhong yingxi jie jing yiyan" [A Few Suggestions for the Hong Kong and Chinese Film Industry], Film Corner, *Chinese Mail*, December 29, 1924, 14.

90. Chan-shek, "Wei duiyu Zhongguo huapian shuoming wen de yijian" [My Views on Language in Chinese Films], Film Corner, *Chinese Mail*, August 30, 1924, 14.

91. Lam King-fei, "Yingxi yu jiaoyu zhi guanxi (xu)" [Film and Education (Continued)], Film Corner, *Chinese Mail*, February 14, 1925, 1.

92. Kok-fei, "Yingxi jinghua shi (yi)" [The Evolution of Film (Part 1)], Film Corner, *Chinese Mail*, July 12, 1924, 13.

93. Kok, "Yingxi xue de fanwei he dingyi" [Definition and Scope of Film Studies], Film Corner, *Chinese Mail*, September 20, 1924, 14.

94. Tsz-suet, "Shezhi yingpian de shouxu (xu)" [How to Shoot a Film (Continued)], Film Corner, *Chinese Mail*, November 8, 1924, 14.

95. Lei-gong, "Yingpian zhong de Zhongguo wushu" [Chinese Kung Fu in Films], Film Corner, *Chinese Mail*, October 4, 1924, 14.

96. Yat-man, "Lun wuguo dianying nüjue zhi fuzhuang" [About the Costume for Chinese Actresses], Film Corner, *Chinese Mail*, December 20, 1924, 14.

97. Kok, "Yingxi xue de fanwei he dingyi (xu)" [Definition and Scope of Film Studies (Continued)], Film Corner, *Chinese Mail*, October 4, 1924, 14.

98. Ba-shi, "Zhipian zuoyi zhi zhongzhong" [Popular Tricks in Film Production], Film Corner, *Chinese Mail*, June 21, 1924, 13.

99. L. Y., "Yingxi de yanjiu (xu)" [A Study of Film (Continued)], Film Corner, *Chinese Mail*, November 15, 1924, 14. See Emilie Yeh's chapter in this volume on the continuity of translation issues in contemporary writings.

100. Kok-fei, "Mingxing zhengming" [Correct Translation of Names of Movie Stars], Film Corner, *Chinese Mail*, May 31, 1924, 13.

101. A-kwok, "Tongxun" [Newsletter], Film Corner, *Chinese Mail*, July 12, 1924, 13.

102. Bao Chun-tsing, "Riben guanxi cuoying shuo fangwen ji" [A Visit to the Kansai Studio in Japan], Film Corner, *Chinese Mail*, August 9, 1924, 14.

103. Sing-co, "Huaming de yanjiu (xu)" [A Study of the Film Titles (continued)], Film Corner, *Chinese Mail*, August 9, 1924, 14.

104. Miriam Hansen, "Early Cinema, Late Cinema: Permutations of the Public Sphere," *Screen* 34, no. 3 (1993): 203.

105. Leo Ou-fan Lee, *Shanghai Modern: The Flowering of a New Urban Culture in China, 1930–1945* (Boston: Harvard University Press, 1999), 47.

106. Emilie Yueh-yu Yeh, "New Takes on Film Historiography: Republican Cinema Redux, an Introduction," *Journal of Chinese Cinemas* 9, no. 1 (2015): 3.

107. Liu, *Jianming xianggang shi*, 147.

108. Chan Him, *Xianggang jiushi jianwen lu* [Stories from Old Hong Kong] (Hong Kong: Zhongyuan Publishing, 1987), 300.

109. Chan, *Xianggang jiushi jianwen lu*, 305.

110. "Xianggang huapian gongsi zhidiaocha" [A Survey of Film Production Companies in Hong Kong], *Chinese Mail*, August 1, 1927, 3.

111. Zhou and Li, *Zaoqi Xianggang dianying shi*, 111.

CHAPTER 4

Enlightenment, Propaganda, and Image Creation

A Descriptive Analysis of the Usage of Film by the Taiwan Education Society and the Colonial Government Before 1937

Daw-Ming Lee

Although film arrived in Taiwan more than a century ago, relatively few books and essays, in any language, have explored Taiwan cinema during the Japanese colonial period. In the past quarter of a century, most film studies on Taiwan cinema in the West discuss only films and their makers after 1950, especially those after the emergence of Taiwan New Cinema.[1]

As for books written in Chinese on the history of Taiwan cinema, only a handful are available. However, most of them are nonscholarly works, including Ye Longyan's *The History of Taiwanese Movies during the Japanese Colonization*, which has been widely quoted by renowned authors such as Guo-juin Hong and Yingjin Zhang.[2] I have studied the historical development of Taiwan cinema under Japanese colonial rule for more than twenty years, and has published many articles in both Chinese and English. My articles are based on original research on primary and secondary sources, including films, books, journals, articles, and references published during and after the colonial period by Japanese and Taiwanese authors.

This chapter is an effort to look into how the colonial government utilized film as a tool to help it rule Taiwan over the fifty years of colonization, particularly before the breakout of the second Sino-Japanese war in 1937.

Misawa Mamie has written a book on the film policy of the Office of the Governor General of Taiwan, which includes similar topics but puts more emphasis on laws and regulations, censorship, and film history in the colonial era. Misawa Mamie focuses her discussion of the use of film by the colonial government on two departments, namely the Police Association, which concentrated its filmmaking and exhibitions on aboriginal affairs, and the Taiwan Education Society, which is also one of the main organizations discussed in this chapter.

Misawa centers her observations on how educators used film as a propaganda tool to affirm their own position in the moral suasion or edification process overseen by the colonial government. She uses several examples to illuminate her points that Japanese educators were preachers of nationalism internally and advocates of ideal images of Taiwan externally. Contrary to Misawa's theoretical hypotheses, this chapter takes a pragmatic approach in finding diachronic and synchronic evidences of government policy (of both the colonial government and imperial Japan) and film organizations in Taiwan, including but not limited to the Taiwan Education Society. I am hoping readers will be able to deduce their own conclusion after inspecting all evidence provided in this chapter.

ITŌ, TAKAMATSU, AND EARLY USAGE OF FILM BY THE COLONIAL GOVERNMENT

Motion pictures arrived in Taiwan at the end of the nineteenth century[3] as an "attraction," as Tom Gunning would call it.[4] Even though the purpose of showing such novelties in the colony was no doubt profit, the tone of reports or advertisements about such events in local newspapers made them sound like scientific demonstrations of a new technology.

Before the film distribution system started to function in 1908, film screenings in Taiwan were run by touring film exhibitors, mostly native Japanese from the homeland, and a handful of Taiwanese who had returned from Tokyo after learning projection skills, then bringing back projectors and films. Early film screenings, an activity usually performed together with other entertainments, were no doubt mainly for profit. However, some Japanese rulers had envisioned the use of motion pictures as a tool of educating (or brainwashing) people of the newly acquired colony.

In 1900, Takamatsu Toyojirō was invited by the director of civil administration, Gotō Shimpei (March 1898–October 1906), to tour Taiwan, exhibiting films on behalf of the colonial government.

According to Kappei Matsumoto, Takamatsu was involved in the labor movement in the late 1890s and early 1900s in Japan. In order to circumvent constraints set by the Police Security Act (*chian iji hō*) of 1900, Takamatsu used verbal *rakugo* entertainment and, later, phonographs and film projectors to carry the movement's messages to the public. Matsumoto cited many sources confirming that Prime Minister Itō Hirobumi (January 1898–June 1898, and October 1900–May 1901), who had noticed Takamatsu's mixed usage of filmed images and speech in 1900, encouraged Takamatsu to show films in the newly acquired colony of Taiwan.[5]

Itō obviously realized the potential of using film as an instrument to enlighten or discipline Japanese from the homeland, and to persuade or indoctrinate Taiwanese to accept Japanese colonial rule. Although Takamatsu was involved in socialist activities, Itō had persuaded Takamatsu not to worry about his leftist background, convincing him that social security and propaganda work in Taiwan required his service.

Takamatsu took an exploratory trip to the island colony in October 1901. He showed films depicting battles of the 1899 Boer War, and the 1900 Boxer Rebellion in Peking, by the Eight-Nation Alliance, to local officials and the gentry, as well as to paying audiences in the major cities of Taiwan.[6]

Such efforts proved, at least on surface, successful to a certain extent. According to a report in *Taiwan Daily News* (*Taiwan nichinichi shimpō*), local administrators and gentry at a screening in a northern town enthusiastically applauded the marvelous scenes from the Battle of Peking.[7] Such were obviously occasions for propaganda, using film to show native Taiwanese that their former motherland had been defeated once again by foreign nations, including imperial Japan.

After the short exhibition tour, Takamatsu returned to Tokyo to start a career as writer-producer of social satire films (called "social puck films") for his own Social Puck Motion Pictures Association.[8] Meanwhile, he was also preparing for annual exhibition trips to Taiwan, which commenced in January 1904, just before the Russo-Japanese War. Takamatsu arrived in the port of Kiryū (Keelung) to start the tour screening of films in Taiwan. While showing the films, he constantly made speeches about labor issues and criticized Japanese officials' behavior in Taiwan. It was obviously due to his relationships with both Itō Hirobumi and Gotō Shimpei that Takamatsu was spared punishment by the police.[9]

The focus in the early years of the fourth governor-general, Kodama Gentarō, and his chief civilian administrator, Gotō Shimpei, was to lay foundations for civil institutions. Educational planning was considered a fundamental part of those measures to establish civil rule. Through the educational system instituted in Meiji Japan, the colonial government hoped to train the population in basic literacy, economic usefulness, and political obedience.[10] Film was used as a medium outside the educational system to win support for the new regime. The use of film by the colonial government, through businessmen such as Takamatsu, was no doubt propaganda.

However, films shown by Takamatsu's projection units in the early 1900s were also meant to enlighten native Taiwanese. Annually Takamatsu would assemble a few dozen narrative and nonfiction shorts from Japan and the West to show audiences in Taiwan "great scientific inventions, advanced civilizations, as well as heritage, scenery, humanities, and the state of Japan and the world."[11] No doubt Takamatsu intended to use film screenings as a novelty to attract native Taiwanese, in order to teach them what the "civilized" way of life was like in Japan and the West.

In 1905, Takamatsu showed a newsreel of the Russo-Japanese War during his tour in ten locations across Taiwan. The screenings became a sensation everywhere they were held. Total donations of 100,000 yen for national defense were gathered during this touring film exhibition.[12] Obviously, the colonial government took the opportunity of these screenings not only to collect donations from colonized native Taiwanese, but also to show them that Japan had the power to defeat Russia, and thus was able to persuade Taiwanese to submit to Japanese rule. In contrast to what other Asians saw, the victory of Japan (a developing Asian country) over Russia (a major European power) "as a portent for their own prospects of breaking free of colonial rule,"[13] the newsreel of the Russo-Japanese War was used by the Japanese colonizer to strengthen its colonial rule in Taiwan.

The newly colonized Taiwanese audience never imagined that the Japanese army had the ability to defeat the Russians. In fact, Fujii Shizue pointed out that when the Russo-Japanese War broke out, the Government-General of Taiwan immediately issued restrictions on reporting the event, for fear that people in Taiwan might find out that the funds for engaging in war were insufficient, because of financial difficulties of the imperial government. There were rumors all over Taiwan about the Japanese capability of ruling Taiwan. People began to sell their bonds and buy silver coins in frenzy. In order to solve the financial crisis, the Government-General of

Taiwan started a monetary reform, unifying the monetary system of Taiwan with that of Japan.[14]

Therefore, it is dubious that Taiwanese could be so impressed by scenes depicted in a Japanese-made newsreel of the Russo-Japanese War that they would decide to succumb to Japanese rule. Though it might be an exaggeration to say that the attitudes of colonized Taiwanese toward their Japanese colonizer could change so drastically after watching a film, the incident does illuminate that such film exhibition was a well-calculated opinion-changing activity used by the colonial government. The success in Taiwan of such newsreels confirms the wisdom of Japanese politicians in realizing film's potential "as a political tool in the management of empire."[15]

In the middle years of the first decade of the century, with native Taiwanese rebellions largely subdued, the use of film by the colonial government started to switch from enlightenment or persuasion of local populace to promotion of government policy.

With the arrival of the fifth governor-general, Sakuma Samata (April 1906–May 1915), in 1906, the policy of the Government-General of Taiwan emphasized wiping out the "raw aborigines."[16] Sakuma's first five-year "Administrating Aborigines Plan" (1906–1910) used a carrot-and-stick policy, which failed miserably, thus forcing the second five-year "Administrating Aborigines Plan" (1910–1915) to move toward fierce military suppression. To support the colonial government's new policy, the early objective of the Taiwan chapter of the Japanese women's group Patriotic Women's Association (PWA), an intermediary organization of the Government-General of Taiwan, was mainly to comfort soldiers and support the war-bereaved families of those involved in fighting indigenous peoples deep in the mountains of Taiwan.

The Patriotic Women's Association (*Aikoku fujinkai*) was established in Japan in 1901 by Okumura Ioko, following her experiences as a member of the imperial comfort delegation to Beijing and Tianjin when the Boxer Rebellion broke out in 1900. The objectives of the organization were primarily to comfort soldiers and support war-bereaved families. Its strong ties with the imperial family made it very popular among the social elites. Local chapters of the organization quickly spread throughout Japan. Chapters in Taichū (Taichung), Tainan, and Taihoku (Taipei) were set up in 1904. The main Taiwan chapter was finally established in 1905. Its membership mainly consisted of the wives of Japanese high officers and businessmen, as well as the wives of Taiwan gentry and social elites. The early film exhibition business of Takamatsu Toyojirō was strongly linked to Taiwan's PWA chapter.

In 1909, in order to raise funds to help it carry out its cause, while at the same time enlightening local residents, the Taiwan PWA chapter established a motion pictures section, supported by Takamatsu, who agreed to organize screenings for nine consecutive days in September in Taipei, followed by screenings throughout Taiwan during the next seven months.[17] The great success of this plan prompted the Taiwan PWA to decide not only to continue the touring film screenings on a regular basis, but also to set up five projection groups within its motion pictures section, to handle film exhibitions across Taiwan. Takamatsu Toyojirō's company, Taiwan Dōjinsha, was once again commissioned to organize all the screenings. Thus, Takamatsu made a great fortune between 1909 and 1915.

The Taiwan PWA became involved not only in the business of exhibiting films, but also in making newsreels, for which Takamatsu's Dōjinsha was also commissioned. According to Ōhashi, in July and October 1910 a camera crew, led by famous cameraman Tsuchiya Tsunekichi, was recruited from Japan to film the military operations against the Atayal "raw aborigines" who were living in the deep northern Taiwan mountains.[18] These military operations were exercised under Governor-General Sakuma's second five-year "Administrating Aborigines Plan."

The newsreels they made were shown first to Governor-General Sakuma and Civil Administration Director Uchida Kakichi (August 1910–October 1915), and soon afterward to soldiers, police, students, and the general public in Taiwan, for propaganda and fund-raising purposes. The newsreels were shown two years later to the press and PWA members at their main office in Tokyo. Special screenings of the films were also arranged for the House of Lords, House of Representatives, and other officials who were concerned with Taiwan.[19] To officially introduce these films to the Japanese society, Uchida Kakichi held a press conference in Tokyo's famous restaurant Seiyoken and screened the films to journalists.[20] Such activities attest to the fact that the Taiwan PWA indeed acted as an intermediary civilian organization producing propaganda films on behalf of the Governor-General's Office, which did not set up its own film projection section until 1914.

These newsreels were also shown later in the Takushoku (Colonization) Expo held in Tokyo's Ueno Park in October and November 1912. A report in the *Tokyo Asahi Shimbun* (October 4) states that the films revealed Taiwan indigenous peoples' savage custom of "head-hunting" and how hard Japanese soldiers and police fought against the "fearsome" natives, finally forcing the "raw aborigines" to surrender by bombarding their villages.[21]

A total of seven films from Taiwan were screened in the Expo. Among them, only one film about sugar companies and Port Takao was related to industrial development in Taiwan. All the rest are about the indigenous culture and the military operation against the "raw aborigines."[22] In comparison, films screened in the Expo that are related to other colonized territories such as Chōsen (Korea), Kantoshu (Kwantung Leased Territory in Manchuria), and Karafuto (Sakhalin) all showed the "development" of these territories under Japanese rule, and prospects for their future industrial development. The fact that newsreels depicting the suppression of Taiwan's indigenous peoples were featured as representative images of Taiwan in the Expo shows how eagerly the colonial government wanted to legitimize its forcible suppression of the Indigenes.[23] Exhibiting these films in Taiwan and Japan had obviously been aimed at enhancing support locally and nationally for suppressing Taiwan indigenous peoples by military means.

A special screening of the films was also arranged for the former director of civil administration, Gotō Shimpei (now minister of communication).[24] According to Fujii Shizue, the imperial government led by Prime Minister Katsura Tarō (July 1908–August 1911) and Minister of Communication Gotō Shimpei (July 1908–August 1911) originally took no interest in supporting Governor-General Sakuma's suppression of indigenous peoples by military means. They changed their position after Emperor Meiji, backed by the most prominent statesman, (*Genrō*) Yamagata Aritomo, supported Sakuma's plan. The Imperial Diet followed suit and passed a fifteen-million-yen budget needed for the second five-year "Administrating Aborigines Plan" (1910–1915).[25]

This is additional evidence that film was primarily considered by the colonial government to be an instrument of propaganda. In total, between 1909 and 1912, the Taiwan PWA completed three field shootings, ending up with twenty film titles.[26]

Another reason for the motion pictures section of Taiwan's PWA to make their 1912 trip to Tokyo, besides showing the newsreels, was to film the activities of a group of fifty-three Taiwan "aborigines" who were visiting Japan.[27] Ōhashi Sutesaburō mentioned that this new documentary film was later shown to (and had astonished) their fellow "aborigines" in Taiwan.[28]

This was the fourth time such "mainland sightseeing" (*naichi kankō*) activity had been sponsored by the colonial government. Although "mainland sightseeing" (inviting leaders of Taiwan's indigenous peoples to visit modernized Japan) had been sponsored by the Taiwan colonial government since 1897,[29] it became policy in 1910, under the chief of the Police Bureau and head of aboriginal affairs, Ōtsu Rinpei.[30] The activities of these aboriginal leaders in modernized Japan, such as sightseeing in the city and visiting military facilities, were filmed and shown to indigenous audiences, who otherwise never would have had such an opportunity.

The purpose of "mainland sightseeing" or "aborigine sightseeing" (*banjin kankō*), as it related to visiting modernized cities in Taiwan by their leaders, was to persuade indigenous people to fear (and not fight against) the mighty military power of great imperial Japan. Showing the filmed record and testimony of their leaders in Japan to indigenous mountain tribes was considered an effective way of convincing "aborigines" to accept Japanese rule. Such usage testifies to the purpose of film for the colonial government in ruling the Aborigines: mainly propaganda.

AN INTRODUCTION TO THE ACTUAL CONDITIONS IN TAIWAN

Utilizing film as a propaganda tool by the colonial government to convince or persuade local Taiwan residents and to inform mainland Japanese, actually started much earlier. A film titled *An Introduction to the Actual Conditions in Taiwan* (*Taiwan jikkyō shōkai, 1907*) was commissioned by the Government-General of Taiwan from Takamatsu's company in 1907. In only two months the camera crew shot more than 20,000 feet of negatives of the actual conditions (and a staged scene about subjugating a tribe of "raw aborigines") of the colonial administration, industrial development, civilian lives, and all types of scenery in more than one hundred locations around Taiwan.

According to Ichikawa, the film was used by the colonial government to brief the representatives during a budgetary subcommittee meeting in the Imperial Diet (*teikoku gikai*).[31] If such was the case, it was obviously a film report by the colonial government to the imperial government, as well as to the people of mainland Japan.

The film was also screened in the "Taiwan Hall" at the 1907 Tokyo Industrial Exposition, and toured all over Japan afterward with a performance group composed of Taiwanese singers and an orchestra, as well as Tsou aborigine performers.[32] The film and live performances were clearly used in the same manner as other custom, cultural, and industrial items exhibited in the Exposition (and the previous 1903 Osaka Industrial Exposition) as proof of the modernized, progressive results of Japanese colonization in Taiwan, as well as an introduction to homeland Japanese about the excellent results of the colonial government's acculturation and industrialization policies.[33]

Many Japanese politicians considered their success in Taiwan as "proof of her worthiness to be admitted into the community of the world's great colonial powers."[34] Therefore, a film such as *An Introduction to the Actual Conditions in Taiwan* was important evidence for the colonial government to show the central government, as well as the general public, that the money spent in the Taiwan colonial adventure was worth every penny.

The success of *An Introduction to the Actual Conditions in Taiwan* in 1907 obviously encouraged the Government-General of Taiwan to continue commissioning Takamatsu[35] or assisting cameramen from mainland Japan to produce newsreels and propaganda films on various administrative subjects in Taiwan.[36] It is reasonable, therefore, to conclude that before the 1920s, film was used mostly as evidential proof of the accomplishment of the Government-General or as a propaganda tool by the colonial government.

Not until the late 1910s was film again used by the Government-General of Taiwan for enlightenment purposes. This may be attributed to the fact that before 1918, education for local residents was not highly valued by the colonial government in Taiwan. According to Yanaihara, the colonial government policy before 1918 was mainly to keep security and stability, to develop industrial capitalism, and to establish the power of bureaucracy and capitalists, all through autocratic police rule.[37]

By 1918, education was emphasized under Governors-General Akashi Motojirō (June 1918–October 1919) and Den Kenjirō (October 1919–September 1923), who both actively pursued an assimilation policy. According to the 1919 Education Rescript, the purpose of education was to cultivate loyal subjects and good citizens. To achieve this purpose, Japanese language became both the means and the content of education in Taiwan. Yanaihara indicated that teaching Japanese in education institutions served three purposes: (1) as a communication tool; (2) as a means to develop culture; and (3) as a means of assimilation.[38]

Baskett points out that in the early 1910s officials of the colonial government (and independent distributors and exhibitors like Takamatsu) believed that film should be used to improve the lives of the population by educating them about modern life in Japan.[39] However, such a description seems more applicable to the colonial officials of 1919. It should be emphasized that the main purpose of education was not necessarily to benefit the colonized Taiwanese, but to "subjectify" them so they would be loyal to the Japanese empire. Education was to further the disconnection between Taiwan and China that had already been achieved by trade and tariff barriers between Taiwan and China after twenty-five years of colonial rule.[40] To Taiwan intellectuals, this policy of ridding them of their own culture was an injury to their national dignity.

After 1914, two important departments of the colonial government most often used films in promoting the government's policy—namely, the Ministry of Educational Affairs and the Bureau of Police Affairs.[41] However, before August 1917 both bureaus were only able to screen films either purchased from homeland Japan and Western nations, or made by commissioned filmmakers such as Takamatsu.

It should be noted that before the end of 1915, the Taiwan PWA was the major institution to tour screenings of administration-backed films. However, in early 1916 the Taiwan PWA abolished its motion pictures section, to avoid conflict of interest with burgeoning local film exhibiting businesses. By the end of the year, all of the Taiwan PWA films were transferred to another intermediary organization of the colonial government, the Taiwan Education Society (Taiwan kyōiku-kai), which was established by the Ministry of Educational Affairs. In a way, the Taiwan Education Society took over the role played by the Taiwan PWA in the use of film for public education purposes.

THE TAIWAN EDUCATION SOCIETY AND ITS USE OF FILM IN SOCIAL EDUCATION

The educational use of film by the Ministry of Educational Affairs in conjunction with the Taiwan Education Society began in December 1914. Thereafter, screenings were delegated to the Taiwan Education Society, making it the main administration-based organization to produce and exhibit nonfiction films in Taiwan through the 1920s.

The Taiwan Education Society (TES) was founded in March 1901 by educators and administrators. In 1907 it became an administration-based organization, executing works commissioned by the Ministry of Educational Affairs. Its budget was allocated by the Education Ministry, with the governor-general serving as its president and the minister of educational affairs as its director.[42]

After 1910, the major functions of the TES were shifted from scholastic research to more practical work, such as holding an annual ceremony to honor deceased Japanese educators in Taiwan, popularizing the Japanese language, conducting seminars with renowned intellectuals for members and community, creating interest in world affairs and other important knowledge, as well as combining film screenings with popular education speeches to achieve better popular educational effects.[43] Such a shift may have been caused by the need found by the Ministry of Educational Affairs for the Taiwanese general population to understand the Japanese language through various means of public education.

By the 1910s, the colonial government had realized that the percentage of those with the ability to understand the Japanese language among the local population was less than desirable.[44] Some Japanese officials believed that those who did not speak Japanese were limited by traditional Chinese ways of living, in their spiritual, professional, social, or family lives. Moreover, very few young Taiwanese were educated in schools or other organizations.[45] Therefore, encouraging local people to learn and use Japanese continued to be a major objective of the colonial government from the late 1910s on. Some form of social education for the uneducated young population was considered vital. Among all vehicles used for social education, film was considered one of the most important.[46] At the time, film had already been used occasionally as a supplement to language instruction in the classroom. The colonial government thought that film was so closely related to the lives of the general public that it could be used to influence them.[47]

In 1914, a motion pictures unit was established in the TES's popular education section. Educational films were purchased, and screenings were held frequently in major cities, as well as in remote locations throughout Taiwan and the offshore islands, beginning in 1915. By 1917, the number of screenings had risen to fifty-two, with a total audience of 96,000.[48] A report to the Assembly of the Taiwan Education Society later that year put the number of viewers at nearly 120,000 for the ninety-one screenings held in 1916 and 1917.[49]

Such use of film as a tool for social education was very different from that of the Ministry of Education in Japan. According to Peter High, it was not until around 1919 that the Ministry in Japan finally began to use film as part of its social education program aimed at staving off the domestic "Red Menace."[50] The more advanced use of film for social education in colonial Taiwan can be attributed to the special circumstances in the colony. As one scholar argued at the time, the island populace, due to their different languages and culture, required a more intuitive media, like film, to change their attitudes and mentality through the eyes and ears.[51]

Even though most of the titles screened by the TES in the 1910s were in essence educational, such as *Civilized Agriculture, Students in Sports, Automobile Racing, Zoo,* and *Observatory and Astronomy,* some films were used to promote patriotic feelings about the Emperor and imperial Japan. This was actually one of the important functions of the TES.

In fact, promoting loyalty to the emperor and the state, with the implication that the emperor *was* the state, had been incorporated in school and social education in Taiwan since late 1890s. The 1890 Imperial Rescript on Education (*Kyōiku ni kansuru chokugo*), which stresses that the loyalty of subjects contributes to the prosperity of the Imperial Throne coeval with heaven and earth, was translated into Chinese, and the administrative order (*kunrei*) that required students to study and memorize the 315-character text was promulgated in February 1897. The colonial government hoped to strengthen local students' loyalty to the empire through ceremonial reading of the document in front of the royal pictures of the emperor and empress.[52]

The date the Rescript was signed by Emperor Meiji had been designated "Education Day" by the colonial government. Ever since then, every year on October 30 the TES would hold a ceremony celebrating Education Day. When the motion pictures unit was formed in 1914, the TES would also screen "educational" films in public places throughout the island on the evening of Education Day. Thus, film was used to promote the idea of "education" to the general public in conjunction with a ceremony and other formal activities.

In February 1916, having purchased a lengthy film (more than 3,500 feet) about Emperor Taishō's accession ceremony, the Land Tenure Foundation for Education (*gakuso zaidan*) leased it to the Taiwan Education Society. The TES quickly arranged thirty screenings, showing the film to more than twenty-eight thousand elementary school students and their parents within one month, all over Taipei.[53] The purpose of these screenings was for Taiwanese schoolchildren and adults to know that they must "venerate the Royal Family and understand the essence of the national polity," according to the report in *Taiwan Education*. It is, therefore, correct for Misawa to point out that it was Japanese nationalism (and modernity) behind the use of motion pictures in popular (social) education by the TES.[54] The formal screening of the 1916 accession ceremony film was the most symbolic example. In 1921, in a similar way the TES screened throughout Taiwan a film about the European visit of the crown prince. Nearly forty-three thousand viewers attended the eleven screenings.[55]

The salute to the royal family had its climax in 1923 when the crown prince paid a visit to the island colony. The royal visit in April lasted twelve days. The TES had already sent cameramen to Tokyo to film the crown prince's departure from the royal residence in Akasaka. Eventually the TES made a fifteen-thousand-foot film about the royal visit to Taiwan. The TES proudly presented the film to Emperor Taishō and the crown prince for their review.[56] Afterward, the film was widely exhibited across Taiwan, "so that the population of the island were able to humbly revere the Holy goodness of the Crown Prince," according to Toda Seizō, head of the TES's motion pictures unit, in an article.[57]

Four months after the royal visit, a 7.9 magnitude earthquake hit Tokyo. The devastating 1923 Great Kantō Earthquake and the blazing aftermath killed at least one hundred thousand people. The disaster caused all subsequent celebrations in Taiwan that year to become occasions for donations to aid "fellow compatriots in the Homeland."[58] This explains why there were very few reports in *Taiwan Education*, the organ of the TES, on the film screenings about the crown prince's Taiwan visit.[59] Yet a great number of copies of the film had actually been made and sent to each local government (*shū* that administered more developed areas or *chō* that administered marginal areas). Most of the island's population went to a screening of the film almost simultaneously in late 1923.[60]

In order for each *shū* or *chō* to do its work in popularizing social education in Taiwan, the TES had already purchased projectors and donated one to each local government in 1922, along with a subsidy to purchase or rent films to show to the public the following year.[61] This policy made the screening of educational films very popular during the 1920s and 1930s.

The screening of education films on the island in early 1920s coincided with the film education movement in Japan, which started in 1917–1918 when film entrepreneurs, cameramen, and some operational officers in the government spontaneously produced documentaries and newsreels for educational, enlightenment, and informational purposes.[62] The film recommendation movement and the motion pictures exposition sponsored by the

Ministry of Education in 1921 finally promoted the educational usage of film into a movement. However, such a movement would not be promoted in Taiwan until 1930, when the TES earned the status of independent incorporated association.

Meanwhile, the Taiwan Education Society was only able to screen films before August 1917. This means that the TES either had to purchase educational films from homeland Japan and the Western nations, or its film productions had to be commissioned to outside filmmakers. Takamatsu Toyojirō's company Dōjinsha, for example, was hired by the TES to film the 1916 Taiwan Industrial Exhibition celebrating the twentieth anniversary of Japanese colonial rule.[63]

The 1916 Taiwan Industrial Exhibition was the first major exhibition held in Taiwan by the Japanese colonial government since its rule over Taiwan began in 1895. It was also the first time the Government-General of Taiwan opened its door to homeland Japanese, as well as to people from other countries. The event was carefully planned and executed. Dignitaries, including members of the royal family, former governors-general, and high officials of the current Government-General of Taiwan, were invited to attend.

The film produced for the 1916 Industrial Exhibition by Takamatsu's Dōjinsha, however, shifted its focus from the Exhibition itself to the visit by HRH Prince Kan'in-no-miya Kotohito Shin'nō, younger brother of Emperor Meiji, and his wife. On the surface, such a major shift in the focus of the documentary film might sound abrupt and strange. Yet it once again confirms the preference for patriotism and nationalism (through paying reverence to the emperor and the royal family) over anything else in the TES's social education program. More than ten thousand feet of negative was shot. The content of the film, with the exception of exteriors, interiors, and night views of the Industrial Exhibition halls, was primarily shots of Prince Kotohito and his wife, including their arrival at the Taihoku (Taipei) Train Station, their visits to the opening ceremony, Taiwan Jinja, the Red Cross, and Taichū Park, their receiving aborigines, and so forth.[64]

The great success of the educational and other nonfiction film screenings in the first decade of the century had obviously prompted the TES to produce films with its own crews. Such a major shift might have also been due to Takamatsu's departure from Taiwan in 1917.[65] In August of that year, Hagiya Kenzō, a veteran cameraman working for the M. Kashī Company, was recruited from Tokyo to be a staff technician in the TES.[66] Hagiya's previous shooting of the 1916 Taiwan Industrial Exhibition film, produced by Takamatsu's Dōjinsha, had tremendously impressed the TES.[67]

By mid-September of 1917, Hagiya was already busy filming events in the Taipei area, such as military training, children practicing at the Kote Shō swimming site next to the Shinten (Hsintien) River, and scenes in the Taipei zoo.[68] At the end of 1917, Hagiya had already filmed important events including the visit in October by HRH Prince Kitashirakawa-no-miya Naruhisa and his wife, and the Hygiene Exhibition in Taichū in November.[69]

Filming the Hygiene Exhibition shows the perceived need to promote popular awareness of hygiene.[70] Epidemic diseases had been serious issues during the early years of colonial rule. In fact, "Taiwan had long experienced plague, malaria, cholera, dysentery, and numerous other contagious diseases."[71] Many scholars have pointed out that more Japanese soldiers died from contagious diseases than on the battlefield when Japan took over Taiwan in 1895.[72] Many Taiwanese, however, either believed in supernatural means to cure disease, or just ignored the colonial government's sanitation campaigns, such as rat extermination. Therefore, the Japanese authorities started to "educate people" by issuing administrative orders, public lecturing, and holding exhibitions.[73]

The motion pictures unit of the TES worked closely with the authorities behind the Hygiene Exhibition, not only by making a documentary of the event, but also by being actively involved in the social education part by designing and reenacting various ways people could become infected with malaria.[74] After that, the motion pictures unit led by Hagiya was instrumental in producing films about epidemic diseases, as well as promoting social awareness of how to prevent them.

For example, in July 1919, when cholera started to spread across Taiwan, the TES sent its cameraman to gather material about the treatment of cholera patients at the Mackay Memorial Hospital in Taihoku. At the request of the Taihoku Chō, the TES screened the film in Taihoku and vicinity, including Kiryū (Keelung) and other cholera-infected areas, in late August and September 1919. Each screening was accompanied by speeches from government-employed or practicing local physicians.

The great success of such endeavors prompted the TES to continue holding screenings across Taiwan to propagate the concept of hygiene among the general public.[75] In 1919, the unit held sixty-seven screenings about such topics in different parts of Taiwan, with more than 125,000 elementary schoolchildren attending.[76] The especially high attendance that year was unusual, because in years without the serious threat of epidemics, the motion pictures unit held fewer screenings with smaller audiences. For example, in 1920 there were only nineteen screenings with about seventy thousand people attending.

By 1918, Japan experienced the so-called Taishō Democracy, after Hara Takashi (September 1918–November 1921) became the first "commoner" prime minister. Military staffs were replaced by civil servants as governors-general of Taiwan. Consequently, Taiwan had its first civil servant, Den Kenjiro, as governor-general in 1919. In the context of the "extension of Japan proper policy" (*naichi enchō shugi*), that is, the policy of ruling Taiwan in the same fashion as homeland Japan, which was initiated by Prime Minister Hara, Governor-General Den Kenjirō began a large-scale reform to integrate the colony into Japan proper.

Before accepting the governor-generalship, Den Kenjirō explained to Hara that an important part of his assimilation policy was educating the Taiwanese to be pure Japanese. Upon assuming his duties in Taiwan, Den proclaimed that Japanization of Taiwan and assimilation of the Taiwanese were the goals of his administration.[77] Taiwanese people were to achieve political equality with the Japanese, so long as the colony could reach a level of development similar to that of Japan.[78] Consequently, the Education Rescript of 1922, also known as an integration rescript, was promulgated by Governor-General Den to abolish the policy of separating Japanese and Taiwanese students based on their race. The curriculum of the public schools, which local Taiwanese attended, was brought closer to that of Japanese students' primary schools. The most important change was the addition of Japanese history. The declared objectives of teaching Japanese history to Taiwanese students were to provide a general introduction to the "national polity" and to cultivate "national spirit" (*kokumin seishin*).[79] This would prepare the Taiwanese to devote themselves to the emperor and imperial Japan in wartime.

In 1922, after the promulgation of the new Education Rescript, the Government-General started rural reform to improve the quality of local manpower. Film screenings were considered a vital part of the program.[80] In order to popularize social education, the TES started to hold training sessions for the staff of local governments that were responsible for such affairs. Twenty-six clerks attended the ten-day session in May 1922, held in the second-floor canteen of the Governor-General's Office.[81] Students studied not only handling of film and operating projectors, but also the history and development of movies, principles of motion picture cameras and projectors, as well as the aesthetics, sociology, and the psychology of film.[82] As part of the Government-General's efforts, many of the local governments started their own film projection training after 1923, with assistance from the TES's motion pictures unit. By the early 1930s, similar training sessions would be held for employees of other governmental institutions, such as schools and the tax bureau.[83]

Interestingly enough, it was around the same time that schools, organizations, and local governments in Japan proper also began to utilize film for education or propaganda purposes. Film was used in both school and social education. In urban and rural areas alike, film screening was extremely popular. In order to enlighten the populace, the Ministry of Education held a training session on motion picture projection techniques in Ueno, Tokyo, in August 1924,[84] almost two years after the TES's similar training sessions held in the governor-general's office building. Once again, Taiwan was more advanced than mainland Japan in the use of film for education and propaganda.

Though most of the public screenings (and some special screenings for the Governor-General's Office) were still held by the motion pictures unit of the TES, starting in October 1922 some screenings were supported by local governments.[85] By 1924, most of the screenings for public education had already been taken over by the local governments' projection units,[86] and by 1930, screenings by local film associations were very common. For example, the Taichū Shū Film Association held 538 screenings in 1930, with more than 220,000 in attendance.[87]

To facilitate public education through film in rural areas, beginning in 1922 the Internal Affairs Bureau (Naimukyoku) used its budget for social affairs to purchase educational films for the TES to screen throughout the island, and gave selected films to local governments to do their own screenings.[88] Head of the motion pictures unit Toda pointed out that the TES made sure each local government received the best possible educational films for regular screenings.[89]

By the mid-1920s the TES would produce about twenty-five films annually using its own cameramen, and purchase another twenty or so Japanese and foreign educational films.[90] By March 1924, the TES had already made eighty-four films with its own cameramen.[91] Though most of the films were about topics related to Taiwan and homeland Japan, fourteen of them (about 17 percent) were records of political events;[92] eleven films (13 percent) depicted local agriculture and fishery products; twenty-two (26 percent) were about cities, offshore islands, scenery, and transportation; five promoted good hygiene and prevention of epidemic diseases; and five showed sports events, mostly athletic meets. Films representing cultural affairs were very few.[93] Only three films were directly related to education.[94] This clearly indicated that the use of film by the Taiwan Education Society was, like its predecessor, the Patriotic Women's Association, for political and propagandistic purposes, rather than educational.

FUTILE EFFORTS BY THE TES TO PROMOTE MODERN IMAGES OF TAIWAN

The Taiwan Education Society not only produced and showed films about mainland Japan to Taiwanese adults and schoolchildren, it also produced and showed films about Taiwan to Japanese in the homeland. In 1920 the Taiwan Education Society started promoting favorable images of Taiwan as one of its functions. Misawa notes that the TES played a dual role in Taiwan—on one hand, it imported the content of Japanese nationalism from mainland Japan; on the other hand, it had to create content representing a positive picture of Taiwan and export it to mainland Japan.[95]

In March and April 1920 the TES dispatched a four-man group to Kyushu and Tokyo with the purpose of presenting the actual situations of Taiwan. A report in *Taiwan Education* on the "Introducing Current Situations in Taiwan" (*Taiwan jijō shōkai*) project once again reveals the frustration felt by the colonial government and Japanese residents in Taiwan about Taiwan's tarnished image in the eyes of the mainland Japanese:

> Even today, twenty-five years after colonization, in homeland Japan Taiwan is still thought to be an inferno—with mountains filled with jungle diseases, and plagued with malaria, constantly in danger of your head being hunted by the savages. One of the reasons for such a misconception to continue is the lack of a factual introduction to today's Taiwanese culture for mainland residents. Consequently, when one tries to invite people from the mainland to work in Taiwan, either in the field of education or any other profession, tangentially they feel the environment in Taiwan is not very convenient.[96]

"In order to eliminate such misunderstanding, to enhance the willingness of the inland people to come to Taiwan to contribute to the development of education and other fields in Taiwan, as well as to understand the relationship between Taiwan (as a southern territory of the empire) and the power of the Japanese empire," the TES felt a need to dispatch a group to homeland Japan to reveal the actual situation of Taiwan.[97]

Each propaganda session consisted of one or two speeches in the daytime and a film screening in the evening. The film the TES showed included shots of aboriginal children riding on small crafts to attend school, which was said to be the most attractive scene to audiences in Japan proper.[98]

In Kyushu, audiences for evening film screenings were much greater than for the morning and afternoon speeches, which were aimed at government officials, entrepreneurs, intellectuals, teachers, and students. An estimated forty-one thousand people attended the screenings in Kyushu.[99] Screenings in Tokyo were more political, in the sense that some sessions were arranged exclusively for the royal family, entrepreneurs, and intelligentsia. Some former and current high officials of the government of Taiwan, including Gotō Shimpei, came to Tokyo specifically to address audiences before the film screenings. Two sessions in Hibiya Park, attended by an estimated eighteen thousand people, indicate the project's popularity.

The Tokyo screenings were highlighted by a special screening for the crown prince and other princes.[100] According to Misawa, the Taiwan Education Society associated its activities with the royal family in order to enhance the image of Taiwan, and to highlight the importance of its project, "Introducing Current Situations in Taiwan."[101] However, I suspect that the crown prince wanted to see the film depicting actual conditions in Taiwan because he wanted to prepare for his visit to the island five months later.

The success of the first group prompted the TES to dispatch a second group to areas west of Nagoya (including two cities and eleven prefectures) in 1921.[102] To prepare for this project, Toda Seizō, head of the motion pictures unit, and cameraman Hagiya Kenzō spent time shooting beautiful spots and exotic scenery throughout Taiwan, months before their Kansai trip.[103]

Hisazumi Eiichi, head of the 1921 group and a former education official for the Government-General of Taiwan, estimated that the twenty-nine screenings in the fifty-five-stop schedule attracted hundreds of thousands of viewers. During their tour, the group not only showed films introducing actual events in Taiwan, they also brought a camera and shot more than three thousand feet of film showing stunning scenes and ancient sites, as well as the royal tour to Kyoto and Osaka by the crown prince.

Nonetheless, Hisazumi pointed out that some Japanese viewers had doubts about the purpose of the screenings—whether the colonial government just wanted to solicit teachers and immigrants to live and work in Taiwan. The source of funding for this TES project was also questioned.[104]

Such criticisms reveal the limits to using speeches and film screenings to lobby the general populace. Even though the TES and the colonial government continued to participate in major events, such as the 1922 Tokyo Peace Expo, and held several large-scale touring exhibitions between 1924 and 1929 to introduce current developments in the Colony, their efforts seemed to be ineffective.

In 1923, the TES solicited assistance from a nongovernmental organization, the Eastern Association (*Toyo Kyokai*). After meeting certain criteria, institutes in Japan, Chōsen (Korea), and Manchuria were allowed to borrow films in the "Introducing Current Situations in Taiwan" series from the Eastern Association.[105] The TES connection with the Eastern Association is a particularly interesting development.

Originally established in 1898 by politicians and the financial world as the Taiwan Association (*Taiwan Kyokai*), to help the Japanese government manage its first colony, the Eastern Association changed its name in 1907 after Japan annexed Korea, in order to include Korea and Manchuria as part of its territories of concern. Therefore, showing the "Introducing Current Situations in Taiwan" films to similarly colonized Korea and Manchuria through the Eastern Association carried certain overtones.

It is not known how successful the efforts by the Eastern Association were. However, individual attempts by the TES to introduce Taiwan to Japan via films continued after 1924.[106] Starting in 1925 such films were shown to visiting Japanese educational groups to introduce education in Taiwan. In April and May 1929, the Government-General of Taiwan held exhibitions in Tokyo and Osaka to promote Taiwan. *Traveling Taiwan* (*Taiwan no tabi*), a film produced by the TES, was screened in Osaka in May.[107]

A major shift happened in the Taiwan Education Society in January 1931. It became an independent incorporated association that owned land, a building, and a women's high school. The TES also expanded its internal structure to include six departments: general affairs, accounting, school education, social education, publications, and photography.

The mission of the TES's photography department would no longer be restricted to showing and making films for social education. It was enthusiastically involved, beginning in 1931, in the production of educational films to be used as supplementary material with textbooks throughout Japan. For example, a twenty-five-hundred-foot film produced by the TES, entitled *Taiwan,* was designated by the imperial government as an educational film to be used for teaching material in Japan proper, when teaching the subject of Taiwan from the designated textbook.[108] *Taiwan* comprehensively presented geography, agriculture, animal husbandry, fisheries, forest products, and minerals, as well as city and rural scenery, historic places, and modern ports. Its main purpose was to clarify the misconception in Japan about Taiwan that Taihoku (Taipei) was a dangerous place, and that malaria was still widespread.

In 1931 the TES also established a policy to produce its own films about Japan's scenery and ancient sites in conjunction with textbooks. Schools in Taiwan would receive these films from the TES, instead of buying them from film companies in Japan. The TES started to work with teachers in normal schools, primary schools, and public schools in Taihoku to illustrate content concerning Japan proper in textbooks for Taiwan students, helping them better understand their unknown "motherland." It was said to be a necessary step in basic education to cultivate students as Japanese nationals.[109]

Ten new titles (8,450 feet) about homeland Japan's scenery and venerable locations were planned in 1931.[110] These films were made by the TES for use in classrooms in Taiwan's primary and public schools because textbooks written for children in Japan proper were deemed too distant from the lives of children in Taiwan.

In 1936, eighteen more titles to be used as supplements to textbooks were produced by the TES, among them fifteen films about Japanese scenic spots and ancient sites. These films were used both in school education and in social education. Some titles in the list featuring beautiful Japanese settings and historic locations, as well as the royal tour to Kyoto and Osaka, were actually shot by TES cameramen dispatched in 1921 for the "Introducing Current Situations in Taiwan" project.

Even though the TES boasted about the great success of these films, as well as the events mentioned above, their actual effectiveness is dubious. The misconceptions of mainland Japanese about Taiwan were so deeply rooted that any effort on the part of the colonial government to correct them seemed futile. According to actor Sawamura Kunitaro, as late as 1942, cast and crews of the "national policy" film *Clan of the Sea* (*Umi no gōzoku, dir.*

Arai Ryōhei, 1942) still dreaded going to Taiwan for location shooting because of their stereotypes about it—a place rife with aborigines, poisonous snakes, and malaria, .[111]

Nakamura lamented that propaganda efforts by institutions such as the Bureau of Colonial Production (*Shokusankyoku*) had put too much stress on Taiwanese culture, aboriginal dances, and exotic produce, such as bananas, coconuts, betel nuts, and so on, and rarely mentioned industrial products, thus creating misconceptions.[112] However, screening *Taiwan*, a film with positive images of industrial development, in elementary schools in Japan proper did not seem to achieve the effects expected by the colonial government in Taiwan.

Twenty-five years of efforts to create a positive image of colonial Taiwan in mainland Japan, starting in 1907 with *An Introduction to the Actual Conditions in Taiwan*, turned out to be an uphill battle by the colonial government and Japanese living in Taiwan. After almost half a century of Japanese rule, Taiwan was still seen by many Japanese in the homeland as a backward area of the empire! No wonder *wansei*, Japanese born and living in Taiwan, were despised by people in Japan proper even after the Second World War.

The Manchurian Incident, and the ensuing Shanghai Incident in January 1932, did not change the direction of the TES's photography department, which continued to make supplementary films and engage in training programs. However, two years later, following the League of Nations' condemnation of the invasion of Manchuria by Japan, the direction of filmmaking and attitudes toward film in Taiwan altered.

Isolation from the world made the Japanese government and military more eager to use film for propaganda purposes, such as "proclamation of a national state of emergency and the need for absolute national unity," to quote from an article in the Home Bureau's Censorship Annual in 1934.[113] In other words, films made by the TES after 1934 showed a tendency to promote patriotism, militarism, and the Japanization of Taiwan.

The use of film by the Taiwan governor-general, and intermediary organizations, thus entered a new phase in film history.

CONCLUSION

Taiwan was imperial Japan's first colony. During the first and last periods, it was ruled by the military, with seventeen years of civilian rule interposed from 1919 to 1936. Because of these changes of administration, as well as the turbulent political and military events during the first half of the twentieth century in Japan and East Asia, when Taiwan was ruled by the Japanese empire, the colonial government's use of film varied in different administrations and different historical periods. In this chapter, I have illuminated how colonial and imperial policies dictated the ways film functioned in Taiwan between 1895 and 1937. We can also deduce, from the ways film had been used before Japan actively engaged in a prolonged war, variations in the focus of different administrations.

Taiwan was one of the earliest territories in the world to use film for political rule, before Japan's other colonies, such as Korea and Manchuria, let alone the Japan home islands itself.

Differential treatment is the basis for colonial rule. One cannot disregard that during Japanese colonial rule of Taiwan, a master-slave relationship existed between the colonizer and the colonized. All Taiwanese, including the indigenous, were deprived of their subjectivity.[114] Thus, as a tool to promote colonial policy, it was natural for film to be used to promote Japanese history and culture, and to help establish identification with the emperor and imperial Japan.

The fifty-year history of film policies of the Government-General in Taiwan may be summarized in three stages: (1) propaganda and enlightenment, between 1900 and 1917, in which films were used to enlighten, and promote government policies among, native Taiwanese, and to promote a modern images of Taiwan among mainland Japanese; (2) social and school education, between 1917 and 1937, at first with emphasis on social education in order to improve the quality of local manpower, and later to make films as supplements to textbooks; (3) propaganda, after 1937, to promote nationalism, militarism, and the policy of Japanization.

Notes

1. Tze-lan Sang took the same view in her recent paper on the state of the field in Taiwan cinema studies. "There are relatively few publications in English that offer a long view of the development of Taiwan cinema." She cited this author's *Historical Dictionary of Taiwan Cinema* (2013) and Guo-juin Hong's *Taiwan Cinema: Contested Nation on Screen* (2011) as two rare examples; Tze-lan Sang, "The State of the Field in Taiwan Film Studies" (presentation at the Second World Congress of Taiwan Studies, London, June 18–20, 2015).

2. Ye's book contains countless errors in fact and far-fetched description or baseless inter-

pretation of historical accounts. Misawa Mamie has pointed out some of these troublesome errors and misinterpretations in her book *The "Screen" under Colonial Rule: The Film Policy in Taiwan in the Japanese Colonial Period (1895–1942)*. One of Ye's most serious mistakes is the claim that Edison's Kinetoscope had been introduced by a Japanese merchant to Taiwan in August 1896, three months earlier than its appearance in Kobe, Japan. Such a claim, highlighted in both Hong's and Zhang's books, was disputed with very strong arguments in Misawa's book; Misawa Mamie, *Zhimindi xia de yinmu: Taiwan zongdufu dianying zhengce zhi yanjiu (1895–1942)* [The "Screen" under Colonial Rule: The Film Policy in Taiwan in the Japanese Colonial Period (1895–1942)] (Taipei: Avanguard Publishing, 2002), 265–268.

3. The Lumière brothers' Cinématographe was shown in Taiwan in June 1900. "Tansuikan getsurei kai yokyōhyō" [A Criticism on the Entertainment Program of Monthly Meeting at Tansui-kan] and "Katsudōshashin" [Motion Pictures], *Taiwan nichinichi shimpō* (Taihoku), June 19, 1900, 5.) It was brought in by a Japanese businessman living in Taipei, Oshima Inoshi, who had invited projectionist Matsuura Shōzō from French Auto Phantom Pictures Association (Futsukoku jidō maboroshi-ga kyōkai) in Osaka to show the Lumières' films in the newly acquired colony. Nine months earlier, in September 1899, an Edison Vitascope was shown in a Taipei theater. ("Jūjikan no katsudōshashin" [Motion Pictures at Jūjikan], *Taiwan nichinichi shimpō* (Taihoku), September 8, 1899, 5.) There was another report in the local newspaper on September 5, which stated that a Cantonese had utilized a "Western Electric Picture Machine" for a show a month ago in a local Chinese community in Taipei. ("Diandeng yingxi" [Electric Lantern Pictures], *Taiwan nichinichi shimpō* (Taihoku), September 5, 1899, 4.) The exact nature of the moving pictures that were shown is not clear, however.

4. Tom Gunning defines "the cinema of attractions," an earlier conception of cinema that dominates cinema until about 1906–1907, "a cinema that bases itself on the quality that *Léger* celebrated: its ability to show something." Tom Gunning, "The Cinema of Attractions: Early Film, Its Spectator and the Avant-Garde," in *Early Cinema: Space, Frame, Narrative*, ed. Thomas Elsaesser (London: BFI Publishing, 1990), 57.

5. Matsumoto Kappei, *Nihon shakai shugi engekishi: Meiji Taishō hen* [History of Japanese Socialist Theater: Meiji Taishō Part] (Tokyo: Chikuma Shobō, 1975), 45–46.

6. Even though no direct evidence can prove it, circumstantial evidence leads Wanshun Shih to conclude in her article "Takamatsu Toyozirō and the Inauguration of Modern Taiwanese Theater" that Takamatsu indeed came to Taiwan in 1901 to screen films. Such evidence includes a report in *Taiwan nichinichi shimpō* in October 1901 describing a film screening activity held in Taipei, which did not specify the person or organization behind the event. Takamatsu Toyojirō is believed to be the one responsible for it because many sources, including his own articles, stated that Takamatsu came to Taiwan to screen films in (October) 1901. A recent discovery by this author of Takamatsu's approved application of a passport to travel from Tainan, a seaport in Southern Taiwan, to Hong Kong and Xiamen on March 25, 1902 reveals that Takamatsu must have been in Taiwan in late 1901 and stayed on until early 1902. His purpose in traveling to Hong Kong and Xiamen needs further exploration. See "Gekisen katsudōshashinkai"

[Fierce Battle Motion Pictures Screening], *Taiwan nichinichi shimpō* (Taihoku), October 23, 1901, n.p.; Ichikawa Sai, "Taiwan eiga jigyō hatsutatsu shikō" [A Preliminary History of the Taiwan Film Industry], in *Ajia eiga no sōzō oyobi kensetsu* [Creating and Developing an Asian Cinema], edited by Ichikawa Sai (Tokyo: Kokusai Eiga Tsūshinsha Shuppanbu, 1941), 86; and Matsumoto, *Nihon shakai shugi engekishi*, 306.

7. "Huodong huandeng" [Moving Magic Lantern], *Taiwan nichinichi shimpō* (Taihoku), November 21, 1901, 4.

8. Okabe Ryū, ed., *Shiryō: Takamatsu Toyojirō to Okasawara Meihō no gyōseki (Nihon eigashi sukō 9)* [Documents: The Business Traces of Takamatsu Toyojirō and Okasawara Meihō (Unedited Manuscripts of Japanese Film History 9)] (Tokyo: Film Library Council, 1974).

9. Matsumoto, *Nihon shakai shugi engekishi*, 306. Gotō was handpicked by Prime Minister Itō Hirobumi to be the chief civilian administrator in Taiwan. It is obvious that Gotō followed Itō's orders and protected Takamatsu's film screenings from being harassed by the police in Taiwan.

10. E. Patricia Tsurumi, *Japanese Colonial Education in Taiwan, 1895–1945* (Cambridge, MA: Harvard University Press, 1977), 10–11.

11. Takamatsu Toyojirō, *Taiwan dōkakai sōsai Itagaki hakusha kukakka kangei no ji* [A Welcome to Count Itagaki, President of the Taiwan Assimilation Society] (Taihoku: Taiwan Dōjinsha, 1914), 6.

12. Ichikawa, "Taiwan eiga jigyō hatsutatsu shikō," 87.

13. Rotem Kowner, "Between a Colonial Clash and World War Zero: The Impact of the Russo-Japanese War in a global perspective," in *The Impact of the Russo-Japanese War*, ed. Rotem Kowner (London: Routledge, 2007), 19.

14. Fujii Shizue, *Lifan: Riben zhili Taiwan de jice* [Administrating Aborigines: The Strategy of Japanese Rule] (Taipei: Wenyingtang, 1997), 181.

15. Isolde Standish, *A New History of Japanese Cinema: A Century of Narrative Film* (New York: Continuum, 2006), 120.

16. Following the advice of Counselor Mochiji Rokusaburō, the Japanese colonial rulers in an Aboriginal Affairs Committee meeting in 1902 decided to divide Taiwan's indigenous people into three groups, based on the degree of "evolution" and their "obedience" to Japanese rule: those who had evolved to the standard of the Chinese, lived in the Japanese administrated area, and obeyed Japanese laws were "ripe aborigines" (*jukuban*); those who had evolved somewhat, lived outside the Japanese administrated area, and obeyed Japanese laws, such as paying taxes, were "acculturated aborigines" (*kaban*); "raw aborigines" (*seiban*) were those who had not evolved much, lived outside the Japanese administrated area, and never obeyed the de facto rule of imperial Japan. See Fujii, *Lifan*, 154–157.

17. Films shown in the touring exhibitions were mainly historical drama, samurai stories, and films adapted from family novels. The total number of film titles was between twenty and thirty. See Ōhashi Sutesaburō, *Aikoku Fujinkai Taiwan Honbu enkakushi* [History of the Development of the Patriotic Women's Association Taiwan Main Office] (Taihoku: Aikoku fujinkai Taiwan honbu, 1941), 137.

18. Ōhashi, *Aikoku Fujinkai Taiwan Honbu enkakushi*, 141–142; Tanaka Jun'ichirō, *Nihoneiga hattatsushi I: katsudōshashin jidai* [A History of the Development of Japanese Cinema I: The Katsudo Shashin Era] (Tokyo: Chūō kōronsha, 1961), 89.

19. See Ōhashi, *Aikoku Fujinkai Taiwan Honbu enkakushi*, 142, as well as "Tōban to aikoku fujinkai" [Subjugating the Aborigines and Patriotic Women's Association], *Taiwan nichinichi shimpō* (Taihoku), February 10, 1912, 7; and "Engei: Zenshin-tai katsudō shashin" [Entertainment: Advance Corps' Motion Pictures], *Taiwan nichinichi shimpō* (Taihoku), April 3, 1912, 7.

20. "Santan taru riban no jikkyō" [Difficult State of Ruling the Aborigines], *Yomiuri Shimbun*, February 12, 1912, 3.

21. "Shokuminchi to katsudō shashin" [Colony and Motion Pictures], *Tokyo Asahi Shimbun*, October 4, 1912, n.p., quoted in Matsuda Kyoko, *Teikoku no shikō: nihon "teikoku" to taiwan genjūmin* [The Thinking of the Empire: The "Empire" of Japan and Taiwan Indigenous Peoples] (Tokyo: Yūshi-sha, 2014), 173.

22. Titles of these films are *Houses of the Aborigines and Aboriginal Woman in Front of Skull Shed, Minister Uchida's Inspection and inside the Village of Gaogan Tribe, Building a Bridge to Link Bonbon Mountain, Marching Police Troupe, Activities of Subjugation Corps,* and *Bombarding Baron Mountain* (Matsuda, *Teikoku no shikō*, 173).

23. Matsuda, *Teikoku no shikō*, 173.

24. Ōhashi, *Aikoku Fujinkai Taiwan Honbu enkakushi*, 141–142.

25. Fujii, *Lifan*, 228.

26. The list of films donated (or deposited) to the Taiwan Education Society showed twenty titles related to the military operations against the aborigines. See "Kaihō: Katsudōshashin fuirumu kizō" [Bulletin: Motion Pictures Films Donation], *Taiwan Education* 176 (1917): 84.

27. See Ōhashi, *Aikoku Fujinkai Taiwan Honbu enkakushi*, 142, as well as "Seiban tsuitachi no yūran" [One Day Sightseeing of Raw Aborigines], *Yomiuri Shimbun*, May 6, 1912, n.p., and "Seiban ikkō kaeru" [The Raw Aborigines Group Returns Home], *Yomiuri Shimbun*, May 13, 1912, 3.

28. Ōhashi, *Aikoku Fujinkai Taiwan Honbu enkakushi*, 142.

29. According to Fujisaki, "mainland sightseeing" began in 1897 when thirteen representatives from four indigenous tribes—Atayal, Bunun, Tsou, and Paiwan—were sent to visit Nagasaki, Osaka, Tokyo, and Yokosuka Port. See Fujisaki Seinosuke, *Taiwan no banzoku* [Aboriginal Tribes of Taiwan] (Tokyo: Kokushi kankōkai, 1936), 874.

30. Fujii, *Lifan*, 258–261. It should be noted that in 1907 when Takamatsu Toyojirō brought *An Introduction to the Actual Conditions in Taiwan*, a film he produced on behalf of the colonial government, to Japan proper to screen at the Tokyo Industrial Exposition, the Reichstag (teikoku gijidō), Eastern Association, as well as the Yūrakuza Thearter in Tokyo, Kakuza Theater in Osaka, and theaters in other major Japanese cities from Hokkaido in the north to Hokuriku, San'in, Chūgoku, and Kyūshū in the south, he had brought with him five young aborigines from Alisan Mountain to perform indig-

enous dances before the screenings. See reports published in *Yomiuri Shimbun*, October 28, 1907, 3, and "Fanren zhi neidi guanguang" [Aborigines' Mainland Sightseeing], *Taiwan nichinichi shimpō* (Chinese edition), December 26, 1907, 5, as well as Toyojirō, *Taiwan dōkakai sōsai Itagaki hakusha kukakka kangei no ji*, 10–11. Takamatsu took these indigenous people to famous sightseeing places and visited troops and warships. The young visitors were summoned by Emperor Meiji in the royal residence in Aoyama. They returned to Taiwan at the end of 1907, and were summoned by Governor-General Sakuma before being sent back to Alisan Mountain. Takamatsu called the trip to Japan for the Tsou indigenous "mainland sightseeing" as well.

31. Ichikawa, "Taiwan eiga jigyō hatsutatsu shikō," 89–90.

32. A report in *Taiwan Daily News* (*Taiwan nichinichi shimpō*) on April 12, 1907 stated that the film would be shown in Taipei in May, and then at the Tokyo Exposition. ("Katsudōshashin satsuei no shūryō" [Photographing of Motion Pictures Ends], *Taiwan nichinichi shimpō*, April 12, 1907, 5.)

33. Hu Chia-yu, "Bolanhui yu Taiwan yuanzhumin: zhimin shiqi de zhanshi zhengzhi yu 'tazhe' yixiang" [Great Exhibitions and the Taiwan Indigenous Peoples: The Politics of Representation and the Images of "Others" in the Colonial Period], *Journal of Archaeology and Anthropology* 62 (2004): 8–9.

34. Yosaburō Takekoshi, *Japanese Rule in Formosa*, trans. George Braithwaite (London, New York, Bombay and Calcutta: Longmans, Green and Co. 1907), 2.

35. For example, when films depicting the military operations against the Atayal "raw aborigines" were screened in the PWA's headquarters in Tokyo in 1912, they were said to include films about the 1911 flood in Taiwan and religious rituals of native Taiwanese as well ("Tōban to aikoku fujinkai"). These films must have been produced by Takamatsu since he was responsible for the screening of these films in Tokyo. Takamatsu's company Dōjinsha was also hired by the Taiwan Education Society, an intermediary organization of the colonial government, to film the 1916 Taiwan Industrial Exhibition, celebrating the twentieth anniversary of Japanese colonial rule. The film was then brought back to Japan by Takamatsu to screen for the royal family and politicians, before touring across Japan.

36. Two news films related to the colonial government's conquering activities were shown in theaters in Tokyo respectively in August and October of 1910. M. Pathé's *Heroes of Taiwan Punitive Expedition* (*Taiwan tōbatsutai no yūshi*) was shown on August 7 in Tokyo's Engiza Theater. Yokota Company's *The Actual Conditions of Conquering Taiwan's Rebels* (*Taiwan dohi seitō no jikkyō*) was shown on October 5 in Tokyo's Seikaikan Theater. Though there's not much detail about these two films, considering the tight control of activities regarding military activities in Taiwan at the time, these films might either have been edited from the existing films or have been invited or assisted by the colonial government.

37. Yanaihara Tadao, *Teikoku shugika no Taiwan* [Taiwan under Japanese Imperialism] (Tokyo: Iwanami Shoten, 1929), 199, 208.

38. Yanaihara, *Teikoku shugika no Taiwan*, 206–207.

39. Michael Baskett, *The Attractive Empire: Transnational Film Culture in Imperial Japan* (Honolulu: University of Hawai'i Press, 2008), 14.

40. Yanaihara, *Teikoku shugika no Taiwan*, 161.

41. Due to the Bureau of Police Affairs' rather limited use of film in administrating "raw aborigines," this chapter will not deal with such usage by the BPA. It will concentrate on the use of film by the Ministry of Educational Affairs of Taiwan colonial government.

42. Some of the TES's budget came from government-related foundations, such as the emperor-endowed Taiwan Beauty Promotion Society Foundation (*onshi zaidan Taiwan saibi-kai*) and the emperor-endowed Taiwan Student Encouragement Society Foundation (*onshi zaidan Taiwan shougaku-kai*), which were both administrated by the Government-General of Taiwan. Some of the money was given specifically for producing or purchasing educational films.

43. *Taiwan gakuji yōran—Taishō yonnen* [Taiwan Educational Affairs Handbook, Taishō Year 4] (Taihoku: Ministry of Educational Affairs, Government-General of Taiwan, 1915), 75–76.

44. According to the Taiwan Education Society, even by early 1930s, almost forty years after colonization, there were still only slightly more than 1 million Taiwanese (around 22 percent of the population) who were able to understand the Japanese language; *Shōwa kyūnen nigatsu Taiwan shakai kyōiku gaiyō* [Summary of Taiwan Social Education—February of Showa Year 9] (Taihoku: Taiwan Education Society, 1934), 3.

45. According to the Taiwan Education Society, by the early 1930s only twenty thousand (less than 3 percent) of young Taiwanese were educated in schools, and another fifty thousand received their education from the Youth Corps or other youth organizations; *Shōwa kyūnen nigatsu Taiwan shakai kyōiku gaiyō*, 3–4.

46. *Shōwa kyūnen nigatsu Taiwan shakai kyōiku gaiyō*.

47. *Shōwa jūnen jūgatsu Taiwan shakai kyōiku gaiyō* [Summary of Taiwan Social Education—October of Showa Year 10] (Taihoku: Government-General of Taiwan, 1935), 98.

48. The statistical numbers were from page 31 of *The 16th Statistical Books of Government-General of Taiwan's Annual Report of Educational Affairs*, which was published annually between 1904 and 1940 by the department in charge of educational affairs for the Government-General of Taiwan.

49. "Kaihō: Dai jūyokai sōkai" [Bulletin: The Fourteenth General Assembly], *Taiwan Education* 186 (1917): 90.

50. Peter B. High, *The Imperial Screen: Japanese Film Culture in the Fifteen Years' War, 1931–1945* (Madison: University of Wisconsin Press, 2003), 10.

51. Nakamura Tsurayuki, "Taiwan ni okeru eiga kyōiku" [Film Education in Taiwan], *Taiwan Education* 360 (1932): 48.

52. Tsai Chin-tang, "Jiaoyu chiyu, yuzhenying yu xiushen jiaokeshu" [The Imperial

Rescript on Education, the Imperial Portrait, and Teaching Morals Education], *Journal of Taiwan History* 2 (2006): 142.

53. Kurita-sei, "Tsūshin ihō: Taihoku tsūshin" [Communication Bulletin: Taipei Correspondence], *Taiwan Education* 166 (1916): 52–53; "Ontairei katsudōshashin haikan" [Have the Honor of Seeing the Film about the Accession Ceremony], *Taiwan Education* 167 (1916): inside front cover.

54. Misawa, *Zhimindi xia de yinmu*, 128–132.

55. Tanaka said that it was the first time ever for an emperor-to-be to travel abroad. Therefore, the crown prince's activities were of great interest for the Japanese at the time. It was estimated that 7 million people, about one-tenth of the population of Japan, had seen the film; Tanaka Jun'ichirō, *Nihon kyōiku eiga hattatsushi* [History of the Development of Japanese Educational Film] (Tokyo: Kagyūsha, 1979), 43–45.

56. "Taiwan kyōikukai sōkai" [General Assembly of Taiwan Education Society], *Taiwan Education* 270 (1924): 87. According to *Taiwan Education*, the film was reviewed by the crown prince on September 30, 1923, almost five months after his departure from the port of Kiryū (Keelung).

57. Toda Seizō, "Katsudōshashin ni tsuite" [About Motion Pictures], *Taiwan Education* 261 (1924): 74.

58. For example, the annual memorial service to celebrate the promulgation of the Education Rescript on October 30, 1923 was canceled. Instead, donation boxes were installed throughout the island to collect money and material to be donated to the student victims of the Kantō Earthquake; "Tsūshin ihō: Taihoku tsūshin" [Communication Bulletin: Taipei Correspondence], *Taiwan Education* 258 (1923): 79.

59. In a rare report that did mention the screening of the film produced by the TES about the crown prince's Taiwan visit, Kaihase-sei said that the touring screening of the film (and some other films) in schools at each village in the Ryūtan area, sponsored by the education department of the Shinchiku Shū government, would begin in September 14, 1923; Kaihase-sei, "Tongxin: Longtan tongxin" [Correspondence: Ryūtan], *Taiwan Education* (Chinese-language edition) 256 (1923): 8.

60. "Taiwan kyōikukai sōkai," 88.

61. "Tsūshin ihō: Taihoku tsūshin," *Taiwan Education* 258, 80–81.

62. Tanaka, *Nihon kyōiku eiga hattatsushi*, 42.

63. Shimo-sei, "Tsūshin ihō: Taihoku tsūshin" [Communication Bulletin: Taipei Correspondence], *Taiwan Education* 168 (1916): 73.

64. Shimo-sei, "Tsūshin ihō: Taihoku tsūshin"; According to a report, the six-thousand-foot film is composed of five reels, three of which are about activities of Prince Kan'in-no-miya Kotohito Shin'nō and his wife, inside and outside the Exhibition; "Kyōshinkai fuirumu kyōikukai nite eisha" [Exhibition Film: Screening by TES], *Taiwan nichinichi shimpō* (Taihoku), April 29, 1907, 7.

65. Takamatsu Toyojirō migrated to Taiwan in 1908, and expanded his business from touring film exhibitions to building theaters for film screenings and stage performances

across the island. He established an entertainment empire in Taiwan through his company Dōjinsha. However, Takamatsu suffered great losses both in show business and for running for political office several times in mainland Japan. Takamatsu closed all his businesses in Taiwan in 1917 and returned to Tokyo to start an educational film production company there.

66. Due to the similarity in Kanji writing and pronunciation of Hagiya Kenzō's family and given names, various references to that name were reported from different information sources in the late 1910s and 1920s in Taiwan. After carefully checking the name used in the first report about him, printed in the *Taiwan Daily News* (*Taiwan nichinichi shimpō*), I found that it was the same as the name used more consistently in reports published in *Taiwan Education*, monthly journal of the Taiwan Education Society, in the 1920s, and confirmed that the correct name of the cameraman hired from M. Kashī in Tokyo by the TES is Hagiya Kenzō. His past employment record is similar to Ogino Kenzō, a cameraman with a similar name in Kanji. According to Tanaka Junichirō, Ogino Kenzō worked for M. Pathé (1906–1912), funded by Umeya Shokichi, who also funded M. Kashī (1915–1916). (Tanaka, *Nihon kyōiku eiga hattatsushi*, 25.) It is very likely that Tanaka Junichirō made a mistake in the mention of the cameraman's name in his book.

67. "Kyōikukai katsudōshashin kiteisō suieijō satsuei" [TES Motion Pictures: Photographing in Kote Shō Swimming Site], *Taiwan nichinichi shimpō* (Taihoku), August 16, 1917, 7.

68. An interesting article in a journal vividly described the filming of Taipei schoolchildren practicing swimming skills in the Kote Shō swimming site. The swimming site was actually part of the Shinten (Hsintien) River. Children were supposed to swim from the swimming site six miles downstream to Monga. Shooting of the activity had to be postponed for a week due to a typhoon. Water was still quite muddy and cold on the day of the shooting. Among the ninety-two students who participated in the long-distance swimming activity, only forty-nine managed to finish the full course; "Shōgakusen no enei: dakuryū wo sagaru sanriyo" [Primary School Students' Long-Distance Swimming: Down the Muddy Stream for More than Three Miles], *Taiwan nichinichi shimpō*, August 25, 1917, 7; Keifū-sei, "Jidō no suiren jikkyō wo mite" [Watching the Actual Scenes of Children Practicing Swimming Skills], *Undō to shumi* 2, no. 9 (1917): 37–39.

69. The need to expand its capability to make and screen more films prompted the TES to hire new technicians. In 1922, cameraman Miura Masao was brought from Japan to work with Hagiya. Between October and December 1922, the two of them produced four nonfiction films, *Hot Springs in Hokutō* (Beitou), *Hygiene Campaign in Taichū Shū* (Taizhong prefecture), *Motorized Military Maneuvering in Taichū Plain*, and *Fire Prevention Campaign in Takao Shū* (Gaoxiong prefecture).

70. It was claimed that such a large-scale exhibition on hygiene had never before been held in Taiwan; "Zappō: Taichū eisei tenrankai" [Miscellaneous Report: Taichū Hygiene Exhibition], *Taiwan Police Association Journal* 4 (1917): 72–73.

71. Caroline Hui-yu Ts'ai, *Taiwan in Japan's Empire Building: An Institutional Approach to Colonial Engineering* (London: Routledge, 2009), 110.

72. Ts'ai, *Taiwan in Japan's Empire Building*; Ming-cheng M. Lo, *Doctors within Borders: Profession, Ethnicity, and Modernity in Colonial Taiwan* (Berkeley: University of California Press, 2002), 40. Ts'ai pointed out that only 164 Japanese died in battle when the Japanese took over Taiwan; in contrast, 4,642 Japanese soldiers died from malaria or other contagious diseases, and an additional 26,094 contracted diseases.

73. Ts'ai, *Taiwan in Japan's Empire Building*, 110.

74. "Kaihō: Katsudōshashin satsuei" [Bulletin: Motion Pictures Photographing], *Taiwan Education* 185 (1917): 66.

75. Katō-sei, "Tsūshin ihō: Taihoku tsūshin" [Communication Bulletin: Taipei Correspondence], *Taiwan Education* 209 (1919): 50.

76. *Taiwan gakuji yōran—Taishō yoūnen* [Taiwan Educational Affairs Handbook, Taishō Year 10 (Taihoku: Ministry of Educational Affairs, Government-General of Taiwan, 1921): 35.

77. Tsurumi, *Japanese Colonial Education*, 93.

78. Ts'ai, *Taiwan in Japan's Empire Building*, 149–150.

79. Tsurumi, *Japanese Colonial Education*, 94–100.

80. Nakamura, "Taiwan ni okeru eiga kyōiku," 48.

81. Two of each from Taihoku (Taipei), Shinchiku (Hsinchu/Xinzhu), Taichū (Taichung/Taizhong), and Taitō (Taidong); seven from Tainan; nine from Takao (Kaohsiung/Gaoxiong); and one each from Hualian and the police bureau; Katō-sei, "Tsūshin ihō: Taihoku tsūshin" [Communication Bulletin: Taipei Correspondence], *Taiwan Education* 241 (1922): 69.

82. "Shinchiku Shū shusai katsudōshashin eishajutsu kōshūkai" [Training Sessions of Motion Picture Projection Techniques Conducted by Shinchiku Shū], *Taiwan Education* 260 (1924): 136.

83. "Eisha gijutsu kōshūkai" [Projection Techniques Training Sessions], *Monthly Report of Taiwan Taxation* 245 (1930): 46.

84. Tanaka, *Nihon kyōiku eiga hattatsushi*, 47.

85. For example, to celebrate Education Day, each year the TES would hold film screenings in the Taipei area. On October 30, 1922, however, the evening screenings in Taipei Park and Monga were funded by the government of Taihoku (Taipei) City, while in Daitōtei they were supported by Taihoku Shū; Katō-sei, "Tsūshin ihō: Taihoku tsūshin" [Communication Bulletin: Taipei Correspondence], *Taiwan Education* 246 (1922): 66.

86. The TES held 70 screenings that year, while local governments' projection units held 561 screenings in total. Of these, Tainan Shū was responsible for 171, and Shinchiku Shū, 102 screenings; "Taiwan kyōikukai dai nijū kai sōkai" [The Twentieth General Assembly], *Taiwan Education* 300 (1927): 150.

87. "Ippan kyōka" [General Education], *Taiwan Education* 351 (1931): 137.

88. *Shōwa kyūnen nigatsu Taiwan shakai kyōiku gaiyō*, 71.

89. Toda, "Katsudōshashin ni tsuite," 74.

90. "Taiwan kyōikukai dai nijū kai sōkai," 151–152.

91. A full list of these films can be found in Toda, "Katsudōshashin ni tsuite," 74–77.

92. Films such as *Funeral of Former Governor-General Akashi, The Landing of a Navy Airplane in Kiryū, The Activities of the Army's Heat-Resisting Automobile Troops in Takao, Scenes of People Celebrating the Tenth Anniversary of the Day for Commemorating the Beginning of the Japanese Rule, Scenes of HRH Prince Kuni-no-miya's Visit, Scenes of HRH Prince Kitashirakawa-no-miya's Visit, Governor-General Uchida's Landing on Taiwan, The Advanced Flying Skill of the Police Air Force, The Submarine in Kiryū Port, Inspecting the Military Parade in Front of the Office of the Governor-General on January 8, 1924*, as well as films about the crown prince's activities (including, of course, his visit to Taiwan) and Taipei citizens celebrating the crown prince's marriage on January 26, 1924.

93. One film was about the ceremony celebrating the birthday of Lord Cheng Huang, one about the ceremony celebrating the birthday of the deity Mazu at the Chaotian Temple in Hokukō (Beigang), one about dragon-boat racing, and one recording indigenous dances.

94. The titles of these films are *Taiwan Education, Kiryū Seaside School Attached Primary School* (*Kiryū rinkai gakkō fushoku shōgakkō*), and *Aborigine Children's Education.*

95. Misawa, *Zhimindi xia de yinmu*, 141–142.

96. Katō-sei, "Tsūshin ihō: Taihoku tsūshin" [Communication Bulletin: Taipei Correspondence], *Taiwan Education* 215 (1920): 51.

97. Katō-sei, "Tsūshin ihō," 51–52.

98. "Xuanchuan Taiwan shiqing" [Publicize Situations of Taiwan], *Taiwan nichinichi shimpō* (Taihoku), May 4, 1920, 5.

99. The total attendance was added up by this author, based on the number of viewers at each screening, which was provided in reports about events taking place at each location in Kyushu and Tokyo. See "Taiwan kyōikukai shusai Taiwan jijō shōkai kōenkai nami katsudōshashinkai jōkyō hōkoku" [A Report on the Situation of TES-Sponsored Lectures and Film Screenings Introducing Current Situations in Taiwan], *Taiwan Education* 218 (1920): 51–53.

100. A special page was dedicated to reporting this great honor in *Taiwan Education* 217; "Honkai sendentai no katsudōshashin Tomiya denka kaku ōji denka no tairan wo tamaharu" [HRH Tomiya and Other Princes Did TES the Favor of Watching Films Screened by Our Propaganda Team], *Taiwan Education* 217 (1920): 46.

101. Misawa, *Zhimindi xia de yinmu*, 142.

102. Hisazumi Eiichi, "Taiwan jijō shōkai zakkan" [Miscellaneous Thoughts about the "Introducing Current Situations in Taiwan" Project], *Taiwan Education* 234 (1921): 33–37. According to *Taiwan Education*, 240, Toda Seizō, head of the motion pictures unit, made a trip to Tokyo in March 1922 to show films introducing the Taiwan situation. This trip was specifically to show the educational affairs situation at the Tokyo

Peace Expo. The motion pictures unit of the TES had been preparing material for the occasion since January. This activity was dissimilar and had no relationship with the previous two "Introducing Current Situations in Taiwan" projects. However, it further confirms the TES's role as "propagator of Taiwan images"; Matsui-sei, "Tsūshin ihō: Taihoku tsūshin" [Communication Bulletin: Taipei Correspondence], *Taiwan Education* 240 (1922): 84.

103. Several issues of *Taiwan Education* had reported about the content shot by the motion pictures unit led by Toda and Hagiya: logging on Alishan Mountain, whaling in Tsuneharu (Hengchun), the salt plains at Hotei Kuchibashi (Budaizui), workers producing camphor in Sankaioku (Sanxia), the Shimotansui (Xiadanshui) River Iron Bridge, Bingdong (Pingtung) Airport, sunrise and moonlit night at Sun Moon Lake, picking tea leaves in Dora (Tongluo), and producing tea in Kansai (Guanxi), etc.

104. Hisazumi, "Taiwan jijō shōkai zakkan," 33–36.

105. "Taiwan kyōikukai sōkai," 90.

106. For example, similar screening sessions took place in 1924, five times in Kyoto, twelve times in Tokyo, and twice in Kumamoto City. ("Taiwan kyōikukai dai nijū kai sōkai," 150.) In March 1925, governor-general of Taiwan Izawa Takio entertained members of the Noble Houses and the House of Representatives at the Imperial Hotel (Teikoku Hotel), showing them films to introduce conditions on the island of Taiwan; "Taishō jūyonnen Taiwan kyōikukai jūyō kiji" [Important Accounts of Taiwan Education Circle in Taishō Year 14], *Taiwan Education* 283 (1926): 95. The TES's head of the motion pictures unit, Toda, went to Osaka and Nagoya for two weeks in May 1926, also to exhibit films about the current situation on Taiwan; "Jinji issoku" [Personnel Notice], *Taiwan Education* 288 (1926): 65.

107. Yasuyama-sei, "Tsūshin ihō: Taihoku tsūshin" [Communication Bulletin: Taipei Correspondence], *Taiwan Education* 322 (1929): 133.

108. Nakamura, "Taiwan ni okeru eiga kyōiku," 51–53.

109. Nakamura, "Taiwan ni okeru eiga kyōiku," 49.

110. Titles included *Tokyo* (three reels), *Kyoto, Osaka, Yokohama, Kamakura, From Kiryū to Kobe, Nagoya, Meiji Jingū, Nikkō,* and *Nara*; "Zappō: honkai sakusei no kyōzai eiga nit suite" [Miscellaneous Report: About the Educational Films produced by the TES], *Taiwan Education* 357 (1932): 150–152.

111. Baskett, *The Attractive Empire,* 15–16.

112. Nakamura, "Taiwan ni okeru eiga kyōiku," 50.

113. Quoted from High, *The Imperial Screen,* 54.

114. Chou Wan-yao, *Taiwan lishi tushuo: Shiqian zhi yijiusiwu nian* [Illustrated History of Taiwan: From Pre-history to 1945] (Taipei: Linking Publishing, 1997), 154–159.

CHAPTER 5

"Guangzhou Film" and Guangzhou Urban Culture

An Overview

Hui Liu, Shi-Yan Chao, and Richard Xiaying Xu

Chinese film historians have generally agreed that film industries have thrived in many large cities in China with different development ecologies.[1] However, current research on the history of Chinese cinema has been too narrowly focused on Shanghai cinema alone. To expand the scope of Chinese film historiography we identified Guangzhou and its cinema history of the early Republican period as a point of departure. Our research found that there is a close connection between the development of Guangzhou city and the cinema history specific to the area of South China, including Guangzhou and Hong Kong.

In the following pages, we will first provide a brief history of the city of Guangzhou. It is the foundation for our subsequent proposal of the idea of "Guangzhou film" in the chapter's second section. By challenging the paradigm in Chinese film history that has been narrowly based on the film industry and urban culture of Shanghai, the idea of "Guangzhou film," as will become clear in the third and fourth sections, materializes through an examination of early Lingnan-based film culture that involved not only production and distribution, but also exhibition and consumption in an evolving urban milieu. Also crucial to this were the geopolitics and historical conditions particular to Guangzhou, as well as the intricate interaction between Guangzhou and Hong Kong. By stressing the significance of a Lingnan-based regional film culture, along with Guangzhou's relative dominance in the early Republican era, we argue for a rethinking of Chinese national cinema from the perspective of regional cinemas and their corresponding urban cultures.

THE CITY OF GUANGZHOU: A BRIEF HISTORY

Guangzhou and the Lingnan area (south of the Five Ridges in Southern China) had profound geopolitical significance in the modern reformation of China. This area was the most typical representative of a marine culture that took shape after 1757, when Guangzhou (then known as Canton) was the only treaty port until after the Opium War (1839–1842), when there were "five treaty ports" dotting five coastal cities of China. Overseas Chinese traveling abroad and foreign merchant ships that docked in Guangzhou brought it a few advantages: it was the first city to be exposed to Western cultures, and it enjoyed more openness than inland cities; it also had the largest number of professionals dealing with foreign affairs. Moreover, overseas students and overseas Chinese brought with them Western education, technology, and media.

It was due to this that Guangzhou played a pivotal role in modern reforms in China. On the map of Chinese geopolitics, Guangdong Province sits in the south of China, and was the first to be assaulted by Western battleships. The cession of Hong Kong in 1841 and Bao'an County in 1898 were two indicators. Within this context, Guangdong also became the birthplace of representative Cantonese talents who had a spirit of anti-imperialism and self-improvement, such as Kang Youwei, Liang Qichao, and Sun Yat-sen. The natural barrier of the five ridges led to an attenuated sense of belonging to inland China in terms of both politics and cultures. While there had been inclinations of autonomy toward the end of the Qing dynasty,[2] a great passion for revolution was manifested among Cantonese talents and capital. From late Qing to the beginning of the Republic of China, Guangzhou displayed a new time and space and showed an eagerness to construct the city according to Western style.

The thirteen sectors of trading along the Pearl River had long broken the scope of traditional city walls and moved the city center of Guangzhou downstream to the north band of the Pearl River. With its proximity to the colonial city of Hong Kong, a place of mainly Cantonese-speaking people, Guangzhou developed a distinct social structure that gravitated toward commerce rather than industry. As foreign trade became the economic pillar of the city, a unique environment was shaped. Financial speculation brought back by overseas Chinese businessmen, frequent smuggling along the coastal areas, and conflicts occasioned by foreign investments and local reactions further helped define the city of Guangzhou.

From 1917 to 1927, Sun Yat-sen and the Nationalist Party (Kuomintang or KMT) established political sovereignty in Guangzhou three times. This period can be called the glorious "Ten Years of Guangzhou,"[3] during which Guangzhou took the lead in city construction in China. For example, Guangzhou learned from European and American models to build the first Chinese modern city with a new municipal system. Sun Yat-sen's son, Sun Fo, then mayor of Guangzhou, launched large-scale city construction activities, including building roads, maintaining riverbanks, improving transportation, building public facilities and commercial residential buildings, and so on. In October 1921, the first public park opened in the city. This park provided recreational spaces to the public; it showcased the development of modern Guangzhou city.[4] Long Bund Road, which was built during 1901–1914, became the new thoroughfare, crossing the east and west of Guangzhou, and it also became the most prosperous business/entertainment district, populated with shops, cinemas, and brothels.[5] On June 21, 1912, China's first department store, Guangzhou Sincere, opened on Long Bund Road. Another major department store, the Sun, and its affiliated Asia Hotel opened on January 4, 1919. The twelve-story building that housed playgrounds, hair salons, and bathhouses was unprecedented in China. These department stores on Long Bund Road set the benchmark for Shanghai's city development. Along with the prosperity of the Long Bund Road district also came the peculiar design of arcade or veranda. A hybridity of Chinese and Western architectural styles, the main objective of this particular design was to facilitate shopping regardless of the weather.[6]

In the 1920s, the traditional Chinese attire was gradually replaced by Western clothing. Imported perfumes, body lotions, leather shoes, foreign houses, and cars were leading the lifestyle of the residents.[7] An article in 1935 titled "Living Conditions in Guangzhou" stated, "Guangdong Province was the first to establish commercial relations with foreigners, and it was also the most prosperous in this. The land of Guangdong is rich, and the living conditions are the best among all provinces. The capital of Guangdong is akin to European and American cities, leaving Shanghai far behind."[8]

Along with this prosperity of Guangzhou city came a robust film culture.

In Guangzhou, there were numerous cinemas dotting the Pearl River banks, the Huiai Road central to the old city, and the then-official Yonghan Road. There were over thirty cinemas in Guangzhou, second only to Shanghai. The cultural atmosphere of film was even more pronounced. The profound influence of film culture on fashion was exemplified by local celebrity Huang Xiulan. The bearer of the title "Miss Xiguan," Huang was representative of Guangzhou fashion. Xiguan is a traditional neighborhood west of the city center known for its Lingnan cultural heritage. Fond of foreign films, Huang would frequently go to movies starring Shirley Temple and would replicate the clothing style of her characters with embroidery. She even changed her named to Xiulan, homophone of the Chinese translation of "Shirley."[9]

Moreover, it may be that Guangzhou residents differed from Shanghai urbanites in taste when it comes to film appreciation. Guangzhou and Hong Kong, so to speak, constituted a unique Cantonese film culture, retaining a particular kind of cinematic experience and urban culture. However, in cinema studies, or even urban cultural studies, few have been done with a clear focus on "Guangzhou" per se. The city of Guangzhou, despite its vital importance and prosperity in the early Republican era, has been largely ignored.

Compared with the limited studies on Guangzhou city, study of Guangzhou film is virtually nonexistent. The film industry was part of the urban history of Guangzhou. However, the study of the history of Guangzhou has been limited to trade and urban development. As a detailed survey in one doctoral thesis in 2005 notes, there are virtually no studies on Guangzhou's consumer culture.[10] While some research showed that Hong Kong began film production in the 1920s with topics exploited from local life, why, then, did Guangzhou not take full advantage of its geographical location and regional culture to become a full-blown cinema city? Somewhat ironically, while Hong Kong is generally regarded as the center of current Cantonese popular culture, it was in effect behind Guangzhou in the 1920s. In respect to the scale of film industry, research released by the U.S. Department of Commerce in 1930 also showed that Guangzhou was the second busiest regional film market in China, second only to Shanghai in terms of both the output of production and the total capacity of the movie theaters (detailed below).

More to the point, since the 1980s, when China opened to the world, Hong Kong has significantly reshaped the identity of Lingnan culture with its Cantonese films and songs. However, the important contribution of Guangzhou to the history of the Republican period and its interaction with Hong Kong has been ignored. Indeed, our proposal of the idea of "Guangzhou film" calls attention to this forgotten history and proffer an embedded account of the Lingnan-based urban film culture during this key era. From the overweening influence of Shanghai then, to the gravitational pull of Hong Kong now, it is advisable to restore Guangzhou's initial clout and natural habitat to the region's cinema and popular culture.

"GUANGZHOU FILM": CINEMA AND URBAN STUDIES BEYOND SHANGHAI

"China's early film production industry developed in parallel lines: one in Shanghai, the other in Guangzhou,"[11] remarked Guan Wenqing (Kwan Manching, Moon Kwan, 1894–1995), a veteran filmmaker who participated in both the Guangdong and the Hong Kong film industries.[12] In the 1910s, few films were made in China. The national film industry essentially took off in the 1920s, with the world recovering from World War I, concomitant with the United States streamlining film production process and formulas.[13] It was documented in the *Yearbook of the Chinese Film Industry 1927* that "film companies have mushroomed since the tenth year of the Republican period (1921), which was truly sensational."[14] By 1925, there were already some 175 film companies in Shanghai, Beijing, Tianjin, Zhenjiang, Wuxi, Hangzhou, Chengdu, Hankou, Xiamen, Shantou, Guangzhou, and Hong Kong altogether. Among them were 141 in Shanghai, followed by Guangzhou with 8, and Hong Kong with 7.[15] In terms of the number of cinemas, before October 1930, there were seventeen cinemas in Guangzhou with 14,300 seats, ranking second in China next to Shanghai, which had fifty-seven movie theaters. Following Guangzhou, Hankou had fifteen, Hong Kong had thirteen, and Xiamen had twelve.[16]

Even though Guangzhou ranked second when judging by number, the two developing lines of Shanghai and Guangzhou mentioned by Guan Wenqing appeared quite unbalanced. Guan's remarks on Guangzhou were nonetheless weighted by the largest region of cinema audiences: the Nanyang Chinese communities in Southeast Asia. Two factors merit attention here. First, the 30 million overseas Chinese consisted mainly of Cantonese, who were the major contributors to the box office of the Chinese film industry in general. And before the advent of sound film, there was no division between Cantonese and Mandarin films. Second, the cinemas in many big coastal cities were then run by foreign businessmen, having screening contracts with American film companies. Domestic films as a result rarely got the chance to be screened in cinemas. "The biggest market (for domestic films), excluding domestic venues, resided primarily in the islands in Southeast Asia, and secondarily in Vietnam," wrote one journalist for *The Public Comment* (*Gongpingbao*).[17] Chinese audiences in the region retained a strong feeling of nostalgia. They cared not so much about the films' quality as about the traditional folklores and fantasies associated with their motherland. Therefore, many film companies in Guangzhou and in Shanghai as well tailored films for the diaspora audience. The same journalist commented:

> Many film companies in Shanghai thought of alternative strategies to avoid direct competition with foreign companies. They drew upon classic novels of gods and spirits, such as *Journey to the West* and *Investiture of the Gods* [*Feng shen bang*] as the sources of film scripts.[18]

Distributors from Southeast Asia also traveled to Shanghai to select, prepay for, and thereby help finance the films they were interested in, well before their completion; they hence established business relationships with production companies (such as the Tianyi Company, one of the top three film companies in Shanghai at that time, forerunner of Shaw Brothers). With the arrival of sound, however, Guangzhou became the privileged center for Cantonese film production. This tremendous audience base also helped explain why Hong Kong became another center of Cantonese films along with the arrival of sound.

With the opening of the Shanghai port in 1843, which was closer to the geopolitical center of China, it quickly replaced Guangzhou as China's foreign trade center, and later became the center of modern and contemporary culture. After the advent of sound film in China in the 1930s, Shanghai cinema, due to its proximity to the political center of Nanjing, produced talkies in Mandarin Chinese and perpetuated the legitimacy of Mandarin as the *lingua franca* for Chinese cinema, with stars like Ruan Lingyu finding themselves marginalized due to their insufficient Mandarin. In contrast, Hong Kong and Guangzhou were trying to develop Cantonese-language films with local talents during the same period. Compared with Shanghai cinema as the representative of Chinese cinema, Cantonese-language films embodied intimate connections to the region in which they were produced. The Cantonese-speaking populations in Guangdong and Guangxi Provinces, together with the 30 million overseas Chinese (over 70 percent of whom were Cantonese-speaking), comprised the major audiences of Cantonese films.

Early cinema cities had to be port cities in order to ensure the importation of film stocks and equipment as well as the distribution of films. Aside from Shanghai, the seven port cities, including Harbin, Dalian, Hankou, Tianjin, Hong Kong, and Guangzhou, accounted for 62 percent of the total cinemas in the entire country and 70 percent of the total seats.[19] Among them, Guangzhou and Hong Kong were the most likely candidates for developing a different film industry vis-à-vis Shanghai. However, much like the discrepant agendas "autonomous governance of united provinces," proposed by Chen Jiongming,[20] and the "great unity," proposed by Sun Yat-sen, the Nanjing government in 1936 went so far as to ban all dialect films in order to promote Mandarin films and enhance the monopoly of Shanghai cinema. This political prohibition ignored the historical fact that Guangzhou had been a cinema city, and it—as will be addressed below—would help reconfigure the intricate dynamic between Guangzhou and Hong Kong.

THE RISE OF "GUANGZHOU FILM" AND ITS EXTERNAL CONSTRAINTS

The earliest film-related activities in China took place in colonial regions or concessions in port cities where foreigners clustered. American Far East shooting teams had arrived in Hong Kong to shoot scenic films in 1898, only three years after the invention of film.[21] As for screening activities, the target audiences consisted initially of foreigners and eventually of Chinese. For Chinese audiences in Guangzhou in particular, early screenings mostly took place in teahouses, or during breaks in Cantonese operas. As one local observer stated, "During the reign of Emperors Guangxu and Xuantong [the first decade of the twentieth century], films arrived in Southern China, first at the 'Pichong Academy' overseen by the Shishi Academy Church located in Daxin Street of Guangzhou. Films were screened as sideline entertainment when classes were over. . . . Not long after that, a new cinema named Jinghuatai opened at Hui'ai Ba Yue. This, as the first cinema in the region, would be later regarded as the ancestor of movie theaters in Southern China."[22] When films were new to Guangzhou, the screening conditions were quite simple: they were mainly arranged in teahouses, academies, or theaters as a sideline business. Between 1911 and 1920, simple screening venues appeared in Minzhi, Tonglingtai, and Xuanyuan Bridge; sideline film projecting businesses appeared in the Yuzhang Academy, Yijing Hotel, Jiutian Dongjia, East Garden, and the rooftop of the Sincere department store.[23]

These screening activities gradually familiarized the Guangzhou residents with films, and a film cultural atmosphere eventually developed.

The city of Guangzhou was undergoing rapid transformation in the early 1920s, and films were one of the most salient factors that represented the modernization (Westernization) of Guangzhou. *The Guangzhou Republican Daily* (*Guangzhou minguo ribao*) launched in June 1923 was the first party newspaper of the KMT. Shortly after its launch, an article titled "Talking about Films" was published on September 25, 1923, which announced the setting up of a special column on films:

> The film industry is booming in China. Guangzhou alone has eight to nine cinemas, and there are film production companies in Hong Kong. Previously movie fans concentrated on one or two actors/actresses, as they appear in feature-length films such as *Huanglian* and *Mo Liqiong*. Most of the film stars in this industry were barely known by our audiences. Nowadays . . . actors and actresses gain more attention. If a film celebrity stars in a new movie, audiences rush to warmly embrace it. This provides evidence for the tremendous pace at which the film industry is developing. To introduce Western civilization and to boost art and education, we specially set up a column for news and reviews on films. We will earnestly introduce valuable films around the world, and spare no efforts in criticizing those we consider harmful to society. We will also release the latest news from film circles, in the hope of stimulating public interest. Essays or opinions from our valued readers would be profusely appreciated.[24]

In terms of the relationship between a city and film, foreign films, especially Hollywood movies, played a leading role in the formation of urban film culture. The closer local showings were to the initial release dates, the more non-Chinese audiences there were. However, during the 1920s, as influenced by Western culture, Chinese people started to display a stronger penchant for movies. In cities where foreigners clustered, Chinese accounted for 30 percent to 70 percent of audiences, depending on the films' appeal. In the inland city of Beijing, Chinese viewers totaled up to 90 percent of audiecnes.[25] Many early cinemas were bought and set up by foreign entrepreneurs and overseas Chinese who had distribution contracts with major Hollywood companies. In light of this, the formation of national film industry served the purpose of countering foreign exploitation and monopoly.

The turning point came in 1925, when Chinese filmmakers became more actively involved at the level of film production. This had everything to do with the market of overseas Chinese in Southeast Asia. As famous early film producer Zhou Jianyun summarized,

> In 1925, there were as many as forty to fifty film production companies in Shanghai, and there were one or two new ones being set up each month. At that time there was a strong demand among the film traders from Southeast Asia for Chinese films: whenever a new film got released, it would be sold at a good price.[26]

In a report on the film markets of Chinese cities conducted in 1930 by J. E. Jacobs, the U.S. Department of Commerce ambassador for Shanghai, the author identified the year 1925 as a turning point for Chinese film production: "From 1921–23, there were only 6 films. But there were 57 in 1926, and the number was no less than that in 1927. The number for 1928 and 1929 was no more than 50."[27] The year 1925 was of special significance for the film industry of Guangzhou: it was the year when the Canton–Hong Kong strike broke out, which prompted the return of many local residents to Guangzhou. The exodus brought an unexpected influx of creative talents and financial capital to Guangzhou. Prior to the strike, there were seventeen film production companies in Hong Kong, including Dahan, Liangyi, Sishi, and Guangya. These film companies had produced a dozen short films, but all of them had to close down in the wake of the strike. Guangzhou seized this opportunity to build up its own film industry. Before the Hong Kong film industry recovered in 1928, Guangzhou took advantage of this golden opportunity to fully utilize its locale and human capital.

The first film production company in Guangzhou is connected to the set located at a Xiguan mansion owned by China Sun (see figure 5.1). It was set up for the film *Love Is Dangerous* (*Rouge, Yanzhi, dir. Li Beihai,* 1925). In 1925, Liang Shaopo from Hong Kong created the Diamond Film Company (Zuanshi) in Guangzhou. He constructed a tent for shooting opposite Rouji Hospital (the third affiliated hospital of Guangzhou Medical College today). *Tidal Wave of Love* (*Aihe chao,* dir. Liang Shaopo, 1926) and *A Small Circle* (*Xiao xunhuan,* dir. Liang Shaopo, 1926) were shot here in 1925–1926. Later Liao Huashen, an overseas Chinese from America, rented the space behind the temple of the city god, and established the Supreme Motion Picture Company (Tian'nan), which produced three films: *The Law Breaker*

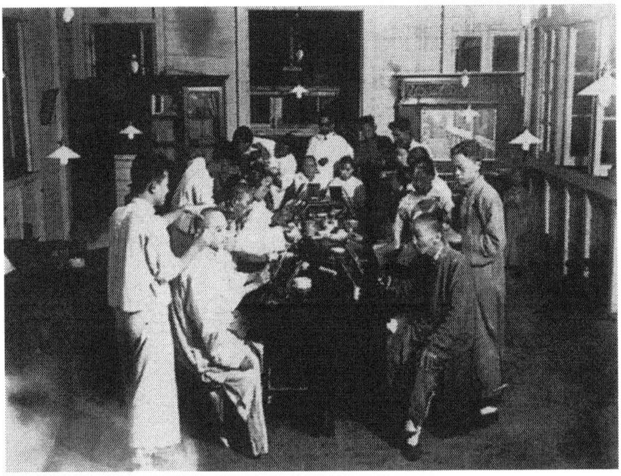

Figure 5.1. Shooting *Love Is Dangerous* (Rouge) in Guangzhou, 1924, with actors putting on makeup

(*Mingjiao zuiren*, dir. Liao Huashen, 1926) and *An Orphan's Escape* (*Gu'er tuoxian ji*, dir. Liao Huashen, 1927). From 1925 to 1927, seven film companies were set up, among them Guangya, Baiyue, and Guangzhou Nanyue. During these three years, they produced eight films (see table 5.1), most of which bore local Guangzhou thematic resonances.

Were these films embraced by the local audiences and markets? To begin with, the cinemas were not agreeable to showing local Cantonese films. Lu Gen (Lo Kan, Lo Gun, 1888–1936), the "King of Cinemas" in Hong Kong and Guangzhou, was not only unsupportive, but actively tried to squeeze them out (detailed below). The cinema owners became cautious, afraid that once they screened Cantonese films, they would be blacklisted by Lu Gen's Mingda Company.[28] Second, to a culture deeply reliant on verbal expressions, Cantonese traits were hard to capture so as to cater to the local audience before the advent of sound film. The films did not feature local characteristics beyond the thematic. *Love Is Dangerous*, *Army Dream* (*Congjun meng*, dir. Chen Junchao, 1926), and *Tidal Wave of Love* reached audiences before June 1926, and their receptions were mixed, to say the least. One movie fan thought that the acting in these three films tended to be either underperformed or overperformed.[29] A film critic also lamented, "It is not that Guangdong does not have enough talent in the film industry. Nor is it that the production companies lack adequate financial capital. There are actually quite a few decent scriptwriters around." Why, then, were these three films "released to such criticism that potential moviegoers might have been discouraged"?[30] In any case, the subsequent release of *The Law Breaker* was applauded by movie fans. Sheng Hua and Huang Yuqi considered the film to have an equal footing with foreign films: the directing was comparable to that of foreign masters, the acting was to the point, and the plot was delicately complex.[31] Another movie writer with the penname of "Dragon Gate Swordsman" commented that he had seen quite a few local productions that turned out to be rather unpleasant experiences, but *The Law Breaker*

Table 5.1. A List of Guangzhou Films, 1925–1927

Title	Production company	Main subject	Premiere date and venue
Love Is Dangerous (*Rouge*) (1925)	Hong Kong Minxin Company, Guangzhou Production Team	Based on the short story "Rouge" in Chinese literary classic *Strange Stories from a Chinese Studio*	February 23, 1925; Minxin World Theatre, Hong Kong
Tidal Wave of Love (1926)	Diamond Film Company	Based on the famous spoken drama produced by the Hong Kong Chung Sing Charity Society	February 24, 1926; Nanguan Theater, Guangzhou
Army Dream (1926)	Guangya Film Company	Depicts the calamities for common people caused by conflicting warlords	May 2, 1926; Hong Kong
A Small Circle (1926)	Diamond Film Company	Depicts the unpredictable human mind and the miseries of workers under economic and imperialist exploitation	N.a.
The Law Breaker (1926)	Supreme Motion Picture Company	Tells the story of a couple fighting against the feudal system to be with each other	September 9, 1926; Mingzhu Theater, Guangzhou
Fake Mask (1927)	Baiyue Film Company	Based on Cantonese folk tale *Killing a Dog to Advise Her Husband*	November 16, 1927; Guomin Theater, Guangzhou
An Orphan's Escape (1927)	Supreme Motion Picture Company	Tells the story of a child breaking free from abduction	November 24, 1927; Xin Guomin Theater, Guangzhou
Multiply and Make a Fortune (1928)	Guangzhou Nanyue Film Company	A satiric comedy with deep social morals	February 8, 1928; Yonghan Theater and Zhongyang Theater

worked at a higher level.[32] Recalling *An Orphan's Escape,* Liu Jintao—a cinematographer at Baiyue Film Company—said that it was ardently embraced by the audiences.[33] Still, the box office of these films could never compete with soaring American and European productions. Nor were they matches for their Shanghai counterparts, especially given that the latter had in recent years gained a handsome industrial scale.

Almost all the film production companies chose to locate around Xiguan district, the well-known business center of Guangzhou in modern times. Over thirty film companies were established in the 1920s and 1930s, spreading around the old city of Guangzhou and Xiguan (see figure 5.2 for the major companies). This indicated that films, as a new form of production, needed support from established businesses, and that they simultaneously benefited the latter with a new form of culture, which was facilitated by the establishment of cinemas in the same neighborhood (see figure 5.3, detailed below). More often than not, new film companies in Guangzhou would simply rent traditional mansions or built tent factories, as opposed to building special shooting sets, as in Shanghai. This exposed the deficiency of the production capacity of the Guangzhou film industry. As a matter of fact, once the Hong Kong film industry recovered after 1928, several companies with their roots in Hong Kong returned home. During 1929–1931, the old companies in Guangzhou slowly closed down, while no new companies opened.

It was not until the 1930s that the Cantonese film market regained its geographic autonomy: twenty to thirty film companies mushroomed into being during 1932–33, as "prosperity made a rare case in the recent decade."[34] In terms of production quantity, Guangzhou also exceeded Hong Kong during this revival. Guangzhou as the center of Cantonese culture appeared to have a particular attraction to local films, with the Cantonese language as its core.

Additionally, unlike other port cities where the cinemas were controlled by foreigners, most of the cinemas in Guangzhou were owned by Chinese nationals. As a native Cantonese, Lu Gen, for instance, reinvented himself from a comprador providing service to foreign banks for their trades with China,[35] into the first Chinese national dedicating to the cinema business in Southern China. His empire of cinemas perfectly demonstrates the trend: that the majority of Hong Kong businessmen were from Guangdong. As Zhang Xiaohui points out, "Many early Cantonese businessmen simultaneously possessed the identities of Hong Kong businessmen or overseas Chinese businessmen."[36] After Lu Gen set up his film distribution outlet

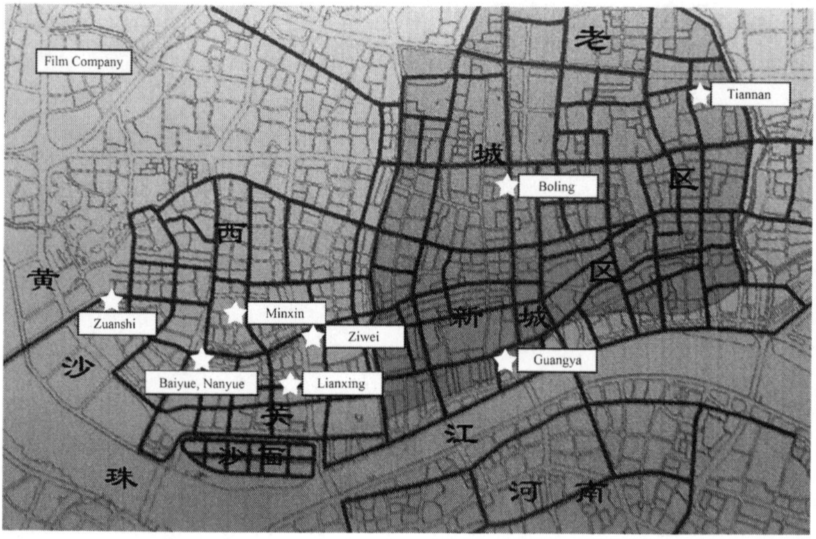

Figure 5.2. The locations of major production companies in 1920s–30s Guangzhou

Mingda and the Coronet Theatre in Hong Kong with around two hundred seats,[37] he built the Mingzhu Theater at the Long Bund with around six to seven hundred seats. That was the first formal movie house in Guangzhou, pivotal to the growth of local film culture.

It is important to note that the Chinese ownership of Guangzhou theaters had much to do with the city's abundant overseas remittances. The decade of 1917 to 1927 saw a peak in this financial flow. According to Zhang Xiaohui, "Overseas remittances were mainly used in speculation businesses, such as real estate in Guangzhou, land transactions, and usury."[38] Guangzhou had a thriving cinema industry, ranking second nationally, and almost all of its cinemas were built by overseas Chinese who returned from aboard.[39] As a result, while there were only thirteen venues involving screening activities in Guangzhou before 1920,[40] new cinemas started to appear thereafter: one in 1920, one in 1922, two in 1923, two in 1924, four in 1925, three in 1926, eight in 1927, three in 1928, two in 1929, four in 1930, one in 1931, three in 1933, one in 1934, and one in 1937. By the time the war broke out in 1937, thirty-nine cinemas had been built in Guangzhou. The biggest five in the early days were Jinsheng, Mingzhu, Guomin, Zhonghua, and Yonghan, which had luxurious "wide seats and grand cinema halls."[41] In the

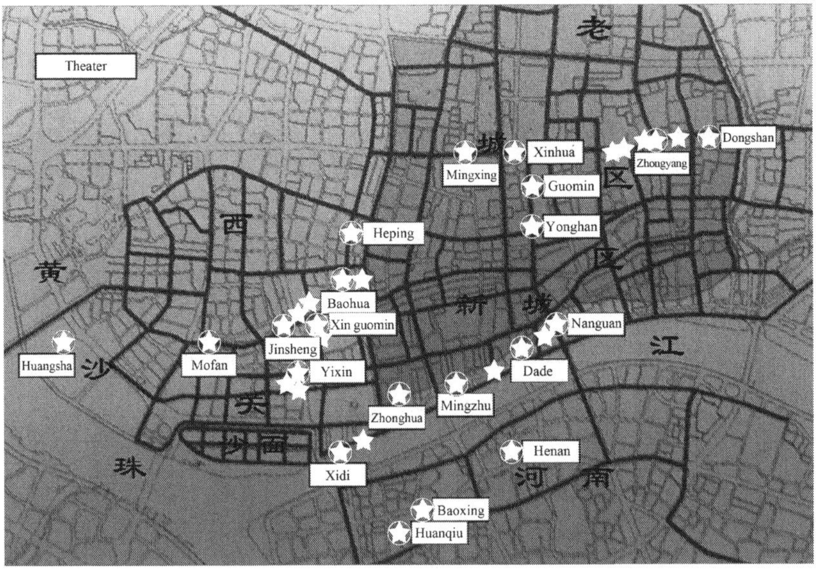

Figure 5.3. The locations of major movie theaters in 1920s–30s Guangzhou

1930s these cinemas were upgraded with sound film projection systems, and luxurious decorations and sofas were added to the interiors. The first-class cinemas with first-run releases included Jinsheng, Mingzhu, Xin Guomin, Zhonghua, and Yonghan: these five cinemas had exclusive screening rights. Jinsheng, Mingzhu, and Yonghan only screened Hollywood films, while Xin Guomin and Zhonghua only screened Chinese films, mainly Shanghai films.[42] These cinemas were located at the business centers in Xiguan and Long Bund. Together with the architectures of the East Asia Hotel and Asia Hotel, they created a prosperous urban milieu in the early Republican period (see figure 5.3 for the major theaters).

There were conspicuous communications and interactions between the early film industries of Guangzhou and Hong Kong. The two cities also manifested a supplementary relation, thanks to different political environments. Though "the two cities were more or less the same, Guangzhou was a bit more prosperous."[43] But in general terms, Hong Kong triumphed over Guangzhou in political stability and financial capital. Accordingly, in 1932, Tianyi Company from Shanghai moved southward, and when the U.S. overseas Chinese Zhao Shushen (Chiu Shu-sun, Joseph Sunn, 1904–1990) and Guan Wenqing returned to China to found the Grandview (Daguan) Film

Company (originally founded in Los Angeles in 1933), they chose to relocate to Hong Kong instead of Guangzhou. These were the two biggest film production companies in Hong Kong in the 1930s, which helped expand the film industry of Hong Kong. These external political and economic factors restricted the further development of Guangzhou film industry. As of August 1935, a local newspaper reported that "the film production companies have all left Guangzhou for Hong Kong."[44] On top of this, the outbreak of the Sino-Japanese War had in fact strangled the development of Chinese national film production industry in general. There were no big film companies even in Shanghai after 1945. Hong Kong, with its peculiar colonial status, by contrast, became a very desirable place to continue the Chinese film industry. Compared with Guangzhou, the advantages of Hong Kong became even more pronounced.

THE DEMISE OF GUANGZHOU FILM

In analyzing the reasons for the failure of Cantonese cinema after the middle of the Republican period, Ming K. Chan pointed out that Guangdong people's personalities were too strong, and there were many internal conflicts. Furthermore, Guangdong had the tradition of giving much weight to trade but less to production. Guangdong is "located on the edge of the coastal borderline, which is vastly different from the central plains . . . [The Cantonese] are less ambitious in politics than in business."[45] Political naïveté could somehow be detected in Cantonese intellectual elites such as Wang Jingwei, Hu Hanmin, and Chen Jitang, who, as cofounders of the Nationalist Party, became gradually marginalized amid the power struggles with political newcomer Chiang Kai-shek. Looking at the national film industry from this perspective, it is notable that Cantonese people and capital constituted the strongest force in the early days. Even in 1926 in Shanghai, there were fifteen film companies, such as Great Wall (Changcheng), Big Asia (Daya), and Pacific (Taipingyang), which were founded by Cantonese, alongside fifty-three Cantonese actors (such as Yang Naimei, Zhang Zhiyun, and Wang Hanlun), and eleven Cantonese directors (like Zhang Huichong).[46] But the Cantonese presence waned in the following decade. In the 1930s, Lianhua Film Company, the biggest film company in Shanghai, aggregated capital from both Guangdong and Hong Kong to run a new cultural enterprise, though it ended in failure. Its entrepreneur, Luo Mingyou (Lo Ming-yau, 1900–1967) spent the rest of his life in missionary service in Hong Kong. Lu Gen, the aforementioned "King of Cinemas" in Guangdong and Hong Kong, was talked into the joint venture Grand Theatre in Shanghai, which directly resulted in his bankruptcy.

Lu Gen owned many luxurious cinemas in various cities, including Hong Kong, Guangzhou, Shanghai, Hankou, and Beijing, and monopolized the distribution of Hollywood films in Hong Kong and some parts of the Mainland. As Lu's business model centered on profitable Hollywood imports, it was not in his interest to see local Guangzhou films flourish. Accordingly, he would, through vicious tactics, cut off supplies to cinemas that screened locally made films. But when American film companies set up distribution offices in Shanghai and became Lu's direct competitors, Lu changed his business strategy by tapping into film production. He rented Mingyuan Studio, which belonged to Luo Mingyou, to establish Zhenye Company, and made a Cantonese film titled *The Fool Pays Respect* (*Dailao baishou*, dir. Hou Yao, 1933). Lu Gen, like many others, held a negative attitude toward regional films. He believed that the center of Chinese film was Shanghai, and had the ambition to capitalize on this with his financial puissance. By contrast, it was two non-Cantonese personalities—Shao Zuiweng (Runje Shaw, 1896–1975; owner of Tianyi) and Shao Shushen (founder of Grandview)—who believed in the value of this regional culture and market. In 1936 when the Nationalist government banned Cantonese-language films in the name of the unification of the Chinese film industry, Shao and Chiu, the bellwethers of the Cantonese film industry, initiated the Huanan Film Association to negotiate with the Nationalist government and earned a three-year grace period.[47]

In tandem with the global distribution of American film and the Mandarin language policy adopted by the Shanghai film establishment, the transition to sound cinema in the 1930s determined the regional character of Guangzhou and Hong Kong films. Produced in vernacular Cantonese, most of these films featured local and historical subjects, and their audiences consisted mainly of moviegoers in Guangdong, Guangxi, and Southeast Asia. However, there was also competition for human resources and capital between these two cities. In the 1919 *Industrial Plans*, Sun Yat-sen drew examples from the common prosperity of the harbor cities such as Victoria and Vancouver in Canada and Seattle and Tacoma in the United States to make the point that Hong Kong and Guangzhou could also enjoy common prosperity. But in fact, political relations between Guangdong and Hong Kong had always been quite fraught. For example, behind the curtain of the 1924 Canton Merchant Volunteers Incident and the 1925 Canton–Hong Kong strike, there were fierce conflicts between the British–Hong Kong government and the Guangzhou government underneath. Within the film industry, although communication between Guangzhou and Hong Kong and the sharing of talents, financial capital, and technology were firmly in place, there was inevitable competition all along. Eventually Hong Kong would replace Guangzhou as the central port city of Southern China, downgrading Guangzhou to a second-tier foreign trade city.

From the 1920s, when the film industry began to develop, to 1937, when the war broke out, it was hard to decide which of the two cities was winning the competition in the film industry: there was no significant difference in their respective film cultures and the scale of their industries. They both remained at low levels of production, and they both enjoyed a stable Cantonese film market. Hong Kong's competitive edge began to show after 1934. This was because Guangzhou had an inferior position in political stability and port trading conditions. The filming equipment and film negatives, for example, had to be imported via Hong Kong, with complicated procedures and taxes.[48] As veteran filmmaker Lu Dun recalled:

> The production institutions were weak in themselves: they had weak economic power, so much so that they did not even build shooting sets. Oftentimes they made films on the rooftop of the Sincere Company, or in the old Xiguan mansions. They had rather primitive equipment. And with the box-office success of the sound film *The Platinum Dragon*, directed by Xue Juexian [Sit Gok-sin, see Kenny Ng's chapter in this volume)] and *Romance of the Songsters*, produced by Grandview (and directed by Zhao Shushen), the Guangzhou film industry, totally lacking filming equipment for sound films, was outcompeted.[49]

A bigger issue lies in the fact that the national film industry developed in sync with the revolutionary history of modern China. The Guangzhou film industry lost the first opportunity with the establishment of the Nanjing government in 1927; it was incapable of catching up with the Shanghai film industry. The second opportunity for Guangzhou film to develop was missed when the war broke out in 1937, and the opportunity was passed to Hong Kong (the sudden fall of which came in 1941). Hong Kong was further empowered by the many filmmakers who fled Shanghai. In the article "Why Wasn't the Base of Cantonese Films Set in Guangzhou?" Lu Dun suggested that "Guangzhou was the most unsettled city, eventful with unsatisfactory living conditions . . . the local bureaucracy was corrupt, and daily life and social security were unstable. Many capitalists were much discouraged. Therefore, the base for Cantonese film production moved to Hong Kong, a place with a more secure environment."[50]

Hong Kong displayed a solid city identity in her films, with pronounced regional culture and language, while Guangzhou became a less visible entity. Despite the famous Pearl River Film Studio, Guangzhou had not been considered the cultural source of Cantonese films, or as a city that would become the center of the regional film industry. Hong Kong benefited from its status as a colony, which protected it from much political turbulence, and finally earned it the opportunity to develop Cantonese-language films into a remarkable cultural product that realized the convergence of technology and art. The flexible and pragmatic overseas Chinese investors would not hesitate to replace Guangzhou with Hong Kong to sustain their film investment. Hong Kong was 200 kilometers from Guangzhou and in the 1920s it took at least half a day to cross the Shenzhen River to arrive in Hong Kong (other than this traditional ferry route, the Guangzhou-Kowloon railway started operation in 1911, and a Guangzhou–Hong Kong airline link became available in 1930). For the film industry, with the change of times and the establishment of cultural trends, it was inevitable for human resources and financial capital to side with one of the two cities. Nevertheless, the opportunities and problems Guangzhou faced in the Republican period are still important topics in the study of Lingnan culture.

CONCLUSION

With the canon of Chinese national cinema firmly in place, we should value the diversity of regional cinemas, and attend to the different ways that people from various regions received movies. While advocating for the importance of other cinema cities besides Shanghai, we are fully aware that this stance may also run the risk of perpetuating Shanghai as the sole representative of Chinese cinema. A characteristic of China lies in its ethnic diversity and geographic expansiveness. If film is deemed a diversifiable cultural expression, it should reflect multiple layers of meanings. When we return to the study of history, however, we find Chinese film history has been portrayed as lacking diversities and complexities; it is unlike a film history of "China," but like a one-dimensional narrative. It even misses the lines of development that really matter: How did films arrive in China? How was Chinese audiences' perception of film shaped? On what ground was the cinematic conception of national film production established? What exactly was the structure of the film industry in the Republican period? None of these questions can be answered by simply referencing Shanghai cinema. Thus the significance of the current study lies not only in presenting new materials, but also in reframing existing film historiography.

Notes

1. Research for this chapter is supported by GRF, "Chinese Film History beyond Shanghai: 1900–1950," funded by the Research Grants Council of Hong Kong (grant number HKBU 245310). This chapter is revised and rewritten from an earlier Chinese article, "Tanjiu minguo shiqi diyu dianying he doushi wenhua de guanxi: cong Guangzhou baozhi chufa" [A Study of the Relationship Between Regional Film and Urban Culture in the Republican Era: Reports from Guangzhou Republican Daily], in *Zouchu Shanghai: Zaoqi dianying de linglei jingguan* [Beyond Shanghai: New Perspectives on Early Chinese Cinema], eds. Emilie Yueh-yu Yeh, Feng Xiaocai, and Liu Hui (Beijing: Beijing University Press, 2016), 69–88.

2. In 1900, the Hong Kong legislator He Qi proposed the "Gengzi Guangdong Independent Plan," which advocated for "saving the nation by cooperation" between Sun Yat-Sen and Li Hongzhang, governor of Guangdong and Guangxi, and proclaimed independence of Guangdong and Guangxi. However, this plan aborted when Li Hongzhang was appointed by the Qing government to a higher position.

3. Chen Mingqiu and Rao Meijiao, eds., *Lingnan jindai shi lun: Guangdong yu yuegang guanxi, 1900–1938* [Modern History of Lingnan: The Relationship between Guangdong and the Hong Kong–Guangdong region, 1900–1938] (Hong Kong: Commercial Press, 2010), 5.

4. Zhan Jinni, "Minguo Guangzhou Zhongyang gongyuan yu shimin shenghuo de gonggong xing" [Guangzhou Central Park and the Public Nature of Civilian Lives during the Period of the Republic of China], *Heilongjiang shizhi* 17 (2009): 117–118.

5. Yang Yingyu, "Jindai Guangzhou changti de xingzhu yu Guangzhou chengshi fazhan de guanxi" [The Relationship between the Construction of the Long Bund of Guangzhou and the Urban Development of Guangzhou in Modern History], *Guangdong shizhi* 4 (2002): 12–17.

6. Pan Anzhu, *Shangdu wangshi: Guangzhou chengshi lishi yanjiu shouji* [History of a

Commercial City: Manuscripts of the Historical Research on Guangzhou City] (Beijing: Chinese Architectural Industry Press, 2010), 157.

7. Zhang Xiaohui, *Minguo shiqi Guangdong de duiwai jingji guanxi* [The Foreign Economic Relations of Guangzhou during the Republican Era] (Beijing: Shehui kexue wenxian chubanshe, 2011), 294–296.

8. "Life Condition of Guangzhou," *Guangzhou minguo ribao*, July 20, 1935, 4.

9. Huang Boli, "Dushi wenhua de xiandaixing xiangxiang—yi xiguan xiaojie wei ge'an de kaocha" [An Imagination of Modernity through Urban Culture—a Case Study of Miss Xiguan], *Jiangxi shehui kexue* 4 (2010): 235–240.

10. Jiang Jianguo, "Wanqing Guangzhou chengshi xiaofei wenhua yanjiu" [A Study of Guangzhou Urban Consumption Culture in the late Qing Dynasty] (PhD diss., Jinan University, 2005), 25.

11. Guan Wenqing, *Zhongguo yintan waishi* [Unofficial History of the Chinese Screen Industry] (Hong Kong: Wide Angle Press, 1976), 127.

12. Guan Wenqing (1894–1995) was born in Chikan village of Kaiping County in Guangdong. He studied English at the University of California in 1911. He then became interested in film and involved in the Hollywood industry. He returned to China in 1920 and devoted himself to the construction the film industries in Hong Kong and Guangzhou. He participated in the scriptwriting, directing, and producing of more than fifty films. His book *Zhongguo yintan waishi* is extremely valuable for its account of the early development of the film industry in the Lingnan area.

13. Lewis Jacobs, *The Rise of the American Film* (New York: Harcourt, Brace & Co., 1939), 305–309.

14. See Cheng Shuren, ed., *Guoren suo jingying zhi yingpian gongsi* [Film Companies Run by the Chinese], in *Zhonghua yingye nianjian* [Yearbook of Chinese Film Industry] (Shanghai: Society for the Yearbook of Chinese Film Industry, 1927), 1.

15. This data is in many ways incomplete and inaccurate. In the report issued by the U.S. Department of Commerce, there were 164 film companies between 1921 and July 1930. Cheng Jihua believed that many companies were "one-off" companies, which didn't make any films after registration. In Cheng's words, "Most of them set up an office and hang a company logo in a symbolic manner, and they are gone before they produce any films." See Cheng Jihua, Li Shaobai, and Xing Zuwen, *Zhongguo dianying fazhan shi* [History of the Development of Chinese Cinema] (Beijing: Zhongguo dianying chubanshe, 1963), 54.

16. The U.S. Department of Commerce, *Motion Pictures in China* (Washington, DC: U.S. Government Printing Office, 1930).

17. "Guochan yingpian zai nanyang zhi jinkuang" [The Current Situation of Chinese Films in Nanyang], *Gongpingbao*, November 9, 1927, 2.

18. "Guochan yingpian zai nanyang zhi jinkuang," 2.

19. U.S. Department of Commerce, *Motion Pictures in China.*

20. Chen Jiongming was the military governor of Guangdong three times (1911–1912, 1913, and 1920–1923) and civil governor of Guangdong from 1920 to 1922. Chen once backed Sun Yat-sen's Constitutional Protection Movement, but he disagreed with Sun on the approaches to reform. Sun wanted to unite the country by force and initiate changes through a centralized government based on a one-party system. Chen advocated a multiparty federalism with Guangdong becoming the model province and a peaceful unification of China. This disagreement led to their breakup. From 1923 to 1925, Sun organized with the Nationalist military forces two eastward campaigns against Chen; Chen fled to Hong Kong, with his remaining forces being completely wiped out by 1925.

21. Kar Law and Frank Bren, *Xianggang dianying kua wenhua guan* [Hong Kong Cinema: A Cross-Cultural View], trans. Liu Hui (Beijing: Beijing University Press, 2012), 13.

22. Zhong Ru, "Huanan di yi jian dianyingyuan tao youshengpian shi shemo?" [Which Was the First Sound Film Shown in Southern China?], *Huanan Dianying* 5 (1944): 8. However, it was suggested in Guangzhou Film Company, *Guangzhou dianyingzhi* [Documents on Guangzhou Film] (Guangzhou: Guangzhou Film Company, 1993) that the first Guangzhou cinema was Tonglingtoi, which opened in 1908.

23. Zhang Fangwei, "Sanshi niandai Guangdong yueju gaikuang" [An Overview of Cantonese Opera of the 1930s], *Chinese opera website*, last modified January 14, 2014, http://www.yuejuopera.org.cn/yjjs2/yjgs/zjlwkzyd/20140114/26.html. See also the chapter of "Fangying" [Screening], in *Guangzhou dianyingzhi*, 27.

24. "Shuo yingxi" [On Photoplay], *Guangzhou minguo ribao*, September 25, 1923, 5.

25. U.S. Department of Commerce, *Motion Pictures in China*.

26. Zhou Jianyun, "Zhongguo yingpian zhi qiantu (1)" [The Future of Chinese Films (1)], in *Dianying yuebao (April 1928—September 1929)*, ed. Feng Pei-ling (Shanghai: Shanghai Academy of Social Sciences Press), 9–11.

27. U.S. Department of Commerce, *Motion Pictures in China*.

28. Liu Jintao, "Guangzhou zaoqi zhipian ye" [Early Film Production Industry in Guangzhou], *Guangzhou cultural history website*, last modified September 17, 2008, http://www.gzzxws.gov.cn/gzws/gzws/ml/28/200809/t20080917_9128_1.htm. Notably, Liu Jintao was a cinematographer at the Bak Yuet Film Company in the 1920s.

29. Langman-sheng, "Yi pie *Aihe chao*" [A Glance at *Tidal Waves of Love*], *Guangzhou minguo ribao*, February 26, 1926, 9.

30. Liang Jiwen, "Wo duiyu guochan yingpian zhi leguan" [My Optimistic View on Domestic Films], *Guangzhou Minguo ribao*, June 7, 1926, 4.

31. Sheng Hua and Huang Yuqi, "*Ming jiao zuiren* shipianji" [Preview of *The Law Breaker*], *Guangzhou minguo ribao*, September 9, 1926, 4.

32. Longmen Jianke, "*Ming jiao zuiren* zhi wo guan" [My View of *The Law Breaker*], *Guangzhou minguo ribao*, September 10, 1926, 4.

33. Lau, "Guangzhou zaoqi zhipian ye."

34. Qilang, "Kai pai nu chao zhi bo ling" [The Booming of Local Film Industry], *Yuet Wa Po*, September 20, 1933, 1.

35. Li Peide, "Guangdong maiban de wangluo yanshen he zhongzhi (1860–1960 niandai)" [The Extension and Termination of the Guangdong Comprador Network (1860–1960)], in *Lingnan jindai shi lun: Guangdong yu yuegang guanxi, 1900–1938* [Modern History of Lingnan: The Relationship between Guangdong and the Hong Kong-Guangdong Region, 1900–1938], ed. Chen Mingqiu and Rao Meijiao (Hong Kong: Commercial Press, 2010), 203–220.

36. Zhang, *Minguo shiqi Guangdong de duiwai jingji guanxi*, 261.

37. Mingming, "Xianggang yingyuan de canghai sangtian" [The Vicissitudes of Hong Kong Movie Theaters], *Youyou zazhi* 2 (1935): 13.

38. Zhang, *Minguo shiqi Guangdong de duiwai jingji guanxi*, 87.

39. Guangdong sheng defangzhi bianzhuan weiyuanhui, ed., *Guangzhou shi zhi* [Guangzhou Municipal History], vol. 18 (Guangzhou: Guangzhou chubanshe, 1996), 176–177.

40. Guangzhou Film Company, *Guangzhou dianyingzhi*.

41. Qingjuan, "Tantan yinghua xiyuan de weisheng" [Remarks on the Hygiene Conditions of Movie Theaters], *Guangzhou minguo ribao*, November 6, 1926, 4.

42. "Bu jingqi niantou: Guangzhou shi jinsui yulejie gaikuang" [The Rainy Days: An Overview of This Year's Guangzhou Entertainment Industry], *Youyou zazhi* 7 (1935): 2.

43. General Ye Jianying was Malaysian Chinese, and was in charge of the overseas Chinese affairs in Guangzhou. Zhou Haibin, "*Jiaguo guangying* kaiguo yuanxun houren koushu (11)" [Light and Shadow of Family and State: Oral Histories by the Heirs of the Founding Fathers of the Country (11)], *Beijing wanbao*, June 15, 2011, retrieved from http://blog.sina.com.cn/s/blog_55dde65f0102eej6.html?tj=1

44. "Xianggang dianying da xiezhen" [Snapshots of Hong Kong Cinema], *Yuet Wa Po*, August 14, 1935, 2.

45. Chen and Rao, *Lingnan jindai shi lun*, 5, 7.

46. "Shanghai dianying ye yu Guangdong ren" [Shanghai Film Industry and the Cantonese], *Guangzhou minguo ribao*, August 31, 1926, 4.

47. Zhou Chengren and Li Yizhuang, *Zaoqi Xianggang dianying shi, 1897–1945* [Early Hong Kong Film History, 1897–1945] (Hong Kong: Joint Publishing, 2005), 211–214. See also Stephanie Po-Yin Chung, *Xianggang yingshiye bainian* [One Hundred Years of Hong Kong Film and Television Industry], expanded ed. (Hong Kong: Joint Publishing, 2011), 92–93.

48. Zhou and Li, *Zouqi xianggang dianying shi, 1897–1945*, 137.

49. Lu Dun, "Yuepian jidi heyi bu she zai Guangzhou?" [Why Wasn't the Base of Cantonese Films Set in Guangzhou?], in *Fengzi shengya ban shiji* [The Life of a Mad Man over Half a Century] (Hong Kong: Xiangjiang chuban youxian gongsi, 1992), 55.

50. Lo, "Yuepian jidi heyi bu she zai Guangzhou?," 55–56.

CHAPTER 6

The Way of The Platinum Dragon

Xue Juexian and the Sound of Politics in 1930s Cantonese Cinema

Kenny K. K. Ng

PROLOGUE

In 1936, a Shanghai movie magazine carried a gossip column on Cantonese opera maestro Xue Juexian (Sit Gok-sin, 1904–1956), titled "Xue Juexian Remakes *The Platinum Dragon: Part Two*."[1] The subtitle of the article, however, issued an unfriendly warning to Xue: "It is hoped that he would better check the censorship order beforehand." Just one year before, another Shanghai journal reported that Xue had set up his own film company in Hong Kong to produce Cantonese sound films. Meanwhile, he was going to refuse to submit his new films to the Nanjing government censors for inspection.[2] The two pieces of entertainment news give us a glimpse of the cultural politics of popular Cantonese talkies in the mid-1930s, namely, the feud between the thriving Cantonese film industries and the Nationalist (Kuomintang) government in Nanjing in enforcing restrictions on Cantonese-speaking films. The 1930s was also a crucial moment for Chinese cinema in its transition from silent picture to sound film productions. In 1933, Shaw Zuiweng (Runje Shaw, 1896–1975) of Shanghai's Unique Film Company (Tianyi) collaborated with Xue to produce the first Cantonese sound film, *The Platinum Dragon* (*Baijinlong*, dir. Tang Xiaodan, 1933), and it became an instant hit at home and abroad. *The Platinum Dragon* was one of the top-grossing films in Shanghai, Guangzhou, Hong Kong, Macau, and

Southeast Asia. Soon Cantonese talkies blossomed and took the market by storm as the lure of lucrative profits attracted both local and foreign capital as well as filmmaking talents to Cantonese filmmaking.

What lies behind Xue Juexian's alleged move to repudiate the Nationalist government's imposed restrictions on Cantonese-language film productions has to do with the politics of sound and spoken language in Chinese cinema. Xue's story constitutes a critical chapter and yet a missing episode of Chinese film historiography and Cantonese film culture during Chinese cinema's transition from the silent to the sound stage. When cultural bureaucrats of the Nationalist regime introduced censorial mechanisms and tried to intervene in Chinese film productions in the 1930s, they campaigned to drive out the martial arts genre, ghost movies, and immoral stories from mainstream cinema houses, as they were deemed a threat to the regime's goal of nation-building. Whereas the tabooed subjects of the superstitious, the supernatural, and the racy in early Republican cinema recently have generated scholarly discussions,[3] Cantonese sound film developments and the linguistic-cultural debates on dialect films have yet to be addressed.

Cantonese filmmaking was always torn between political alignment with the nation and its pursuits of commercial interest and entertainment value. Nationalist screen policies went on offense against Cantonese talkies because censors suspected that they would hinder the linguistic and political unification of the nation. Besides obvious political motivations on the side of the government, the campaign to curb Cantonese-dialect films manifested the enduring rivalry between Cantonese- and Mandarin-speaking pictures that was born alongside Chinese sound films. With the arrival of sound in Chinese films, the Hong Kong–Guangdong region emerged as the largest production center of Cantonese talkies, exporting its product not only to Cantonese-speaking communities in South China, but also to the Chinese diaspora in Southeast Asia and North America. Furthermore, the assimilation of Cantonese opera performance into talking pictures with the popularization of gramophone records created a vibrant commercial cinema with lucrative profits. In its rivalry with Shanghai-based Mandarin films for market share and cultural supremacy, Cantonese cinema was inevitably engaged in cultural politics on local, national, and transnational levels.

The Platinum Dragon, the first Cantonese talkie, is no longer extant, as many Cantonese films made before the 1950s have been lost. But the recent rediscovery of a corpus of early Cantonese talkies in the 1930s and 1940s, including Xue Juexian's *The Platinum Dragon: Part Two* (*Xu Baijinlong*, 1937), has provided archivists and scholars new access and renewed perspectives from which to reconstruct early Cantonese film history and aesthetics.[4] What prompted the Cantonese opera artist to remake *The Platinum Dragon* in 1936? Did Xue use the remake of his film to respond to the Nationalist regime's challenging political demands and market constraints on Cantonese pictures? What does the sequel tell us about the generic and artistic characteristics of Cantonese cinema as a crossover between Cantonese theater and screen, and between Hollywood and Cantonese opera and film?

To begin with, *The Platinum Dragon* was initially one of Xue's successful opera-and-film fusions and theatrical productions of "Western-costume Cantonese opera" (*xizhuang yueju*). Xue's opera performance was adapted from the Hollywood film *The Grand Duchess and the Waiter (dir. Malcolm St. Clair)*, released in 1926. After producing the film sequel *The Platinum Dragon: Part Two* in 1937 (codirected by Gao Lihen [Ko Lei-hen] and Xue himself), Xue remade part 1 of the story in 1947 as *The New Platinum Dragon* (*Xin Baijinlong*, dir. Yang Gongliang [Yeung Kung-leong]), which is similar to his 1933 film in terms of themes and plots.

The Platinum Dragon was obviously not a singular case (but the most successful one) of operatic adaptations and filmic remaking in early Cantonese film culture. But Xue's successful film marked a significant change by spawning a wave of popularity for Cantonese opera films in the 1930s. Yu Mo-wan argues that in their heyday, Cantonese opera films constituted a significant portion of Cantonese film production during the 1930s. These films were mostly based on old Cantonese opera plots, restaging the stories in contemporary contexts using modern costumes and scenery and still employing Cantonese opera songs.[5] But the highly popular Cantonese opera cinema in early Chinese film historiography has been forgotten partly because most of these films no longer exist, and partly because they have been considered secondary in artistic merit in comparison with either stage opera performances or cinema itself, treated as mere popular entertainments for mass consumption.[6]

Among the many Cantonese opera films of merely entertainment value, however, the Cantonese operatic remakes of Ernst Lubitsch's *The Love Parade* (1929) stand out as among the best works in the category. The Hollywood film was adapted into two "Western-costume Cantonese operas" in Shanghai's theaters in the early 1930s, starring respectively Xue Juexian and Ma Shizeng (1900–1964). It was Xue Juexian who went on to transform the Hollywood picture into a Cantonese film version, as *Xuangong yanshi* (literally, "An Amorous History in the Jade Palace," dir. Shao Zuiweng [Runje Shaw]) in 1934.[7] A versatile and leading opera performer with star power established on stage, Xue was quick to capitalize on the new media and delivery channels of gramophone, radio, and film, which in tandem gave birth to a new audiovisual entertainment culture in urban China during the early Republican era.[8] Further, Xue's creative talents and entrepreneurial zeal enabled him to move between the various modes of cultural productions and across different fields of artistic and commercial activities.

Early Cantonese sound films drew on Western and Hollywood inspirations. They also had a close relationship with Cantonese theater, singers and actors crossing between the stage and screen in Hong Kong, Guangdong, Shanghai, and Southeast Asia.[9] These intricate cultural-geographical circuits, with their constant transfer of capital, technology, agency, and talent, allow a critical conception of Cantonese cinema as translocal and transnational from its inception. This chapter offers a study of the texts and contexts of these two extant films of Xue, and seeks to raise issues of transnationality and intermediality in relation to Xue's pioneering Cantonese opera-film crossovers, and to ponder the political-cultural meanings of his Cantonese film-remaking in Cantonese cinema. Yiman Wang's study of the remakes of Lubitsch's *The Love Parade* by Xue Juexian and Ma Shizeng in their Cantonese opera film versions indicates the quintessential transborder flows between foreign cultures and local traditions in the development of Cantonese films, and in Xue's case, the abundant transcultural appropriations of stories, styles, and performance between Hollywood, Shanghai, Hong Kong, and Southeast Asia. Using Cantonese cinema as a prime example, Wang proposes the "transnational" as a methodology to "address the cultural politics in Chinese film production, distribution and exhibition."[10] Resisting the claim of transnational cinema as an outcome of economic globalism and commodification, Wang seeks to redirect criticism to the importance of intercultural exchange and negotiation. She considers the "Western-costume Cantonese operas" as "foreignizing remakes," in which "the 'foreign' contributes to formulating Cantonese (and later on Hong Kong) cinema and the correlated lingual-cultural subject positioning" from the 1930s on.[11] It is in the vigorous interregional film activities that one finds the interplay between various Chinese filmmaking communities (especially between Shanghai, Guangzhou, and Hong Kong) highly interactive, whereas their cultural borders are invariably being reshaped.

In distinction from Wang's ultimately theoretical reflection of "border cultural politics in its enunciation, modes of address and exhibition" in transnational film studies, I am concerned about how Xue's adventurous and commercial Westernized Cantonese opera films assimilate foreign elements in the Cantonese performance tradition and strategic practice to engage cultural politics on regional and national levels. My study of Xue's Cantonese opera film remaking and adaptation of Hollywood puts his ventures within historical contexts in relation to the cultural politics of Cantonese- versus Mandarin-language cinema, dynamic regional flows between Shanghai, Hong Kong, and Southeast Asia, and intergeneric adaptations between stage and screen. Historically, Xue's artistic innovation and entrepreneurial vision could only be achieved in an intermediated environment with new technology transfer and exchange between the local theater and foreign cinema, a permeable border between performative art and commercial entertainment for urban consumers, and the transregional flow of capital and talent between Hong Kong, Guangzhou, Shanghai, and Southeast Asia in which the craze for profit and the cultural politics of regional and national identities are contested. In studying Xue's moves between different physical places and his strategy to reinvent Cantonese operatic and filmic genres, as a response to commercial and political crises confronting Cantonese cinema, we need to consider the artistic and pragmatic choices he made and how he wagered on the new genres and representations at various stages.

ENTER *THE PLATINUM DRAGON*: TRANSNATIONAL CIRCUITS OF COMMERCE, CANTONESE CINEMA, AND HOLLYWOOD

"The Platinum Dragon," the hero played by Xue Juexian in 1933, unmistakably spells out the intimate interplay between early Cantonese movie culture and commercial business when entrepreneurs and performing artists joined hands to brand their products for mass consumption. It was a marketing strategy for Xue to name his Cantonese opera adaptation as *The Platinum Dragon* after the cigarette brand Golden Dragon produced by Nanyang Brothers Tobacco Company. Golden Dragon Cigarettes was launched in 1925 and targeted local Chinese as well as overseas Chinese consumers in Southeast Asia. In the late 1920s, Nanyang approached Xue to help advertise its cigarette brand. Xue adapted his favorite Hollywood silent film *The*

Grand Duchess and the Waiter for the stage, and named his Western-style Cantonese opera fusion *The Platinum Dragon*.

By 1930, Shanghai had become a cultural and commercial hub for migrants from various regions in China with a sizable Cantonese-speaking community. Indeed, there were intimate triangular business and cultural connections between Hong Kong, Guangzhou, and Shanghai.[12] The market for Cantonese operas and films was promising enough for Xue to expand his operatic territory.[13] When Xue's new Cantonese opera debuted in Shanghai in 1930, Nanyang gave the show a commercial boost by dispensing free cigarettes to theatergoers. Promotional banners were hung with the slogan "Watch *The Platinum Dragon*, Smoke Golden Dragon Cigarettes" (*Guan Baijinlong mingju, xi Baijinlong xiangyan*).[14] Similar commercial gimmicks were reprised by Nanyang and Xue in promoting the film in 1933 with resounding success. Xue's "Western-costume Cantonese opera" reportedly won the favor of massive Cantonese audiences, including overseas Chinese in Vietnam and Cambodia. Apparently, the Cantonese sound film had a wide appeal to Cantonese-speaking spectators. *The Platinum Dragon* failed to impress the Shanghai audience due to dialectic differences, whereas it enjoyed extraordinary runs in Guangzhou, Hong Kong, and Macau, and later in Southeast Asia.[15] Besides the factor of commercial collaboration that partially accounted for the success of the opera, the popularity of *The Platinum Dragon* can also be attributed to its variegated and mixed entertaining performances on stage, which made Cantonese opera look like a Hollywood vaudeville theater—a variety show featuring individual and social dancing, fighting scenes, and magic and hypnotic performances with modern music (electronic guitar) accompaniment within a Western-style stage set.[16] It was a perfect case of "cross-media promotion" as the opera, the film, and the cigarette all won the (Cantonese) people over.[17]

Xue Juexian's enterprising crossover and visionary experimentation with new media technologies and genres are emblematic of the notion of "cultural entrepreneurship" in early twentieth-century Asia, which evinces "a pluralistic approach to the art and business of culture characterized by active participation in multiple modes of cultural production," and "involves the investment of both talent and capital in new enterprises."[18] But Xue's biographical ventures and the historical vicissitudes of Cantonese operatic film experimentation certainly go beyond the surface of any general description of cultural risk-taking or entrepreneurship. Surviving the downturn of

Cantonese theaters in the late 1920s, Xue managed to build his stardom with his dynamic performances and eclectic style; his flair for crossing between different role-types on stage earned him the title "all-around master performer" (*wanneng laoguan*). In developing the hybrid genres of Western-style Cantonese opera and film, he was eager to learn from Beijing opera, modern spoken drama, and Hollywood cinema, absorbing elements "from facial cosmetics application to the introduction of violin and saxophone as regular instruments, from the more agile northern martial arts (of Peking [Beijing] opera) to the aesthetic of the silver screen."[19] Xue's idea of artistic interaction between different cultural media and cultural expressions can be aptly summarized by his own projection on the Cantonese opera dream, which he considered a cross-fertilization of "the Cantonese-opera essence; northern-style technique; Beijing-opera martial arts; Shanghai-style tricks; the movie's expression; drama ideologies, and Western stage settings."[20] It is not difficult to surmise that his idea of Cantonese cinema should exhibit similar generic flexibility in assimilating foreign influences and diverse performative traditions into native styles.

Xue Juexian was brought up and educated in Hong Kong. He studied at St. Paul's College, a well-known English-language school, but quit school at the age of sixteen because of family economic hardship. He embarked on his theatrical career when he was introduced to a troupe in Guangzhou in 1921. After a few years of apprenticeship and training, the young Xue was able to gain an early foothold in Guangzhou's theatrical troupes with his assiduousness and gift for performance. He managed to get leading roles on stage in a few years. Soon after, Xue would make his dramatic move to Shanghai, where he had firsthand experience with the movie world. But his move to Shanghai was an expedient decision dictated by circumstances. In 1925, he was embroiled in a deadly gang fight in which Xue's protector was gunned down. Xue had a narrow escape from death. Feeling that his life was threatened, Xue took off immediately for Shanghai and stayed there for over a year.[21] His first brief sojourn in Shanghai proved to be an eye-opening and life-changing experience. More importantly, Xue saw the great potential of cinema as a new entertainment medium. In 1926, Xue founded the Feifei Movie Production Company in Shanghai. As the manager and director, he involved himself in the movie industry; he changed his name to Zhang Fei. He acted in the movie *The Shameless Girl* (*Lang die*, literally meaning "Waves of Butterflies", dir. Zhang Fei, 1926), in which he played the male lead in the inaugural silent movie, with Tang Xueqing (1908–1955) in the leading female role.[22] Xue and Tang later got married, and Tang then played the female lead in *The Platinum Dragon* (1933) and *The Platinum Dragon: Part Two* (1937). In 1932, when the Cantonese theater market in South China experienced an epic collapse, Xue went back to Shanghai to look for new opportunities. Xue used his contacts in the nascent filmmaking industry in Shanghai to make his popular film *The Platinum Dragon*.[23]

Xue Juexian's venture into filmmaking in Shanghai coincided with the business ambition of Unique (later the Shaw Brothers) in extending its movie network across British Malaya and Singapore. *The Platinum Dragon* enjoyed such an enormous success that Runme and Run Run Shaw were convinced to turn to Cantonese filmmaking for the Southeast Asian market. In fact, the artistic and commercial achievements that Xue demonstrated in the early sound film helped to lay a foundation for Unique's populist approach and market scheme. The studio strategically used Hong Kong as a base of production in fostering the development of early Cantonese films in Southeast Asia.[24] But how should we reassess Xue as the cultural pioneer who hastened the artistic blending of Cantonese opera, Western theater, and modern cinema in his Western-style Cantonese opera-and-film? Significantly, how do we make sense of *The Platinum Dragon* and early Cantonese cinema's transnational encounter with Hollywood and the West within the cultural and historical contexts of the 1930s and 1940s? With no known copy of Xue Juexian's 1933 film extant, my study concerns *The New Platinum Dragon* in 1947. Based on the commonality of their story plots, Xue's 1947 remake was largely based on the 1933 film with some changes in plots and narrations.

Xue Juexian's filmic adaptation was inspired by *The Grand Duchess and the Waiter*, his favorite Hollywood silent picture. The Hollywood comedy is about a Parisian millionaire's (Albert Durant, played by Adolphe Menjou) efforts to woo the elegant Duchess Zenia (Florence Vidor), an exiled Russian aristocrat, by posing as a waiter in her service. Though the wealthy man is famous as a playboy with multiple assignations at the film's opening, he becomes devoted to the noblewoman from the first moment he sees her and is determined to win her over after some whimsical twists and turns. Recognized as a sophisticated comedy of 1920s akin to the high comedy of manners (best epitomized by the silent films of Ernst Lubitsch), *The Grand Duchess and the Waiter* was praised by American film critics as having "the high standard of the wit" to delight the sophisticated audience as well as "the humor of the situations and lines" that could be grasped by anyone.[25]

I argue that it was the game of love, the masquerade in performance, and the foreign/exotic spectacles offered by the Hollywood film that prompted Xue Juexian to re-create indigenized versions of the romantic comedy in Cantonese theater and onscreen. Love is central to Xue's film comedy, as in the American silent. In *The New Platinum Dragon*, a young and wealthy Chinese businessman, Bai Jinlong (Platinum Dragon, played by Xue) returns from San Francisco to Shanghai. On board a cruise ship he chances to meet Zhang Yuniang (Cheung Yuk-neung; played by Zheng Mengxia [Cheng Mang-ha]) and develops a crush on her. The man vows to marry her. Xue's adapted film gained much from Hollywood's sophisticated comedy—love is never taken for granted as a naively romantic idea; it has to be achieved with effort, care, and risk-taking. The plot unfolds as the hero, though rich and charming, has yet to undertake actions and make sacrifices to win the woman's heart and authenticate his sincere love. The male's courtship continues when he meets the woman for the second time at a New Year's costume ball. The ballroom scene is significant not because the Cantonese film can in any sense reproduce the glamorous mise-en-scène of the ballroom dancing in its Hollywood counterpart, which provides the fantasy of upper-class living. Rather, it gives Xue Juexian a chance for tour de force singing (for more than ten minutes) with the actress in the famous scene of "Arguing with each other in the garden" (*Huayuan xiangma*). This episode in the garden showcases Xue's characteristic performative style and the cinematic art of Cantonese film-opera crossover.[26] Moreover, the singing episode delivers cues that are pivotal for understanding the film's critique of appearance and reality, and of the deluded vision of the beautiful and the rich. When the couple bickers and mocks each other behind their masks (during the costume party) in the backyard, the hero implies he may well be a dandyish and handsome bachelor in disguise. The woman in return declares that she really does not care about who the man implies he is. She refuses to confess her love, a gesture showing that it takes human effort and care to vindicate true love, which has nothing to do with beauty or fortune.

For Yuniang, indeed, love is the last bastion to resist the world of deceit and desire around her. Her father, suspected of fraud and embezzlement in Shanghai, leaves for Hong Kong, where he plans to scam rich and powerful men and to marry his daughter to one of them. The costume party is important as the venue of human masquerades—it is where the father meets a "banker" who turns out to belong to a syndicate of con artists. Meanwhile, for Platinum Dragon, it is ironically through the act of impersonating and putting on a false human identity that he is going to prove his true love for the heroine. So he disguises himself as a waiter at the hotel in the service of the woman in order to have an intimate relationship with her.

The games of courtship and false identity develop further when Yuniang's father finds himself unable to afford his rent at the hotel. In the American movie, the duchess soon discovers that her family and highborn relatives can no longer pay for their grand expenses. The Cantonese adaptation re-creates a similar situation, with even more compelling twists and turns. To ease his financial crisis, the father wants to pawn his daughter's diamond brooch pin—a love token given by her mother—to pay the rent. When Platinum Dragon (the waiter) notices, he helps to deposit the woman's precious article in the hotel in return for the money that Yuniang needs. Hence, the brooch pin serves as a functional cue that motivates the plot of the film. Earlier in the party scene, the "banker" observes that Yuniang puts on the diamond brooch pin and decides to befriend her father and the family. Toward the end of the film, the trickster and his criminal gang capture the woman to ask for a ransom of the diamond pin. Again, Platinum Dragon has to go through his last ordeal by cross-dressing as a woman (a familiar gender role-play for Xue Juexian, who also specialized in acting female roles as the male *dan* on stage) to negotiate with the gang and rescue his love. The ending may be flawed by an occasional dash of slapstick and farce. But when Yuniang accepts Platinum Dragon's marriage proposal for what he has done, not for who he is, the ending becomes more convincing, not as a forgone conclusion but as the film's cogent effort to humanize sexual and conjugal relationships.

My brief analysis of *The New Platinum Dragon* shed lights on the cinematic features of the first 1933 sound film, and may partially explain why Xue Juexian's new Cantonese venture held such a wide appeal for native Cantonese, if not all Chinese, audiences. Yet, despite its embrace of American and Hollywood culture, *The Platinum Dragon* was denigrated as a frivolous entertainment, an escapist fantasy of an Americanized bourgeois lifestyle, and worse still, a slavish devotion to capitalism (especially in the portrayal of the chivalrous hero). Negative commentaries appeared in the current criticism between 1933 and 1937; the film was despised for glorifying the "magic power of money" (*jinqian de moli*), whereas the Westernized Cantonese opera production was lampooned for making "senseless fuss" (*hun nao*) as a chaotically mixed stage play that was "neither Chinese nor Western" (*buzhong buxi*) and "neither contemporary nor traditional" (*feijin feigu*).[27] Such artistic depreciation of the Cantonese opera-film crossover, of course, recalled a similarly simplistic rationale for the moral and political criticisms of magical-fantastic genres in 1920s Shanghai. It overlooks the Cantonese film pioneer's effort to articulate a localized vision of the modern by assimilating Hollywood in Cantonese theater and screen, and fails to understand how the "foreign" contributes to formulating Cantonese (and later Hong Kong) cinema from the 1930s to the 1950s.[28] As Cantonese cinema continued to flourish as a quintessentially popular entertainment mixing the foreign with the local, it increasingly became a target of political and moral criticism in the decades to come. *The Platinum Dragon* and the film's metamorphosis exemplify the fate of the cinema itself.

SUBDUING *THE PLATINUM DRAGON*: SURVIVAL OF CANTONESE-DIALECT CINEMA

The national polemics against Cantonese filmmaking continued into the 1940s when Xue Juexian remade *The New Platinum Dragon*. Just a year after Xue's new film production, an article published in the *Qingqing* movie magazine launched an abusive attack on Cantonese film circles, predicting extinction of Cantonese pictures as cheap, low-quality entertainments that contaminated the mind. The article denigrated popular Cantonese pictures as a "contagious disease that not only can eradicate the whole film community of the southern Chinese region, but even more abominably, can kill off the 'conscience' of the good people of China."[29]

Such a forthright denunciation of the Cantonese movie industry on moral grounds indeed perpetrated the bitter tug-of-war between Mandarin and Cantonese cinemas, in which Shanghai's media had consistently picked on Cantonese talkies and slandered them as "shoddy quickies" (*cuzhi lanzao*). The disparagement of Cantonese productions as backward and nonsensical was part of the media discourse concomitant with the national government's coercive measures to drive out Cantonese and all dialectal pictures through censorship. In 1930 the Film Censorship Committee in Nanjing issued a formal ban on all dialectal pictures in the country, with a political agenda to promote Mandarin as the national language. Nonetheless, Cantonese film companies could still enjoy a boom regardless of the announcement of the ban under the protection of a separatist provincial government in Guangdong. The national government could not reinforce the dialect film ban until 1936, when it regained control of Guangdong and other South China provinces. Frantic responses were made by filmmakers and representatives of the industry from Guangdong and Hong Kong. They quickly formed an alliance and founded the South China Film Association, chaired by Runje Shaw. These representatives petitioned Nanjing and strongly opposed that hostile ban that would put Cantonese cinema in peril, as the authorities was ready to implement wholesale restrictions on Cantonese talkies in July 1937.[30]

The process of bargaining between Guangdong and Hong Kong filmmakers, and the countermeasures and arguments proposed by the Cantonese delegates, were documented in *Yilin* (*Artland*), an émigré movie magazine that had wide readerships in South China and overseas Chinese communities, in the issues between 1937 and 1939. The statutory ban was suspended with a three-year grace period until 1940, when Cantonese pictures would be gradually phased out in the mainland market. Despite the postponement of the ban, negotiations and disputes were ongoing, with strife and distrust between the two sides. Cantonese filmmakers were doubtful that Mandarin filmmakers in Shanghai had a vested interest in pushing the draconian censorship policies that would eventually expelled Cantonese talkies from the mainland market. To counter these adverse policies, the Cantonese representatives argued that because Mandarin was far from popular in South China, language unification should be implemented in phases. Some insisted that Cantonese films were popular among the local populace in South China, and so Cantonese-dialect pictures were crucial and functional in promoting the cause of science and progress for the nation.[31] This kind of nationalistic rhetoric understandably veiled Hong Kong filmmakers' fear of losing the vast Southern China market once the ban was strictly executed. The negotiations reached such a deadlock that some Cantonese filmmakers harbored antinortherner sentiments, and some had already refused to submit their films to the government censors. Ironically, it was the outbreak of the Sino-Japanese War that spoiled the mainland government's plan to impose the ban on Cantonese pictures.

The making of *The Platinum Dragon* and *The Platinum Dragon: Part Two* is illustrative of the polemical and volatile transformation of 1930s Cantonese cinema, surviving the politics of the dialect film ban, on the one hand, and encountering vehement media censure of the worth and artistic merits of Cantonese pictures, on the other. The huge commercial success of *The Platinum Dragon* in 1933 spawned dozens of Cantonese film studios in the coming years to tap into the new markets, but the quality of the new films declined just when investment and production reached a fervent pitch.[32] In

1934 and 1935, Runje Shaw became the target of finger-pointing by Shanghai's media and film distributors, bearing the brunt of their criticism for churning out shoddy pictures, largely the product of other Cantonese filmmakers. [33] Meanwhile, overproduction in this period led to a box-office slump for Cantonese movies. As the chairman of the South China Film Association, Shaw was committed to fighting for the legitimacy of Cantonese films, and he also voiced discontent with his fellow Cantonese filmmakers for failing to elevate the standards of Cantonese filmmaking.[34]

One can surmise that, under these hostile attacks, Shaw must have been eager to produce good Cantonese pictures with both artistic and commercial values. It was in response to the market crisis that Shaw teamed up with Xue Juexian again to make the second part of *The Platinum Dragon* (though their partnership disintegrated during the shooting of the film). The filming of *The Platinum Dragon: Part Two* was delayed by many unfavorable incidents. In 1934, Xue was brutally attacked by a Cantonese gang after a performance in Shanghai. He survived the assault, but it nearly blinded him. Film stocks were destroyed by fire three times during the filming, including two disastrous fires that broke out at the Unique studio in 1936. The crew had to reshoot the film a fourth time.[35] Eventually, Xue finished the film production, possibly during his longer visit to Southeast Asia (reportedly at the invitation of Run Run Shaw).[36] In 1935 he toured Southeast Asia to conduct research on the film industry and explore the business of doing theatrical performance there. Xue formed an itinerant theatrical troupe to tour Singapore in 1936, the same year he filmed the second part of *The Platinum Dragon*. The sequel was produced by Nanyang Studio, a company restructured by Shaw after fire destroyed the Unique Studio in 1936. Hence, in *The Platinum Dragon: Part Two*, geographical and cultural spaces in Southeast Asia prominently figured in its relationships with Shanghai and China. I shall tease out the historical and cinematic significance in the context of the film's transnational making and consumption.

The Platinum Dragon: Part Two is a romantic comedy that revolves around Platinum Dragon (Xue Juexian) and three women. The Cantonese film takes a rare look at the cutthroat business world of overseas Chinese business in Southeast Asia in connection with Shanghai. The sequel is a loose extension of the story in *The Platinum Dragon*. Platinum Dragon is now engaged with Zhang Yuniang (Tang Xueqing), and he has moved with her family to Southeast Asia to assist his future father-in-law in running his rubber manufacture company. Platinum Dragon is able to show his caliber and an astute mind in administration of the company. Yet he cannot gain the favor and trust of Zhang's father, who thinks of him as "hypocritical." Platinum Dragon feels dejected after rows with Yuniang's father, which reveal the maladies of life in the Chinese upper middle class. Meanwhile, Platinum Dragon is quickly taken in by the charm and attention of Wu Mali (Mary) (Lin Meimei [Lam Mui-mui]), without knowing that she is a family member of his business rival in the rubber industry. Disguised as the romantic lover, Mary intends to seduce Platinum Dragon and talk him into investing his money in her company so as to undercut the business of the Zhang family, for which he is working. After the fiancée discovers the man's infidelity, the couple is on the verge of breaking their engagement. The crisis of their disengagement is overcome by Yuniang's sister, Yuchan (played by Huang Manli [Wong Man-lei]), who intervenes in the man's affair by using her appeal on him. Succumbing to the sister's ingenious scheme and the spell of her charms, Platinum Dragon leaves Mary and proposes marriage to Yuchan. The plot of romantic intrigues is, however, brought to a twisted ending when the bride at the marriage ceremony turns out to be Yuniang. The game of love comes full circle when Platinum Dragon and Yuniang return to where they started and to the roles they intended to play, husband and wife.

Adopting the narrative interest of Hollywood-style romantic comedies, Xue Juexian's sequel also reveals a desire to expand Cantonese talkies in the Southeast Asian market after the commercial success of his first sound film. The first shot of *The Platinum Dragon: Part Two* shows a map of Southeast Asia with an animated image of a steamship sailing across the globe. This opening scene illustrates vividly the ambitions of both Xue and Unique (Nanyang) to explore the new southern markets, navigating their movie business from Shanghai via Hong Kong to Southeast Asia. The move to Southeast Asia was a strategic plan when the Cantonese film business was being censored and censured in Mainland China.

Under the veneer of film comedy lies the subtext of the lingual-cultural and transnational politics of Cantonese cinema, which started to build its base at the margins of Mainland China and yet strove to respond to the call for national progress. Thus, the amusing moral drama of family problem, male infidelity, triangular love, and marriage is subtly intertwined with the world of crafty business schemes, transnational capital flows, and a sense of saving China's industries and economy. In the latter part of the film, as Yuchan captivates Platinum Dragon with her sex appeal, she convinces him to redirect the huge sum of money he promised to give Mary for a private investment, to donate for the cause of education for Chinese children in Nanyang (Southeast Asia). Following the finale of the happy reunion and wedding of the couple, the film ends with Platinum Dragon paying his farewell speech to the company chiefs before he returns with his wife to Shanghai. He makes a passionate speech to encourage overseas Chinese businessman to make investments in Mainland China so as to contribute to China's national industry and economy. Produced at the time of political turmoil in 1936, Xue attempted to maintain a good balance between commercial and political interests, and demonstrated a sharp historical sensitivity in the film.[37] Overseas Chinese donations indeed became an important source of funding for China in the War of Resistance. And it turned out that the Southeast Asian market was congenial to the growth of the Cantonese movie industry in the coming decades.

Yet, despite the slight trace of national sentiment in the film, for the majority of Cantonese-speaking and general Chinese audiences in 1930s China, Hong Kong, and Southeast Asia, the popularity of Xue Juexian's sequel had much to do with the portrayal of Platinum Dragon—a high-society Chinese dandy, a profligate man of manners, a chivalrous gentleman, and above all, an object of desire for women (whom they hankered after) and men (whom they wished to become). The allure of Xue's screen presence was augmented by his stardom in Cantonese theater.[38] The merger of Cantonese opera and Western cinema that highlighted the performances of masquerade and role-playing, and the plots of human scheming and money swindling, contributed to its box-office success.[39] The film's scandalous and humorous ending—in which the man cheats on his fiancée, gets separated from her, but eventually finds himself tricked into marrying her—recalls the "comedy of remarriage" in 1930s–1940s Hollywood cinema.[40] The core of this comedy concerns the threat of separation or divorce, which spurs the couple to seek mutual understanding of their romantic liaison and to put love and gender equality back in a conjugal relationship. Along the lines of Hollywood's comic construction of the modern woman, Xue's sequel compellingly features Yuchan not so much as a seductress or social flapper but as a strong-willed and scheming woman who gains the upper hand over the man to handle the family crisis and manages to seal the couple's broken relationship with the final ritual of marriage. The film's unique way of incorporating foreign genres, visualizing new ways of modern life, and addressing changing social mores and lifestyles not only offered audiences entertaining plots and visual spectacles, but also productively engaged with issues of cinematic modernity, gender, intermedia performance, and spectatorship as a form of urban entertainment—an artistic experiment that was undertaken ahead of its time.

CODA: CIRCUITS OF EARLY CANTONESE CINEMA

The rise and fall of *The Platinum Dragon* exemplified early Cantonese-language cinema in its dynamic interactions within the larger map of Chinese-language cinemas and the transnational connections between Hong Kong, Guangdong and South China, Shanghai, Southeast Asia, and Hollywood. With the advent of sound film technology in the 1930s, the Hong Kong–Guangdong region emerged as the largest production center of Cantonese talkies, exporting its product not only to Cantonese-speaking communities in South China, but also to the Chinese diaspora in Southeast Asia and North America. The assimilation of Cantonese opera performance in talking pictures with the popularization of gramophone records created a vibrant commercial cinema with lucrative profits. The emergence of Cantonese-speaking pictures and the dialect movie industry led to political and cultural contradictions when the ideology of state-building with rising nationalist discourse and censorship practice got in the way of moviemaking and consumption, with complex political, commercial, and cultural implications. In its rivalry with Shanghai-based Mandarin films for market share and cultural supremacy, Cantonese cinema was inevitably engaged in cultural politics on local, national, and transnational levels. Cantonese filmmakers were always torn between political alignment with the nation and pursuit of commercial interest and entertainment value.

Xue Juexian's cinematic series of *The Platinum Dragon* was emblematic of Cantonese cinema's effort to respond to the political imperative of the nation and regionally commercial interest in the volatile 1930s. By blending the art of Hollywood romantic comedy with a Westernized form of Cantonese opera, Xue also made ingenious efforts to modernize Cantonese cinema by rejecting the highly popular genres of martial arts and magic spirit films prevalent in Shanghai and Hong Kong. Whereas Xue's theater and cinema were significantly based in the transregional networks of Shanghai, Guangzhou, and Hong Kong, his Cantonese films indeed smacked of "Shanghai styles" (*haipai*) in assimilating foreign cultural imports and projecting modern lifestyle. But Xue's idiosyncratic creative flair and his market sense as the pioneer of Cantonese (Chinese) cinema was soon forgotten, if not entirely erased from historiography and cinematic memory (dozens of his films are no longer extant)[41] when Cantonese cinema was submerged in discourse of the "national defense cinema" (*guofang dianying*), followed by a number of "cleansing movements" (*qingjie yundong*) of Cantonese films in the late 1930s and 1940s. *The Platinum Dragon*, as a popular and intricate romance and a modernist blending of Cantonese theater and Western cinema, would surely have offended moralistic and political critics at that time and thereafter.[42]

With a renewed focus on Chinese-language cinemas as comprising pluralistic linguistic registers and diversified regional traditions in recent studies of Chinese cinema, this preliminary examination of *The Platinum Dragon* and Xue Juexian's early cinematic venture begins to address unresolved questions in the field of Cantonese cinema historiography and aesthetics. The case of *The Platinum Dragon* and the early Cantonese filmic tradition it represents bespeak the presence of dialects, accents, and music, disputing the uniformity and commonality of national identity in cinematic history. *The Platinum Dragon* created a new genre of the musical film, and the dynamic blending of opera and cinema in various degrees would be sustained well into the 1960s. Xue's successful move between theater and cinema also hastened the crossing over of opera artists and screen stars, which consolidated a distinctively Cantonese performance culture in Hong Kong. On the other hand, it is worth further studying the Hong Kong–Shanghai connections in the formation of early Cantonese cinema, as seen in Xue's embrace of Hollywood's global appeal and his creation of a dandyish gentleman in *The Platinum Dragon*.[43] The recent rediscovery of early Cantonese film texts provides the impetus for a transregional inquiry into the sound, dialect, and cultural politics of Cantonese film culture and the close ties between Hong Kong, Shanghai, Guangzhou, and Southeast Asia.

ACKNOWLEDGMENT

This chapter is an outcome of my project, namely, "The Sound of Politics: Cantophone Cinema in 1930s–1960s" (11673616), under the support of the General Research Fund (GRF) granted by the Research Grants Council of Hong Kong.

Notes

1. "Xue Juexian chongpai *Xu Baijinlong*: Xiwang ta xian cha yi cha jiancha ling" [Xue Juexian Remakes *The Platinum Dragon: Part Two*: He Better Check the Censorship Order Beforehand], *Ying yu xi* 1, no. 4 (1936): 6.

2. "Xue Juexian zai Xianggang zuzhi gongsi: Pai yueyu shengpian busong Nanjing jiancha" [Xue Juexian Has Established His Own Company in Hong Kong to Make Sound Films, Which He Will Not Submit to Nanjing for Inspection], *Yule* 1 (Inauguration issue) (1935): 25.

3. See Zhiwei Xiao, "Constructing a New National Culture: Film Censorship and the Issues of Cantonese Dialect, Superstition, and Sex in the Nanjing Decade," in *Cinema and Urban Culture in Shanghai, 1922–1943*, ed. Yingjin Zhang (Stanford, CA: Stanford University Press, 1999), 183–99; Wang Chaoguang, *Yingyi de zhengzhi: Minguo dianying jiancha zhidu yanjiu* [The Politics of Film Art: A Study of the Institution of Film Censorship in the Republican Era] (Beijing: Zhongguo renmin daxue chubanshe, 2013).

4. More than a dozen Hong Kong films from the 1930s and 1940s were discovered in San Francisco in 2012. After repair work and technical preservation, the Hong Kong Film Archive screened eight of the early Cantonese film productions in early 2015, including *The Platinum Dragon: Part Two*.

5. Yu Mo-wan, "Xianggang yueju dianying fazhan shihua" [Words on the History of Development of the Hong Kong Cantonese Opera Film], in *The 11th Hong Kong Film Festival: Cantonese Opera Film Retrospective* (Hong Kong: Hong Kong Urban Council, 1987), 18–21.

6. Kevin Latham, "Consuming Fantasies: Mediated Stardom in Hong Kong Cantonese Opera and Cinema," *Modern China* 26, no. 3 (2000): 329–30.

7. Lubitsch's *The Love Parade* was so popular among Cantonese filmmakers that there were two more remakes of the Hollywood comedy by veteran Cantonese film director Zuo Ji (Tso Kea, 1916–1997) in 1957 and 1958, known as *My Kingdom for a Husband* (1957) and *My Kingdom for a Honeymoon* (1958), and both retained the Chinese title *Xuangong yanshi*. For a study of the remakes, see Yiman Wang, "*The Love Parade* Goes On: 'Western-Costume Cantonese Opera Film' and the Foreignizing Remake," in *Remaking Chinese Cinema: Through the Prism of Shanghai, Hong Kong, and Hollywood* (Honolulu: University of Hawai'i Press, 2013), 82–112.

8. For a cultural history of gramophone records and radio broadcasting in Hong Kong and Guangdong, see Yung Sai-shing, *Yueyun Liusheng: Changpian gongye yu Guangdong quyi 1903–1953* [Recording Cantonese Tunes: The Gramophone Industry and Cantonese Folk Arts, 1903–1953] (Hong Kong: Cosmic Books, 2006).

9. For a study of the modernization of Cantonese opera and its transnational circuits in the 1920s and 1930s, see Yung Sai-shing, *Xunmi Yueju shengying: Cong Hongchuan*

dao Shuiyindeng [Tracing Cantonese Opera: From Red Boat to Silver Light] (Hong Kong: Oxford University Press, 2012).

10. Yiman Wang, "The 'Transnational' as Methodology: Transnationalizing Chinese Film Studies through the Example of *The Love Parade* and Its Chinese Remakes," *Journal of Chinese Cinemas* 2, no. 1 (2008): 10.

11. Wang, "*The Love Parade* Goes On," 83.

12. As May-bo Ching points out, there had been close commercial and cultural interconnections between Guangzhou, Shanghai, and Hong Kong since the early twentieth century. Whereas Guangzhou and the Pearl River Delta hinterland exported commercial talents with rich experience in Sino-foreign trade, Shanghai congregated human, material, and technological resources from the country and abroad. Hong Kong served as a stable and secure haven for trading against the political turmoil occurring in the Mainland. See May-bo Ching, "Where Guangdong Meets Shanghai: Hong Kong Culture in a Trans-regional Context," in *Hong Kong Mobile: Making a Global Population*, ed. Helen F. Siu and Agnes S. Ku (Hong Kong: Hong Kong University Press, 2008), 45–62.

13. According to Pui-tak Lee in his study of the interflow of Guangdong and Shanghai film culture in the 1930s, Cantonese filmmakers had been rather active in Shanghai cinema, taking up positions from studio owners, theater owners, film distributors and dealers to directors, actors, technicians, and musicians. See Pui-tak Lee, "To Ban and Counter Ban: Cantonese Cinema Caught between Shanghai and Hong Kong in the 1930s," in *The Hong Kong-Guangdong Film Connection*, ed. Ain-ling Wong (Hong Kong: Hong Kong Film Archive, 2005), 30–49. Lee also estimates that there were about three hundred thousand Guangdong natives in Shanghai in 1930; see Lee, 32.

14. Lee, "To Ban and Counter Ban," 35.

15. Chengren Zhou, "Shanghai's Unique Film Productions and Hong Kong's Early Cinema," in *The Shaw Screen: A Preliminary Study*, ed. Ain-ling Wong (Hong Kong: Hong Kong Film Archive, 2003), 33.

16. Liu Zhenggang, *Huashuo Yueshang* [On Cantonese merchants] (Beijing: Zhonghua gongshang lianhe chubanshe, 2008), 151–54.

17. Lee, "To Ban and Counter Ban," 35.

18. Christopher Rea, "Enter the Cultural Entrepreneur," in *The Business of Culture: Cultural Entrepreneurs in China and Southeast Asia, 1900–65*, ed. Christopher Rea and Nicolai Volland (Vancouver: UBC Press, 2015), 10.

19. Wing-chung Ng, *The Rise of Cantonese Opera* (Urbana: University of Illinois Press, 2015), 72.

20. In spring 1938, Xue Juexian wrote about his opera dream in *Yilin* (*Artland*). Quoted from Cui Songming, ed., *Tushuo Xue Juexian yishu rensheng* [Pictorial Illustration of Xue Juexian's Artistic Life] (Guangzhou: Guangdong Bahe huiguan, 2013), 92.

21. Gang violence was prevalent in the world of Cantonese theaters and business in the 1920s and 1930s. See Ng, *Rise of Cantonese Opera*, 26.

22. The movie was adapted from Xue Juexian's Cantonese opera with the same title, in

which he played the main character, with Tang Xueqing in the female leading role. Tang was born to a senior office member's family, a well-off household with reputation and fame. Her grandfather was one of the brothers of Tang Shaoyi (1863–1938) who served as ministers and ambassadors in the Qing dynasty and later became the first prime minister of the Republic of China. Xue hired her as the female lead in the movie after many twists and turns. Xue and Tang finally got married.

23. In 1931, Xue Juexian moved back to Shanghai. He then ran the Nanfang Movie Production Company and filmed *The Platinum Dragon* in 1933. The late 1920s saw the epic collapse of the Cantonese opera business in Guangzhou and Hong Kong. See Ng, *Rise of Cantonese Opera*, 56–77.

24. For a discussion of *The Platinum Dragon*'s potential impact on early Cantonese cinema, see Zhou, "Shanghai's Unique Film Productions," 80–84. Hong Kong film historian Yu Mo-wan believes that the success of *The Platinum Dragon* was crucial for the rise of Cantonese cinema in the 1930s, as well as for Shaw to establish a firm market base in Southeast Asia. See Yu Mo-wan, "Xue Juexian yu dianying" [Xue Juexian and Cinema], in *Zhen shan mei: Xue Juexian yishu rensheng* [The Authentic, the Good, and the Beautiful: Xue Juexian's Artistic Life], ed. Guangdong Bihe huiguan and the Hong Kong University Art Museum (Hong Kong: Hong Kong University Art Museum, 2009), 70–74.

25. Lea Jacobs, *The Decline of Sentiment: American Film in the 1920s* (Berkeley: University of California Press, 2008), 123.

26. Victor Fan gives a detailed cinematic analysis of this singing scene in the garden in *The New Platinum Dragon*. See Victor Fan, *Cinema Approaching Reality: Locating Chinese Film Theory* (Minneapolis: University of Minnesota Press, 2015), 178–86.

27. Li Yi, "Xue Juexian yu yueju *Baijinlong*" [Xue Juexian and Cantonese Opera *The Platinum Dragon*], *Nanguo hongdou* 3 (2009): 16–19. Quoted from Li, 17.

28. Wang, "*The Love Parade* Goes On," 83.

29. "Yueyupian jiangqu juejing" [Cantonese Films Soon to Be Extinct], *Qingqing Dianying* 32 (1948): n.p.

30. For a detailed account of the censorship of Cantonese film in the 1930s, see Lee, "To Ban and Counter Ban," 30–49, esp. 41–44; Stephanie Po-yin Chung, "A Tale of Two Cinemas: Prewar Tug-of-War between North and South," in Wong, *The Hong Kong-Guangdong Film Connection*, 50–67. Also see Stephen Teo, "The Hong Kong Cantonese Cinema: Emergence, Development and Decline," in *The Chinese Cinema Book*, ed. Song Hwee Lim and Julian Ward (London: British Film Institute, 2011), 103–110.

31. See, for example, Ji Chen, "Guanyu jinying yueyupian zhi mianmianguan" [A Look at the Ban on Cantonese Films in Different Aspects], *Yilin* 3 (1937): n.p.

32. According to Zhou Chengren's survey, there were only three film production companies in Hong Kong in 1933. In 1936, there were twenty-five companies—eight times as many. In 1933, only five films were produced. The output surged to forty-nine films in 1936. Zhou, "Shanghai's Unique Film Productions," 33.

33. See Zhi Qing, "Tianyi gongsi de yueyu yousheng pian wenti" [Questions Concerning Tianyi's Cantonese Sound Films], *Diansheng zhoukan* 3, no. 17 (1934): n.p.; "Yueyu shengpian kaishi moluo, Shao Zuiweng deng dashou shenchi" [Cantonese Films in Decline: Shao Zuiweng Gets Reprimanded], *Yule* 1, no. 24 (1935): 593.

34. Chung, "Tale of Two Cinemas," 42.

35. Yu, "Xue Juexian yu dianying," 71.

36. Ng, *Rise of Cantonese Opera*, 72.

37. A nationalist message was put in the film's advertisement in *Zhongshan ribao* (June 15, 1937) in Guangzhou, which read: "Qingchang li: Fazhan gongyi! Gequ zhong: Tichang shiye" [Develop Arts and Crafts in Love. Advocate Manufacturing Industries in Songs]. Quoted from May Gwan-yuk Ng: "*Xu Baijinlong* de qingchang, shangchang, yangchang" [The Love Battlefield, Business World and Foreign Influence in *The White Gold Dragon, Part Two*], in *Early Cinematic Treasures Rediscovered*, ed. Winne Fu and May Gwan-yuk Ng (Hong Kong: Hong Kong Film Archive, 2015, exhibition program brochure), 33.

38. For an analysis of stardom in Cantonese theater and performance culture, see Latham, "Consuming Fantasies."

39. According to Yu Mo-wan, *The Platinum Dragon: Part Two* was the top-grossing film in Guangzhou in 1937. The film had a continuous run of fifteen days with full-house attendance. See Yu, "Xue Juexian yu dianying," 71.

40. Stanley Cavell, *Pursuits of Happiness: The Hollywood Comedy of Remarriage* (Cambridge, MA: Harvard University Press, 1981).

41. According to Yu Mo-wan, Xue Juexian had thirty-five films to his credit. He was most likely the first Chinese opera actor who successfully turned to filmmaking when he made *The Shameless Girl* in 1926. See Yu, "Xue Juexian yu dianying," 70–73.

42. *The Platinum Dragon* continued to receive political criticisms because the "Western-costume Cantonese opera" embraced Americanization and Western comprador capitalism, and the play's mixture of Chinese and Western elements was deemed vulgar, frivolous, and pornographic, as the story contained elements of robbery, adventure, hooliganism, adultery, and sexual immorality. See Li, "Xue Juexian yu yueju *Baijinlong*," 17.

43. For the global appeal of Hollywood, see Miriam Hansen, "The Mass Production of the Senses," in *Reinventing Film Studies*, ed. Christine Gledhill and Linda Williams (New York: Oxford University Press, 2000), 332–350.

PART II

Intermediaries, Cinephiles, and Film Literati

CHAPTER 7

Toward the Opposite Side of "Vulgarity"

The Birth of Cinema as a "Healthful Entertainment" and the Shanghai YMCA

Yoshino Sugawara

EMERGENCE OF MODERN MOVIEGOING: MOVIE EXHIBITION AT THE SHANGHAI YMCA

Almost a decade after the arrival of movies at the end of the nineteenth century, movies were exhibited in Shanghai as one of the attractions or stage performances at various amusement venues, which varied from traditional theaters to teahouses.[1] Throughout the twentieth century, alongside the gradual increase in the number of movie houses owned by foreigners, movies became increasingly popularized. The stable supply of electricity through the River Power Plant, established in 1913, accelerated the greater accessibility of movies in the city. At this point, so-called civilized drama, an elementary style of modern drama, became popular and was frequently performed in theaters; at the same time, a new style of amusement hall called *youxichang* gained in popularity with the community. These newly emerged venues for various styles of attractions and performing arts became the main stage for movie exhibitions.

Simultaneously, the transition and diversion of movie exhibition venues brought about a change in spectatorship; in other words, drama and movie journalism set up particular discourses revealing how "modern" and "civilized" audiences were different from "traditional" audiences. At traditional drama theaters and teahouses—which had been the favorite venues for movie exhibitions before the emergence of exclusive movie houses—"Usually, the people in the audience drank tea, cracked nuts, ate candies, talked with each other, and joked and laughed among themselves during the performance."[2] Along with the emergence of exclusive movie houses, these attitudes of traditional theatergoers became problematic, especially with regard to managing movie spectators' manners and the hygiene of the exhibition venues.[3] Moviegoing at *youxichang* was no exception. Though these novel amusement halls were gradually gaining popularity in Shanghai, they were also turning into a target of social criticism wherein they were accused of causing disruption in the social order. While some said that *youxichang* was the favorite venue for prostitutes and married people having secret love affairs, others spread the rumors that gave the amusement halls an immoral reputation.[4] The social criticism was also directed against the values in the exhibited films; among these, female nudity and cruel depictions of crime in detective movies were the main target.[5] Just after a murder case in 1920, one in which a white-collar worker killed a prostitute, many newspapers in Shanghai sensationally reported the case on a daily basis, with some of them pointing out that the murderer had been influenced by detective movies.[6] A year after the murder, China's first full-length feature film, *Yan Ruisheng* (dir. Ren Pengnian, 1921), was based on the case; journalists maintained discourses according to which similar criminal cases were frequently portrayed, which resulted in the accusation that movies had a destructive influence on society.[7]

Accordingly, what these discourses regarding movies implied was their apparent intention to identify two definite styles of movie sphere; movies in Shanghai were inseparable from "vulgarity" during the early decades, very different from later decades in which another sphere of movie culture had emerged. In fact, by the second and third decades of the twentieth century, the various activities of educational institutes and students tried to remove what were called "vulgar" elements from the context of movie exhibition.[8] Most of these activities were merely onetime events and were not perpetual; however, one exception was the Shanghai YMCA, which is this article's focus. The Shanghai YMCA not only conducted periodic movie exhibition programs as, in their words, a "wholesome and healthful entertainment,"[9] it also clearly recognized the role of movies in social education; this organization played an unequivocal role in the cinema history of Shanghai.

Furthermore, the Association's "wholesome and healthful" movie shows promoted a new attitude toward movie spectatorship as well as its modernization in the same way as the movie journalism discourses. With this novel movie spectatorship, the popular attitude of moviegoers who took over that of the traditional theatergoers, such as "eating, drinking, chatting while laughing with each other, simultaneously watching and listening to drama performances,"[10] would shortly be challenged and so resulted in the modernization of traditional theaters. That is to say, the Association's movie exhibitions were intended to invent the "modern" movie sphere wherein "modern" spectatorship, definitely divided from that of traditional theatergoing, was exclusively conducted; through this the YMCA desired to be a part of social reform, which originated from the May Fourth Movement as well as the new cultural elites in the new era.

With regard to the relationship between the movies and the disruption of social orders, some governmental and police agencies tried to keep "unfavorable" situations under control; however, Shanghai's semicolonized and dividedly ruled political circumstances did not allow them to successfully do so. Instead of controlling them, some organizations began to authorize "favorable" movies and other visual aids that were considered positive and useful for social reform. Accordingly, these movements were synchronized with conservatism prevalent in the United States, Great Britain, and Japan. At this juncture, we can say that the movie reform conducted by the Shanghai YMCA was a different version of this global conservatism. With its claim to be "wholesome and healthful," regardless of the dubiousness of the slogan itself, the Association's movie exhibition venue was the first institute that renewed the experience of moviegoing, which later became the norm during the reform and gentrifying of commercial movie houses in the 1920s. In addition, the YMCA also created an advantageous condition for developing China's earliest film productions, which aimed at reforming society through movies; establishment of the Film Section of the Commercial Press was one of the most significant by-products of the Association's movie activities. Not only were several members of the Film Section of that company members of the YMCA,[11] the section's activities also took on the Association's principle of "wholesome and healthful" moviegoing.

Although the film exhibitions by the Shanghai YMCA had a broad influence on China's film history, the historical significance of the Association's role has not been paid much attention by scholarship. Therefore, this chapter will reevaluate the Shanghai YMCA's film exhibitions, with focus on the

Association's earliest film activities. Although some difficulties remain in terms of primary source materials, I will nevertheless envisage what these film exhibition activities were like, as well as their significance for China's early film history.

CULTURAL SALON OF NEW ELITES: THE SOCIAL AND CULTURAL ROLE OF THE SHANGHAI YMCA

Shanghai became one of the most important commercial ports in China after the Opium War. The Bund, located running along the Huangpu River, which crossed the city vertically and divided it into east and west shores, was Shanghai's earliest developed area. Important administrative offices of the Municipal Council of International Settlement were located in this area, as well as skyscrapers of large-scale foreign and multinational firms, such as banks and trading companies. Northward from this area, the Garden Bridge was built across the Suzhou River and toward Hongkew, the opposite side of the Bund. In 1900, Robert E. Lewis, an American missionary, opened the Shanghai YMCA in Hongkew with the support of Cao Xuegeng. The early activities of the Association were simple and small-scale; the members held periodical meetings for prayer and gatherings for Bible readings at Lewis's home on Broadway Road (present-day Daming lu). When established, the Association was anxious that "Shanghai's culture and society was extravagant, which might wreck young men's morality"; hence the Association aimed "to plant three disciplines: the education of moral, intellectual, and physical discipline."[12] Although it had only thirty-five members just after establishment,[13] it grew rapidly when the meeting venue was transferred to the Bund; in 1902, membership reached more than 650.[14]

In 1907, the Shanghai YMCA moved its meeting venue to the Bund, No. 120 Sichuan Road. The building consisted of four flours with a modern design; there was a gymnasium with professional equipment at the ground level, and a reading room and library were located at the first level, where electric fans and cold drinks were provided to members during summer.[15] Members enjoyed the latest issues of magazines that many elites preferred to read, such as *Oriental Magazine*, *Women's Magazine*, and *Educational Magazine*, as well as *Science*, which was edited by the Chinese Association for Science, with the aim of expanding scientific knowledge among a broader range of readers.[16] The number of library visitors reached more than one hundred.[17] Another feature at the second level was the large hall; located at the west side of the building, this hall was capable of hosting seven hundred people. The "Martyrs' Hall," named after the martyrs of the Boxer Rebellion at the turn of the twentieth century, had a stage at the front and furnished theater seats imported from Grand Rapids, Michigan, a city famous for manufacturing furniture.[18] In 1915, the hall was also equipped with electric fans, so as to "keep the inside of the hall cool during the high-temperature season."[19] Moreover, the building ran a restaurant that provided both Chinese and Western cuisine, and had a modern stage where the members enjoyed performances of orchestras.[20] Overall, there seemed to be no question that the Association had great advantages in terms of its equipment and facilities compared to other educational and entertainment institutes.

Varied institutes for sports with brand-new equipment were another reason why many young people were attracted to the Shanghai YMCA. The Association offered not only a gymnasium and track field, but also a swimming pool—the first one in China—located inside the building and filled with warm water; the number of pool users reached more than twenty-seven thousand within one year of its opening.[21] Other examples that reinforce how attractive the Association was include its night school for education in various professions as well as its middle school, and its support for various types of education, including information about studying abroad. Its collective service regarding education increased the number of those that attended the Association. In 1918, addressing the increase in the number of automobiles, the Shanghai YMCA opened a driver's school; the Association had the good sense to take up such new opportunities. The YMCA building would be "easy to access" one could "conduct academic research, enjoy hobbies and entertainments, gentrify hygiene and cultivation, and seek morals." The Association took pride in its uniqueness, as there were "no such clubs like ours."[22] The Shanghai YMCA's practice of carrying out modern recreation was, indeed, quite radical.

After the system of the imperial examination was abolished in China, a number of newly emerged elites, instead of the traditional literati, became the core of society in large cities in China, and Shanghai was no exception. These newly established elites displayed common characteristics that were particular to their strata: speaking good English, having a strong and healthy body, and being profoundly interested in improving society. The Shanghai YMCA was the right venue for them if they hoped to succeed in business as well as in self-actualization; indeed, it became a cultural salon for them. Many of those that gathered at the venue did not have much interest in religion; for those who "wanted to learn English, and were interested in sports," the Shanghai YMCA was "extraordinarily attractive."[23] There seems to be no doubt that many of the big wheels in the political and commercial society of Shanghai were also the members of the Association. In addition, famous novelists, performers, and filmmakers joined the members' list, one after another.[24]

Among the various activities, occasional entertainment meetings allowed people without membership to participate. It is worth noticing that the entertainment meetings included magic shows, modern drama, singing, and dances—which were typical favorite performances for students' entertainment in that era—as well as speeches with magic lantern slides and movie exhibitions, that is, performances making use of modern media. The Shanghai YMCA recognized that such entertainment activities could supply, for its members and their families, opportunities to "enjoy the best sort of entertainment," and believed that "music, storytelling, sleight-of-hand, the illustrated lecture, and the moving pictures are principal features of such entertainments."[25] According to the Association, participating in its activities could not only improve social skills,[26] but also provide opportunities for the members to communicate with others of different ages and from different professions.[27] The members would get together at the Association beyond their traditional human networks, based on blood relationships and regional ties; in this modern sphere, members trained in modern learning and sociability, which was especially significant when considering the social role of the Association.[28] When entertainment meetings were initiated in the second decade of the twentieth century, the YMCA's activities for improving and educating society had just been set up. Members who had learned how to be "free of the suspicion of self-interest and trained in pooling the energies of the middle class" through the Association, "the only place where all the guilds could meet on neutral ground," were "in a unique position to bring together the scattered energies of different groups within the middle class," and had unequivocal influence to conduct social reforms.[29]

"WHOLESOME AND HEALTHFUL" ENTERTAINMENT: MOVIE EXHIBITIONS BY THE SHANGHAI YMCA

As indicated in table 7.1, the Association ran three different styles of movie exhibition events during the 1910s; among these, movie exhibitions "(1) as entertainment" and "(2) as visual aids for lectures (including utilizing lantern slides)" were the most prominent. It is notable that the aim of watching movies in this context was exclusively to create a "healthful" entertainment in order to improve society, while simultaneously strengthening members' chances of getting better occupations, which were novel attitudes for moviegoers. In the following sections, I will sketch the actual conditions of the Association's movie exhibitions as concretely as possible, while focusing especially on exhibition types (1) and (2), as previously mentioned.[30]

Movie Exhibitions as Entertainment

The Shanghai YMCA had begun to show movies as early as in 1907. According to a newspaper article,[31] movie exhibition was at first a onetime activity, not periodic. Because of the lack of available historical materials, there are no remaining sources that tell us anything about the actual situation of the exhibition, which makes it difficult to conclude to what extent the Association recognized the significance of movies for society. However, along with the proliferation of movie exhibitions, which developed early in the second decade of the century, the occasions for entertaining and communicating with members had started. Grand Entertainment and Members' Entertainment were the favorite occasions. When they were set up in 1907, such entertaining and communicating activities were primarily regarded as occasions for cultivating individuals; among them, meetings for Bible reading were the most popular. However, the aim of these activities was soon changed, and entertainment became the highest priority, while drama, games, and magic became the favorite programs.[32] Movie exhibition was no exception, and became highly popular. Due to its members' needs, the Association set up periodic movie programs in 1913, which ran once a month, apart from the summer and winter vacations. Two years later, along with the increased frequency of Grand Entertainment, which now occurred once a week, the frequency of movie exhibitions also increased rapidly, and the times and dates of the exhibitions were regularized to every Saturday at eight o'clock.[33]

Compared with other commercial movie exhibitions, the Shanghai YMCA's periodic movie exhibitions were advantageous in terms of the ticket price, the capacity, and the equipment at the venue, as well as its way of selecting movies. The representative movie exhibition venues in Shanghai during the 1910s are shown in table 7.2, and it is quite obvious that the Association, as a movie house, offered ticket prices that rivaled those of commercial movie houses, which offered the cheapest ticket prices.[34] Furthermore, the capacity of the Association's hall was in no way inferior to that of movie houses run by foreigners.[35] In the middle of the 1910s, the Association held its Grand Entertainment twenty-seven times a year, and almost three hundred members and related individuals, on average, took part in each of these meetings.[36] During this period, small and middle-scale movie houses held approximately four to five hundred seats. From these facts, it can be concluded that the Association's movie exhibition was inclusive and professional and that it was not inferior to commercial movie houses.

In its management of movie exhibitions, the Shanghai YMCA was superior to other movie houses. Utilizing ticket numbers for seats is one of many examples: the Association decided to sell tickets with seat numbers as early as in 1913, when it set up their once-a-month movie exhibition. Distributing commentary books or pamphlets is another good example. Although publishing such printed materials for audiences became more popular in the 1920s, the Association distributed these print media as early as 1914.

It is notable that the Association, unlike commercial movie houses, did not aim to earn a profit; in some cases exhibiting movies actually lost money.[37] In fact, the purpose of movie exhibitions was firmly set on advancing the Association's own principles. One important reason for the Association's movie exhibitions became popular was that many of the participants were newly emerged urban elites who spoke good English, had a substantial knowledge of commerce, science, and public health, and preferred physical training—that is to say, those who enjoyed the modern way of life and modern values. It can be said that the Association's principles of "wholesome and healthful" entertainment were welcomed widely by these urban elites.[38]

The wholesome fare that the Shanghai YMCA tried to offer can also be observed in the movies exhibited. Its principles for selecting movies appeared explicitly in magazine advertisement. The Association repeatedly stressed its way of "selecting academic and moral movies,"[39] offering a cheap price, but also supplying refined tastes that would be effective for both mind and body.[40] According to these sources, it is clear that the Association defined itself as utterly different from commercial movie houses.

Taking the above into consideration, one simple question arises: which films did the Association actually project? It is hard to specify the titles of the films that were screened, primarily because of the deficiency of historical source materials that indicate particular titles and other details about the movies that were exhibited, either in the Association's magazine or in advertisement for the events. Even if some sources remain, in most cases they are written in Chinese characters, thus lacking the original movie titles. In spite of this, reliable sources show that the Association's principle for selection was that movies "not only . . . be interesting, but also . . . have good influences on both mind and soul." Films about industry, education, comedy, and science were preferred.[41] Although highly distinguished movies were limited, the Association generally preferred movies with stories. Despite the Shanghai YMCA's desire for highly cultivated movie selection, the Association also wanted to entertain its members and their companions, who were family members or friends in most cases, by simultaneously supplying opportunities for communicating with each other as part of the movie exhibition events.

Among the story films screened by the Association, serial short movies were favorites, as well as films based on history and literature. Many French films were selected until the middle of the 1910s: for example, *Les Misérables* (dir. Albert Capellani, 1912, shown in May 1913), probably *Zigomar* (dir. Victorin-Hippolyte Jasset, 1911) and its predecessors (screened in September 1913),[42] and the *Fantômas* series directed by Louis Feuillade (screened intermittently from March to November 1914). In addition, the Association started to show documentary films about World War I much earlier than commercial movie houses (titles are unknown, screened September 1914). After regular movie screenings were set up in 1917, American films constituted the main program for the events. Literary films, such as *Julius Caesar,* based on the Shakespeare's play (title unknown, screened in September 1916) became popular, as well as other story films, especially those concerning World War I. Detective movies also entertained members, including serial short movies like *The Strange Case of Mary Page* (dir. J. Charles Haydon, 1916; from this series, four titles were screened in March 1917), and *Graft* (dir. Richard Stanton, 1916, screened from April to June 1916), as well as full-length detective feature films, *For the Defense* (dir. Frank Reicher, 1916, screened in November 1916). Those movies, especially the presentation of full-length feature films, were very rare and had not been exhibited in commercial movie houses in Shanghai, which exclusively and repeatedly screened short serials.[43] Exhibiting full-length feature films was a significant characteristic of the Association's movie selection.

Documentaries and newsreels reporting current world trends were selected as frequently as story films. Among them, those about World War I were highly popular. Other specific films included private travelogues shot on the occasion of members' trips abroad,[44] which in most cases were shot in the United States. An explicit, recurring trend of the movies selected by the Shanghai YMCA is that the Association recognized watching movies as pure recreation, rather than as a strictly academic activity. However, in regard to the attitude of the moviegoers, it was also significant that the members attending the movie exhibitions were more concentrated on the act of watching the movies than traditional theatergoers were, as they acquired new knowledge and enjoyed modern and intelligent recreation simultaneously by means of watching movies.

The reform of spaces for movie exhibition was another aim of the Shanghai YMCA's desire to provide "wholesome and healthful" entertainment. As previously mentioned, commercial movie houses in Shanghai in the 1910s were full of "vulgarity" and noise because of their unruly audiences. However, at the Association's movie exhibitions, "inside the venue there was neither noise nor smoking," and it was "quite orderly,"[45] because the audiences gathered, more or less, under the name of religious faith. Among the audience members were many interested in reforming society, and this kept away "immature" or "backward" audiences from a "modern" and "homogeneous" community.[46] In another words, the Shanghai YMCA tried to take going to the movies away from traditional theatergoing, and establish a space for modern movie exhibition in the context of modernization and the reform of society.

Movie and Lantern Slide Exhibitions as Visual Aids for Lectures

As early as 1903, the Shanghai YMCA had already utilized magic lantern slides as visual aids for lectures, with satisfying results.[47] However, it was not until 1911 that the Association started showing magic lantern slides abundantly and periodically. That year, Clarence H. Robertson, a missionary who held a doctorate in engineering, set up a series of science lectures with some other colleagues that used a large number of magic lantern slides. Robertson's science series consisted of five lectures regarding scientific knowledge, which were offered seventy-eight times during the first four years, and the number of attendees for each lecture reached more than three hundred.[48] In 1913, they again organized another lantern slide lecture on public health, aiming to reduce the risk of infection that had been threatening Chinese society. This lantern slide lecture, again, was a great success, which led the Association to establish an exclusive section regarding developing, promoting, and even producing magic lantern slides that were particular to their own purposes. For this reason, William Wesley Peter, who had formerly lived in Beijing as a medical missionary, was invited to the Shanghai YMCA to set up the Health Section under the jurisdiction of the Religious Department, which controlled the series of lectures. From that time on, the Association became more amenable to presentation of magic lantern slides, and later movies, as part of lecture series. In the second year after the establishment of this new section for lantern slide lectures, the Association began to produce its own lantern slides; under the direction of Peter, the lecture section designed, produced, and purchased visual aids for its lectures.

During the 1910s, other educational institutes, such as the Association for Social Education and the Society for Education in Kiangsu Province, took a great interest in lantern slides for pedagogical use and social reform. In 1914, a representative culture industry firm, Commercial Press, started selling magic lantern slides as visual aids for education, which satisfied the social demands for social education and reform. It is worth noting that, before the Commercial Press started selling sets of magic lantern slides, it held a premiere screening of them at the Shanghai YMCA.[49] This indicates that the audience that gathered at the Association had reliable aesthetic views of modern visual culture and was capable of reviewing them.

It can be said that lectures with visual aids were "wholesome" entertainment that met the demand of the Association's principles. According to the Association's annual reports, the lectures were held once a week, every Wednesday night at eight o'clock, and each time 100 to 250 audience members participated.[50] After 1917, another lecture series was set up, intended for moral education; these attracted 80 to 100 attendees.[51] During the 1910s, lantern slides were still the core medium for these lectures, but they were gradually replaced by movies after the middle of the decade.

The titles of lectures that used visual aids can be seen in table 7.3. It is evident that the Association, apart from religious titles, most likely favored topics regarding social education and public health and those that provided better knowledge of industrial techniques.[52] Shortly after the arrival of movies in Shanghai, a reviewer noticed that movies could be very useful for spreading knowledge, especially regarding techniques from the field of medical studies.[53] However, the commercial movie spaces in Shanghai were filled with "vulgarity," as previously mentioned, which made it impossible for movies to take any responsibility for social education and reform. It was the Shanghai YMCA that uncovered the educational value of movies, which had been buried beneath the context of the traditional amusement, and thereby offered many opportunities to enjoy the stimulating experiments in synergy between this modern visual medium and social education. Furthermore, the Association also eagerly supported E. D. Douty, a representative of the United States Conditioning and Testing Co., who visited the Association in order to develop the silk industry in the Far East and hold a lantern slide lecture in Shanghai (indicated in table 7.3) with the aim of improving industrial lectures.[54]

For improving industrial movies, the significance of the American consulate in Shanghai is unmistakable. Among the consulate's bureaucrats, Julean Arnold, a trade commissioner dispatched from the Bureau of Foreign and Domestic Commerce of the Commerce Department, played an important role in distributing American industrial movies. Having stayed in the Far East for many years, Arnold recognized the importance of movies for educational use.[55] World War I had just been declared, and the United States aimed to extract large profits from the Far East. At the end of 1918, the Consulate General of Shanghai held a large-scale industrial movie exhibition meeting with more than one thousand invited guests, including important politicians and influential persons from Shanghai's economic society.[56] Arnold was the guest of honor, which suggests that both the Shanghai Consulate General and the Bureau of Foreign and Domestic Commerce were aware of the significance of industrial movies in China.[57] The Shanghai YMCA and the Consulate General maintained a close relationship,[58] as the institutions shared common interests, even in the distributing of American industrial movies in China. From this point of view, it can also be said that the exhibition of industrial movies by the Shanghai YMCA promoted American interests against the Chinese movie market, and simultaneously created the foundation for American movies to be spread throughout China.

Throughout the 1910s, the relation between movies and education was strengthened; the Shanghai YMCA's movie exhibition activities contributed to this connection. Since the arrival of the May Fourth Movement, science and democracy had become the mainstay for China's establishment of modern culture, which involved a large number of intellectuals. In the middle of the 1910s, magazines about general interest and enlightenment of society, such as *Oriental Magazine* and *Women's Magazine*, set up columns that exclusively focused on science, aiming to spread the general and practical knowledge of science across a broader range of readers. In these science columns, academism was maintained to some extent; however, new scientific knowledge was also popularized so that ordinary readers could grasp it. Movies were introduced in these columns as an application of modern technology, primarily emphasizing the system and construction of projecting techniques. Movies also became a favorite theme in *Science*, a famous magazine edited and published by the Chinese Association for Science, which had a tremendous influence on the development of science knowledge in China, and which suggested that movies were—contrary to commercial movie exhibitions in which movies were consumed as entertainment products—accepted by all as a new and advanced modern technology. Eventually, during the second decade of the twentieth century in Shanghai, movies found and established a strong connection with education; the Shanghai YMCA was certainly one of the catalysts that brought about this connection.

The Shanghai YMCA's educational and industrial usage of movies makes it apparent what role the Association played in advocating movie exhibitions; namely, it recognized movies as an intelligent entertainment and utilized them not purely for sensory stimuli, but also to dispense knowledge. Movies, therefore, broke away from the cultural customs of traditional entertainment and were established as a contemporary medium.

CONCLUSION

The movie exhibition activities of the Shanghai YMCA seem to be erased from the history of Chinese cinema, primarily because of the anti-Christianity movement that reached its zenith in 1924 and the anti-imperialism that spread during the same era.[59] The improvement and development of commercial movie exhibition venues in the middle of the 1920s also eroded the advantages of the Association's film exhibitions: namely, their novelty and rarity.

Nevertheless, the Shanghai YMCA's movie exhibitions indeed demonstrated crucial influences. In particular, it cannot be ignored that the Association was well aware of the significance of utilizing movies as a visual tool for social education and proved this through its own operations. The direct and deep relationship between the YMCA and the Film Division of the Commercial Press, one of the earliest film producers in China, was significant. It was, according to the general discourse of Chinese film history, an American cinematographer traveling through China with his companions to shoot short movies in China who introduced a cinematographic camera to the

Commercial Press, inciting that company to produce movies. However, this was merely one of the motives for the firm to begin film production. Bao Qingjia, one of the important founders of the Film Division of the Commercial Press, was a member of the Shanghai YMCA and, when establishing the Division, he adhered to the same principles as the Association. The Association for Encouraging Good Will, a recreation group among workers at the Commercial Press, is a good example of how deeply the Film Division shared the Association's principles. Established in 1913 by a few workers, including Bao Qingjia, the Association for Encouraging Good Will declared that its goas was "educating good workers through the three principles of intellectual, moral, and physical discipline," and the Shanghai YMCA was the very venue of these activities.[60] Thus, the Film Division of the Commercial Press maintained close relations with the Association; the Division learned skills in producing magic lantern slides and movies from the Association, as well as how to develop various visual aids for social education.[61]

Moreover, the Shanghai YMCA strongly stressed the importance of improving movie exhibition venues and equipment. He Tingran was one of the enthusiastic members of the Association, who later became a representative entrepreneur of a movie house business in Shanghai, which maintained the principle of supplying "highly and purely cultivated" movies.[62] Graduated from St. John's University in 1916, He Tingran taught English at a school that was run by the Association, and also worked for Isis Theatre, the first movie house established by a Chinese. As the manager of this theater, He engaged

Table 7.1 Three Styles of Movie Exhibition by the Shanghai YMCA in the 1920s

Style	Organized by	Aim of exhibition	Frequency of exhibition	Primary type of movie exhibited
1. As entertainment	Social Department (formerly Department of Friendship and Entertainment)	Entertainment	Once a week	Feature films (long length, serials) Travelogues, newsreels, etc.
2. As visual aid for lectures (including utilizing lantern slides)	Social Department / Religious Department	Entertainment / Social Education	Once or twice a week[a]	Industrial movies Educational movies
3. As other style	Each related department	Recreation	Irregular	Feature films Newsreels, etc.

Source: Issues of *Shanghai qingnian* and *Shenbao*.

[a]Although lectures were given once or twice a week, not every lecture exhibited movies or slides.

Table 7.2. Movie Houses in Shanghai during the 1910s

Type of exhibition venue		Name of venue	Established in	Number of seats	Most expensive ticket	Least expensive ticket
Commercial exhibition venue run by foreigners		Apollo	1910	700	[1.5 yuan]	[1 yuan]
		Embassy	1914	850	[1.5 yuan]	[1 yuan]
		New Helen	1913	500	0.3 yuan	0.1 yuan
Commercial exhibition venues (run by Chinese)	Movie houses	Isis	1917	1,000	0.5 yuan	0.1 yuan
		Republic	1915	400	0.2 yuan	0.1 yuan
	Amusement halls	New World	1915	[600]	0.3 yuan (admission fee)	
		Great World	1917	[600]	0.2 yuan (admission fee)	
Non-commercial exhibition venues		Shanghai YMCA	1900	[800]	0.2 yuan (if not holding the membership)	0.1 yuan (if holding the membership)

Source: S. Cheng, ed., *China Cinema Year Book*. Numbers of seats in brackets are derived from C. J. North, *Chinese Motion Picture Market* (U.S. Department of Commerce, 1927); ticket prices from ads in *Shenbao* in January 1918; and prices in brackets from *Film Magazine* 1, no. 2.

Table 7.3. Lectures with Visual Aids at the Shanghai YMCA in 1917

Date	Subject	Lecturer	Type of visual aid
March 28	Brain health	Yu Huangbin (medical doctor)	Movie
April 8	Rebirth and renewal	Guo Bingjun (Commercial Press, the YMCA member)	Movie
June 27	Education of blind children	Fu Bulan (president of Shanghai school for the blind	Lantern slides and movie
July 6	Advantages and disadvantages of usage of Chinese silk by American silk industry and Japanese methods for sericulture	D. E. Douty (United States Conditioning and Testing Co.)	Movie
September 9	Christianity can improve the society	Feng Jianguang (minister)	Movie
November 14	Individual hygiene	Hu Xuanming (alumnus of Johns Hopkins University, medical doctor)	Movie
December 28	Methods of farming and agriculture	Zhang Tiancai (alumnus of Cornell University)	Movie

Source: Issues of *Shanghai qingnian* and *Shenbao*.

in various improvements and developments, which included programming loftier movies and improving movie pamphlets. In 1926, He became independent from Isis and established his own movie exhibition network, after which he dominated Shanghai's movie market, with the aim of modernizing movie exhibition circles, until he moved to Hong Kong after World War II. As a scholar of Chinese cinema history, Xiao Zhiwei, points out, "Movie house etiquette in China was developed deliberately and consciously by the modernizing elite in order to shift away from and provide a contrast to the traditional theater."[63] According to the arguments above, by using the term "elite," Xiao does not merely intend its surface meaning, but also includes merchants who sought profits as well as a loftier vision of social well-being. He Tingran is a typical example of such a newly emerged merchant. He maintained few documents that showed his principles or philosophy, as he was not an intellectual who expressed his ideas with words. However, some newspaper and magazine articles reported on his way of managing film theater companies, and clearly show that he shared the Association's principles for entertainment: namely, contributing to society by supplying "wholesome and healthful" movies.[64]

The Boy Scout Section of the Shanghai YMCA renovated the building in 1914 and opened a new garden on the roof; from this open-roof garden, the panoramic scenery of the entire city of Shanghai could be enjoyed. Especially at night, when the commercial neon signs of Great World, one of Shanghai's famous amusement halls, shone like stars, a large number of brilliant neon signs spread through the nightly scene.[65] During the 1910s, the open-roof garden was the primary venue for the Association's recreation events, during which a cool breeze outside the building could be enjoyed: members enjoyed their "wholesome and healthful" entertainment while watching the neon signs, symbols of the "vulgarity" of commercial entertainments. That venue emerged as the opposite of vulgarity, and contributed to the establishment of a new film culture in China. The attempt by the Shanghai YMCA to break from traditional theatergoing and construct a new way of viewing movies promoted more space for modern moviegoers.

Notes

1. The original work on this chapter was published in *Japanese Journal of Image Arts and Sciences* 90 (2013): 41–56, while the Chinese version appeared in *Communication and Society* 29 (2014): 151–175. Each version was supported by Grants-in-Aid for Sci-

entific Research funded by the Japan Society for the Promotion of Science (21720129 and 25870929). In the English version, I have slightly adjusted the first section according to the reviewer's comments.

2. Zhiwei Xiao, "Movie House Etiquette Reform in Early-Twentieth-Century China," *Modern China* 32, no. 4 (2006): 516.

3. Ken, "Yingxi guanzhong zhi shijie" [Ten Prohibitions of Moviegoers], *Film Magazine* 1, no. 3 (1922): 202. Citation refers to the following reprint edition: Jiang Yasha, Jing Li, and Chen Zhanqi, eds., *Zhongguo zaoqi dianying huakan* [Chinese Early Movie Magazines], vol. 1 (Beijing: Quanguo tushuguan wenxian suowei fuzhi zhongxin, 2004). This article appeared in one of the earliest movie magazines in China and itemized ten prohibitions that would improve people's manners in movie houses; these included refraining from "putting your legs under your front chair" and "speaking in loud voices that bother calmness and comfort," as well as recommendations "to put your hand on the seat when you stand up"; with respect to hygiene of the movie houses, it also prohibited "to bring food with hulls," "to wipe your snot on the surface of the chair," as well as "to smoke inside the auditorium, so as not to obscure the screen with smoke". Furthermore, some reminiscences regarding the early memories of movie houses in Shanghai, for example, A'na pointed out the loudness and bad manners at Hongkew Cinema and Victoria Cinema in the following article: "Shanghai dianyingyuan de jinxi" [Old and New Stories about Film Theaters in Shanghai: Part I], *Shenbao*, November 2, 1938, 13. As to the manners of moviegoers and improving the circumstances of movie houses, there were continued arguments among journalists until the middle of the 1930s. Among them, the most representative "bad" behavior was the following: "Inside a small or middle scale movie house, if there appeared a man and a woman kissing on the screen, the audiences get excited, shouting 'Good!' and whistling too enthusiastically, which makes me suffer a headache" ("Dianying zatan (er)" [A Sequel to Miscellaneous Impressions about Movies], *Shenbao*, January 14, 1925, 8).

4. Great World, a famous amusement hall, was one explicit example of the "immorality" of those venues, which "was full of prostitutes in such quantity that almost every guest could get one"; Nakagawa Yoichi, "Shina no eiga" [Movies in China], *Eiga jidai* (1926): 34. Great World was also notorious as a spot where many couples could meet in secret and enjoy adultery (Lubinsheng, "Jiating zhi heimu" [Gossips about Families], in *Zhongguo heimu daguan* [Collections of Gossips in China], the first issue of vol. 1 (Shanghai: Zhonghua tushu jicheng gongsi, 1918), 5–6.

5. For example, *Her Painted Hero* (dir. F. Richard Jones, 1915), exhibited at the Apollo Theatre in June 1918, was criticized by one person who accused it of containing a woman's nudity. The audience member wrote a letter and reported it to the Municipal Council of International Settlement, which conducted an investigation regarding the movie ("Viloudaki to Canning," June 5, 1918, U1-2-548. Shanghai Municipal Archives). With respect to the control "immoral" movies by the Shanghai Municipal Council, see Zhao Weiqing, *Shanghai gonggong zujie dianying shencha (1927–1937)* [The Film Cen-

sorship of the Shanghai International Settlement (1927–1937)] (Shanghai: Shanghai jiaotong daxue chubanshe, 2012), especially chapter 2.

6. "Maitian faxian nushi sizhi" [The Fourth Report on Finding a Woman's Body in a Wheat Field], *Xinwenbao*, June 19, 1920, n.p.

7. In his reminiscences, the famous film director Cheng Bugao describes how many crimes of the era were influenced by American detective movies and how those criminals learned criminal techniques through such movies. Cheng Bugao, *Yingtan yijiu* [Reminiscences of the Film World] (Beijing: Zhongguo dianying chubanshe, 1983), 38–41.

8. The World Chinese Student's Federation and the Society for Education in Kiangsu Province were the representatives.

9. Providing "wholesome and healthful entertainment" was the aim of the recreation meetings by the Shanghai YMCA (Shanghai YMCA, "Annual Report for 1917," *Shanghai qingnian* 17, no. 11 (1918): 17).

10. Xu Jianxiong, *Jingju yu Shanghai dushi shehui (1867–1949)* [Peking Opera and the Urban Society in Shanghai] (Shanghai: Shanghai sanlian shudian, 2012), 238.

11. The list of the Association's members, including employees of the Commercial Press, appears in "Huiyuan timing" [List of Members], which was published in *Shanghai qingnian* 16, no. 31 (1917): n.p. *Shanghai qingnian* was edited in both Chinese and English by the Shanghai YMCA; because some of the early Chinese issues of the magazine were deficient in page numbers, I am unable to list some the page numbers of the sources from this magazine.

12. "Qingnianhui ershinian lai zhi xiaoshi" [A Short History of the YMCA's Last Twenty Years], *Shenbao*, April 20, 1918.

13. Shanghai YMCA, "Benhui huiwu baogao jilue" [A Brief Report of the Association], *Shanghai qingnian* 18, no. 43 (1919): n.p.

14. Kenneth Latourette, *A History of Christian Missions in China* (Piscataway, NJ: Gorgias Press, 2009), 586.

15. For the original literature, see the Shanghai YMCA's report "Rizeng yuesheng" [Gradual Development], *Huiwu zazhi* 6, no. 18 (1908): n.p., the predecessor of *Shanghai qingnian*. Because of the difficulty in accessing the original source, I have referred to the phrases quoted in the following source: Zhang Zhiwei, *Jiduhua yu shisuhua de zhengzha: Shanghai jidujiao qingnianhui yanjiu 1900–1922* [The Struggle between Christianity and Secularization: Research on the Shanghai YMCA, 1900–1922] (Taipei: Taiwan daxue chubanshe, 2010), 192.

16. Shanghai YMCA, "Cangshushi tonggao" [An Announcement from the Library], *Shanghai qingnian* 16, no. 32 (1917): n.p.

17. Shanghai YMCA, "Qingnianhui cangshushi qishi" [Information from the YMCA Library], *Shanghai qingnian* 14, no. 15 (1915): 8.

18. Robert E. Lewis, *Search of Far Horizons* (West Conshohocken, PA: Infinity Publishing, 2003), 100.

19. Shanghai YMCA, "Jiaoji bu" [Department of Friendship and Entertainment], *Shanghai qingnian* 14, no. 24 (1915): 6.

20. Regarding the equipment in the new building, see the following source: Robert E. Lewis, "Report of Robert E. Lewis, Shanghai, 1907," in *The Archives of the Young Men's Christian Association in China at the University of Minnesota Libraries: The Annual Reports 1896–1949*, ed. Chen Su, Dagmar Getz, and David Klaassen (Guilin, Guangxi: Guangxi Normal University Press, 2012), 3:79.

21. Shanghai YMCA, "Annual Report for Year 1916," *Shanghai qingnian* 16, no. 8 (1917): 11.

22. Shanghai YMCA, "Qingnian julebu" [The Club of the Youth], *Huiwu zazhi* 6, no. 18 (1908): n.p. Due to the difficulty in accessing the primary source, I refer to the quotation in the following source: Zhang, *Jiduhua yu shisuhua de zhengzha*, 191.

Other magazine articles reported on the pride of the Shanghai YMCA in how modern its services were; the Association's building was equipped with new furniture and electronic fans and provided cold drinks as well as ice cream, which proved the Association was "not to be compared with other amusement open-roof gardens in Shanghai" (Shanghai YMCA, "Jiaoji bu," 6). Compared to the Carlton Hotel, one of the finest hotels in the city, the services and equipment of the Association were indeed in no way inferior.

23. Hiratsuka Yoshinori, *Hiratsuka Yoshinori chosaku shū II: Chūgoku kindai kyōikushi* [Selected Works by Hiratsuka Yoshinori II: The Modern History of Education in China] (Tokyo: Kyōiku kaihatsu kenkyūsyo, 1985), 142. Original work published 1942.

24. As to the relation between the Association and the politics and financial society in Shanghai, see Zhang, *Jidujiao yu shisuhua de zhengzha*, 157–172. With respect to its relation with Shanghai's film and arts circles, the following persons were members of the Association: Yuan Lüdeng, one of the directors of Star Motion Picture Company, Fang Shubo and Bian Shuying, both engaged in the management of Star Motion Picture Company: Bao Qingjia from the Film Division of the Commercial Press; Shi Shanyuan and Lu Jie, core members of the Film Association in China; Tang Jishan, a member of United Photoplay; He Tingran, the owner of a representative movie house chain in Shanghai, and Wang Dungen, a multitalented artist also known as journalist and drama critic.

25. Shanghai YMCA, "Annual Report for Year 1915," *Shanghai qingnian*, n.d.: 9.

26. Shanghai YMCA," Annual Report for Year 1915."

27. Shanghai YMCA, "Minguo wunian ji yujiuyiliunian Shanghai jidujiao qingnianhui baogao" [Social Department, Annual Report for 1916 by the Shanghai YMCA], *Shanghai qingnian* 16, no. 8 (1917): n.p.

28. Several articles in the Association's magazine repeatedly stressed the importance of new communication between young men beyond their traditional ties (Shanghai YMCA, "Minguo wunian ji yujiuyiliunian Shanghai jidujiao qingnianhui baogao," 19; Hu Yongqi, "Qingnianhui yu qingnian zhi guanxi" [The Relation between the YMCA and Young Men], *Shanghai qingnian* 17, no. 1 (1918): n.p.)

29. Shirley S. Garret, *Social Reformers in Urban China: The Chinese Y.M.C.A., 1895–1926* (Cambridge, MA: Harvard University Press, 1970), 127–128. According to Alain Corbin, recreational activities in the United States developed as self-training and self-

empowerment, rather than as entertainment during spare time in between work (Alain Corbin, dir., *Rejā no tanjō* [The Birth of Recreation], trans. Watanabe Kyōko (Tokyo: Hujiwara shoten, 2010), 13–14. Original work published as *L'avènement des loisirs, 1850–1960* (Paris: Aubier, 1995). Therefore, the Shanghai YMCA's recreational activities can be said to reify the principle of the American way of recreation.

30. Here I want to make a brief remark on the third type of movie exhibition run by the Association. This type was conducted primarily on the occasion of various religious activities, meetings for special events, as well as ceremonies arranged by the schools that were run by the Association. During religious activities, movies were often screened with a somewhat religious subject, although among the various movies exhibited on the other occasions, majorities were for entertainment purposes.

31. "Qingnianhui xuyan dianguang yingxi" [The Sequel Movie Exhibition by the YMCA], *Shenbao*, September 27, 1907, 19.

32. Zhang, *Jiduhua yu shisuhua de zhengzha*, 199.

33. Shanghai YMCA, "Qing kan yingxi" [Watch the Movies], *Shanghai qingnian* 16, no. 48 (1917): n.p.

34. In other cases, showing a membership card instead of paying the admission fee was also popular.

35. Until the middle of the 1920s, the audience of the Carlton Theatre, Apollo Theatre, Embassy Theatre, and Isis Theatre, which exclusively exhibited European and American movies, were primarily foreigners and the upper-class Chinese, though most of those who preferred attending Hongkew Cinema, New Helen Theatre, Republic Theatre, Faguo Theatre, and Chapei Cinema were middle- and lower-class Chinese and children ("Dianying zatan" [Miscellaneous Impressions about Movies], *Shenbao*, January 13, 1925, 8).

36. According to annual reports published by the Association, the number of participants in Grand Entertainment in each year were as follows: in 1915, 33 occasions with 11,356 participants: in 1916, 23 occasions with 8,449 participants: in 1917, 22 occasions with 4,980 participants: in 1918, 32 occasions with 9,262 participants: in 1919, 24 occasions with 7,854 participants.

37. The activities provided by the Shanghai YMCA were mainly supported by membership fees, tuition at its attached schools, admission fees for the gymnasium, and donations; therefore, it can be said that the ticket fees for the Association's movie exhibitions were not for gaining profits. The report on its activities in 1919 indicates that the income of the Social Department, which managed various entertainment activities, remained at only 211.35 yuan, while its expenses exceeded 1,000 yuan (Shanghai YMCA, "Annual Report for Year 1919," *Shanghai qingnian* 19, no. 8 [1920]: 31–33). Although the YMCA's income was apparently deficient compared to its expenses, it sometimes did not dare to ask ticket fees, as aforementioned, which implies that the Association's movie exhibitions were not aimed at profits. Another point worth noting is that the rental fees for movie prints for the Association's activities were extraordinarily inexpensive. According to a newspaper report, the rental fee for each one thousand feet of newsreel,

produced by the Film Division of Commercial Press, was 180 to 190 yuan. The report also indicates that one thousand feet of a regular feature-length film was rented at 220 yuan, while *Flesh Soup* (*Xiaofu geng*, dir. Ren Pengnian, 1922), a longer feature film with eight reels, was rented at 2,000 yuan ("Shangwu yinshuguan suochu yingpian zhi tongji" [Statistics about the Movies Produced by Commercial Press], *Shenbao*, May 10, 1923, 17). On the other hand, the rental fees for movie prints exhibited at the Association in 1919 were only 266.38 yuan overall (Shanghai YMCA, "Annual Report for Year 1919," 33). Furthermore, the film prints were often forwarded from other YMCAs, in different areas, to the Shanghai YMCA, which suggests that the Association established its own network of film distribution in the area, which made it possible for the Association to provide such cheaply priced movie screenings. In the Chinese version of this article published in *Communication and Society*, the figures listed for the Social Division's income and expenses for film rental fees in 1919 contained typographical errors; the numbers presented in this English version are correct.

38. Zhang points out: "The reason Grand Entertainment gained such popularity was deeply related with the strong social demand for entertainments, as well as the deficiency of amusement venues during the 1910s" (*Jiduhua yu shisuhua de zhengzha*, 201).

39. "Qingnianhui jinwan zhi lequ" [Tonight's Entertainments at YMCA], *Shenbao*, April 13, 1918, 10.

40. Ad of the Shanghai YMCA, *Yingxi zazhi* 1, no. 2 (1922): 80. Reprint, Jiang, Jing, and Chen, *Zhongguo zaoqi dianying huakan*, 166.

41. Shanghai YMCA, "Qing kan yingxi."

42. The particular title of the series that was screened cannot be distinguished, as the newspaper advertisements for the movie exhibition only indicate the name of the protagonist, "Nieke wentuo zhentan an" [The detective cases of Nick Carter], and do not include the original title (ad for Shanghai YMCA movie exhibition, *Shenbao*, September 24–26, 1913).

43. With respect to the exhibition of foreign movies in Shanghai during this era, there have not been enough inclusive works; however, Qin Xiqing's "1920 niandai: minzu rentong yu Zhongguo zaoqi dianying de queli" [The 1920s: National Identity and Establishment of the Early Chinese Cinemas], (PhD diss., Film Art Research Center of China, 2006) provides an elemental but essential understanding of it.

44. Exhibiting travelogues shot by Tang Jishan, one of the founders of the China Photoplay Company, from his trip to the United States are one representative example of such movies. See "Qingnianhui jinwan zhi yingxi" [Tonight's Movies at the YMCA], *Shenbao*, April 20, 1918, 11.

45. Shanghai YMCA, "Tonglehui zhaochang kaihui" [Grand Entertainment Is Opening as Announced], *Shanghai qingnian* 16, no. 37 (1917): n.p.

46. The Association's tendency to establish its own institutes, instead of attending those of the local society, for avoiding "vulgarity" is also recognized in the case of the barber inside the Association's building. According to the Association's explanation, as the ordinary barbers in the city were much inferior in terms of hygiene and held no official

license, the Association uniquely opened its own barbershop for its members (Shanghai YMCA, "Qingnianhui lifachu" [The Barber of the YMCA], *Shanghai qingnian* 14, no. 15 (1915): 14).

47. Charles W. Harvey, "Annual Reports of Foreign Secretaries of the International Committee, October 1, 1902 to September 30, 1903," in Su, Getz, and Klaassen, *Archives*, 2:164.

48. William Wesley Peter, "Annual Report for the Year Ending September 30, 1914," in Su, Getz and Klaassen, *Archives*, 7:192.

49. Ad for Commercial Press, *Xinwenbao*, January 11, 1914. Regarding the production of lantern slides by Commercial Press, Huang Dequan's article ("Shanghai shangwu yinshuguan chuchuang huodong yingpian kao" [Study of Early Filmmaking by Commercial Press in Shanghai], *Contemporary Cinema* 170 (2010): 56–63) presents a predominant and significant study. However, while it can be determined at what particular time Commercial Press started to produce lantern slides by merely employing historical resources—including the diary of the founder of that company—these sources do not pay attention to why and how they started to do so in terms of their relationship with the Shanghai YMCA.

50. According to the annual reports of the Association, the numbers of lecture series held on every Wednesday night and their attendants were as follows: in 1916, they were held 23 times with 6,154 attendants; in 1917, 50 times with 5,167 attendants; in 1918, 52 times with 5,229 attendants; in 1919, 23 times with 5,140 attendants.

51. "Minguo qinian ji yiqian jiubai shiba nian Shanghai jidujiao qingnainhui baogao—deyu bu baogao" [Report of the Lecture Department, in the Annual Report for 1918 by Shanghai YMCA], *Shanghai qingnian* 18, no. 4 (1919): n.p.

52. Overall, the screening of travelogues was also popular in the series, with a few exceptions where movies were provided that were not related to the theme of the lectures.

53. An allegedly first report of watching movies in China, "Weichunyuan guanyingxi ji xuqiangao" [Sequel Article about Watching Movies in Weichunyuan], *Xinwenbao*, June 13, 1897, n.p., pointed out the effectiveness of utilizing movies for learning medical techniques and other practical skills.

54. E. A. Turner, "Annual Report for the Year Ending September 30, 1917," in Su, Getz, and Klaassen, *Archives*, 11:79.

55. Arnold believed that various types of educations were needed in China that went beyond classrooms; he suggested that various styles of media, including lecture meetings, printed media, and movies, would be helpful for education ("Shina to kinsei teki kōgyō (shita)" [The Sequel of New China, and Modern Commerce and Industry], *Taiwan nichinichi shimpō*, February 22, 1918, n.p.).

56. The industrial movie exhibition was held on December 18 of that year. The exhibition was held from 9:00 p.m. until 11:45 p.m., and consisted of the following titles: the first section projected *How to Manage Trades and Management of Retail Shops*, *How to Produce Glasses*, and *Short Comedy: The Lamb*, while the second section screened *The*

Latest Way to Manufacture Watches, *The Process of Producing Exquisite Crafts*, and *Short Comedy: Revealing That Man's Ghost* ("Guan Meiguo shiye yingpian ji" [A Record of Watching American Industrial Movies], *Shenbao*, December 19, 1918, 10).

57. See "Guan Meiguo shiye yingpian ji." Other guests at the exhibition included Zhu Baosan and Lao Jingxiu from financial society in Shanghai; and Ge Gonzhen, Zhao Zhonghui, and Zhu Shaobing from the journalist community. There were also representative individuals from famous foreign firms and institutes, such as Standard-Vacuum Oil Co., Steiner & Co. Representatives from the educational society also participated, which included G. A. Fitch and Li Qifan from the Shanghai YMCA, Zhu Youyu and Naodeng (allegedly the name of a foreign teacher) from Saint John's University, as well as Kuang Fuzhuo and Jiang Menglin from the Commercial Press.

58. Zhang, *Jiduhua yu shisuhua de zhengzha*, 159.

59. About the influence of the anti-Christianity movement against the Association, see Zhang, *Jiduhua yu shisuhua de zhengzha*, 382–389.

60. "Gongjie qingnianhui zhi chengji" [The Activities of the Young Men Association in the Laborers' Society], *Shenbao*, September 15, 1914, 10.

61. For example, just after the Shanghai YMCA set up its lecture series with lantern slides, it imported slides from the United States. Later, when the Association decided to produce its own original slides, it entrusted the production to the Commercial Press (G. H. Cole, "Annual Report for the Year Ending September 30, 1914," in Su, Getz, and Klaassen, *Archives*, 7:170). Another example shows the deep relation between these two institutes; when the Film Division of the Commercial Press was shooting one of its earliest newsreels, *The Fifth Athletic Meeting in Far East*, W. W. Peter, a significant person who managed the visual aids of the Association, supervised the filmmaking ("Shangwu yinshuguan huodongbu jinkuang" [The Recent Situation of the Film Division of Commercial Press], *Shenbao*, June 11, 1921, 11).

62. "Beijing daxiyuan kaimu guanggao" [Ad for the Opening of the Peking Theatre], *Shenbao*, November 7, 1926, 1.

63. Xiao, "Movie House Etiquette Reform," 515.

64. The Shanghai Amusement Company, a film theater company run by He Tingran, had several directors that were simultaneously members of the Association. Regarding this issue, see Yoshino Sugawara, "Beyond the Boundary between China and the West: Changing Identities of Foreign-Registered Film Theatre Companies in Republican Shanghai," *Journal of Chinese Cinemas* 9, no. 1 (2015): 23–41.

65. Shanghai YMCA, "Jiaoyi dahui zhi sheng" [The Success of the Member's Entertainment], *Shanghai qingnian* 16, no. 27 (1917): n.p. The open-roof night gardens where people could enjoy eating and drinking among various attractions gained popularity just after the start of stable electricity distribution in 1913. Identical to the case of the barber aforementioned in this chapter, the Association's summer entertainment on the roof garden of its own building provided a "healthful" night garden, without "vulgarity."

CHAPTER 8

Movie Matchmakers

The Intermediaries between Hollywood and China in the Early Twentieth Century

Yongchun Fu

This chapter considers at length the perception and practices of intermediaries during the early twentieth century, with the focus on their contributions to the Chinese film industry. It is a cliché to say that Chinese filmmakers learned from Hollywood in the first half of the twentieth century. However, major executives and directors in the Chinese film industry such as Zhang Shichuan never visited Hollywood. Their perceptions of the American film industry were largely obtained through American filmmakers who came to China and through watching American movies, many of which were imported by Chinese distributors. Such an interesting phenomenon calls for light on a group of figures who have long since passed into oblivion or are misunderstood in the history of Chinese cinema: the intermediaries. Who are they? To what extent were they responsible for the expansion of Hollywood business in China? What did the intermediaries bring to the Chinese film industry? In the literature on Chinese film history fueled by nationalism, a number of intermediaries are either buried in the dust or labeled as "aggressors" or "traitors," since they are regarded as helping the expansion of Hollywood's business and thus oppressing the domestic film industry. In my view, this nationalistic film historiography reduces the complex role that the intermediaries played in Chinese film history. Employing extensive research in Chinese and American archives, this chapter attempts to demonstrate that the intermediaries served as "matchmakers" between Hollywood and the Chinese film industry. I argue that the intermediaries bridged the film industries of Hollywood and China and made significant contributions to the evolution of the Chinese film industry.

Intermediary in this chapter refers to the figures and enterprises responsible for the intercommunication between Hollywood and the Chinese film industry. Hao Yen-p'ing's seminal account on the compradors in modern China provides an excellent model for my study on the intermediaries between Hollywood and the Chinese film industry.[1] Hao articulates the significance of the comprador as a middleman to China's early industrialization. In contrast to the criticism that the compradors were the "spearheads of foreign colonialism and economic imperialism," Hao points out that the compradors in some extent "competed with foreign merchants in the management of modern enterprises, and thus in a way functioned to prevent the unchecked foreign incursion."[2] Xiao Zhiwei is one pioneer who notices the significance of the intermediaries in Chinese film studies. Xiao incisively introduces the notion of "in-between production" into the history of how distributors appropriated Hollywood content in the Chinese cultural context.[3] "In-between production" refers to a process of "repetitions, evocations, translations and reproductions" in areas like the introduction of English words into Chinese in linguistic studies.[4] In the vein of Hao and Xiao, I intend to address the functions of the intermediaries between Hollywood and the Chinese film industry in the early twentieth century. Two types of intermediaries are stressed here, that is, (1) American citizens who came to China for the film business, exemplified by William Henry Lynch; and (2) Chinese merchants who did business with American corporations, in particular, film distributors, exemplified by Lo Kan (Lu Gun, Lu Gen). It should be noted that the intermediaries between Hollywood and China are not limited to these two groups. The students who returned from an American study background, such as Hong Shen, marked themselves as prominent intermediaries in Chinese film history by introducing American film knowledge and importing sound film equipment to the Chinese film industry. In addition, it is necessary to point out that the functions of intermediaries are reciprocal. While this study focuses on the influence of the intermediaries from Hollywood on China, the opposite deserves critical attention as well.

To provide a background, I start with a brief introduction of the nationalistic approach to Chinese film studies and the attitudes of its proponents about intermediaries. The chapter then follows the contributions of American practitioners to the Chinese film industry, a group of intermediaries who are labeled "aggressors" in nationalistic writings. I identify William Lynch, the cinematographer of the Asiatic Film Company, as someone who played a crucial role in developing the skills and careers of the first generation of Chinese directors. The chapter then investigates Chinese merchants distributing Hollywood films in China, as the other type of intermediary. On one hand, these intermediaries helped the exploration by Hollywood in China as a critical sector in Hollywood's strategy of localization, while on the other hand they benefited the Chinese film industry in various ways. The chapter concludes by suggesting in broader terms that patriotic sentiment should not be the only criterion in the study of Chinese film history.

NATIONALISM IN CHINESE FILM STUDIES

The nationalistic approach dominates the study of Chinese film history. Nationalism is defined as a concept that emphasizes "national identity as that aspect of individuals' self-image that is tied to their nation."[5] China's nationalism emerged along with the rise of the nation-state in modern China from the late nineteenth century. Nationalism grew into a major ideology of the Nationalist Party in the first half of the twentieth century. The nationalistic approach in the history texts coincides with the broad social context. As early as the 1930s, Gu Jianchen, one of the first film historians, subscribed to nationalism in his research.[6] Gu's nationalistic sentiment is well expressed in his statement on the cinema department of the British American Tobacco Company, which produced films with Chinese casts and purchased small cinemas in 1920s China. The commercial expansion of the cinema department, from Gu's point of view, was an example of "economic oppression" of the Chinese film industry.[7]

The nationalistic sentiment went further after the Communist Party takeover in 1949. According to Dirlik, Mao Zedong developed his ideas by "subsum[ing] Marxism with nationalism" and structured Chinese society with such a theory in mind.[8] In *History of the Development of Chinese Film*, Cheng Jihua and his colleagues consciously employ Mao Zedong's thought in their study of Chinese film history. Cheng and his colleagues consider Chinese film history to be a struggle between "the progressive culture for socialism, national liberation and people's democracy" and "imperialist and other reactive cultures."[9] The contribution of the Chinese "national capitalists" prior to 1949 is only acknowledged due to their efforts to build a national film industry and their patriotic sentiments. American merchants, together with Hollywood films, are regarded as a force of economic and cultural aggression against the national industry.

Within the theoretical framework of "national cinema," the recent literature avoids the overideologization found in the previous literature; however, a focus on national building makes the role of foreigners a blind spot. In the wake of focusing on national cinema, Hu Jubin positions nationalism as a principal axis in Chinese films prior to 1949.[10] According to Hu, "What the Chinese cinema, as a national cinema, participated in and reflected, was a nationalism about politics."[11] Hu divides the pre-1949 history of Chinese cinema into five periods and characterizes each period with a different type of nationalism. For instance, the 1920s saw the upsurge of industrial nationalism, which prioritized "the establishment of the film industry as the Chinese nation's domestic industry."[12] However, an exaggerated emphasis on nationalism in the Chinese film industry is liable to neglect the contribution of figures who had few connections with nation-building. For instance, American film merchants, in Hu's account, are merely the rivals of the Chinese national industry, whose intention was to monopolize the film industry.[13] Apart from their stimulating the "advocacy of a national cinema" in China, Hu remains silent on the contributions of American merchants to the domestic film industry.[14]

AMERICAN FILM PRACTITIONERS IN CHINA

In Chinese film history, Zhang Shichuan is known as the investor in, founder of, and executive of Mingxing (Star Motion Picture Company) from its inception. In addition, Zhang, together with Zheng Zhengqiu, is regarded as the "Father of Chinese Cinema." During his forty-year film career, Zhang Shichuan directed over 150 silent and sound films. However, prior to becoming involved in the film business, Zhang confessed that he seldom watched movies.[15] It was his experience as director of the Asiatic Film Company that inspired his interests in filmmaking and increased his film knowledge. The Asiatic Film Company was the first professional company in Chinese film history, but with staff from the United States and China. The following passage examines the contributions of the American film practitioners to the Chinese film industry, with special attention on William H. Lynch, the cinematographer and executive of the Asiatic Film Company.

Oddly enough, the Asiatic Film Company has received little attention in Chinese film studies. The name of the corporation is misspelled as "China Cinema Company" or "Asia Film Company" in the existing literature.[16] Early historical writings identified Benjamin Brodsky, the owner of China Cinema Company and the Variety Film Exchange, as the organizer of the Asiatic Film Company.[17] However, recent research suggests that Brodsky did not involve himself in the film business in China until the 1910s and his business had little connection with the Asiatic Film Company.[18] At this stage, it is safe to say that the Asiatic was in the hands of two American merchants in 1910s Shanghai: Thomas Henry Suffert (1869–1941) and Arthur Julius Israel (1875–1948). Like the mangling of its corporation name, these two names are mistakenly referred to as "Yashell" or "Elsser" and "Lehrmann."[19] The Asiatic Film Company perhaps commenced its business in 1913 and was defunct after 1915.[20]

The contribution of Thomas H. Suffert to the Asiatic and Zhang Shichuan is very likely to remain in the financial and executive sections. Thomas Suffert was born in Cleveland, Ohio. He moved to Shanghai in 1895 for commercial exploration. The historical record shows that Suffert mainly served as a speculator in Shanghai.[21] In a 1916 passport application, Suffert is referred to as "the owner and manager of an American registered firm which engaged in the import and export trade with the United States and other countries," the Central Trading Company in Shanghai.[22] With respect to the operation of the Asiatic, Suffert seems to have been its executive. A 1913 source shows that Suffert, representing the Asiatic Film Company, applied for permission to show films at the Little Street Theatre (*de la Rue Petit*) in Shanghai.[23] In addition, Suffert attended the Annual Meeting of Ratepayers under the name of the Asiatic Film Company in 1918.[24] As a friend of Zhang Shichuan, Suffert continued to participate in Zhang's late film business, after the demise of the Asiatic. When Zhang Shichuan was organizing the Mutual Stock and Produce Company in 1921, the predecessor company of Mingxing, Suffert served as a consultant.[25] It was Suffert who introduced his friend Carl Louis Gregory to Zhang Shichuan. As a foremost cinematographer and a professor at Columbia University, Gregory favored Zhang Shichuan and his Mingxing in various ways, including film shooting, film printing, and script writing.[26] Suffert was also involved in the management of the Mingxing Film School in 1921. In addition, Mingxing's affiliated cinema, Star, was registered under the name of Suffert in the United States for the sake of avoiding taxation.[27]

In comparison with Suffert, Arthur J. Israel appeared to have played a lesser role. The existing literature identifies Israel as the cameraman of the Asiatic.[28] However, no certain evidence has come to light so far to support this identification. Arthur Israel was born in San Francisco in 1875. In his twenties, Israel became a cigar dealer in California. His passport application records showed that Israel went to China as early as 1902.[29] In his thirty years in Shanghai, Israel mainly focused on the business in the Shanghai Life Insurance Company, a British Company with mostly American capital.[30] During the period from 1913 to 1915, Israel served as a director, the third highest position, in the company. In addition, he was occupied as the director of the Consolidated Rubber Estates Limited, a member of the board of directors of the Laou Kung Mow Cotton Spinning & Weaving Company, and an executive committee of the Shanghai Amateur Baseball League.[31] Moreover, during the period 1913–1915 when the Asiatic was active, Israel had to spend several months on a business trip to Vancouver and Hong Kong from November 1913 to March 1914.[32] Even if he did operate a camera, Israel could not have had enough time to produce more than a dozen films during this period. It seems that Israel was merely an investor in the Asiatic Film Company, given his abundant experience in finance and investment.[33] The credit of projecting films and the daily operation of the Asiatic should go to other figures.

I believe that an American citizen named William H. Lynch is owed the credit for this enterprise. Apart from English sources, one Chinese source supports my speculation.[34] Prior to becoming involved in the film business, William Lynch operated a photo studio named the North Beach Studio in Santa Monica (a city close to Hollywood) starting in 1905.[35] His experience in the photo studio facilitated his job in the motion picture industry as a cinematographer. In 1912, Lynch was hired to be a film cameraman by the Globe Motion Picture Company. Lynch, together with Rochefort Johns, initiated a three-month trip to Asia to film in locations including China.[36] This trip probably generated Lynch's interest in the Orient. Therefore, he agreed to join the Asiatic Film Company in Shanghai as early as January 27, 1913.[37]

The date when Lynch joined the Asiatic cannot be later than March 1913. The reason is that on that date, he wrote back from China to the *Daily Outlook*, a local newspaper issued in Santa Monica.[38] Lynch first described his experience in the Asiatic Film Company.

> We have located a moving picture studio and complete plant for making and finishing moving pictures here. We are starting in a new field

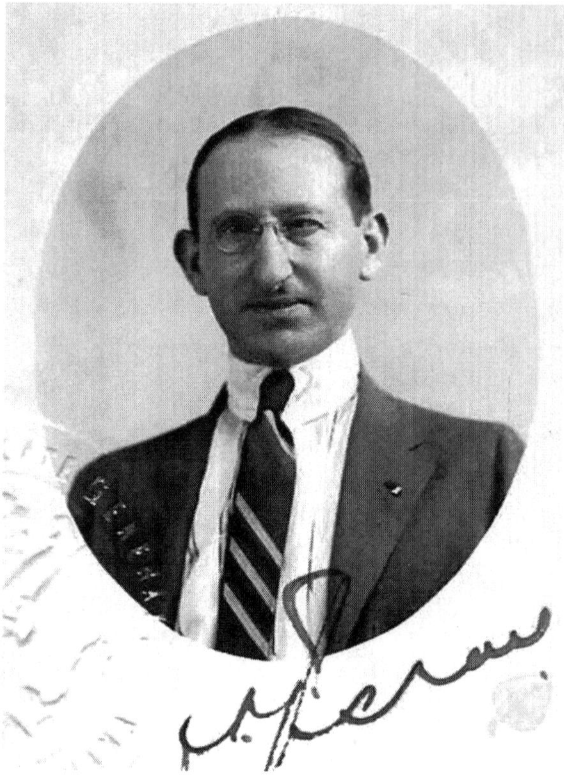

Figure 8.1. Arthur Israel. Source: U.S. Passport Application of Arthur Israel 1918. Photo courtesy of National Archives and Records Administration and www.ancestry.com

> and pictures made with Chinese actors are to be shown to the Chinese people. It is something that has not been done to this date and from reports we believe it will be a big success. We will also operate in connection with the production of the films, several theaters throughout China for the purpose of creating a greater demand and later on will put our entire time and efforts to the production of film only.[39]

According to this letter, it is clear that using Chinese actors was a deliberate production and marketing strategy for the Asiatic with the purpose of satisfying its target consumers: Chinese audiences. In addition, the letter demonstrates that even if the Asiatic Film Company was not originally organized by Israel and Suffert, their alleged predecessor, Benjamin Brodsky, might not have produced substantial movies, as is suggested in the existing literature.[40] To Lynch, a film-producing career seemed promising, and therefore he "decided to make [his] permanent home abroad (in China)" in 1913.[41]

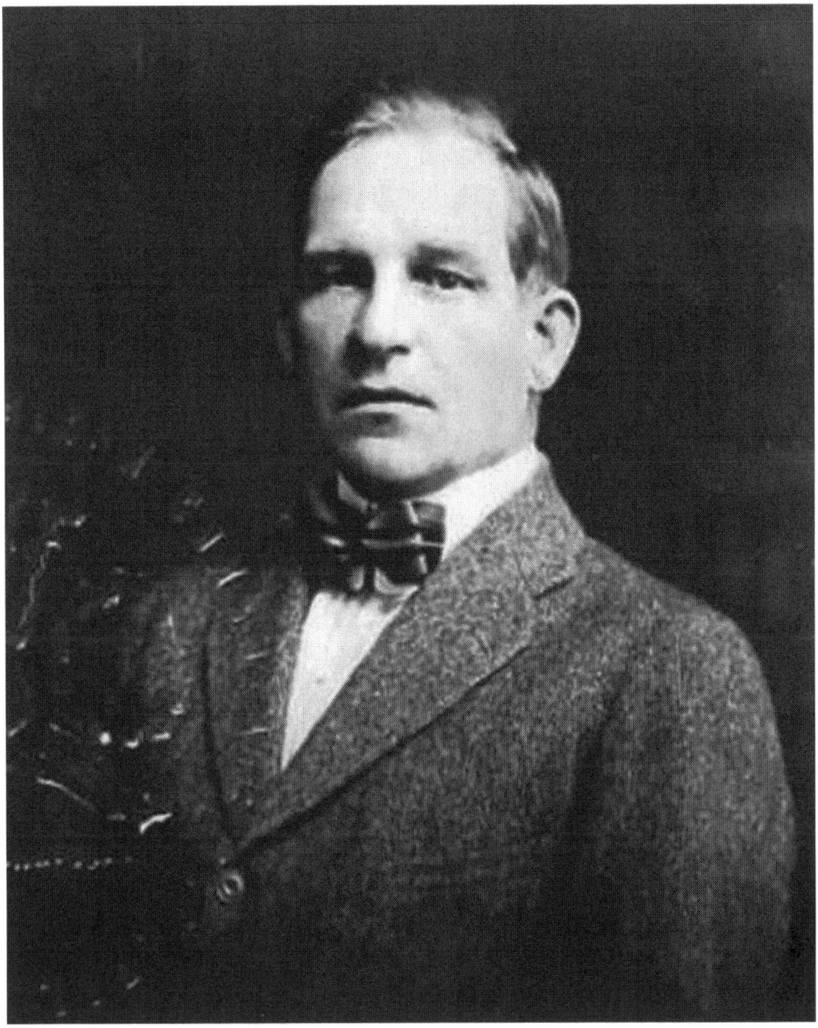

Figure 8.2. Thomas Suffert. Source: U.S. Passport Application of Thomas Suffert 1916. Photo courtesy of National Archives and Records Administration and www.ancestry.com

A 1914 report of *The Moving Picture World* provided a detailed illustration of the operation of the Asiatic.[42] The report is fairly reliable since the author, Clarke Irvine, wrote the report based on his meeting with William Lynch in China in 1913.[43] According to this report, William Lynch, the "Shanghai manager of the Asiatic Film Company," was making films for the Asiatic, "which ha[d] many releases each month."[44] In addition,

> The Asiatic Film Company maintains a large studio in Shanghai, where sixteen star actors are daily posing before the camera. These men—no women are allowed to do this kind of work—are the first, and so far, the only Chinese to act before the camera. There are two directors and two interpreters who work under the supervision of Mr. Lynch. These stars are supported by a well-organized company of twenty-five actors. The laboratory and finishing plant is equipped to turn out 10,000 feet of finished film a day. The supply is for the entire country, and the releases are made just as in America and Europe. There are a number of theaters in Shanghai, two of which are operated by this company.[45]

The above passage clearly shows the significance of William Lynch to the Asiatic Film Company and by extension to the Chinese film industry in its initial stage. According to this passage, Lynch was in charge of not only projecting films, but also of all productions of the Asiatic Film Company. It was the most prominent position in the Asiatic, given that none of the other staff, foreigners or Chinese, had professional knowledge of how to produce motion pictures. Zhang Shichuan and Zheng Zhengqiu were arguably the two directors under the supervision of William Lynch. With respect to the division of labor in the Asiatic Film Company, Zhang Shichuan claimed that he was responsible for supervising camera movement, while Zheng was in charge of guiding the actors' performance.[46] However, in the early 1910s, the perception and practice of director was not well developed within the Chinese film industry. In addition, the initial productions of Chinese films were close to a documentary of the original *wenmingxi* (civilized drama).[47] There were few jobs left for the directors once actors started to perform. Furthermore, as I mentioned earlier, Zhang's directing knowledge was next to nothing at the beginning.[48] Therefore, the position of Lynch in the productions of the Asiatic is likely to have been more significant than that of directors such as Zhang Shichuan and Zheng Zhengqiu.

William Lynch returned to the United States in June 1914. His initial plan was to return to China as long as "the revolution in China subside[d] enough for operations to continue."[49] However, why Lynch did not manage to travel back to China remains unclear. Lynch's departure is one major reason why the Asiatic went into decline, apart from the shortage of film stock due to the outbreak of World War I.

Apart from the presence of Lynch, the Asiatic Film Company deserves notice because it is one of the first Chinese concerns that distributed films in overseas markets. In September 1913, Arthur R. Oberle, representing the Asiatic Film Company, passed by Honolulu when traveling back to the United States. Oberle stated that he secured "many thousand feet of pictures depicting actual scenes in the series of battles" in China.[50] Arguably, this is the documentary titled *Shanghai Battles* (1913) referred to in the Chinese records.[51] Unfortunately, I am unable to identify any exhibition information in the United States regarding the documentary. Nevertheless, the Asiatic Film Company successfully circulated its productions in Southeast Asia. An advertisement shows that *Khoojin Whatchay* (*A Poor Man Wins a Lottery*, 1913), a production of the Asiatic, was exhibited at the Empire Theatre in Singapore in 1917.[52] *Khoojin Whatchay* was arguably the first Chinese mainland film screened in Southeast Asia, the largest Chinese diasporic community. Chinese film companies then followed the pathway of the Asiatic and turned Southeast Asia into the largest overseas market for Chinese films in the first half of the twentieth century.

The contribution of the American intermediaries in many cases is not valued but attacked by Chinese historians blinded by nationalism. For instance, foreign figures in the Asiatic Film Company are described as imperialists who part of the economic and cultural aggression against China.[53] If we understand the political context in which these figures were denounced, the contribution of foreign figures in the Asiatic such as Lynch, I would argue, is greater than their potential threat to the Chinese film industry. In fact, the Asiatic can be seen as crucial to the emergence of the Chinese film industry. In addition, the films made by the company, as the first trial cooperation between foreign and Chinese practitioners, solicited the latters' interest in filmmaking.[54] Therefore, it is not exaggerating to say that William Lynch was a "torchbearer" for Zhang Shichuan and Zheng Zhengqiu, the so-called fathers of Chinese cinema, showing them how to handle the equipment, providing them knowledge in running the business. As a result, Zhang and Zheng set up Mingxing in 1922, which became the leader in the film industry for more than a decade.

William Lynch and his Asiatic Film Company are merely one example of numerous American practitioners who were active in modern China. American film practitioners facilitated the formation of Chinese film industry by systematically introducing filmmaking techniques and importing film equipment. With respect to the evaluation of the foreign intermediaries, Zheng Junli is balanced when he admits that much film knowledge of Chinese filmmakers was obtained from their working experiences with American intermediaries, apart from the "colonial aggression" supposedly perpetrated by these American merchants.[55]

CHINESE MERCHANTS STRADDLING THE DIVIDE BETWEEN HOLLYWOOD AND CHINA

We may now return to Zhang Shichuan. Apart from his early experience with the Asiatic, Zhang continuously updated his skills as a director through watching Hollywood films.[56] A large number of these Hollywood films were distributed by Chinese distributors, who constitute the second type of intermediary between Hollywood and the Chinese film industry. In this section, I examine this type of intermediary and their contributions to the domestic film industry, with a focus on Lo Kan.

In the teens, American films were mainly brought to China by British and French film exchange corporations. The outbreak of World War I resulted in the upsurge of requests for American films due to the unavailability of French films. In 1921, Universal studio set up its distribution subsidiary in Shanghai. Fox, Paramount, and Metro-Goldwyn-Mayer followed suit in the 1930s. These Hollywood subsidiaries and some local distributors were the major players in the Chinese film market.[57] Powerful Chinese distributors often secured exclusive rights to exhibiting American films throughout China. A case in point is Lo Kan. Born in Canton in 1888, Lo became involved in the distribution business by establishing Hong Kong Amusements in 1921. In its heyday, from 1922 to 1923, Hong Kong Amusements almost monopolized the distribution of Hollywood films in China.[58] Even in the 1930s, when major Hollywood studios operated through their branch offices, Hong Kong Amusements maintained its close ties with Hollywood.[59]

In addition to Hong Kong Amusements, Lo operated and owned several large film firms involving equipment, distribution, and exhibition. These firms included China Theatre, Yangtze Amusements, Eastern Amusements,

Cathay Amusements, Puma Films, Theatre Equipment Company, and North China Amusements.[60] Film exhibition was one of his key businesses. In the 1930s, Lo Kan directed and controlled "more than thirty of the leading cinema-theaters in China and Hong Kong, several of which he owned."[61] The highlight in Lo's legend is his rebuilding Grand Theatre in Shanghai, updating it into a superior first-run cinema in the Far East. In 1932, Lo set up the United Theatres Corporation and registered it in the United States with 5 million Mexican dollars. It was probably the largest film business in China in the first half of the twentieth century in terms of registered capital. The United Theatres Corporation was designed to be a vertically integrated film enterprise including production, distribution, and exhibition. One intention of the company was to organize a theater chain that could monopolize the exhibition of Hollywood films in Shanghai. In its heyday, United Theatres encompassed nine movie houses, including the Grand, Cathay, Carlton, Isis, Paris, Crystal Palace, Ritz, Ward, and Pearl.[62]

As intermediaries, domestic film distributors such as Lo Kan benefited Hollywood's expansion in unfamiliar markets like China. To Hollywood executives, the political, economic, and cultural situation in China was quite different from that in the United States. Domestic distributors could smooth the way for the business of Hollywood in China. For instance, the Isis theater served as the second-run theater for the United Artists in Shanghai. According to a resource in 1927, "The theater [was] located in Chinese territory and suffered very much from the strict Chinese martial law regulations."[63] Under the management of Lo Kan, Isis changed its entrance to open into the International Settlement territory. Thereby, it successfully bypassed the Chinese military troubles. In addition, Lo's expansion into the interior cities benefited the exhibition of United Artists movies. In 1928, Lo contemplated opening cinemas in interior cities including Ningbo, Hangzhou, Nanjing, Yantai, Jinan, and Wuxi. Lo's plan brought an opportunity for the expansion of United Artists' film business. United Artists noted in 1928 that "we [had] been able to negotiate for a number of our old pictures to play at these interior cities."[64]

One prominent feature of the foreign film distributors was the position they straddled between America and China. Although the entire business of the distributors focused on the Chinese film market, most of the corporations owned and operated by the distributors were registered in the United States. There were several advantages in being an American corporation, one of which I want to stress. As an American corporation, Lo's company could seek support from the American authorities once conflicts happened. The American government was known for protecting its citizens and their economic interests in China. An instance is the opening of a theater in Changsha, an inner city of China. In 1923, Joseph Y. Tsau, an American citizen who opened the Lyceum theater within the walls of the city in Changsha, filed a complaint with American consuls against the Chinese government. The Chinese authorities requested Tsau move the theater outside the walls, since the inner city was not a commercial port. Such a move would jeopardize Tsau's business. With the help of the American vice consul and the Changsha Foreign Office, Tsau obtained permission to continue operating his theater within the city walls.[65] It is certain that Tsau would not have enjoyed such treatment if his theater were registered in China. The benefit Tsau obtained stands as one of the most important reasons to register a corporation in the United States. Similarly, for the sake of seeking protection from the British government, Lo Kan became a British citizen.

Nationalistic writings are hostile to foreign film distributors like Lo Kan. Radical nationalists labeled Lo a "traitor" or "imperialist" who betrayed China's economic rights while benefiting from Hollywood's exploration in China. Cheng Jihua and his colleagues equate Lo's United Theatre Company with American imperialism and treat its appearance as "a further development of American intention toward aggression against the Chinese film industry," because it was registered in the United States.[66] However, it is necessary to point out that such attacks on Sino-American companies were highly selective. As I mentioned previously, the Peacock Motion Pictures Company and the Star theater were all registered in the United States, yet were free from nationalistic attacks. Recent nationalist historians such as Hu Jubin, however, remain silent on Lo's company. Due to the distribution of films from Hollywood, an economic rival of the national industry, Lo's company, from Hu's point of view, did not benefit the national film industry, even if it did not hinder it.

The question here is the extent to which the distribution of Hollywood films threatened the development of the domestic film industry. The expansion of Hollywood and the development of the Chinese film industry are not necessarily mutually exclusive. In a rapidly growing market such as China in the 1920s, the output of the Chinese film industry and Hollywood could increase simultaneously. A gauge is the footage of film stock imported from the United States to China. The linear feet of exposed film stock for exhibition purposes in 1929 was more than twenty times larger than in 1913.

The expansion of unexposed films for producing Chinese films was more striking; this figure in 1925 was 220 times larger than in 1920.[67] Even if there may be something to Hollywood's threat, the other side of the coin should not be neglected. In some cases, the competition from Hollywood became an inspiration for the Chinese film industry. Additionally, Hollywood films circulated by Chinese distributors provided one of the few channels for Chinese practitioners to learn from Hollywood. In the first half of twentieth century, American films remained a vital resource for China to imitate in terms of camera movement, direction, performance, and industrial systems. Hollywood brought to China film equipment and production techniques during the period of China's transition to talkies. If nationalists intend to recognize the positive contribution of Hollywood films to China, the function of Chinese distributors as intermediaries introducing Hollywood films into China should not be neglected.

In addition, nationalistic accounts excluding foreign film distributors from their historiography ignore the multiple identifications of these distributors. In many cases, distributing Hollywood films was merely one part of a complex enterprise operated by these intermediaries. The intermediaries usually participated in other sectors of the film industry, and therefore blurred the boundary between national capitalists and intermediaries. Lo Kan, for instance, apart from distributing and exhibiting Hollywood films, was responsible for distributing domestic films in Hong Kong. In the 1920s, Lo's Hong Kong Amusements circulated *The Burning of Red Lotus Temple* (*Huoshao hongliansi*, dir. Zhang Shichuan, 1928) in Hong Kong.[68] In addition, Lo was one of key shareholders of Lianhua (the United Photoplay Service), a prominent force in the Chinese film industry in the 1930s.[69] There was even a chance that Lo would buy Lianhua in 1932.[70] Sometimes, intermediaries would even compete directly with Hollywood counterparts through involvement in domestic film productions. Possessing abundant capital, they turned out to be the most effective rival to foreign merchants. At the moment of China's conversion to talkies, Lo's United Theatres had "a definite project of establishing a modern sound studio and leasing it to Chinese producing companies."[71] An advertisement for United Theatres mentioned that Lo had already purchased modern sound equipment and had invited an expert from the Radio Corporation of America to supervise the construction of studios and installation of equipment.[72] If the plan bore fruit, through leasing the studios to Chinese filmmakers, United Theatres would not only "obtain a handsome return on its capital," but also "obtain a first refusal on all pictures produced at the studios."[73] The number of sound pictures produced in China would increase from fifteen per annum to at least forty in the 1930s. As analysts for the American consul pointed out, such a substantial increase in the number of Chinese talkies would "curtail the demand for foreign pictures."[74] Unfortunately, Lo's plan was aborted due to unexpected economic barriers. However, Lo did not terminate his investment in film production. In 1933, employing the sound equipment purchased for United Theatres, Lo released the box-office hit *The Fool Pays Respect* (*Dailao baishou*, dir. Hou Yao, 1933), and in 1935, Lo finally erected a sound studio in Hong Kong.[75] Here what I want to stress is the multifunction role of distributing merchants like Lo Kan. It is true that they assisted the expansion of Hollywood's business in China, serving as so-called traitors. Nevertheless, the multiple role these intermediaries played in the relationship between Hollywood and China should not be ignored. Some of them benefited the Chinese film industry in various ways.

CONCLUSION

When one discusses China's response to Hollywood, the implied discourse is that China had already built relations with Hollywood. However, "building relations" is not an abstract process. Figures and enterprises were necessary to develop the relations between Hollywood and China. As this chapter has shown, these figures, that is, intermediaries, bridged the communication gap between Hollywood and Chinese cinema.

The study of the intermediaries between Hollywood and the Chinese film industry is linked to transnational Chinese cinemas studies. In the past two decades, transnationalism has become a key word in Chinese cinemas studies. With few exceptions, academic discussion has centered on the period after 1978, when Mainland China began to invite transnational capital and cooperation in the film industry.[76] Inviting transnationalism into film history can fill an intellectual void, noticing "phenomena that [not] only cross but straddle and defy borders."[77] Over the national cinema paradigm, the contribution of board-crossing figures like the intermediaries between Hollywood and China has been neglected. As this chapter demonstrates, intermediaries in the early twentieth century bridged relations between Hollywood and the Chinese film industry. The development of the domestic film industry would have been slower without the contributions of these intermediaries. The complexity of history risks simplification in the shadow of nationalism.

ACKNOWLEDGMENTS

The author would like to thank Zhou Xuelin, Laurence Simmons, Zheng Han, Paul Clark, and Suguwara Yoshino for their perceptive advice on the chapter. It was made possible by help from the Interlibrary Loan and Document Delivery Service in the University of Auckland Library (New Zealand), in particular Alice Mendoza; the Auckland City Library; and the Santa Monica Public Library. An early version of this chapter was published in the *Journal of Chinese Cinemas* (www.tandfonline.com). The author would like to thank the journal editor, Song Hwee Lim, and the two anonymous reviewers for their suggestions.

Notes

1. Yen-p'ing Hao, *The Comprador in Nineteenth Century China: Bridge between East and West* (Cambridge, MA: Harvard University Press, 1970); Cheng Shuren, *Zhonghua yingye nianjian* [China Cinema Yearbook] (Shanghai: Zhonghua yingye nianjian she, 1927), 10.

2. Hao, *Comprador*, 5.

3. Zhiwei Xiao, "Translating American Films into Chinese Audiences," in *Transnational Asian Identities in Pan-Pacific Cinemas: The Reel Asian Exchange*, ed. Philippa Gates and Lisa Funnell (New York: Routledge, 2012), 88–100.

4. Lydia H. Liu, *Translingual Practice: Literature, National Culture, and Translated Modernity-China, 1900–1937* (Stanford, CA: Stanford University Press, 1995), xvii.

5. Peter Hays Greis, *China's New Nationalism: Pride, Politics, and Diplomacy* (Berkeley: University of California Press, 2004), 9.

6. Gu Jianchen, "Zhongguo dianying fadashi" [The Development of Chinese Film], in *Zhongguo dianying nianjian 1934* [Chinese Film Yearbook 1934], ed. Zhongguo jiaoyu dianying xiehui (Beijing: Zhongguo guangbo dianshi chubanshe, 2008), 321–346.

7. Gu, "Zhongguo dianying fadashi, 15.

8. Arif Dirlik, *Marxism in the Chinese Revolution* (Lanham, MD: Rowman & Littlefield, 2005), 129.

9. Cheng Jihua, Li Shaobai, and Xing Zuwen, *Zhongguo dianying fazhan shi* [History of the Development of Chinese Cinema], vol. 1 (Beijing: China Film Press, 1980), 3.

10. Jubin Hu, *Projecting a Nation: Chinese National Cinema before 1949* (Hong Kong: Hong Kong University Press, 2003), 25–27.

11. Hu, *Projecting a Nation*, 19.

12. Hu, *Projecting a Nation*, 48.

13. Hu, *Projecting a Nation*, 20.

14. Hu, *Projecting a Nation*, 20.

15. Zhang Shichuan, "Zi wo daoyan yilai" [Since My Director Career Commenced], *Minxin* 3 (1935): 11.

16. Yingjin Zhang and Zhiwei Xiao, *Encyclopaedia of Chinese Cinema* (London: Routledge, 1998); Zhen Zhang, *An Amorous History of the Silver Screen: Shanghai Cinema, 1896–1937* (Chicago: University of Chicago Press, 2005); Kar Law and Frank Bren, *Hong Kong Cinema: A Cross-Cultural View* (Lanham, MD: Scarecrow, 2004). I identify the English name of this company based on an English yellow page book published in Shanghai titled *1915 North China Desk-Hong List* (Shanghai: North China Daily News Publishing House, 1915).

17. Cheng, *Zhonghua yingye nianjian*; Cheng, Li, and Xing, *Zhongguo dianying fazhan shi*; Jay Leyda, *Dianying/Electric Shadows: An Account of Films and the Film Audience in China* (Cambridge, MA: MIT Press, 1972).

18. Law Kar, "Jiekai Xianggang dianying qiyuan de mituan" [The Doubts and Suspicions about Hong Kong Movie's Origin], *Contemporary Cinema* 4 (2010): 78–85; Huang Dequan, *Zhongguo zaoqi dianying shishi kaozheng* [A Textual Critique of Early Chinese Film History] (Beijing: China Film Press, 2012). The relationship between Benjamin Brodsky and the Asiatic Film Company is still open to study. I note that one still picture that Brodsky provided to the *New York Tribune* (George Kaufman, "Bret Harte Said It: The Heathen Chinese Is Peculiar," *New York Tribune*, August 27, 1916) is the same as the picture (which appeared as a still picture named *La Ha Naung Middong*) in a report about the Asiatic Film Company in the *Moving Picture World* (Clarke Irvine, "Chinese Photoplays," *Moving Picture World* 19, no. 8 [1914]: 935.) Second, another still picture is labeled *The Three Thieves* in the report on Brodsky, which is believed to be a production of the Asiatic Film Company. See Huang, *Zhongguo zaoqi dianying shishi kaozheng*, 73. Third, William H. Lynch, the cinematographer of the Asiatic Film Company, claimed that he was one cinematographer for *A Trip through China*, a documentary by Brodsky's China Cinema Company (*Daily Outlook*, October 27, 1916). Fourth, the office and sales room of Brodsky's China Cinema Company was located at 2 Hongkong Road (*1916 North China Desk-Hong List*), while the same address appeared as the Asiatic Film Company in *Shanghai Street Directory*, another part of the same publication. See *1916 North China Desk-Hong List* (Shanghai: North China Daily News Publishing House, 1916), 47, 200.

19. Yingjin Zhang, *Chinese National Cinema* (New York: Routledge, 2004), 19; Leyda, *Dianying/Electric Shadows*, 15.

20. Huang, *Zhongguo zaoqi dianying shishi kaozheng*, 62.

21. Charles Lobingier, "Toeg & Read v. Suffert, Sept. 3, 1907," in *Extraterritorial Cases*, ed. Charles Lobingier (Manila: Bureau of Printing, 1920), 112–120.

22. "U.S. Passport Application of Thomas Suffert (1916)," *Passport Applications for Travel to China, 1906–1925*, Washington, DC: National Archives and Records Administration, ARC Identifier 1244180/MLR Number A1540, NARA Series: M4419, vol. 7.

23. Municipal Administrative Council, *Compte rendu de la gestion pour l'exercice 1913* [Account Management of 1913] (Shanghai: Imprimerie Muncipale, 1913), 65.

24. "The Municipal Gazette," *North-China Herald*, March 14, 1918, n. p.

25. "Datong jiaoyisuo chuangli huiji" [Minutes of the Commencement of the Mutual Stock & Produce Company], *Shenbao*, November 28, 1921, n. p.

26. Guan Ji'an, "Naimei nushi" [Miss Anna May Yang], *Dianying zazhi* 1, no. 1 (1924): 46.

27. Yoshino Sugawara, "Minkokuki Shanghai no eigakan ni tsuite: kokusan eiga jōeikan to eigakan no keiei jōkyo o chūshin ni" [Film Theaters in Shanghai in the Republic of China: Research on the Business Operations of Theaters Showing Chinese Films], *Yaso* 81 (2008): 94–111.

28. Cheng, *Zhonghua yingye nianjian*; Cheng, Li, and Xing, *Zhongguo dianying fazhan shi*, 1, 18; Zhang, *Amorous History*, 431–439. My identification of Arthur Israel as the mysterious Yishier in Chinese literature is based on three reasons: (1) Israel's employee record. Israel worked in the Shanghai Life Insurance Company ("U. S. Passport Application of Arthur Israel [1917]," Emergency Passport Applications, Argentina thru Venezuela, 1906–1925, ARC Identifier 1244183/MLR Number A1544, Box 4485, vol. 2, Washington, DC, National Archives and Records Administration), which is supported by a Chinese source (Gongsu, "Xinju tuibian ji" [A Record of New Play's Degradation], *Xinju zazhi* 1 (1922): 9. (2). Israel's visa application records. In his records, Israel identified his own Chinese name as Yisier ("U. S. Passport Application of Arthur Israel [1918]," Passport Applications, January 2, 1906–March 31, 1925, ARC Identifier 583830/MLR Number A1534, NARA Series: M1490, Roll 626, Washington, DC: National Archives and Records Administration) and Yishuoer ("U. S. Consular Registration Certificates of Arthur Israel (1914)," U. S. Consular Registration Certificates, 1907–1918, General Records of the Department of State, 1763–2002, Record Group 59, Washington, DC: National Archives and Records Administration), which are phonetically similar with the word *Yishier* in Chinese; and (3) the close relationship between Israel and Suffert. In Suffert's visa application record in 1916, Israel wrote the identification letter and claimed that Israel had known Suffert since 1902 ("U.S. Passport Application of Thomas Suffert [1916]"). I take this opportunity to thank Professor Ramona Curry at the University of Illinois, whose seminar account on Brodsky enlightened me to search passport application records.

29. "U. S. Passport Application of Arthur Israel (1917)."

30. The Chinese name of the corporation is Huayang renshou baoxian gongsi, not Shanghai Nanyang renshou baoxian gongsi (Shanghai Nanyang Life Insurance Company) as suggested in the existing literature; Zheng Junli, *Xiandai Zhongguo dianying shi lue* [Modern Chinese Film History] (Shanghai: Liangyou Book Store, 1936), 12; Cheng,

Li, and Xing, *Zhongguo dianying fazhan shi*, 16. As a matter of fact, there does not exist a company named Shanghai Nanyang renshou baoxian gongsi in China in the 1910s. In addition, I am unable to find evidence regarding Israel and the Asiatic attending the Panama Pacific International Exposition as suggested in the existing literature; Zhou Jianyun et al., *Dianying jiangyi* [Syllabus on Introduction to Motion Pictures] (Shanghai: Dadong Book Store, 1924); Cheng, *Zhonghua yingye nianjian*. Israel stayed in Shanghai at least up to 1922, while Suffert died in Shanghai in 1941.

31. "Consolidated Rubber Estates Limited," *North-China Herald*, December 13, 1913, n.p.; "Sport, Baseball," *North-China Herald*, March 21, 1914, n.p.; "Meeting, Shanghai Life Insurance Co.," *North-China Herald*, June 12, 1914, n.p.; "Laou Kung Mow Cotton S. & W. Co.," *North-China Herald*, February 19, 1915, n. p.

32. "Passengers," *North-China Herald*, November 15, 1913; "Passengers," *North-China Herald*, March 28, 1914, n. p.

33. The claimed studio manager of the Asiatic Film Company was E. M. Gross, according to *1915 North China Desk-Hong List*. The detail of E. M. Gross is open to study.

34. Irvine, "Chinese Photoplays"; Zhou et al., *Dianying jiangyi*.

35. "Advertisement," *Daily Outlook*, August 30, 1905, n. p.

36. "Start on Trip," *Daily Outlook*, September 5, 1912, n. p. Another report showed that Lynch would "stop first at Honolulu, then to Guam, Manila and the countries of the Orient" ("Moving Pictures of the Fire," *Daily Outlook*, September 5, 1912, n.p.). The "countries of the Orient" here should include China. The passenger list shows that William Lynch departed Shanghai to Kobe on October 26, 1912. See "Women's World," *Daily Outlook*, January 27, 1913, n. p.; "Passengers," *North-China Herald*, October 26, 1912, n. p.

37. "Women's World."

38. I found Lynch's name in the published hotel register of Kalee Hotel in Shanghai from June 23, 1913, to March 14, 1914. See *North China Daily News*.

39. "Lynch Writes to the Outlook," *Daily Outlook*, April 9, 1913, n. p.

40. Some scholars argued that before Israel and Suffert took over the Asiatic, Benjamin Brodsky had produced at least two films. See Cheng, *Zhonghua yingye nianjian*; and Cheng, Li, and Xing, *Zhongguo dianying fazhan shi*.

41. *Daily Outlook*, October 27, 1916, n. p.

42. Irvine, "Chinese Photoplays."

43. Irvine, "Chinese Photoplays."

44. Irvine, "Chinese Photoplays."

45. Irvine, "Chinese Photoplays."

46. Zhang, "Zi wo daoyan yilai," 11.

47. Law, "Jiekai Xianggang dianying qiyuan de mituan," 81.

48. Zhang, "Zi wo daoyan yilai," 11.

49. "Home from Orient," *Daily Outlook*, June 29, 1914, n.p.; Clarke Irvine, "Doings at

Los Angeles," *Moving Picture World* 21, no. 10 (1914): 1360. Lynch quit the film industry after returning to the United States and became an agent in a real estate company (see "10 Lots Sold in Topanga," *Daily Outlook*, July 19, 1915, n.p.) and later a farmer. It seems that Lynch has no descendant.

50. *Honolulu Star-Bulletin*, September 15, 1913, n. p.

51. Huang, *Zhongguo zaoqi dianying shishi kaozheng*, 56.

52. "Advertisement," *Singapore Free Press and Mercantile Advertiser*, July 11, 1917, n. p.

53. Cheng, Li, and Xing, *Zhongguo dianying fazhan shi*, 1.

54. Law, "Jiekai Xianggang dianying qiyuan de mituan," 84.

55. Zheng, *Xiandai Zhongguo dianying shi lue*, 18.

56. He Xiujun, "Zhang Shichuan he Mingxing yingpian gongsi" [Zhang Shichuan and His Star Motion Picture Company], in *Wenshi ziliao xuanji* [Anthology of Literature and History Materials], vol. 67, ed. Quanguo zhengxie wenshi he xuexi weiyuanhui (Beijing: China Literature and History Press, 1980), 194.

57. Richard P. Butrick, "The Motion Picture Industry in China," 893.4061/69, Confidential U.S. State Department Central Files, China, Internal Affairs, 1930–1939, Washington, DC: National Archives and Records Administration, 1932.

58. Law and Bren, *Hong Kong Cinema*, 121.

59. "General Ledgers and Producers Account," Series 5C: Foreign General Ledgers and Journals, Reel 3, China, United Artists Corporation Archive, Madison: Wisconsin Historical Society.

60. "Shanghai shangye chuxu yinhang youguan yingxiyuan de diaocha baogao" [On the Theater Houses Industries, a Survey Conducted by the Shanghai Commercial & Saving Bank], n.d., Q275-1-2041, Shanghai Municipal Archive.

61. "Shanghai shangye chuxu yinhang youguan yingxiyuan de diaocha baogao."

62. "Shanghai shangye chuxu yinhang youguan yingxiyuan de diaocha baogao."

63. Qian Zhang, "From Hollywood to Shanghai, American Silent Films in China" (PhD diss., University of Pittsburgh, 2009), 48.

64. "General Report for Two Months Ending 20 June 1928," Series 2A: O'Brien Legal File, 1919–1951, Folder 95, Box 4, United Artists Corporation Archive, Madison: Wisconsin Historical Society.

65. "Motion Picture Theatre Permitted within the Walls of Changsha, Letter from C. D. Meinhardt to American Consulate, January 30, 1923," Record of the Department of State Relating to Internal Affairs of China, 1910–1929, Washington, DC: National Archives and Records Service, 1923.

66. Cheng, Li, and Xing, *Zhongguo dianying fazhan shi*, 188.

67. Butrick, "The Motion Picture Industry in China," 101.

68. Yu Mo-wan, *Xianggang dianying shihua (juan yi)-mopian niandai: 1896–1929* [Notes on Hong Kong Film History I: The Silent Era, 1896–1929] (Hong Kong: Sub-Culture Press, 1996), 102.

69. "Shanghai shangye chuxu yinhang youguan yingxiyuan de diaocha baogao" [On the Theater Houses Industries, a Survey Conducted by the Shanghai Commercial & Saving Bank], n.d., Q275–1-1949, Shanghai Municipal Archive.

70. Lu Jie, *Lu Jie riji zhaicun* [The Dairy of Lu Jie Diaries] (Beijing: Zhongguo dianying ziliao guan, 1962), March 28, 1932.

71. Butrick, "Motion Picture Industry in China," 49.

72. "Shanghai shangye chuxu yinhang youguan yingxiyuan de diaocha baogao," Q275–1-2041.

73. "Shanghai shangye chuxu yinhang youguan yingxiyuan de diaocha baogao."

74. "Shanghai shangye chuxu yinhang youguan yingxiyuan de diaocha baogao."

75. Law and Bren, *Hong Kong Cinema*, 121.

76. Cf. Chris Berry, "Sino-Korean Screen Connections: Towards a History of Fragments," *Journal of Chinese Cinemas* 10, no. 3 (2016): 247–264; Jeremy Taylor, *Rethinking Transnational Chinese Cinemas: The Amoy-Dialect Film Industry in Cold War Asia* (New York: Routledge, 2011).

77. Chris Berry, "Transnational Chinese Cinema Studies," in *The Chinese Cinema Book*, ed. Song Hwee Lim and Julian Ward (London: British Film Institute, 2011), 11.

CHAPTER 9

The Silver Star Group

A First Attempt at Theorizing *Wenyi* in the 1920s

Enoch Yee-lok Tam

Wenyi film has been a research focus of Chinese film studies since the 1980s. An abundant number of scholars have written on the topic of *wenyi* film, defining its generic nature as "literature and art film" or film adaptation of great literature, or understanding in relation to themes of love and human relationship. Many scholars have explored the role of *wenyi* films in the postwar Hong Kong and Taiwan cinemas. Yet, in terms of prewar Chinese cinema, only brief accounts on some *wenyi* directors or works can be found. This chapter thus asks the following questions: When and how was the notion of *wenyi* introduced into the field of Chinese cinematic production? How was it defined and received by film theorists of the time? Through a close reading of some early film magazines and journals in the 1920s, this chapter traces how the film journal *Silver Star* (*Yinxing*, 1926–1928) published a large amount of articles concerning the articulation of *wenyi* in films. In addition, a special issue, *Film and Wenyi* (*Dianying yu wenyi*, 1928), by the same publisher further highlights the fact that the journal strove to articulate the relationship between film and *wenyi*. Through a close reading of these texts, the chapter traces how the first attempt to theorize *wenyi* in film emerged in the 1920s and how, in turn, this attempt related to the appropriation of Romain Rolland's heroism as new heroism and Kuriyagawa Hakuson's symbols of anguish. But before reading these theoretical texts, I review the current studies of *wenyi* film in order to better position this chapter in the discussion of *wenyi* and film.

CONTEMPORARY DISCUSSIONS ON *WENYI* FILMS

Wang Molin's two books in the late 1970s and early 1980s indicated that *wenyi* is an established genre and a critical perspective in discussing Chinese directors and their works.[1] Wang examines directors from China, Hong Kong, and Taiwan—including Li Xing, Bu Wancang, Doe Ching (Tao Qin), and Chin Chien (Qin Jian)—and points out that *wenyi* films can be understood as a genre of ethical conflict and romance pervaded with tragic sentiments.[2] In the mid-1980s, Liang Liang wrote an article on Chinese *wenyi* film, listing films from Republican China, Hong Kong, and Taiwan.[3] Liang traces the origin of *wenyi* film in Republican China and extends the discussion to postwar Hong Kong, Qiong Yao's romance in Taiwan, and "pure *wenyi*" in Taiwan New Cinema. This informative article demonstrates that *wenyi* films, generally understood as a filmic adaptation of literary work, have been an established film genre for a century.

Around the same time, Cai Guorong published his seminal book *Studies on Contemporary Chinese Wenyi Film*.[4] He confirmed that the genre mainly dealt with family relationships and ethics; the genre also embraced romantic elements, which allowed it to represent the finer aspects of human emotions. Sharing a line of thinking with Liang, Cai regards lyrical feeling as a crucial aspect of *wenyi* films from the Republican period to Taiwan New Cinema. Contrary to Liang's orientation is that Cai focuses on postwar Hong Kong and Taiwan, first, by highlighting the contribution of various film production companies, and, second, by indicating how adaptation from an original novel influences the style of the film. In the anthology published by the Tenth Hong Kong International Film Festival for its retrospective on Cantonese *wenyipian* (*wenyi* film), Law Kar adopts Cai's definition of *wenyi* film in discussing the archetypes and variations of Cantonese *wenyi* film.[5] These four examples illustrate how *wenyi* film was defined and applied to film study in the 1980s.

In later scholarship on Chinese cinema, *wenyi* became an oft-studied research focus. Scholars expanded the discussion of *wenyi* film directors and their cinematic styles[6] while locating the relationship between *wenyi* film and healthy realism,[7] ethics,[8] and politics.[9] While some scholars have attempted to highlight the issue of adaptation in *wenyi* films,[10] others have reinterrogated the definition of *wenyi* and its relation to melodrama.[11] In these examples, most literature focuses on postwar Hong Kong and Taiwan cinemas.[12] However, the relationship between *wenyi* and film in the earlier eras of Chinese cinema remains an unanswered question.

There have been a few attempts to figure out this *wenyi* tradition. In relation to the world cinema tradition, Teo puts forward the *wenyi* genre as the tradition of Chinese filmmaking. When dealing with the origin of *wenyipian*, he cites the incorporation of *wenmingxi* ("civilized dramas") in the Shanghai film industry in the 1920s. Teo further proposes that later in the "Orphan Island" period (1937–1941), "the term *wenyipian* referred to adaptations of Chinese and foreign novels."[13] Yet his brief account of the origin of *wenyipian* does not conceal the fact that "*wenyipian* . . . is an enigmatic nomenclature even to the Chinese."[14]

To resolve this enigma, Yeh traces the introduction of *wenyi* to the field of cinematic production in early Chinese cinema. She confirms that "the term *wenyi* is derived from a Japanese literary concept, bungei"[15] and was used by Xu Zhuodai as one of his genre classifications in his book *Studies on Photoplay* (*Yingxi xue*, 1924).[16] On the application of the *wenyi* film genre in early Chinese film production, Yeh, in another article, provides a list of films related to *wenyi* in terms of their advertisements in *Shenbao*, a prestigious newspaper in the late Qing and Republican period. Her list shows that the term "literature and art blockbuster" (*wenyi jupian*) first appeared in 1931 and was widely circulated after 1935.[17] In the conclusion of her research, she lists thirteen articles written by critics and literati discussing the relationship between film-as-art and the notion of *wenyi* in the 1920s.[18] However, the list omits many primary sources, such as the film journal *Silver Star*, which this chapter investigates, that contribute to the discussion of the relationship between film and *wenyi* or among film, literature, and other arts.

Besides tracing the origin of *wenyi* film, the scholars mentioned above also stressed the significance of *wenyi* directors and *wenyi* film in the Republican period. Cai briefly outlines the debate over romantic and realistic style in *wenyi* works such as Zhang Shichuan's *Fate in Tears and Laughter* (*Tixiao yinyuan*, 1932), Fei Mu's *Spring in a Small Town* (*Xiaocheng zhi chun*, 1948), Zheng Zhengqiu's *Twin Sisters* (*Zimei hua*, 1933), and Bu Wancang's *The Peach Girl* (*Taohua qixue ji*, 1931).[19] Wang also cites Bu Wancang's other films and points to the fact that *Love and Duty* (*Lianai yu yiwu*, 1931) and *Conscienceless* (*Rendao*, 1932) were well-known *wenyi* films in the 1930s.[20] Liang highlights the relationship between "Mandarin Ducks and Butterflies" literature and film and underlines the influence of Zhang Henshui's novels on *wenyi* filmmaking.[21] According to Liang, *Fate in Tears and Laughter* was the only literary work that had been adapted into film twice before 1938. Zhang Zhen traces the practice of *wenyi* filmmaking back to the 1920s, citing Dan Duyu's *Swear and Oath* (*Haishi*, 1921) and Zheng Zhengqiu and Zhang Shichuan's *An Orphan Rescues His Grandpa* (*Gu'er jiuzu ji*, 1923) as the most recognized origins of the *wenyi* tradition, and analyzing "the exaltation of a lyrical modernist subjectivity and art cinema (or *wenyi* style)"[22] in Hou Yao's *A Poet from the Sea* (*Haijiao shiren*, 1927).

From these literatures, one can observe that *wenyi* filmmaking was practiced in the early 1920s and named a film genre by Xu Zhuodai in 1924, although the term was never in extensive circulation before the 1930s. In the next two decades, *wenyi* became an established film genre and was widely practiced by filmmakers. However, questions about the early introduction of the notion of *wenyi* remain unanswered, especially with respect to the theorization of *wenyi* in films. More precisely: How was the notion, in the 1920s, theoretically and discursively introduced into the field of cinematic production? How was it defined in its introduction? Why did theorists then appropriate the notion from the field of literary production to cinematic production? Lastly: How did its introduction respond to the larger political and social context at the time?

I single out the film journal *Silver Star* as an exemplary case for a study of the early theorization of *wenyi* in films. *Silver Star* was published by Lu Mengshu, a prestigious film critic, and aimed to promote *wenyi* films as an art. He clearly stated in the editorial of the first issue of *Silver Star* that the objective of the magazine was "to let common people know that 'film is an art' and eliminate the undesired phenomenon of understanding 'film as only a tool' [for entertainment]."[23] Nor was the idea of film as an art form invented by Lu alone. Similar statements can be found in earlier film journals such as *Film Magazine* (*Yingxi zazhi*, 1921–1922), and the idea was spread among film critic circles throughout the decade. What singles out *Silver Star* in the discussion of the relationship between film and *wenyi* is that a special issue called *Film and Wenyi*, also edited by Lu Mengshu, was published. As will be demonstrated, Lu and other contributors to the film journal put tremendous effort into articulating the relationship between film and *wenyi*, as well as theorizing the notion of *wenyi* in cinema. Although there were internal differences among individual contributors, the journal was rather homogenous in its ideology. In this sense, Michel Hockx's argument about a literary journal is beneficial here. He states that a literary journal "can be considered in three alternative ways: as a collectively authored text, as the product of a single editor, or as an authorless collection of 'voices.'"[24] Hockx further suggests that for a journal seen as a collectively authored text or an authorless collection of voices, its entire content, including texts and visual materials, should be subject to analysis. In the case of *Silver Star*, these three alternative ways of studying a journal can be applied. For the purpose of discussion, this group of contributors is designated the *Silver Star group* in the rest of the chapter—a group that demonstrated a collective will in promoting film as an art with respect to the notion of *wenyi*.

Through a close reading of the materials produced by the Silver Star group, this chapter aims to (1) examine the theorization of *wenyi* in terms of its relation to literature and art through the adaptation of Kuriyagawa Hakuson's symbols of anguish, a process that elevates film into a serious form of art; (2) pinpoint the function of *wenyi* film in moving and touching common people in order to highlight the educational power of film; and (3) display how the appropriation of new heroism in *wenyi* film leads to the emancipation of the underclass and, moreover, to revolution. The relationship between *wenyi* literature, film, and art will be demonstrated in the following section.

WENYI: LITERATURE, FILM, AND ART

According to Yeh, the term *wenyi* in Chinese is derived from a concept in Japanese literature, *bungei*, and is "a synonym for Western literature and an art form that is explicitly foreign, outside of Chinese conventions."[25] In the *Wenyi Dictionary*, edited by Sun Lianggong and published in 1928, the entry for *wenyi* states:

> *Wenyi*: Generally, it is a noun for literature and art. Its meaning is narrower than that of art while broader than that of literature. Sometime it designates literature (namely pure literature); and sometime it is used to denote the totality of art.[26]

While confirming the explanation given by Yeh, this definition of *wenyi* also demonstrates the inherent ambivalence of the term. Sun's definition oscillates between literature and art, as it sometimes refers to literature, sometimes to art, and sometimes to both simultaneously. Nevertheless, the dictionary definition shows that the term remains closely related to art and literature. Interestingly, the Silver Star group also dealt with this triangular relationship among film, literature, and art.

While discussing the idea of film as an art, the young litterateur Zhang Rougu (1905–1960) of the Silver Star group claimed that "film is an integrated art, combining *wenyi* and science. *Wenyi* can be regarded as its base."[27] This view of film as an integrated art based on *wenyi* was common among the group. Adopting the definition in the *Bungei Dictionary*, which was edited and published in Japan, the group saw film as the eighth art, placing it alongside literature, music, painting, drama, architecture, sculpture, and dancing.[28] Yu Dafu (1896–1945) later asserted that "film is an art that possesses actualizing power."[29]

The idea of film as an integrated art combining art, literature, and science was not new to the cinematic landscape of the time. For example, in the "Inaugurating Preface" of *Film Magazine*, Gu Kenfu (189?–1932) suggested that "the nature of motion picture is the combination of technology, literature, and science"[30] and pointed to the relationship between motion pictures and modern drama. When talking about the mission of *Mingxing Special* (*Mingxing tekan*), Zhou Jianyun (1893–1967) also underlined the fact that a "motion picture is an integrated art; it reflects the reality of humankind. Those who promote it should carry the knowledge of literature, science, optics, aesthetics, philosophy, history, psychology, and sociology."[31] These examples show that the common understanding of film as an integrated art had already been established at the time *Silver Star* was in circulation. The perspectival shift that the Silver Star group brought in was to replace art and literature with the notion of *wenyi*. Such a replacement was not merely rhetorical. By substituting *wenyi* for art and literature, Zhang Rougu and other members in the Silver Star group, as will be shown later, brought a new perspective to film.

The concept of film as an integrated art of *wenyi* further implied that, after poetry, novels, and drama, film was the fourth subgenre of literature (the fourth literature).[32] Members in the group therefore appealed to directors and scriptwriters to acquaint themselves with literature for the purpose of producing better pictures.[33] To assert that film was a subgenre of literature was to highlight its "literariness," which was mainly revealed in film scriptwriting. Chen Zhiqing (?–1931) shared Hou Yao's (1903–1942) view that a scriptwriter is the soul of cinema. He therefore proclaimed that "the scriptwriter is the one who actually produces a motion picture, not the director"[34] and that "the director is only responsible for actualizing the continuity that the scriptwriter has written."[35] The privileging of the scriptwriter and the categorization of film as a subgenre of literature in the early theorization of *wenyi* in films were a result of the close affiliation of motion pictures (*yingxi*) with other forms of drama (modern drama [*wenmingxi* or *xiju*] and Chinese opera [*xiqu*]). From a historical perspective, Hu Jubin and others show that in the early years the venues for the exhibition of film coincided with those for *xiqu*.[36] He further points out that early film production practices borrowed from the production of spoken drama and opera films.[37] The early film historian Zheng Junli (1911–1969) also indicated that the scriptwriters of spoken drama brought new scriptwriting techniques to the field of cinematic production.[38]

Yet, what counted as, or contributed to, the literary quality or "literariness" of film? Lu Mengshu, Chen Zhiqing, and others kept referring to the term "symbols of anguish" (*Kumon no shocho, Kumen de xiangzeng*), coined by the Japanese literary critic Kuriyagawa Hakuson, to develop their own theory of scriptwriting. The book *Symbols of Anguish* was published posthumously in 1923 in Japan, and a year later Lu Xun (1881–1936) translated it from Japanese to Chinese. In his monograph, Kuriyagawa suggested that anguish (*kumon, kumen*) was the source of literary creativity. Through Lu Xun's translation, the Silver Star group was heavily influenced by this proposition in their scriptwriting. Lu Mengshu defines *wenyi* work as "the reflection of the time, symbols of anguish. In general, it is the outcry (*nahan*) of the oppressed people."[39] Here, Lu, on one hand, defined *wenyi* in terms of the symbols of anguish, and, on the other hand, incorporated Lu Xun's notion of outcry (*nahan*), which in turn was heavily influenced by Kuriyagawa's symbols of anguish.[40] On the same page, Lu Mengshu cited Kuriyagawa in *Symbols of Anguish* to illustrate the dialectic between two archetypal forces, namely the force of oppression and the force of vitality, an idea that can be traced back to Sigmund Freud's theory of the id and Henry Bergson's concept of the élan vital. Lu notes that vitality

> never falls into impasse or standstill, never compromise or surrender. It seeks only the vitality of freedom and liberation. Whether consciously or unconsciously, it burns us from within, deep in our hearts, like raging flames.[41]

Kuriyagawa postulates that creativity in literature and art springs from living in, as well as fighting against, anguish:

> On the one hand, we experience this anguish; on the other hand, we participate in severe struggle. On the road to our life, we groan, shout, resent, and weep, and at the same time we often immerse ourselves in the happiness and praise of triumph. The cry from within forms what I call *wenyi*.[42]

Following Kuriyagawa's formulation, Lu Mengshu asserted that "*wenyi* is an expression of life."[43] Again Lu cites Kuriyagawa by way of Lu Xun's translation:

> *Wenyi* is purely an expression of life; it is the only world in which people can leave completely the oppression and compression of the outside world, can stand on the absolute freedom of the mind, and can express their own individuality.[44]

In this sense, artistic creativity and human individuality are "mobilized by the conflict between the uninhibited, freedom-seeking 'life-force' and external social constraints."[45] Kuriyagawa's celebration of individuality is the reason why he was embraced by the May Fourth writers, the same writers who also celebrated individual liberation from feudal and traditional China. Here a certain continuity between the May Fourth Movement and the Silver Star group can be established, not only because *Silver Star* invited Yu Dafu to contribute to the journal, but also because of a shared idea of *wenyi* as symbols of anguish.[46]

Besides defining the nature of *wenyi*, the group also attempted to define the function of *wenyi* film. Zhang Rougu proclaimed that the function of *wenyi* film is "to revitalize the dead *wenyi* works in living motion pictures and at the same time let people understand the moving and touching power of the narration in *wenyi*."[47] For Zhang, *wenyi* film is a genre that adapts from *wenyi* works, and is capable for moving and touching people. While Zhang did not state who the target audience of *wenyi* films was, Lu Mengshu, the chief editor of *Silver Star*, continued from Zhang's line of thought and stated clearly that *wenyi* films are produced for every single person, including the illiterate. In the concluding chapter of his anthology *Film and Wenyi*, Lu said:

> The only way is to inflame our fire of life, ardently and fiercely making new heroic *wenyi* works into films, so that illiterate people can enjoy art and culture. Consequently this can revitalize an aged and antiquated China, creating a new and energetic nation.[48]

Here, in addition to pointing out that *wenyi* films were for all, Lu enthusiastically revealed his belief that *wenyi* films could help reinvigorate the nation. At the time, this was a common belief about the function of art, ever since Liang Chi-chao (1873–1929) published his famous article "On the Relationship between Fiction and the Government of the People" (1902). Liang indicated from the very beginning of the article that "to renovate the people of a nation, one must first renovate its fiction." Liang saw literary writing as a means to alter the morale of his compatriots. With a similar understanding of cultural production in the age of reform, Lu strongly believed that film had the potential to renew a nation. After all, it was a "democratic" art that even illiterate people could enjoy. Hence, elevating the status of film to art via the *wenyi* discourse was never merely a *l'art pour l'art* project imagined by the critics and artists. Rather, it was intimately tied to the project of nation-building.

The Silver Star group formulated the relationship between film and *wenyi* from the perspective of literature and art and defined its function in relation to nation-building. The group regarded film as a literary genre while privileging scriptwriters over directors. Borrowing from Kuriyagawa's conception of *wenyi*, the group sees the symbols of anguish as a driving force for creating *wenyi* films, just like their literary counterpart. From this, Sun Shiyi and Lu Menghsu concluded that a "motion picture is an expression of life, a criticism of life, a reflection of the time, and symbols of anguish."[49] Not only was film a literary genre, it could bring anachronistic *wenyi* works to life for every person, including the illiterate. In its theorization of *wenyi* in films, the Silver Star group pinpointed the function of *wenyi* film in moving and touching the common people. Thus, the ensuing inquiry would be how *wenyi* films worked on the common people.

GOING TO THE PEOPLE: *WENYI* FILM AND LITERATURE

Compared to literature, members of the Silver Star group saw films as a closer, more popular and economic medium for the common people. Xin

Min asserted that the main difference between film and literature lay in their respective popularity:

> Readers of *literature* should have a certain level of literacy. . . . However, film does not work in that way. In every theater, there are men and women, the elderly and the young, and people with all kinds of occupations. All are included in spite of the difference in their level of cultivation.[50]

Chun Bing also agreed that film was the most economic and popular form of art, because every person in a society would be able to see, read, and understand films.[51] In this vein, film became an excellent tool for educating the masses. Cinema as an educational instrument for common people was not a new idea in the 1920s. Victor Fan argues that even in the famous "hard film versus soft film" debate "these two theoretical positions in fact share a common belief: that cinema is an educational instrument for political ends."[52] Therefore, it was not surprising that the members of the group saw film as a tool for mass education. Li Baijin extrapolated what film education could bring to the people, the nation, and its time:

> Regardless of the purpose and attitude you have for watching a film, it can affect your mind, pushing your mind to critique, to research—this can influence your life and actions. Without being aware of the changes, you are transformed. . . . This can lead society to honesty and nobility, to enhance the spirit of race, to fortify the foundation of a nation.[53]

Again, Li revealed a strong tendency to link film to nationalism and socialism, especially since film was a democratic tool to address common people from all walks of life. In the theorization of *wenyi*, the mass was a prominent term that many contributors of *Silver Star* could not avoid. For instance, Tian Han (1898–1968) mentioned in *Silver Star* his unfinished film project *Into the People* (*Dao minjian qu*) and the social movement that happened in Russia with the same name: "Those who have done research on Russian history, especially modern Russia *wenyi* (literature and arts), should be aware of the 'going to the people' movement among the Russia youths in the 1870s."[54]

This may be regarded as one of the clues to Tian's leftist turn in the 1930s. However, in the late 1920s, as a member of the Silver Star group, Tian's rhetoric in his long article "Silver Dream" was as romantic as that of

Lu Mengshu's, since the former underlined "'love for sex' and 'love for nature' as the important themes for contemporary literature as well as modern film art."[55] His literary examples included William Wordsworth and Charles Baudelaire. He also provided examples in films like Kurihara Kisaburô's adaptation of Tanizaki Jun'ichirō's novel *Jasei no Midara* (1921) and Charles Bryant's adaptation of Oscar Wilde's play *Salome* (1922) to illustrate his point. What Tian witnessed in the "going to the people" movement was the passion and fantasy of the Russian youths and their belief in the peasants' bearing a kind of "sublimated honesty and simplicity."

This romanticism was indeed at the core of the Silver Star group's understanding of *wenyi*, an impulse that will be discussed in the next section. Yet Tian's fascination with the peasants was not shared by other members in the Silver Star group, especially when the readers of the film journal were living in the modern city of Shanghai. Therefore, Sun Shiyi (1904–1966), one of the editors of *Shenzhou tekan* (*Shenzhou Special*, 1925–1927) and the scriptwriter for *New Woman* (*Xin nüxing*, dir. Cai Chusheng, 1935), and others preferred to use the term "underclass" rather than "people." Sun articulated the relation between film and the people and demarcated the history of drama in the West into four periods: mythological drama, aristocratic drama, bourgeois drama, and democratic drama. He proclaimed that the history of drama had already evolved into the stage of democratic drama (drama for all people).[56] At this stage, the content of drama should be extracted from, as well as be about, the underclass, as it was the majority among all social classes. Chen Zhiqing took a similar stance toward common people. He claimed that the upper class was the minority in society and that "the life of upper-class people is utterly deprived of humanity [and] is incomparable to the sincerity of the underclass."[57] Therefore, he advised scriptwriters to extract materials from the life of the public: "Be attentive to the lives of the modern ordinary people; be attentive to their needs, since the audience is tightly tied to motion pictures, a relation that is closer than that between education and the masses."[58] Lu Mengshu agreed with Sun and Chen that artistic dramatization should focus on ordinary people.[59] Film "has already taken the responsibility of instructing life because it describes real life more thoroughly."[60] To Lu, film transformed dead *wenyi* (i.e., drama and literature) into living (animated dramatic events) art.

In the article "Film and Wenyi," Yu Dafu further linked the popularity of film to the ideal of socialism. According to Yu, film was more economic than literature because it was less time-consuming and as a result would attract more common people. He stressed this point and extended the discussion of the popularity of film to the ideal of socialism:

> We all know that film is cheap, economic, simple, and easy to read. These advantages of film are self-explanatory in its correspondence to the ideal of socialism of our time. With its enormous power in propaganda, we all understand how good it can be for social education and the education of common people.[61]

He further remarked that "to popularize is not to vulgarize, to simplify is not to monotonize. . . . In sum, these should be done on the spiritual level, not losing the temperament of the taste of arts."[62] Yu understood the value of the popularity of films for the purpose of serving ordinary people and emancipating them from oppression.

Ying Dou went even further to assert that film-as-art should be revolutionized and publicized: "Art should stand with the troops of underclass people, leading them, instructing them to take part in the upward struggle and battle."[63] Ying's military rhetoric expressed the urgency of extrapolating film art into revolution and emancipation of the masses.

The Silver Star group advised scriptwriters of *wenyi* films to be aware of the propagandistic and educational power of films, which could move people and instruct them how to think, feel, and live. As film was the most democratic form of art, its content should be derived from the majority of people, that is, the underclass. Furthermore, the group proposed that, instead of simply aiming to emancipate the individual from oppression by bestowing individuality upon the audience, *wenyi* films also possessed the potential to lead the masses to participate in nationalistic and socialistic revolutions. However, portraying the lives of the underclass alone could not lead to emancipation and revolution. In order to see how this works, we must turn to the concept of new heroism that was proposed by the group.

New Heroism: Wenyi Facing Revolution

The Silver Star group, especially Lu Mengshu and Chen Zhiqing, advocated the notion of new heroism (*xinyingxiong zhuyi*), allegedly derived from Romain Rolland's thinking.[64] From Rolland's *Jean-Christophe* and *Life of Beethoven* Lu Mengshu derived his idea of new heroic film. For Lu, China at that time was severely under the influence of egoism (*liji zhuyi*), which exploited the proletarians as much as it could. Egoistic and individualistic people indulged themselves in materialism and became, in Lu's words, "nonhumans." By paraphrasing Arthur Schopenhauer's "will to live," Lu claimed that suffering people should "fight bravely. Even though they are trapped and severely injured, they should fight bravely."[65] A new hero fights against inhuman oppressors and makes reality a better living circumstance for common people. However, a new hero is not someone who possesses qualities superior to the common person:

> A new hero is not a person with superpower. Women and children are qualified to be new heroes provided that they are enthusiastic, with sacrificing spirit, to selflessly fight for the whole nation, to sacrifice, to fight against oppression, and to improve the abominable living situation.[66]

For Lu Mengshu, these constituted the qualities of a new hero. He understood film as an art for representing human lives, and for instructing and educating. New heroic film in his eyes is

> like a huge mirror that reflects the characters and their background completely and colorfully, to frighten the people, to provoke them, to inflame the fire in their hearts, to encourage them to be better persons, and to ardently fight for their lives.[67]

One can easily discern how the notion of new heroism may be linked to the symbols of anguish, in which Kuriyagawa highlights Bergson's "life-force." By embracing their "life-force," common people could potentially become new heroes.

Lu admitted that his idea of new heroic film was indeed influenced by Chen Zhiqing.[68] In an article on writing a good script, Chen Zhiqing stated that "for modern people, especially Chinese people, all they need is the spirit of new heroism. . . . He is a hero that is willing to sacrifice, to suffer, to fight, to rebel, and to improve the abominable living situation."[69] Like Lu, Chen also thought that film as an art form reflected the living conditions of humans. Furthermore, he extended the idea of reflection and regarded film as a means to manifest "national spirit" or "national character." He recognized the persistent and courageous spirit that he found in German films. He criticized Chinese producers for their lack of urgency in cultivating a national spirit in their films. As a result, the films produced could never acquire a high quality, never become art or *wenyi* films. The major reason was that films obtained plot materials from the lives of the upper class, which, to Chen, was shallow, hollow and nonrepresentative.

Here one can see how new heroism harked back to the advocacy of "going to the people" or underclass. The notion of going to people or underclass is in fact imbued with romanticism. In the anthology *Film and Wenyi*, Du Shihuan discusses what he calls "neo-romanticist film." He briefly traces the emergence of neoromanticism via the linear progression from classicism, romanticism, and naturalism to neoromanticism. For Du, neoromanticism is a combination of naturalism and romanticism: "It takes 'the attitude of natural scientific observation' in naturalism and 'the style of using mystical symbolism to express reality' in romanticism for its attitude and style respectively."[70] He concludes that "neo-romanticism does not describe life in an aloof manner. Rather, it guides life with impassioned tears; it guides people away from their dark and mundane life, and bears forth a world of poetic beauty."[71] Du's suggestion that neoromanticist film echoed the positive side of neoromanticism suggested by Yu Dafu in the context of literature. "Yu Ta-fu [Yu Dafu] divided neo-romanticism into two categories: the positive kind of new heroic and new idealistic literature (represented by Rolland, Barbusse, and Anatole France); and the negative type of symbolist poets who followed the decadent nihilism and moral anarchism of Baudelaire and Verlaine."[72] Though one may discover the negative type in the writing of Tian Han, the general take on neo-romanticism in the Silver Star group follow Du's articulation of guiding people to the beautiful, new world through the act of new heroism.

Illuminated by the spirits of new heroism and symbols of anguish, and with their eagerness to embrace production from the West, Lu and others replaced the traditional Chinese spirit with a rigorous spirit and emotional outburst. For the group, the traditional Chinese spirit was static and passive, while the Western spirit was dynamic and rigorous. Huang Zhen's article is a typical example to show how the Silver Star group construed the dichotomy between the West and China. "Westerners (especially the Greeks) are a dynamic, living, young and enthusiastic ethnicity that is not afraid of hardship."[73] With this spirit in mind, it could be argued that *wenyi* works in the West "are all living and aggressive, so the people over there are also aggressive. They are so confident that they are able to conquer the heaven and God."[74] In contrast, Eastern *wenyi*, and in particular its Chinese manifestation, was dying and passive, and was destined to fade out in the course of world history: "The passive *wenyi* is fatal; it diminished the Jew, depreciated Persia, and also weakened China."[75] In the end of the article, Huang called for embracing the living art and art with a rigorous spirit (of the West); he also suggested abandoning the decaying, dying, and passive art of old China.

Following this line, Lu condemned the passive spirit of China, making its people into slaves, making them submissive and inert to any change from the outside world. Hence, to Lu the mission of *wenyi* was to save people from slavery, remaking them into living people and renewing the whole nation:

> After all, film is an art. Its core is to criticize life, to depict life, to set life as its background. On the silver screen of cinema, it ought to cry out with anger over the oppressed people, and express their rebellion, resistance, and sacrificing spirit and through this to light the fire of life in people, to reform the passive and inert national spirit.[76]

At the turn of the twentieth century, with Liang Chi-chao's proposal mentioned above, it was nothing new for people to see literature and art as tools for transforming the nation, or as art forms that participate in revolution. By defining *wenyi* films as an expression of internal anguish and by redefining Chinese people as new heroes, the group linked *wenyi* films to revolution. Here revolution should be understood as an abrupt change from the old to the new, from the traditional to modernity, from generic mass productions to refined, well-scripted *wenyi* productions for the sake of common people, and for enlightening them to assist their transition from nonhumanity to new heroism.

CONCLUSION

After the cultural translation of *wenyi* from Japan to China in the early twentieth century, the notion gradually gained serious attention in the 1910s in the field of literary production. Numerous literary journals and magazines with the term *wenyi* in their title indicated how seamlessly the term was incorporated into the discursive practices of literature. Desiring to elevate the status of film to art, a group of people began in the 1920s to redefine film by using the notion of *wenyi*. *Silver Star*, and its related book publications, was the crystallization of the thought of this group of people. The Silver Star group pondered the question of the relationship among *wenyi*, art, literature, common people, and revolution. To them, not every film was a work of art, but *wenyi* film was definitely a form of art. Their understanding of *wenyi* was heavily influenced by Kuriyagawa Hakuson by way of Lu Xun. *Wenyi* was an art of symbols of anguish, which was understood as a form of expression of the inner outburst arising from the external oppression of life. This outburst became a strong means of reflecting the lives of people, the spirit of the time as well as the spirit of the nation. The group considered this reflection to be the ultimate mission of *wenyi* films. Its objective was to reconfigure underclass people into new heroes and prepare them to participate in the revolution and renovation of the whole nation—making the weak strong, the old new, the passive active, the inert aggressive.

Given the tendency for film scholars to understand *wenyi* as family melodramas and romances, it is necessary to locate a more illuminating theorization of *wenyi* in relation to the representation of underclass people (socialist realism) and revolution (new heroism). By rehistoricizing *wenyi* in this way, one can uncover a trajectory of *wenyi* film across different movements and debates in Republican China, such as the New Life Movement (*xin shenghuo yundong*), the hard/soft debate in which film thinkers pondered which spectators were best educated via the cinema as an educational tool, "The Yan'an Forum on Literature and Art" in which Mao Zedong argued that the arts (including film) were a pedagogic tool to reflect the life of the working class and to serve the advancement of socialism, and so on. In this regard, *wenyi* studies are a means to conceive a new approach to Chinese film historiography. This chapter outlines the first attempt at theorization of *wenyi* by the Silver Star group and provides a point of departure for richer *wenyi* studies to emerge in the future.

ACKNOWLEDGMENT

An earlier version of this chapter appeared as "The Silver Star Group: A First Attempt at Theorizing *Wenyi* in the 1920s," *Journal of Chinese Cinemas* 9.1 (2015): 62–75.

Notes

1. Wang Molin argues in *Daoyan yu zuopin* that *wenyi* is an established genre and performs critical analyses of Chinese directors and their works from *wenyi* perspective

in *Zhongguo dianying yu xiju*. See Wang Molin, *Daoyan yu zuopin* [Directors and Their Works] (Taipei: Lianya chubanshe, 1978); Wang Molin, *Zhongguo dianying yu xiju* [Chinese Film and Drama] (Taipei: Lianya chubanshe, 1981).

2. Wang, *Zhongguo dianying yu xiju*.

3. Liang Liang, "Zhongguo wenyi dianying yu dangdia xiaoshuo, shang" [Chinese Wenyi Film and Contemporary Novel, Part 1], *Wenhsun* 26 (1986): 257–262; Liang Liang, "Zhongguo wenyi dianying yu dangdia xiaoshuo, xia" [Chinese *Wenyi* Film and the Contemporary Novel, Part 2], *Wenhsun* 27 (1986): 266–277.

4. Cai Guorong, *Zhongguo jindai wenyi dianying yanjiu* [Studies on Contemporary Chinese *Wenyi* Film] (Taipei: Zhonghunminguo dianying tushuguan chubanbu, 1985).

5. Kar Law, "Archetypes and Variations: Observation on Six Cantonese Films," in *Cantonese Melodrama, 1950–1969*, ed. Li Cheuk-to (Hong Kong: Urban Council, 1986), 15–20.

6. Liu Xiancheng, "Zhongguo yixu: Li Xing dianying tanyuan" [Chinese Remnant: The Origin of Li Xing's Films], *Journal of Beijing Film Academy* 4 (1998): 50–62; Stephen Teo, *Wong Kar-wai* (London: BFI Publishing, 2005); and Emilie Yueh-yu Yeh, "The Road Home: Stylistic Renovations of Chinese Mandarin Classics," in *Cinema Taiwan: Politics, Popularity and State of Arts*, ed. Darrell William Davis and Ru-shou Robert Chen (Oxford: Routledge, 2007), 203–216.

7. Tang Weimin, "Youyi wenyi zhandou fusheng, dianying zhengjing jiankong qifei, xushiwenben meixue zaixian: Liushi niandai Taiwan jiankangxieshi dianying de jueqi" [Recurring Right-Wing *Wenyi* Discursive Tactics, Policing Political Economy of Cinematic Production, and Representing Narrative aesthetic: The Rise of Healthy Realistic Cinema in Taiwan] (PhD diss., Fu Jen Catholic University, 2008).

8. Wang Chunchi, "Xiandai lianai yu chuantong jiating de lunli chongtu: Cong Taiyu dianying jiating lunli wenyi aiqing leix- ing kan 1950–1960 niandai aiqing, hunting, jianting de daode xiangxiang" [Ethical Conflicts between Modern Romance Relationships and Traditional Family: An Investigation of the Moral Imagination of Romance, Marriage, and Family in the 1950s and 1960s through the Lens of Tai-Language Familial Ethic and Romantic *Wenyi* Film], *Applied Ethics Review* 53 (2012): 57–81.

9. Stephanie Po-yin Chung, "Xinlian gushi: Zhengzhi wenyi he yueyu yingye" [Sun Luen Story: Politics, Wenyi and Cantonese Film Industry], in *Wenyi renwu, Xinlian qiusuo* [The Mission of *Wenyi*, the Searching of Sun Luen], ed. Sam Ho (Hong Kong: Hong Kong Film Archive, 2011), 35–52.

10. Leung Ping-kwan, "Cong guozu dao siqing: Huayu tongsu qingjieyu de bianhua, Lanyuhei de lizi" [From Nation-Building to Private Passion: The Changes in Chinese Melodrama], in *Shaoshi yingshi digou: Wenhuua Zhongguo de xiangxiang* [Shaw Bros. Enterprise: Cultural China Imaginary], ed. Liao Jinfeng et al. (Taipei: Rye Field Publishing, 2003), 295–306; Huang Yikuan, "Taiwan yanqing xushi yu dianying gaibian zhi kongjian zaxian: Yi liuling zhi baling niandai wenhua changyu wei zhu" [Space Representations in Taiwan Love Narratives and Their Film Adaptations: From the 1960s–

1980s Literary Field], *Zhongxzheng daxue zhongwen xueshu niankan* 14 (2009): 135–164; and Huang Yikuan, "Yanqing xushi yu wenyipian: Qiong Yao xiaoshuo gaibian dianying zhi kongjian xinggou yu xiandai lianai xiangxiang" [Love Narrative and *Wenyi* Film: Space Construction and Modern Love Imagination in Film Adaptations of Qiong Yao's Novels], *Dong Hwa Journal of Chinese Studies* 19 (2014): 329–372.

11. Stephen Teo, "Chinese Melodrama: The Wenyi Genre," in *Traditions in World Cinema*, ed. Linda Badley et al. (Edinburgh: Edinburgh University Press, 2006), 203–213; Ain-ling Wong, "The Black-and-White Wenyi Films of Shaws," in *China Forever: The Shaw Brothers and Diasporic Cinema*, ed. Poshek Fu (Urbana: University of Illinois Press, 2008), 115–132; Han Yanli, "Butan zhengzhi de zhengzhixue: Gangchan lunli qinqing pian shixi" [Political Discourse without Politics: An Analysis of Hong Kong–Produced Familial Ethic Film], in *Lengzhan yu Xiangang dianyin* [The Cold War and Hong Kong Cinema], ed. Wong Ain-ling and Lee Pui-tak (Hong Kong: Hong Kong Film Archive, 2009), 209–219; Emilie Yueh-yu Yeh, "Pitfalls of Cross-Cultural Analysis: Chinese *Wenyi* Film and Melodrama," *Asian Journal of Communication* 19, no. 4 (2009): 438–452; Emilie Yueh-yu Yeh, "From Foreign Word to Genre Concept: Meaning and Application of 'Wenyi' in Early Film," in *Chinese Cinema: Tracing the Origins*, ed. Ain-ling Wong (Hong Kong: Hong Kong Film Archive, 2011), 182–205; Zhen Zhang, "Transplanting Melodrama: Observations on the Emergence of Early Chinese Narrative Film," in *A Companion to Chinese Cinema*, ed. Yingjin Zhang (Malden, MA: Wiley-Blackwell, 2012), 25–41.

12. Liu, "Zhongguo yixu"; Leung, "Cong guozu dao siqing"; Wong, " Black-and-White Wenyi Films"; Han, "Butan zhengzhi de zhengzhixue"; Tang, "Youyi wenyi zhandou fusheng"; Huang, "Taiwan yanqing xushi yu dianying gaibian zhi kongjian zaxian"; Huang, "Yanqing xushi yu wenyipian"; Chung, "Xinlian yushi"; Wang, "Xiandai lianai yu chuantong jiating de lunli chongtu."

13. Teo, "Chinese Melodrama," 205.

14. Teo, "Chinese Melodrama," 203.

15. Emilie Yueh-yu Yeh, "Wenyi and the Branding of Early Chinese Film," *Journal of Chinese Cinemas* 6, no. 1 (2012): 73.

16. Yeh, "Wenyi and the Branding"; and Yeh, "Pitfalls of Cross-Cultural Analysis."

17. Yeh, "From Foreign Word to Genre Concept," 187.

18. Yeh, "From Foreign Word to Genre Concept," 202.

19. Cai, *Zhongguo jindai wenyi dianying yanjiu*.

20. Wang, *Zhongguo dianying yu xiju*.

21. Liang, "Zhongguo wenyi dianying yu dangdia xiaoshuo, shang."

22. Zhang, "Transplanting Melodrama," 34.

23. Lu Mengshu, "Juantouyu" [Editorial], *Yinxing* 1 (1926): 4.

24. Michel Hockx, *Questions of Style: Literary Societies and Literary Journals in Modern China, 1911–1937* (Leiden: Brill, 2003), 124–125.

25. Yeh, "Wenyi and the Branding," 72.

26. Sun Lianggong, *Wenyi cidian* [*Wenyi* Dictionary] (Shanghai: Minzhi shuju, 1928), 55.

27. Zhang Rougu, "Dianying yu shengjing" [Film and the Bible], *Yingxin* 5 (1927): 22.

28. Zhang Rougu, "Diba yishu" [The Eighth Art], *Yingxin* 8 (1927): 20–24; Bai He, "Xiwang Zhongguo diba yishu zhi jianglai" [Hoping for the Future of the Eighth Art of China], *Yinxing* 14 (1927): 28–29.

29. Yu Dafu, "Dianying yu wenyi" [Film and *Wenyi*], *Yinxing* 12 (1927): 13.

30. Gu Kenfu, "Fakan ci" [Inaugurating Preface], *Yingxi zazhi* 1, no. 1 (1920): 8.

31. Zhou Jianyun, "Benkan Zhi Shiming" [The Mission of the Journal], *Mingxing tekan* 1 (1925): 1.

32. Chun Bing, "Yinmu shang de wenxue" [Literature on the Silver Screen], in *Dianying yu wenyi* [Film and *Wenyi*], ed. Lu Mengshu (Shanghai: Liangyou tushu, 1928), 18–19.

33. Chen Zhiqing, "Zhongguo yingju zhong jige zhongyao de wenti, shang" [Some Important Issues of Chinese Cinema, Part 1], *Yinxing* 3 (1926): 6–12; Wei Nan, "Dianying de wenyihua" [Making Film *Wenyi*], in Lu, *Dianying yu wenyi*, 1–15.

34. Chen Zhiqing, "Zhongguo yingju zhong jige zhongyao de wenti, zhong" [Some Important Issues of Chinese Cinema, Part 2], *Yinxing* 4 (1926): 6.

35. Chen, "Zhongguo yingju zhong jige zhongyao de wenti, zhong," 7.

36. Jubin Hu, *Projecting a Nation: Chinese National Cinema before 1949* (Hong Kong: Hong Kong University Press, 2003), 29–38. See also Zhen Zhang, *An Amorous History of the Silver Screen: Shanghai Cinema, 1896–1937* (Chicago: University of Chicago Press, 2005), 89–117; Laikwan Pang, *The Distorting Mirror: Visual Modernity in China* (Honolulu: University of Hawai'i Press, 2007), 164–183.

37. Hu, *Projecting a Nation*, 38–44.

38. See Zheng Junli, *Xiandai Zhongguo dianying shi lue* [A Brief History of Modern Chinese Cinema] (Shanghai: Shanghai liangyou, 1936), 35.

39. Lu Mengshu, "Yingju juben de shangque" [Reflection on Motion Picture Scriptwriting], in *Xinghuo* [A Little Sparkle], ed. Lu Mengshu (Shanghai: Liangyou tushu, 1927), 87.

40. Tsau Shu-ying, "They Learn in Suffering What They Teach in Song: Lu Xun and Kuriyagawa Hakuson's Symbols of Anguish," in *Symbols of Anguish: In Search of Melancholy in China*, ed. Wolfgang Kubin (Bern: Peter Lang, 2001), 441–469.

41. Lu Xun, *Lu Xun quanji di shisan juan* [Collection of Lu Xun, Book 13] (Beijing: Renmin wenxue chubanshe, 1973), 23.

42. Lu, *Lu Xun quanji di shisan juan*, 44.

43. Lu, "Yingju juben de shangque," 90.

44. Lu, *Lu Xun quanji di shisan juan*, 32.

45. Weihong Bao, "Baptism by Fire: Aesthetic Affect and Spectatorship in Chinese Cinema from Shanghai to Chongqing" (PhD diss., University of Illinois, Chicago, 2006), 177–178.

46. See, for example, Zhang, "Diba yishu"; Chen, "Zhongguo yingju zhong jige zhongyao de wenti, shang"; Chen Zhiqing, "Lun shezhi guzhuang yingju" [On Producing Costume Film], *Shenzhou tekan* 6 (1927): 24–34; Chen Zhiqing, "Zailun xinyingxiong zhuyi de yingju" [Revisiting New Heroic Film], *Yinxing* 8 (1927): 10–13; Sun Shiyi, "Wan xiaceng de yingju" [Motion Picture for the Underclass], *Yinxing* 1 (1926): 6–8; Lu Mengshu, "Dianying yu geming" [Film and Revolution], *Yinxing* 9 (1927): 36–42; Li Baijin, "Lun dianyin yu jiaoyu" [On Film and Education], *Yinxing* 12 (1927): 36–39.

47. Zhang, "Dianying yu shengjing," 22.

48. Lu Mengshu, "Dianying wenyi hua yu wenyi dianying hua" [*Wenyi* Film and Cinematic *Wenyi*], in Lu, *Dianying yu wenyi*, 146.

49. Sun, "Wan xiaceng de yingju," 8; Lu, "Dianying yu geming," 41.

50. Xin Min, "Yingpian yu xiaoshuo zhi butong" [The Differences between Film and Literature], *Yinxing* 3 (1926): 37.

51. Chun, "Yinmu shang de wenxue," 28.

52. Victor Fan, "The Cinema of Sun Yu: Ice Cream for the Eye . . . but with a Homo Sacer." *Journal of Chinese Cinemas* 5, no. 3 (2001): 226.

53. Li, "Lun dianyin yu jiaoyu," 38.

54. Tian Han, "Yinse de meng xu" [The Silver Dream con't], *Yinxing* 6 (1927): 14.

55. Tian, "Yinse de meng xu," 14.

56. Sun, "Wan xiaceng de yingju."

57. Chen, "Zhongguo yingju zhong jige zhongyao de wenti, zhong," 8.

58. Chen, "Zhongguo yingju zhong jige zhongyao de wenti, zhong," 8.

59. Lu Mengshu, "Zai heian de yingjuchang zhong" [In a Dark Motion Picture Theater], *Yinxing* 13 (1927): 21.

60. Lu, "Zai heian de yingjuchang zhong," 22.

61. Yu, "Dianying yu wenyi," 14.

62. Yu, "Dianying yu wenyi," 17.

63. Ying Dou, "Yingzu zai wenyi shang zhi jiazhi" [The Value of Photoplay in *Wenyi*], in Lu, *Dianying yu wenyi*, 80.

64. Lu Mengshu, "Xin yingxiong zhuyi" [New heroism], *Yinxing* 4 (1926): 16–18; Lu Mengshu, "Guochan dianying jinhou yingyou de xinqushi" [The Expected Tendency of Local Film], *Yinxing* 3 (1926): 24–25; Lu Mengshu, "Xin ying xiong zhuyi de yingju" [New Heroic Motion Picture], in Lu, *Xinghuo*, 1–11; Chen, "Zhongguo yingju zhong jige zhongyao de wenti, zhong"; Chen, "Zailun xinyingxiong zhuyi de yingju"; Yu, "Dianying de wenyihua," 67–77; Ying Dou, "Zhipian gongsi ying jiqi zhuyi zhege wenti, shang" [The Urgent Issues Concerning Production Companies, Part 1], *Yinxing* 16 (1928): 10–13.

65. Lu, "Xin yingxiong zhuyi de yingju," 5.

66. Lu, "Xin yingxiong zhuyi de yingju," 9.

67. Lu, "Xin yingxiong zhuyi de yingju," 10.

68. See Lu, "Xin yingxiong zhuyi."

69. Chen, "Zhongguo yingju zhong jige zhongyao de wenti, zhong," 8.

70. Du Shihuan, "Xin langman zhuyi de dianying" [Neoromanticist Film], in Lu, *Dianying yu wenyi*, 114.

71. Du, "Xin langman zhuyi de dianying," 117.

72. Leo Ou-fan Lee, "Literary Trends: The Quest for Modernity, 1895–1927," in *An Intellectual History of Modern China*, ed. Merle Goldman and Leo Ou-fan Lee (Cambridge: Cambridge University Press, 2002), 189.

73. Huang Zhen, "Dongxi liangfang de wenyi" [The *Wenyi* of the East and the West], *Yinxing* 12 (1927): 30.

74. Huang, "Dongxi liangfang de wenyi," 31.

75. Huang Zhen, "Dongxi liangfang de wenyi," 31.

76. Lu, "Zai heian de yingjuchang zhong 2," 32.

CHAPTER 10

Forming the Movie Field

Film Literati in Republican China

Emilie Yueh-yu Yeh and Enoch Yee-lok Tam

REVISIONIST HISTORIOGRAPHY AND "FILM LITERATI"

Chinese film historiography of Maoist China, by design, writes off motion pictures, filmmakers, publications, and organizations that were not viewed as offering good support to the founding of the People's Republic.[1] Likewise, the account told by the other side, that of the Republic of China, also excluded instances and figures that failed to support the Kuomintang (KMT), the Nationalist Party. Political historiography is hence limiting because of its need to follow a linear, teleological narrative that precludes ambiguity, contradictions, and betrayals. These politicized linear, teleological principles have dictated the writing of Chinese film history and, to some extent, Chinese diaspora film historiography. As a result, the past of Chinese-language, or Sinophone cinema, is fraught with glaring omissions, deliberate exclusions, and discrimination.

As one of the authors of this chapter has written previously, this orientation has resulted in a grim memory loss in Chinese film history.[2] The systematic discrimination against the so-called Mandarin Ducks and Butterflies Literature (hereafter Butterfly) writers and their film activities is one of the worst instances. In the first two decades of the Republican period, most popular films were adaptations from Butterfly bestsellers, including *Hei ji yuanhun* (*Wretched Spirit*, dir. Zhang Shichuan, 1916), written by Wu Jianren, and *Yu li hun* (*Jade Pear Spirit*, dir. Zhang Shichuan, 1924), by Xu Zhenya. Some of the major filmmakers of the 1920s also came from the

Butterfly school. But for a long period of time apathy toward these works and writers was so complete that their names and works were banned from the history of Chinese cinema. Inevitably the exclusion of the Butterfly filmmakers obscured early film history, leaving the documentation on cinema's development in the 1920s incomplete. Luckily this political historiography began to relax in the early 1980s, with the efforts of pioneering historians who illuminated the significance of Butterfly authors and their works, especially with respect to modernity, social reform, sexual politics, and the culture industry in the Republican era.[3] Though varying in scope and perspective, these founding works set the stage for a line of critical historiography on modern Chinese literature: David Der-wei Wang, Chen Jianhua, Carlos Rojas, Eileen Chow, and Zhao Xiaoxuan have made substantial additions to the growing studies on Butterfly literature.[4] These works corrected the notion that Butterfly literature was minor, frivolous, or negligible. Instead, they proposed that it played a pivotal role in making Republican literature a multifaceted, sometimes divergent, field of cultural production.

Similarly in the 1980s a gradual dissolve of the opposition between China and the West and subsequent political reform in the Asia Pacific region triggered relaxation of censorship. Amendments and corrections to the omissions and exclusions in film history were hence made one after another in remarkable works by historians and institutions from all over East Asia. To name just a few: the pioneering oral histories on Taiwanese dialect films published by the Taipei Film Archive in the 1990s;[5] the Hong Kong International Film Festival catalogs published by the Hong Kong Urban Council in the 1990s;[6] the exhibitions and their attendant curating publications edited by the team of researchers at the Hong Kong Film Archive;[7] and many film historians working on the pre-PRC history in the Mainland, Hong Kong, Taiwan, Singapore, and beyond.[8] These diverse works not only filled blank pages in the history of cinema; they also altered our vision of the past.

The revisionist historiography has been in fashion for some time now. Central to our discussion is the relation between the Butterfly writers and the film industry in Republican Shanghai. Emerging in the late Qing, Butterfly literature flourished during the transition between two epochs—one feudal and the other republican. The incredible shift allowed Butterfly literature to be fully blended into dual temporalities and styles: conserving the classics while experimenting with emergent liberalism and technology. And it is in the latter where the Butterfly writers formed a close alliance with cinema, a burgeoning narrative and technological apparatus that would impact ways of writing, thinking, and seeing in the new century. The Butterfly writers were among those who quickly grasped the opportunities provided by motion pictures to refashion an increasingly competitive leisure market. They used their professional network in journalism and translation to tap into the nascent film business, which needed source material for publicity and production. In the 1910s and 1920s, Butterfly writers were active in building the film culture by translating movie terms and subtitles and writing film and movie star reviews. It is safe to say that in the first decade of the Republic, Chinese cinema had the fingerprints of Butterfly literature all over it, and the rewriting of the Republican cinema will not be inclusive without acknowledging and examining these fingerprints.

According to the literary historians, over twenty writers were associated with Butterfly literature between 1900 and 1930.[9] In Yeh's study, she identifies fourteen Butterfly writers who crossed over to the motion picture industry, as producer, scriptwriter, director, actor, publicist, or critic. Frequently they played more than one role at a time, and often they performed in multiple capacities.[10] Among these, some were more active in building the new industry than others. Bao Tianxiao, Zhu Shouju, Zhou Shoujuan, Xu Zhuodai, Cheng Xiaoqing, Gu Mingdao, Yan Duhe, and Xu Bibo, for instance, were entrenched in the thriving film scene in the 1920s. Zhang Henshui and Wang Dungen were less invested, though their fingerprints on the screen were no less visible. Several of Zhang Henshui's works were high-profile screen adaptations,[11] while Wang Dungen wrote two filmscripts.[12]

Contributions by these Butterfly authors to the film industry, particularly works by Bao Tianxiao and Zhou Shoujuan, have been gradually unveiled.[13] These discoveries are groundbreaking, calling for further, advanced studies of the interstices between literary and filmic practices. Following this path, we identify Bao Tianxiao, Zhu Shouju, Zhou Shoujuan, Xu Zhuodai, and Yan Duhe as film literati for their involvement with motion pictures, as critics, publishers, editors, scriptwriters, directors, producers, or translators of foreign film stories called "cine-fiction" (*yingxi xiaoshuo*). We argue that the early filmscape, and more specifically, the formation of the movie field in Republican China, may not be sufficiently delineated without taking stock of these people and their various works. By treating them as decisive players in early Chinese film industry, we hope to address their contributions in hybridizing letters and images and in allying screenplays and cine-fiction—in sum, the unique position of "film literati" in bridging the filmic and literary fields.

We introduce the term *film literati* (*dianying wenren*) to label this group of writers for the purpose of highlighting their versatility as players in both fields. "Literati" (*wenren*) is a loaded term in Chinese history. Literally it means the "learned" or "man of letters," referring to social elites, the backbone of the civil service in imperial China. But a more common usage of "literati" in late Qing and early Republican period refers to literary professionals in general. They might or might not always "sell their writing" (*mai wen*) for a living, though most of them did. *Literati* by the turn of the twentieth century therefore has at least two connotations: a class identity as well as a vocational classification. With these two distinct identities, we coin the term *film literati* to foreground these writers' movement from an elite precinct to a marketplace of popular culture, from a respectable field of letters and arts to a commercial sphere of visual splendor. Unlike the leading intellectuals of early Republican years (e.g., Lu Xun, Chen Duxiou, and Li Dazhao), who sought social change by means of grandiloquent rhetoric, film literati found their niche in the culture industry through ingenious applications of their writing techniques, including the two-way translation of turning foreign film stories into a new genre called "cine-fiction," and adapting their own novels as screenplays. The new space in the culture industry allowed them to occupy a peculiar position in the intersection of the movie and literary fields by utilizing the cultural and social capital they possessed.

Film literati is a composite term to indicate writers who utilized their writing for the advancement of the emergent movie field, in criticism, scripts, story ideas, and publicity. Previous studies established Zhou Shoujuan's track record as a film critic and Bao Tianxiao as a scriptwriter. They transported their transcultural expertise—through their translating practice—to structure the movie field, which was nonnative to begin with and required translating and rewriting for the local audience. In other words, the capital they offered to the formation of motion pictures as a new field was not merely technical know-how, but also epistemological. A parallel can also be drawn between the introduction of cinema to China and the overall ethos of Butterfly literature—a fascination with the foreign, yet an insistence on local identity, resulting in a noticeable drift between the so-called old and the new eras, the archaic and a contemporary sensibility. Here we find an uncanny resonance between early cinema and popular literature when they were engulfed by the new wave of capitalism in the early 1920s. Cinema and vernacular literature were both seen as viable forms to approach the contemporary and apprehend the modern, including practice in newly emerging culture industries of publishing, publicity, and image-making. This appreciation mobilized ample crossover between the two constituencies, despite their seeming contrasts.

Film literati's intervention in the movie field resonated far beyond their conventional reputation. Their sway can hardly be measured according to a simple method of content analysis, that is, how many pieces of film work they wrote or produced, including their market share and economic value accumulated at the time. More than that, we argue that film literati were instrumental in setting the precepts of the cinema institution in the Republican era. They guided both industry novices and the new converts to standards of watching, receiving, evaluating, and making movies, based on their experience in reading and translating foreign literature. By these means film literati also intended to benchmark film's aesthetic and social value against prevailing norms of image production of the Other. They often used cinema to intervene in the existing conventions of visual representation of the foreign, be it people, customs, scenery, landscape, or objects. These interventions were crucial in structuring the movie field in its formative stage, by drawing its boundaries, mapping and regulating its sphere.

The phrase *movie field* is coined from Pierre Bourdieu's concept of "field" in cultural production.[14] Bourdieu developed his social theory by means of three key terms: *habitus*, *field*, and *capital* in an attempt to reconceive the formation of a class society.[15] To Bourdieu class division or class identity is created symbolically and culturally, rather than merely by social or economic terms. The process is often determined by the interplay between agent and the social structure, which takes place in the habitus, a socialized norm or tendency where people tend to think or act. For example a group of people are socialized through a set of dispositions within a socially determined environment. The habitus is not fixed and can change over time, depending on specific needs, circumstances, and contexts. In tandem with "habitus," Bourdieu introduced noneconomic dimensions to the analysis of the concept of "capital" in class structure. In addition to the notion of monetary or material resources, Bourdieu added that the idea of "capital" as cultural and symbolic resources. In the field of arts, education and culture particularly, cultural or symbolic capital is more significant in shaping the power relations, determining the classification of a class hierarchy. The notion of "fields" refers to an area, or a network where people express and reproduce their dispositions (habitus), to accumulate cultural capital, thereby establishing a recognized status.

Habitus, fields, and cultural, symbolic capital were proposed as new forms in understanding the complex formation of class and power, as fundamentals of social theory. Bourdieu was especially concerned with the diverse forms of "capital," in which symbolic and cultural capital are as important as financial means in forming a class identity. Hence the power attached to a given class is never a simple process. Instead, it requires vectors of interaction with various forms of capital, within the operations of fields and habitus. With these notions in mind, power becomes a much more nuanced system of interplay and exchange of cultural, symbolic, and economic capital. Bourdieu leads us to rethink art, film, and literary production not as individual activities, but as fields of cultural production: "The field of production and circulation of symbolic goods is defined as the system of objective relations among different instances, functionally defined by their role in the division of labor of production, reproduction and diffusion of symbolic goods."[16]

The world of the Butterfly authors can thus be described as a field where they produced (writing), reproduced (translation, adaptation), and disseminated (publishing, printing) their letters and thoughts. By putting their labor in these divisions, they formed a network of shared taste, interest, and information where they accumulated and displayed their cultural capital. Note that many of these writers were migrants from the provinces, and it was crucial for them to work as cognate agents of a field striving for capital and power. Producing literary goods was one option; making movies was possibly an even more profitable alternative.

We isolate Zhou Shoujuan as a case study to provide an illustration of film literati and their crossover movement. As an early film practitioner, Zhou's role as a film critic has already been explored. For example, Chen Jianhua studied Zhou's film review column entitled "Yingxi hua" ("On the Cinematograph"). Between June 20, 1919, and January 17, 1920 Zhou wrote over a dozen film articles for the literary page called "Ziyou tan" ("Talking Freely") in *Shenbao*, where he introduced foreign films and treated these films as a means of enlightening his readers.[17] *Shenbao* was a major Chinese-language newspaper in Shanghai known for its coverage of culture, leisure, literature, and mass media. One of its signature features was Zhou's column, which attracted a wide readership, and hence Zhou's interest in motion pictures had an extensive influence in shaping cinema's reception by China's urbanites. Precisely because of the immensity of Zhou's contribution to early film culture, we argue that his other roles in film culture are in need of further elucidation, especially pertaining to our term *film literati*.

We delineate Zhou as a leading film literatus in fields of interlocking relations and exchanges by piecing together his practices as film critic (writing reviews in *Shenbao, Mingxing Special Issue, Shanghai Pictorial, Film Pictorial,* etc.), scriptwriter (writing scripts for films such as *Shuihuo yuanyang* [*An Ill-Fated Couple*, dir. Cheng Bugao, 1924], *Huan jin ji* [*Money Returned*, dir. Dan Duyu, 1926], *Ma Jiefu* [dir. Zhu Shouju, 1926], *Meiren guan* [*A Beauty's Seduction*, dir. Bu Wancang, 1928], etc.), and cine-fiction writer (rewriting movies as short stories). Tracing his multivalent activities in print media and film industry lets us see the dynamics between the movie and literary fields and put forward a new understanding of the early filmscape as an evolving, cross-disciplinary terrain. We will first discuss Bao Tianxiao, Zhu Shouju, Xu Zhuodai, and Yan Duhe. The last part of the chapter focuses on Zhou Shoujuan to corroborate the concept of film literati.

FILM MEETS BUTTERFLY LITERATURE: CROSSOVER BETWEEN THE MOVIE AND THE LITERARY FIELD

Bao Tianxiao (1876–1973)

Bao Tianxiao, originally named Bao Qingzhu, had varied professional experiences before he became involved in film. As literatus Bao was extremely prolific and versatile. His career crossed many different genres (romance, children literature, detective, science fiction) through a span of more than three decades, from around 1900 to the 1930s.[18] In many ways Bao exemplified the "modern" literati, making a successful transition from the traditional type of scholar to a professional writer in the new century. Bao came from Suzhou, a river town outside Shanghai known for its literary and artistic ambience, including its traditional Chinese gardens and private *écoles*. For centuries, Suzhou was a hotbed producing literati proficient in poetry, calligraphy, painting, and music. When the national civil service examination system (*keju zhidu*) was abolished in 1905, literati residing in the provinces migrated en masse to metropolitan cities to find a new identity for themselves. Shanghai with its burgeoning publishing industry was where these skilled writers found a new professional environment, a new habitus of long-term prospects and sustainability.[19]

Bao, like most of his peers, worked primarily as an editor and translator of foreign literature. Between 1901 and 1919 he edited more than a dozen magazines, for which he was also a contributing writer. Bao was particularly known for translated novels that featured children and education.[20] For example, the novel *Xin'er jiuxue ji* (*The Schooling of Xin'er*) was a translation of *Heart: An Italian Schoolboy's Journal* (*Cuore*, Edmondo de Amicis) and won a prize from the Ministry of Education.[21] His novel *Ku'er liulang ji* (*The Story of a Poor Vagrant Boy*) was also a translation based on Yuho Kikuchi's *A Child without Family* (a Japanese translation from Hector Malot's *Sans Famille*). This work was adapted by Zhang Shichuan and Zheng Zhengqiu into *Xiao pengyou* (*Little Friends*, 1925). Bao's own novel *Yi lü ma* (*A Thread of Hemp*) was adapted into *Guaming fuqi* (*The Couple in Name Only*, dir. Bu Wancang, 1927). Both pictures were produced by the Mingxing yingpian gongsi (Star Motion Picture Company). The popularity of his fictions, most of which were translated works, made him a sought-after literatus by the nascent film industry. Bao recalled his recruitment meeting with Star's production head, Zheng Zhengqiu:

> Zhengqiu explained: "... We've read some of your short stories. You could simply write a story like those, or shorter. Then we can add additional materials, divide it into scenes, and expand it into a filmscript. What do you think?" ... Zhengqiu continued: "My colleagues suggested that you write a filmscript for us each month, and we will pay you one hundred yuan. We can sign a one-year contract first. No hurry about writing new filmscripts just yet. In the first place, you can rewrite your two novels, *Orchid of the Valley* and *Fallen Plum Blossoms*, and give us a synopsis for each. We will put them on the screen. You will agree, won't you?"[22]

Bao took only seven days to write the synopses for *Kong'gu lan* (*Orchid of the Valley*, dir. Zhang Shichuan, 1925) and *Meihua luo* (*Fallen Plum Blossoms*, dir. Zheng Zhengqiu and Zhang Shichuan, 1927). The two films achieved a spectacular box-office success, especially *Orchid of the Valley*, proving market potential for literary adaptation. Bao then became Star's chief writer.[23] In addition, he wrote stories for other film companies. Between 1925 and 1927 eleven films (see table 10.1) credited his contributions, either as scriptwriter or translator of the handbill. Handbills were key promotional tools and allowed greater mobility of screen culture to wider circles, especially for foreign movies glossed for Chinese audiences.

Another important feature of Bao's film literati career, besides the various things he did for film companies, was cine-fiction. Bao produced a large number of cine-fictions. Many of these works were literary versions of Star's productions, and, in fact, some of these films were adapted from Bao's own works (see table 10.1). As film literatus, Bao achieved a prolific career by recycling his own work in multiple platforms, characterized by a circuit of reproduction; that is, by rendering his original or translated works into screenplays on one part of the loop, and by rewriting his film adaptations or foreign film stories into cine-fiction, at the other end.

Zhu Shouju (1892–1966)

Zhu Shouju, a Shanghai native, was the most prolific Butterfly author-filmmaker. Under the pen name "Shanghai Dream Narrator" (*Haishang shuomengren*), he published his influential novel *Xiepu chao* (*Tides of Huangpu*), which was serialized in *Xin Shenbao* (*New Shenbao*) from 1916 to 1921.[24] *The Waves of the River Huangpu* was a type of pulp fiction derived from tabloid journalism prevalent in Shanghai beginning in the late Qing period. This genre boasted a candid depiction of all walks of life in Shanghai, with embellished details and sultry anecdotes. Zhu's novel presents a slice of the private lives of Shanghai celebrities (corrupt officials, reckless concubines, hapless opera performers, fickle revolutionaries, and dishonest dramatists) and their sexual indulgences. It was an instant hit. May Fourth critics attacked it for its sensationalism and cheap thrills. Eileen Chang, however, repeatedly referred to it as an influence on her work, claiming that it was the best "naturalist" novel in China.[25]

Apart from being a pulp fiction writer, Zhu was an avid cinephile, and his path to directing seemed predetermined. With the funds from several investors, in 1920 he partnered with his cinematographer friend Dan Duyu to found the Shanghai yingxi gongsi (Shanghai Film Company).[26] The company's debut was the 1921 *Haishi* (*Swear and Oath*, dir. Dan Duyu). Zhu wrote his first screenplay, *Gujing chongbo ji* (*The Revival of an Old Well*), also directed by Dan, in 1923. A huge hit in Shanghai and overseas, *The Revival of an Old Well* was credited as the first feature film that inaugurated the *aiqing dianying* (tragic love) genre. From then on Zhu went full speed to expand his career from literatus to full-fledged filmmaker. He sold the copyright of *The Waves of the River Huangpu* to upgrade the company's infrastructure.[27] In 1924, Zhu headed the Shanghai yingxi yanjiu hui (Shanghai Film Study Society) and Baihe yingpian gongsi (Lilium Pictures) For Lilium, he directed two pictures, both of which were adaptations of Butterfly fiction.

Lilium shortly merged with Dazhonghua yingpian gongsi (Great China Film Company) into Dazhonghua baihe (Great China Lilium Pictures) and Zhu remained as chief director of the company, making a major contribution to its growth.

On the other side of the business, Zhu did not forgo his film literati practice. He cofounded a film magazine, *Dianying zahi* (*Film Magazine*), with Gu Kenfu and Cheng Bugao in 1925. Zhu edited the first nine issues, collaborating with other Butterfly writers to secure their footholds in the movie field. During the production of *Swear and Oath*, Zhou Shoujuan, chief editor of *Banyue* (*Biweekly*), provided much-needed publicity for the film's lead, Yin Mingzhu, in his magazine.[28] A symbiotic relation thus arose between the two fields, which not only accelerated the growth of the film industry, but also accumulated necessary cultural capital for those on both sides to utilize. During Zhu's tenure in Lilium and Great China Lilium, he claimed directing and writing credits for nearly twenty titles (see table 10.2). Zhu exited the film industry in 1935 briefly but returned in 1940, primarily as a scriptwriter.[29]

For a long time Zhu's only surviving film was believed to be an incomplete print of *Ersun fu* (*Mother's Happiness*, 1926), housed in Beijing's Film Archive. This film was written by Zhu and directed by Shi Dongshan. In 2011 Japan's National Film Center recovered *Fengyu zhi ye* (*On a Stormy Night*, 1925), directed and written by Zhu Shouju. The print was found from the Kinugasa Teinosuke collection donated by his family after Kinugasa passed away in 2006. The print found in Tokyo comprises eight reels, only one reel short of the original length.[30] The surviving print of *On a Stormy Night*, though incomplete, gives us access to a film directed by a representative film literatus.

Xu Zhuodai (1881–1958)

Xu Zhuodai (Xu Fulin; Xu Banmei), commonly known as a humorist within the Butterfly school, directed, wrote, and starred in more than fifteen films. Xu wrote hundreds of satiric pieces and many film articles promoting artistic value (*wenyi*) in local film production. Xu studied physical education in Japan, though his interest was much broader. Before becoming a filmmaker and film critic, Xu was a dramatist, writing scripts for the westernized Chinese stage show called new drama (*xinju*). Xu's memoir indicates that he wrote more than thirty comedies and put them on stage daily over a month's time. Xu later tried his hand at the comic novel.[31] Xu's flexible, chameleonic adjustment prompted Butterfly historian Fan Yanqiao to describe his career in three distinct phases, after his three different names: "The first was the Xu Fulin phase, in which he was a physical educator and children's fiction writer; the second one was the Xu Banmei time, in which he was a scriptwriter for the new drama; the third phase was Xu Zhuodai, in which he was a novelist."[32] Yet in most of the accounts of Xu Zhuodai, his contributions to the movie field are omitted, and so is his role as film literatus.

Xu's most remarkable contribution as a film literatus was his partly translated, partly edited *Yingxi xue* (*Studies on Photoplay*, 1924). This is one of the earliest film theory books in China, in which Xu discussed aspects of film genre, scriptwriting, directing, cinematography, performance, and editing. In addition, Xu's 1922 essay "The Art of *Women Skeletons*" ("Yishu shang de *Hongfen kulou*"), published in *Shenbao*, was one of the very first writings to advocate artistic value as a criterion in film criticism.[33] As film literati Xu advocated the precepts of *wenyi*—art and literary treatment—as guiding principles in Chinese filmmaking.[34]

Like Zhu Shouju, Xu also made a quick crossover from writer to film director and producer. In 1925, he founded a small production house, Kaixin yingpian gongsi (Happy Film Company), with Wang Youyou. Contrary to Xu's film reviews that propagated *wenyi*, artistic aspirations, and literary merit, Xu seemed to have a relaxed attitude about film production. His production firm Happy Film focused on slapstick, comedies, special effects films, and supernatural films to surprise and amuse audiences.[35] Xu also edited the company's in-house magazine *Kaixin tekan* (*Happy Special Issue*). According to his partner Wang, the company's goal was to make fun movies, silly, even mindless, but fitting for average audiences."[36] Xu used his Japanese connection to bring in Japanese cinematographer Kawatani Shohei to shoot the first batch of shorts in 1925, *Yinshen yi* (*The Invisible Cloak*), *Linshi gongguan* (*Temporary Residence*), and *Aishen zhi feiliao* (*Cupid's Feed*).[37] Tricks (*qulike* or *tuolike*, transliterating the English term "trick") were always used in Happy Film's line of production as main attractions. For instance, *Shenxian bang* (*The Magic Club*, dir. Wang Youyou, 1926) applied tricks to send the actors to the moon. This reminds us of Georges Méliès's famous *A Trip to the Moon* (1902). Happy's mode of production was exceptionally flexible and circumstantial, according to Xu's remark on the company's "scavenger mode" (*shi xiangyan pigu zhuyi*), referring to its lack of resources.[38] Happy Film was closed in 1928. At the short-lived Happy Film Company Xu scripted and directed twelve films (see table 10.3). In the end Xu considered Happy Film a failure because of the company's inability to produce feature-length films, which foreclosed its long-term prospects.[39] In the mid-1930s, Xu joined Yihua yingye gongsi (Yihua Film Company) as an actor and also wrote scripts for Star.

Yan Duhe (1889–1968)

Originally named Yan Zhen, Yan Duhe was best known as a newspaper editor. Yan edited the supplement *Kuaihuo lin* (*Happy Forest*, later renamed *Xin yuanlin* [*New Garden*]) of *Xinwenbao* for more than thirty years, beginning in 1914. In Shanghai *Xinwenbao* was comparable to *Shenbao*, while Yan's *Happy Forest* is compared with Zhou Shoujuan's *Talking Freely* as two leading supplements. The sobriquet *Yi juan yi he* ("Cuckoo and Crane") was coined after the first names of the two leading editors Zhou Shoujuan (*juan* for cuckoo) and Yan Duhe (*he* for crane) at the time. Yan also translated *The Complete Works of Sherlock Holmes*. His editorship was so prominent that it was possible his film works were overshadowed.

Like many other film literati, Yan's entry to the movie field was through editorials. *Xinren tekan* (*Xinren Special Issue*), coedited with Zhou Shixun, for the film company Xinren is one of these editorial venues. More importantly, he contributed to *Zhongguo yingxi daguan* (*Grand View of Chinese Cinema*, 1927), along with Xu Zhuodai and others. The book is one of the earliest reference books on Chinese cinema, with complete entries on individual film companies, directors, actors, and film journals.

Although he never served as regular staff in Star, Yan Duhe maintained a close relationship with the company. In 1926, Star announced a call for share subscriptions, and Yan drafted the subscription in the paper.[40] In addition, Yan served as script consultant for Star's first sound film, *Genü Hongmudan* (*The Songstress Red Peony*, dir. Zhang Shichuan, 1930).[41] According to our survey, Yan was credited in fifteen films (see table 10.4) as scriptwriter, consultant, and publicist. Beyond any doubt, his most acclaimed film work was the adaptation of Zhang Henshui's *Tixiao yinyuan* (*Fate in Tears and Laughter*, dir. Zhang Shichuan, 1932) in six installments. Indeed, Huang Xuelei argues that Yan Duhe "was not the only qualified candidate for these tasks. It was Yan's fame and stature that the Mingxing [Star] leadership regarded as crucially important."[42] Here we see that the cultural capital Yan accumulated in the print media significantly eased his crossover to the movie field.

Scriptwriting was one of Yan's major commitments. He taught scriptwriting in Zhonghua dianying xuexiao (China Film School), a feeder school set up by a film company of the same name in 1924. Following this, with Butterfly colleagues Zhou Shoujuan, Pan Gongzhan, and Yao Sufeng, Yan formed Zhongguo dianying yishu yanjiuhui (Society of Chinese Film Art Studies). In 1932 he also took up the scriptwriting consultant role at the Tianyi Film Company. Yan's long-term engagement as film literatus would continue until the mid-1930s. For a detailed list of his scripts please see table 10.4.

In her studies on Hollywood, Janet Wasko emphasizes the film industry's reliance on literary source materials. According to her, nearly half of Hollywood's production in the studio era came from literature, Broadway theater, or other published materials.[43] Our survey of the number of films produced between the 1910s and 1920s also showed the close relationship between the movie field and the vernacular literature established since the late Qing period. The affinity between cinema and literature is demonstrated in the preceding discussion of the various roles the Butterfly writers took on; these roles typified many forms in which the film industry utilized literary resources and the conditions in which the Butterfly writers made themselves useful to the movie field.

Zhou Shoujuan (1895–1968) and Cine-Fiction

Zhou Shoujuan (Zhou Zufu) was considered the premium Butterfly writer[44] and a representative figure in the crossover between the literary and the film spheres. Zhou's literary career began in 1912 with the publication of his fiction *Ai zhi hua* (*Flower of Love*). His translation of *Oumei mingjia duanpian xiaoshuo congkan* (*Selected Short Stories by Famous European and American Writers*) won him recognition from Lu Xun.[45] Besides fiction and translation, Zhou was active in editing literary and film magazines, including *Ziluolan* (*The Violet*), *Libai liu* (*The Saturday*), *Dianying huabao* (*Film Pictorial*), *Shanghai huabao* (*Shanghai Pictorial*), and *Yinguang* (*Silver Light*). *The Violet* and *Libai liu* were considered premium outlets among major Butterfly periodicals. Like a typical Butterfly literatus, Zhou's professional identity was multilayered and his presence in the literary field ubiquitous. Among these activities, Zhou's most cited film achievement is the reviews he wrote for *Ziyou tan* (*Talking Freely*), the literary supplement of *Shenbao*. Between 1919 and 1920, Zhou published a total of sixteen movie reviews, covering narrative, performance, direction, and set design. In many ways Zhou can be regarded one of the earliest cinephiles in China, along with Gu Kenfu and Lu Jie (Lok Key), publishers of *Yingxi zazhi* (*The Motion Picture Review*) in 1921. *The Motion Picture Review* is the earliest film publication that survived history.

As film literatus Zhou was not limited to theory and criticism, however. Like most other literati that crossed over to the movie field, Zhou was involved in production, writing scripts, and publicity. His debut as a scriptwriter took place in 1924, for *An Ill-Fated Couple*, directed by Cheng Bugao. Subsequently he wrote five additional scripts (see table 10.5). He also worked as a publicist for Great China Lilium and Star in the 1920s and for Tianyi in the 1930s.

Zhou was a pioneer in film criticism—the reviews on *Shenbao*'s *Talking Freely* were ahead of their time in terms of scope and perspectives. They broke new ground, bringing in a new crop of film devotees. Hence Chen Jianhua suggested that Zhou introduced the film genre to the Chinese audience,[46] while Xue Feng argued that Zhou's film reviews enlightened his readers no less than did the May Fourth intellectuals.[47] Nevertheless, we consider Zhou's major undertaking as film literatus should be extended beyond those initial sixteen articles. We suggest taking into account his output in cine-fiction, the new literary genre created by film literati, to further assess Zhou's crossover career. Zhou was eager to transform his moviegoing routine to letters, keeping a record of the stories he watched on screen or read in foreign publications. This is the background from which Zhou produced his film reviews. Zhou wrote in a fashion of reportage, sharing with the readers his spectatorship, perhaps as a movie guide as well. Movies provided him with raw materials and inspiration.

Years before he published his movie articles in *Shenbao*, Zhou began writing cine-fiction, a journal or record of the movies he watched. From 1914 to 1922 Zhou published ten cine-fictions based on foreign films he had seen: *Waiting* (1911), Georges Monca's *Le Petit Chose* (1912), *How Heroes are Made* (dir. Enrico Guazzoni, 1912), Mario Caserini and Eleuterio Rodolfi's *The Last Days of Pompeii* (1913), *War is Hell* (dir. Alfred Machin, 1914), *A Woman's Sacrifice* (dir. Tom Green, 1906), D. W. Griffith's *The Open Gate* (1909), *Purity* (dir. Rae Berger, 1916), *The Woman Thou Gavest Me* (dir. Hugh Ford, 1919), and *Trumpet Island* (dir. Tom Terriss, 1920).[48] For more details, see table 10.5. Most of these works were published in *Saturday*, a key Butterfly literary magazine with which Zhou was closely affiliated. The symbiosis between cine-fiction and Butterfly outlets affirms the claim we made at the beginning of our chapter regarding the close connection between popular literature and cinema in the early Republican era. Throughout the teens and the early 1920s, Butterfly writers like Zhou and Bao Tianxiao penned cine-fiction. By the mid-1920s, cine-fiction had become a routine genre, having been institutionalized as a staple in film publications. This is clearly demonstrated in an exclusive cine-fiction section in the magazine *Dianying Yuebao* (*Film Monthly*). Stories published in this section featured both foreign and domestic sources, indicating the adaptable multiplicity of the genre, as publicity and literature East and West, or in between.[49]

Zhou Shoujuan specialist Chen Jianhua argues that Zhou's oeuvre manifests the cultural production in the Republican era as a complex constitution of reception, translation, and rewriting.[50] We add that Zhou's multifaceted career mimics the interlocking network of letters and moving images, testifying to a symbiotic linkage of literature and film in Chinese film history. This was made possible by the constant interplay and exchanges of these two fields. As evidenced by Zhou Shoujuan's film reviews, especially his transmutation of screen stories into a new form of cine-fiction, the relationship between fiction and film, the two major sources of popular cultural consumption in Republican times, is proven to be much more intimate and intense than was previously imagined.

In 1925 Zhou published a short story, "Xiao changzhu" ("The Boy Heiress"), as a piece of cine-fiction based on a silent film of the same title, directed by Lu Jie and produced by Great China Lilium.[51] The film was inspired by Mary Pickford's boy role in the American picture *Little Lord Fauntleroy* (dir. Alfred E. Green and Jack Pickford, 1921), also a literary adaptation from Frances Hodgson Burnett's novel of the same title published in 1886. A wealthy old man separates from his only son because he is disappointed with the son's marriage. Years goes by, and the old man is facing death without an heir. Unable to locate his son, the old master's staff finds the son's daughter as a surrogate. But a girl cannot be an heir, according to the custom. So she is made up as a boy to console the grandfather and to fend off relatives coveting her grandfather's wealth. When the girl's gender is disclosed, the succession plan becomes unfeasible. Just when the evil relatives are about to prevail, the girl's father suddenly returns to resume his place as heir.[52] "The Boy Heiress" was the first cine-fiction based on a Chinese picture that Zhou had written; before this, Zhou only worked on foreign films he watched at the cinema. Lu's diary recorded that prior to "The Boy

Heiress," Zhou occasionally wrote handbills and publicity materials for the company and also used his name and influence to promote films released by Great China Lilium.[53] *The Boy Heiress* (dir. Lu Jie [Lok Key], 1925) would be the first Chinese picture in which Zhou was fully involved as a publicist. He edited *The Boy Heiress Special Issue*, which contains several important written records of the film: a synopsis, a full script and credits, the cine-fiction, publicity and production stills, and a couple of short pieces written on location shooting and preproduction.[54] As a film *The Boy Heiress* has been lost; and if not for Zhou's cine-fiction the film would remain buried in the abyss of historical wreckage.

Existing literature suggests Butterfly literature's inherent ambivalence toward modernity and its anxiety to overcome that uncertain state. Reading a few representative texts, including *Zhou Shoujuan shuoji xiace* (*Collected Fiction of Zhou Shoujuan*), volume 2, and the short stories collected in Fan Boqun's *Mandarin Ducks and Butterflies: Selected Works of the "Saturday,"* including "Aiqing daili ren" ("Love Letters") written by Xu Zhuodai and "Zai jiaceng li" ("The Room Next to the Staircase") by Bao Tianxiao, we observe a consistent pattern.[55] The authors paused on conventional tropes of victimized women, children, and the poor to advocate a mild version of scientific rationality and liberalism. It appears that when Butterfly literati wrote cine-fiction, both the tropes and the underlined ideologies were sustained. *The Boy Heiress* unfolds with a familiar setting of traditional values under siege, resulting in family disintegration; eventually blood relations unlock the conflict and unite the family. Furthermore, the value under question is recuperated by the return of the wayward son. Clearly the film sides with the idea of individualism when it comes to marriage; nevertheless, when it faces the issue of inherence, male lineage remains an unbending concept. The oxymoron of the film's English title—"a boy heiress"—is a decoy within the plot to pacify the grandfather and trick the relatives. But when the daughter's father—the true heir—returns, crises are dissipated, and order is resumed. Perhaps it is implied that the young daughter will eventually be accepted as the heiress of the family. But for the time being, only male members of the family have legitimacy to carry on the family tree. The film's ideological position on the issue of gender equality takes many steps backward.

The cine-fiction of "The Boy Heiress" is a by-product of the film. It is a publicity tool. Though it may be a true record of the film's narrative, it can hardly be mistaken as a copy of the film. And without seeing the film, we cannot truly have a credible examination of the relationship between cine-fiction and its filmic version. In what way can we identify cine-fiction as an interface between motion pictures and vernacular literature? Does cine-fiction exemplify the convergence of images and literature? To answer these questions we will compare the Italian epic *The Last Days of Pompeii* (1913) and Zhou Shoujuan's rewrite. Our comparison sheds light on the impact of the new visual medium of the twentieth century in Chinese vernacular literature, in its imagery, narrative, and ideology.

From Italy to China, from Film to Fiction: Two Versions of the Fallen Pompeii

Zhou watched *The Last Days of Pompeii* on its second run in Shanghai's Tokyo Theatre (March 13–16, 1914)[56] and subsequently published his cine-fiction of the same title in *Saturday* in 1915. In his introduction Zhou described the popularity of the film in Shanghai, though he had missed it in its first run shown in the Victoria Theatre (March 3–11, 1914)[57]: "I was not into movies, so I did not see this famous picture though I had heard so much about it. Recently I was bored to death, with grudges and desolation besieging me, so I began to frequent cinemas, for relief and pleasure."[58] Zhou went on to express his amusement over the plot and the set of *Pompeii*. At the advice of his friend, he decided to rewrite the movie into a tragic love (*aiqing*) story, based on the film's melodramatic ending.

Last Days of Pompeii (1913, hereafter *Pompeii*) is an Italian period film with international impact. The story centers on a triangular relationship between Glaucus, a noble Athenian, his love interest Jone, and Glaucus's blind slave Nidia. The evildoer is the high priest Arbace, who headed the Egyptian cult Isis, which spellbound the people of Pompeii. Arbace covets the beauty of Jone and vows to possess her. Nidia, desperate to win her master's love, collaborates unknowingly with Arbace to poison Glaucus, who is then framed as a murderer by Arbace for a crime Arbace himself commits. Glaucus faces the cruel Roman law of pitting his survival against hungry lions in the Colosseum. All of these events take place against the looming eruption of Mt. Vesuvius in A.D. 79. *Pompeii*'s scale, length (running time eighty-eight minutes) and operatic majesty put the rest of the world on notice that cinema was a medium of monumental potential. In her discussion of modern "American" narratives in early cinema, Miriam Hansen argues that the success of the Italian spectacles is indebted to the themes from Mediterranean antiquity, which she calls the Babylonian narrative.[59] This narrative "portrayed the challenge of

Christian values to pagan Rome. Unlike their rivals (the thrillers that turned on kidnapping and torture, while hinting at other depravities), these Christian epics judiciously balanced their portrayal of decadence with the eventual triumph of Christianity."[60] *Pompeii* and other Italian epics such as *Quo Vadis?* (dir. Enrico Guazzoni, 1913) and *Cabiria* (dir. Giovanni Pastrone, 1914) were particularly admired by Cecil B. DeMille and D. W. Griffith, whose *Intolerance* (1916) was inspired by these Italian spectaculars. The Italian pictures were instrumental in transitioning to feature-length, prestige events that addressed middle- and upper-class patrons.[61]

The Italian film epics owe debts to literature. *Last Days of Pompeii*, *Quo Vadis*, and *Cabiria* were all adaptations from prior literary properties. *Pompeii*, for instance, was based on a novel of the same title written by Edward George Bulwer-Lytton in 1834. But this is not the sole reason why they exerted worldwide influence, including their popularity in China. In *Pompeii*, Mario Caserini and Eleuterio Rodolfi trimmed down the scale of the novel by de-emphasizing the religious conflicts between the Egyptian cult Isis and Christianity. They also reduced the complex relationships among several key characters into a love triangle vis-à-vis a ruthless predator. The cinematic scale alternates between romance, drawing-room intrigue, and Roman eroticism (scenes depicting beautiful Jone taking the baths with her maids). Explicit parallels are made between innocent lovers—figured as immaculate doves—and the wicked priest of Isis Arbace, who is likened to a predatory owl. This is a literary technique derived from contemporary fiction, appealing to literate audiences accustomed to poetic metaphors, figure of speech visualized in images. Acting for the most part is physical and externalized, especially the distinct body movement of the blind Nidia, though the story hews to elements that psychologize the behavior of principal characters. Another appeal of the story is its appropriation of the tragic burial of the city of Pompeii, domesticating its destruction by embedding the spectacle into a story of unrequited love and sacrifice. This personifies the natural disaster, and brings intimacy, emotions, and tenderness to a world-famous epic of volcanic obliteration. Magic and spirituality (Isis), special effects and spectacle, echo the power of motion pictures.

In general, Zhou Shoujuan did not depart extensively from the diegesis of *Pompeii* in his rewrite. He follows the narrative structure chronologically, depicting the principal characters of Glaucus (in Zhou's version Clauous), Jone (Zhou's Ions), Nidia (Zhou's Nydia), and Arbace accordingly, and brings in the volcanic eruption as deux ex machina at the end. Despite these

Table 10.1. Bao Tianxiao Filmography

Year	Title	Director	Scriptwriter	Author of the original story or cine-fiction, handbill
1925	*Kelian de guinü* (*My Pitiful Daughter*)	Zhang Shichuan	Bao Tianxiao	Cine-fiction rewritten as *Youhuo* (*Seduction*)
1925	*Xiao pengyou* (*Little Friends*)	Zhang Shichuan	Zheng Zhengqiu	Adapted from Bao's novel *Ku'er liuleng ji* (*The Story of a Poor Vagrant Boy*), a translation of Yuho Kikuchi's *Ie naki ko (A Child without Family)*, based on Hector Malot's *Sans Famille*
1925	*Xinren de jiating* (*The Newlyweds*)	Ren Jinping	Gu Kenfu	Handbill written by Bao Tianxiao
1925	*Kong'gu lan* (*Orchid of the Valley*)	Zhang Shichuan	Bao Tianxiao	Bao's original novel
1926	*Duoqing de nüling* (*A Lovelorn Actress*)	Zhang Shichuan	Bao Tianxiao	Cine-fiction rewritten as *En yu chou* (*Grace and Hate*)
1926	*Hao nan'er* (*A Good Guy*)	Zhang Shichuan	Bao Tianxiao	N.a.
1926	*Ta de tongku* (*Her Sorrows*)	Zhang Shichuan	Bao Tianxiao	N.a.
1926	*Furen zhi nü* (*The Daughter of a Wealthy Family*)	Zhang Shichuan	Bao Tianxiao	Cine-fiction rewritten under the same title; also wrote handbill.
1926	*Liangxin fuhuo* (*Resurrection*)	Bu Wancang	Bao Tianxiao	Adaptation of Leo Tolstoy's *Resurrection*; also wrote handbill
1927	*Guaming fuqi* (*The Couple in Name Only*)	Bu Wancang	Zheng Zhengqiu	Adapted from Bao's novel *Yi lü ma* (*A Thread of Hemp*)
1927	*Fengliu shaonainai* (*An Amorous Wife*)	Ren Jinping	Bao Tianxiao	Adapted from Bao's fiction *Qing zhi maoyi* (*Trading of Love*)
1927	*Meihua luo* (*Fallen Plum Blossoms*)	Zhang Shichuan, Zheng Zhengqiu	Bao Tianxiao	Adapted from Bao's translation of Kuroiwa Shūroku's *Suteobune* (*Abandoned Ship*), a Japanese translation of Mary Elizabeth Braddon's *Diavola*
1928	*Duoqing de gege* (*An Amorous Man*)	Ren Jinping	Bao Tianxiao	N.a.
1929	*Mangmu de aiqing* (*Blind Love*)	Bu Wangcang	Bao Tianxiao	Adapted from Bao's *Nüling Fuchou ji* (*Blind Love*, 1928–1929)

Table 10.2. Zhu Shouju Filmography

Year	Title	Director	Scriptwriter
1923	*Gujing chongbo ji* (*The Revival of an Old Well*)	Dan Duyu	Zhu Shouju
1923	*Qi er* (*Son Abandoned*)	Dan Duyu	Zhu Shouju
1924	*Caicha nü* (*The Tea Picking Girl*)	Xu Hu	Zhu Shouju
1925	*Fengyu zhi ye* (*On a Stormy Night*)	Zhu Shouju	Zhu Shouju
1925	*Qianqing* (*An Old Affair*)	Zhu Shouju	Zhu Shouju
1925	*Dai zhong fu* (*The Lucky Man*)	Zhu Shouju	Wang Bei'er
1926	*Ersun fu* (*Mother's Happiness*)	Shi Dongshan	Zhu Shouju
1926	*Ma Jiefu* (*Ma Jiefu*)	Zhu Shouju	Zhou Shoujuan
1926	*Lianhuan zhai* (*Chains of Debt*)	Zhu Shouju	Zhu Shouju
1927	*Meiren ji* (*A Beauty's Trap*)	Lu Jie, Zhu Shouju, Wang Yuanlong, Shi Dongshan	Zhu Shouju
1927	*Wupen ji* (*Redress a Grievance*)	Zhu Shouju	Zhu Shouju
1927	*Dapo Gaotangzhou* (*Victory at Gaotangzhou*)	Zhu Shouju	Zhu Shouju
1928	*Jiushi wo* (*Here I am*)	Zhu Shouju	Zhu Shouju
1928	*Erdu mei* (*The Second Spring*)	Zhu Shouju	Zhu Shouju
1928	*Gugong moying* (*Shadows in the Old Palace*)	Jiang Qifeng	Zhu Shouju
1928	*Ma Zhenhua* (*Ma Zhenhua*)	Zhu Shouju, Wang Yuanlong	Zhu Shouju
1929	*Zhenzhu guan* (*The Pearl Crown*)	Zhu Shouju	Zhu Shouju
1929	*Qingyu baojian* (*Karma of Love*)	Li Pingqian	Zhu Shouju
1929	*Jiuhua niang* (*Madam Nine Flowers*)	Zhu Shouju	Zhu Shouju
1929	*Yinmu zhi hua* (*Queen of the Silver Screen*)	Zheng Jiduo	Zhu Shouju
1930	*Huoshao Jiulongshan* (*Burning of the Nine-Dragon Mountain*)	Zhu Shouju	Zhu Shouju
1930	*Dapo Jiulongshan* (*Victory at the Nine-Dragon Mountain*)	Zhu Shouju	Zhu Shouju

"faithful" reproductions, we observe the following changes in Zhou's cine-fiction that might thicken our conception of cine-fiction.

Zhou's presence as a first-person narrator is made explicit from the outset, and continues throughout the story. At the beginning, Zhou sets the backdrop where the adaptation takes place. He begins the story by telling his audience the history of Pompeii, personifying Pompeii as "an old folk" with glorious past and a metropolitan outlook, like contemporary London and Paris. Such a beginning reiterates the narrative mode used in vernacular Chinese storytelling, citing history and geography to astonish readers. Here

Table 10.3. Xu Zhuodai Filmography

Year	Title	Director	Scriptwriter	Actor	Author of the original story or cine-fiction, handbill
1925	*Linshi gonggua (Temporary Residence)*	Xu Zhuodai, Wang Youyou	Xu Zhuodai	Xu Zhuodai, Wang Youyou	NA
1925	*Aishen zhi feiliao (Cupid's Feed)*	Xu Zhuodai, Wang Youyou	Xu Zhuodai	Xu Zhuodai, Wang Youyou	NA
1925	*Yinshen yi (The Invisible Cloak)*	Xu Zhuodai, Wang Youyou	Xu Zhuodai	Wang Youyou, Xu Zhuodai	NA
1926	*Huodong yinxiang (The Moving Safe)*	Xu Zhuodai, Wang Youyou	Xu Zhuodai	Wang Youyou, Xu Zhuodai	NA
1926	*Huo zhaopai (A Living Billboard)*	Xu Zhuodai, Wang Youyou	Xu Zhuodai	Xu Zhuodai, Wang Youyou	NA
1926	*Shenxian bang (The Magic Club)*	Wang Youyou	Unknown	Wang Youyou, Xu Zhuodai, Ouyang Yuqian	NA
1926	*Guai yisheng (The Odd Doctor)*	Xu Zhuodai, Wang Youyou	Xu Zhuodai	Wang Youyou, Xu Zhuodai	NA
1926	*Xiong xifu (The Heroic Wife)*	Xu Zhuodai, Wang Youyou	Xu Zhuodai	Xu Zhuodai, Wang Youyou	NA
1926	*Hong meigui (The Red Rose)*	Xu Zhuodai, Wang Youyou	Zhu Shuangyun	Xu Zhuodai	NA
1926	*Lingbo xianzi (Daffodil Fairies)*	Xu Zhuodai	Xu Zhuodai, Wang Youyou	Xu Zhuodai	NA
1926	*Jigong huofo 1 (Living Buddha Ji Gong 1)*	Wang Youyou	Xu Zhuodai	Wang Youyou, Xu Zhuodai	NA
1927	*Jigong huofo 2 (Living Buddha Ji Gong 2)*	Wang Youyou	Xu Zhuodai	Wang Youyou, Xu Banmei	NA
1927	*Jigong huofo 3 (Living Buddha Ji Gong 3)*	Wang Youyou	Xu Zhuodai	Wang Youyou, Xu Banmei	NA
1927	*Jianxia qizhongqi 1 (Swordsmen Legends 1)*	Xu Zhuodai	Xu Zhuodai	Zheng Chaofan, Wang Youyou	NA
1927	*Jianxia qizhongqi 2 (Swordsmen Legends 2)*	Xu Zhuodai	Xu Zhuodai	Zheng Chaofan, Wang Youyou	NA

Table 10.3.—*Continued*

Year	Title	Director	Scriptwriter	Actor	Author of the original story or cine-fiction, handbill
1927	*Qianli yan* (*The Magic Eyes*)	Wang Youyou	Wang Youyou	Wang Youyou, Xu Zhuodai	NA
1928	*Sanya qiwen* (*Three Deaf-mutes*)	Wang Youyou	Xu Zhuodai	Unknown	NA
1933	*Pinming* (*Fighting for life*)	Liu Chungshan	Liu Chungshan	Liu Chung-shan	Xu Zhuodai
1937	*Huangjin wanliang* (*Ten Thousand Taels of Gold*)	Huang Kuaisheng	Xu Zhuodai	Hong Jingling	NA

Table 10.4. Yan Duhe Filmography

Year	Film Title	Director	Scriptwriter	Other
1925	*Renmian taohua* (*A Beauty Remembered*)	Chen Shouyin, Chen Baoqi	Yan Duhe, Lu Danan	
1926	*Kongmen xianxi* (*A Virtuous Daughter-in-law*)	Cheng Bugao	Yan Duhe	Title cards
1926	*Gu'er jiuzu ji* (*An Orphan Rescues His Grandpa*)	Zhang Shichuan	Zheng Zhengqiu	Handbill
1927	*Fengliu shaonainai* (*An Amorous Wife*)	Ren Jinping	Bao Tianxiao	Title cards
1928	*Guai nülang* (*A Strange Girl*)	Chen Shouyin	Yan Duhe	
1928	*Wu Song danao shizilou* (*Wu Song Makes Havoc in the Lion Building*)	Zhao Chen	Yan Duhe	
1928	*Guangong ci Cao* (*Guan Yu Fooled Cao Cao*)	Cheng Bugao	Unknown	Handbill
1928	*Duoqing de gege* (*An Amorous Man*)	Ren Jinping	Bao Tianxiao	Handbill
1931	*Gechang chunse* (*The Romance of the Opera*)	Li Pingqian	Yao Sufeng	Film consultant
1931	*Genühen* (*The Regret of the Songstress*)	Ren Jinping	Unknown	Handbill
1931	*Genü Hongmudan* (*Songstress Red Peony*)	Zhang Shichuan, Cheng Bugao	Hong Shen	Film consultant
1932	*Tixiao yinyuan* (*Fate in of Tears and Laughter*)	Zhang Shichuan	Yan Duhe	
1932	*Zuihou zhi ai* (*The Last Love*)	Shaw Runje	Yao Sugeng	Script consultant
1932	*Yiye haohua* (*A Night of Glamour*)	Shaw Runje	Su Yi, Gao Jilin	Script consultant
1933	*Chunfeng yangliu* (*Spring Willow in the Wind*)	Wang Fuqing	Gong Lusu	Film consultant

Table 10.5. Zhou Shoujuan Filmography

Year	Title	Director	Scriptwriter	Author of the original story, cine-fiction, handbill
1924	*Shuihuo yuanyang (An Ill-Fated Couple)*	Cheng Bugao	Zhou Shoujuan	N.a.
1925	*Zhen'ai (True Love)*	Chen Tian	Zhou Shixun	Adapted from Zhou's original novel *Zhen/Truth*
1926	*Ma Jiefu (Ma Jiefu)*	Zhu Shouju	Zhu Shoujuan	N.a.
1926	*Huan jin ji (Money Returned)*	Dan Duyu	Zhou Shoujuan	N.a.
1926	*Lüyang honglei (Green Poplar, Red Tears)*	Dan Duyu	Zhou Shoujuan	N.a.
1928	*Meiren guan (A Beauty's Seduction)*	Bu Wancang	Zheng Zhengqiu	Adapted from Zhou's novel *Ai zhihua (The Flower of Love)*
1931	*Gechang chunse (The Romance of the Opera)*	Li Pingqian	Yao Sufeng	Film consultant
1932	*Zuihou zhi ai (The Last Love)*	Shaw Runje	Yao Sugeng	Script consultant
1932	*Yiye haohua (A Night of Glamour)*	Shaw Runje	Su Yi, Gao Jilin	Script consultant
1933	*Chunfeng yangliu (Spring Willow in the Wind)*	Wang Fuqing	Gong Lusu	Film consultant

Zhou foregrounds the presence of the storyteller, playing down the invisibility of the omniscient narration commonly seen in early motion pictures. For instance, when he introduces Glaucus and Jone as a couple, he suddenly breaks into the diegesis by telling the audience that his account must stop short because as a storyteller he lacks a firsthand knowledge (of intimate courtship) in giving out further details to his readers.[62] Another salient feature in Zhou's version is the considerable dialogue he adds in major scenes. In the sequence where Arbace reveals his desire for Jone, his attempted rape is primarily depicted through acting and staging, such as Arbace's physical aggression toward Jone and her expression of fear and resistance. Because Arbace's desire to take possession of Jone has been premised in a prior close-up of an owl labeled "predatory," the filmmakers directed this sequence rather economically by inserting only one title card ("predatory"--in explaining the meaning of the owl) on Arbace's lie about Glaucus.

Zhou, however, uses dialogue between Arbace and Jone to render this pivotal sequence. Arbace says: "Let me kiss your cherry lips. I can wait no longer." Jone replies: "High priest, are you drunk? What is this place? How dare you touch me? I will not let you smear my innocence."[63] Clearly the lascivious speech pronounced by Arbace and Jone's furious response intensify the dramatic situation of her plight. Prior to this Zhou adds a prop missing from the film—a telescope—to depict Arbace's voyeurism toward Jone when she enjoys a romantic sail with Glaucus. For this, the film only shows the back of Arbace, who spots the couple on their boat from his balcony. There is no shot reverse shot indicating Arbace's sight of the couple on the sea and how he reacts. Zhou, however, focuses on Arbace's intense lust for Jone—so much that he picks up a telescope to survey Jone. The close-up view of the distant Jone brought to Arbace by a telescope, according to Zhou, adds to his jealousy and his craving. The sight of the telescope is anachronistic, as this instrument was not invented until the seventeenth century. Despite the glaring anachronism, the use of a telescope to capture the object of male desire is a device carrying a contemporary touch. It not only advances the plot but also brings voyeurism forward, reminding readers of the visual provenance (cinematic) of the fiction (cine-fiction).

Zhou also pinpoints the victimization of woman as the story's pathos. Zhou's rewrite centers on Nidia—her angelic beauty, her misfortune, her unrequited love, and her eventual sacrifice. Clearly Nidia is the muse to Zhou, who uses two full pages to introduce her, focusing on her incredible beauty in embroidered and erotic language typically seen in the Butterfly fiction.

The lengthy description of Nidia may result in a "slow" start of the story (story economy) but it is imperative to the "scholar and the beauty" trope in Butterfly romance. "Scholar and the beauty" is an ideal matrimony in the Butterfly romance—centering on a heterosexual couple with distinct outlook and division of quality—a beautiful virgin paired with a learned gentleman. The essential pathos then becomes an amorous destiny, but an ideal unfulfilled, hence the tragic love ending. Zhou's deployment of the generic pocket of "scholar and the beauty" hence leads him to foreground the inconceivable beauty of the blind slave, and to retell the story by focusing on the slave's perspective and her desire. The subjectivity of Nidia is thus empathically depicted, compared to the film version. For instance, the film shows the happy, domestic life of Nidia after she's settled in Glaucus's house in a sequence of three scenes. First she is seen spending her time by feeding the birds in the courtyard until Glaucus passes by for a chat; in the next scene of a similar setting, he surprises her while she carries a jar of water; they chat some more. In the scene that follows, she is in the garden, picking up roses and kissing them. No title cards inserted in this sequence further explain the plot; hence a certain degree of temporal ellipsis arises, promoting the audience to infer the story. Audiences are presented the happy time Nidia and Glaucus spend together, but there is little indication of what exactly is being exchanged between them, and what motivates her strong passion for Glaucus. Gratitude? His personality? Or his money? All are possible. The audience is compelled to deduce the story based what is given on screen. In Zhou's version, however, instead of depicting the scenes as they are, he offers an account of Nidia's reflection to frame the sequence where her passion for her master quickly accelerates:

> She has little to do in Glaucus's house. She spends her day singing, picking flowers, feeding doves, or chatting with Glaucus in the drawing room. . . . Even if she cannot see the young master's beautiful face, she has an image of him clearly inscribed in her mind. . . . Nidia is a mature and intelligent woman, and her prior life did not allow her a chance of romance. But with the reversal of fortune and now the amorous young master, she cannot help but fall in love with him.[64]

Zhou delineates Nidia's routine, adding a drawing room sitting to the film version. Romance in the drawing room is imperative to the "scholar and the beauty" narrative. More importantly, Zhou explains the cause of her passion, not out of gratitude, but a longing for romantic exchange, like those intimate interactions between Glaucus and Jone. But because of Jone, Nidia's love goes unanswered. The unrequited burning desire prompts her collaboration with Arbace. All of these details fulfill the pathos of the Butterfly tragic love narrative. This underlies Zhou's rendition of Nidia's death into melodramatic hyperbole. The closing of the film shows Nidia leading Glaucus and Jone to the shore, where a boat is about to depart. Glaucus takes Jone on board while Nidia bids them farewell. Nidia then sinks herself into the water. End of the film. The tragic end, however, in Zhou's account is elaborated as follows:

> Just when Nidia tries to step into the boat, the boat sails away. Disappointed, Nidia stands on the beach, smiling, looking up to the sky, and says: "Nidia, you've carried out your duty. It is time to die." As she says these words, she smiles and puts her arms into the water . . . just when we have lost sight of her, her head comes out from the water, her face wet with tears. At the top of her lungs she cries out: "Farewell Glaucus, my love . . . don't forget me, the poor Nidia." Suddenly a big wave pushes her into a swirl. All that is left to be seen is her golden locks.[65]

Zhou's hyperbolic account of Nidia's death is rendered by standard melodramatic formulas, using emotion, tears, cries, and the physical evidence of the departed heroine to tell us her resignation to fate and her remorse. These vivid images and sounds Zhou intends to crystallize the pathos of the sacrificial woman—her wretched life and the unalterable course of her destiny. Zhou's story of the last days of Pompeii is indeed the last days of Nidia the blind flower girl.

Because Zhou intended to domesticate and indigenize the story, his version, in terms of pathos and languages, was by virtue a tour de force Butterfly transcription, and hence becomes a distinct text of its own. Zhou's rewrite is by no means inferior. Instead, with unique visualization and incorporation of Western culture and technology, Zhou remade the Italian epic and its Babylonian narrative with distinct, palpable Butterfly ingredients. In hindsight, one should wonder if these two narratives have something in common. By rewriting a Roman natural disaster as a Butterfly tragic love story, Zhou performed a tour de force, putting two distant narratives together through superimposing local popular fiction on a foreign film. A cine-fiction piece like Zhao's *Last Days of Pompeii* exemplifies the surplus value of motion pictures for the literary establishment; in turn, the sphere of the movie field expands further with the aid of literature.

CODA

This chapter focuses on several key popular authors instrumental in constructing the movie field in Republican China, especially their activities in hybridizing letters and images, and in transforming fiction into screenplays and vice versa. We call these authors *film literati*, referring to their dual positions in the literary and the movie fields. We discuss their negotiation between traditional and emergent forms of narrative, and their crossover from the literary to the movie field. We highlight a hybrid genre known as "cine-fiction," that is, the literary adaption of motion pictures, to examine the symbiosis between the two fields. Finally, by comparing the 1913 film *The Last Days of Pompeii* and its fiction version written by Zhou Shoujuan, we've come to a more informed account of the dynamics between literature and cinema. The study on film literati reveals interstices between Butterfly literature and the Republican cinema. Butterfly authors' contribution to the formation of China's movie field is too important to overlook, and we hope our chapter will provoke more interest in this line of enquiry.

Notes

1. Research for this chapter is supported by a research grant awarded by Chiang Ching-kuo Foundation for International Scholarly Exchange (Project Number: RG013-P-12). We thank CCK's support and the assistance of Nicolas Li Ling and Yan Wai Ka.

2. Emilie Yueh-yu Yeh, "New Takes on Film Historiography: Republican Cinema Redux, an Introduction," *Journal of Chinese Cinemas* 9, no. 1 (2015): 1–7.

3. Perry Link, *Mandarin Ducks and Butterflies: Popular Fiction in Early Twentieth-Century Chinese Cities* (Berkeley: University of California Press, 1981); Wei Shaochang, *Wo kan yuanyang hudie pai* [My View of the Mandarin Ducks and Butterflies School] (Hong Kong: Chung Hwa, 1990); Fan Boqun, *Minguo tongsu xiaoshuo yuanyang hudie pai* [Mandarin Ducks and Butterflies School: The Popular Fiction in Republican China] (Taipei: Guowen tiandi zazhi she, 1990); Rey Chow, *Woman and Chinese Modernity: The Politics of Reading between West and East* (Minneapolis: University of Minnesota Press, 1991).

4. David Der-wei Wang, *Fin-de-siecle Splendor: Repressed Modernities of Late Qing Fiction, 1849–1911* (Stanford, CA: Stanford University Press, 1997); Chen Jianhua, "Zhongguo dianying piping de xianqu: Zhou Shoujuan 'Yingxi hua' dujie" [Pioneer of Chinese Film Criticism: A Reading of Zhou Shoujuan's "Shadow Play" Discourses], *Xiandai zhongguo* 9 (2007): 53–76; and Carlos Rojas and Eileen Chow, eds., *Rethinking Chinese Popular Culture: Cannibalizations of the Canon* (New York: Routledge, 2009); Zhao Xiaoxuan, *Yuanyang hudie pai xinlun* [The New Discussion and Evaluation of the Mandarin Ducks and Butterflies School] (Lanzhou: Lanzhou University Press, 2004).

5. See Dianying ziliaoguan koushu dianying shi xiaozu (The Oral History Unit of the Film Archive), *Taiyupian shidai* [The Era of the Taiwanese Dialect Film] (Taipei: Taiwan Film Archive, 1994).

6. See, for examples, *The China Factor in Hong Kong Cinema* (Hong Kong: Urban Council, 1990); *Hong Kong Cinema in the Eighties: A Comparative Study with Western*

Cinema (Hong Kong: Urban Council, 1991); *Overseas Chinese Figures in Cinema* (Hong Kong: Urban Council, 1992); *Mandarin Films and Popular Songs: 40's-60's* (Hong Kong: Urban Council, 1993); *Cinema of Two Cities, Hong Kong-Shanghai* (Hong Kong: Urban Council, 1994); *Early Images of Hong Kong and China* (Hong Kong: Urban Council, 1995).

7. For oral histories of filmmakers, see Kwok Ching-ling, ed., *Hong Kong Here I Come* (Hong Kong: Hong Kong Film Archive, 2000); Wong Ain-ling, ed., *An Age of Idealism: Great Wall & Feng Huang Days* (Hong Kong: Hong Kong Film Archive, 2001); Kwok Ching-ling and Grace Ng, eds., *Director Chor Yuen* (Hong Kong: Hong Kong Film Archive, 2006); Wong Ain-ling and Angel Shing, eds., *Wang Tianlin* [Director Wong Tin-lam] (Hong Kong: Hong Kong Film Archive, 2007). For studio studies, see, for example, Agnes Lam, Maggie Lee, and Wong Kee-chee, eds., *The Glorious Modernity of Kong Ngee* (Hong Kong: Hong Kong Film Archive, 2006) and Grace Ng, ed., *One for All: The Union Film Spirit* (Hong Kong: Hong Kong Film Archive, 2011). For studies of individual filmmakers, see Wong Ain-ling, ed., *The Cinema of Lee Sun-fung* (Hong Kong: Hong Kong Film Archive, 2004); Wong Ain-ling, ed., *Li Han-hsiang, Storyteller* (Hong Kong: Hong Kong Film Archive, 2007); Wong Ain-ling, ed., *Zhu Shilin: A Filmmaker of His Times* (Hong Kong: Hong Kong Film Archive, 2008). For dialect film studies, see, for example, May Gwan-yuk Ng, ed., *Xianggang Xiayu dianying fangzong* [The Amoy-dialect Films of Hong Kong] (Hong Kong: Hong Kong Film Archive, 2012); and May Gwan-yuk Ng, ed., *Xianggang Chaoyu dianying xunji* [The Chaozhou-dialect Films of Hong Kong] (Hong Kong: Hong Kong Film Archive, 2013). For exhibition-turned-book publications, see, for example, Wong Lai-ming, ed., *Bujing moshushi: Chen Qirui, Chen Jingsen fuzi de bujing meixue* [A Touch of Magic: Veteran Set Designers Chan Ki-yui & Chan King-sam] (Hong Kong: Hong Kong Film Archive, 2013).

8. See, for example, Qing Xiqin, *Oumei dianying yu Zhongguo zaoqi dianying, 1920–1930* [European Film and Chinese Early Cinema, 1920–1930] (Beijing: China Film Press, 2008); Wong Ain-ling, ed., *Zhongguo dianying suyuan* [Chinese Cinema: Tracing the Origins] (Hong Kong: Hong Kong Film Archive, 2011); Emilie Yueh-yu Yeh, ed., *Huayu dianying gongye: Fangfa yu lishi de xin tansuo* [Rethinking Chinese Film Industry: New Histories, New Methods] (Beijing: Beijing University Press, 2011). See also Zhang Zhen, *An Amorous History of the Silver Screen: Shanghai Cinema, 1896–1937* (Chicago.: University of Chicago Press, 2005); Xuelei Huang, *Shanghai Filmmaking: Crossing Borders, Connecting to the Globe, 1922–1938* (Leiden: Brill, 2014); and Weihong Bao, *Fiery Cinema: The Emergence of an Affective Medium in China, 1915–1945* (Minneapolis: University of Minnesota Press, 2015).

9. Fan, *Minguo tongsu xiaoshuo yuanyang hudie pai*. See also Xue Feng, "'Fuxian lishi piping' yu Zhongguo chuantong de xiandai huixiang: yi ershi shiji er san shi niandai 'yuanyang hudie pai' wenren de dianying piping wei zhongxin" ["Bifurcated Historic Review" and Modern Echo of Chinese Tradition: Using Mandarin Ducks and Butterflies Literati's Film Criticisms in the 1920s and 1930s as Examples], *Dangdai dianying* 5 (2010): 101–107.

10. Emilie Yueh-yu Yeh, "*Wenyi* and the Branding of Early Chinese Film," *Journal of Chinese Cinemas* 6, no. 1 (2012): 82–94.

11. Zhang's works adapted to the silver screen include *Yinhan shuangxing* (*Two Stars*, dir. Shi Dongshan, 1931), *Tixiao yinyuan* (*Fate in Tears and Laughter*, 1932), *Luoxia guwu* (*Runaway Lovers*, dir. Cheng Bugao, 1932), *Man jiang hong* (*For My Country*, dir. Cheng Bugao, 1933), *Meiren en* (*When a Lovely Girl Bestows her Favors*, dir. Wen Yimin, 1935). Among these titles, *Fate in Tears and Laughter* has been adapted seven times for the movie screen and a number of television series; the most recent one was in 2004.

12. The two titles are *Jie hou yan* (*Out of the Hell*, dir. Zhang Huichong, 1925) and *Gongren zhi qi* (*The Wife of a Worker*, dir. Ren Pengnian, 1926).

13. Mei Wen, *Posui de yingxiang yu shiyi de lishi: Cong jiupai yuanhu dianying de shuailuo kan Zhongguo zhishi fanxing de zhuanbian* [Broken Images and Forgotten History: The Shift in the Chinese Intellectual Paradigm through the Lens of Mandarin Ducks and Butterflies Films] (Beijing: China Film Press, 2004), 193; see also Feng Min, "Bao Tianxiao yu Zhongguo dianying" [Bao Tianxiao and Chinese Cinema], *Dangdai dianying* 1 (1997): 46–49; Zhang Wei, *Yuanyang hudie pai wenxue yu zaoqi Zhongguo dianying de chuangzuo* [Mandarin Ducks and Butterflies Literature and Early Chinese Film Production] (Beijing: China Film Press, 2004); Chen, "Zhongguo dianying piping de xianqu"; Li Bin, "Yuanyang hudie pai wenren: Di yi dai Zhongguo dianying ren" [Literati of the Mandarin Ducks and Butterflies School: Pioneers of Chinese Cinema], *Suzhou keji xueyuan xuebao (shehui kexue ban)* 28, no. 3 (2011): 96–102; Xue Feng, "'Richang wenhua piping': xiandai Zhongguo chenshi pingmin shenghuo de zhinan yu xiangxiang—yi ershi shiji er san shiniandai 'yuanyang hudie pai' wenren de yingping shuxie wei zhongxin" ["Everyday Cultural Criticism": Guidance and Imagination of the Everyday Life in Modern Chinese Cities—from the Perspective of Film Criticism of Mandarin Ducks and Butterflies Literati in the 1920s and 1930s], *Dangdai dianying* 10 (2012): 101–106.

14. Pierre Bourdieu, *The Field of Cultural Production: Essays on Art and Literature*, ed. Randal Johnson (New York: Columbia University Press, 1993).

15. Pierre Bourdieu, *Distinction: A Social Critique of the Judgment of Taste*, trans. Richard Nice (Cambridge, MA: Harvard University Press, 1987).

16. Bourdieu, *Distinction*, 115.

17. See Chen, "Zhongguo dianying piping de xianqu."

18. Mei Chia-ling, *Cong shaonian Zhongguo dao shaonian Taiwan: ershi shiji Zhongwen xiaoshuo de qingchun xiangxiang yu guozu lunshu* [From Young China to Young Taiwan: Youth Imagination and National Discourse in Chinese Novels in the Twentieth Century] (Taipei: Maitian chuban, 2013), 82–83.

19. Bourdieu, *Field of Cultural Production*, 165–177.

20. Chinese literary historian Chen Pingyuan highly praised Bao for his translations, comparing him with Lin Zhu. See Chen Pingyuan, *Ershi shiji Zhongguo xiaoshuo shi*

[History of Chinese Novels in the Twentieth Century] (Beijing: Beijing University Press, 1989), 61.

21. See Huang, *Shanghai Filmmaking*, 87.

22. Bao Tianxiao, *Chuanying lou huiyi lu* [Chuanying lou Memoirs] (Taipei: Longwen chuban gongsi, 1990), 654–655.

23. Cheng Jihua, Li Shaobai, and Xing Zuwen, *Zhoungguo dianying fazhan shi* [History of the Development of Chinese Cinema] (Beijing: China Film Press, 1980), 56.

24. The sequel *Xin xiepu chao* (The New Tides of Huangpu) was published in *Hong zazhi* (Red Magazine), of which Yan Duhe was the chief editor.

25. See Shu Jing, "Chan: yefang Zhang Ailing" [Cicadas: Evening Chat with Eileen Chang], in *Zhang Ailing pingshuo liushi nian* [Sixty-Year Criticisms of Eileen Chang], ed. Zi Tong and Yi Qing (Beijing: Zhongguo huaqiao, 2001), 146–158. Theodore Huters may not agree with Eileen Chang's appraisal, but he confirms the riveting anxiety, social undercurrents, and desire that the novel unveiled; see Theodore Huters, *Bringing the World Home: Appropriating the West in Late Qing and Early Republican China* (Honolulu: University of Hawai'i Press, 2005), 229–251.

26. For the details of the establishment of the film company, see Zhu Shouju, "Shu Shanghai Yingxi Gongsi chungli jingguo" [On the Establishment of the Shanghai Film Company], *Yue du MOOK* 33 (2013): 88–95. Also see Fan Boqun, "Zhu Shouju lun" [On Zhu Shouju], *Xin wenxue shiliao* 1 (2013): 103–124.

27. See Fan, "Zhu Shouju lun," 119.

28. Chen Jianhua, "Cong yingmi dao yinmu qingyuan: Dan Duyu, Ying Mingzhu yu zaoqi Zhongguo dianying de shenti zhengzhi" [From Cinephile to Lovers on the Silver Screen: Dan Duyu, Yin Mingzhu, and Body Politic in Early Chinese Cinema], *Zhongguo bijiao wenxue* 1 (2015): 9–24.

29. At first, he bought a share of the Fair Steel and Iron Factory (Gongping gangtiechang) to retire, but he came back to the movie field, writing scripts for Cathy, including *Lüsi niang* (*Madam Lü Si*, dir. Xu Xinfu, 1948) and *Meiren xue* (*Blood of the Beauty*, dir. Xu Xinfu, 1948).

30. See Sato Akinari, "Zhu Shouju yu tade dianying zuopin *Fengyu zhi ye*: Zhongguo wusheng dianying Dongjing jianding shouji" [Zhu Shouju and His Film *Stormy Night*: Notes on Authentication of Chinese Silent Film from Tokyo], *Ming Pao Weekly*, June 1 2011.

31. For a substantial collection of Xu Zhuodai's comic novels, see Fan Boqun, ed., *Huaji dashi: Xu Zhuodai* [The Master of Comedy: Xu Zhuodai] (Taipei: Yeqiang, 1993).

32. Fan Yanqiao, "Xu Zhuodai de huaji shi" [The History of Xu Zhuodai's Comedy], *Banyue* 4, no. 12. Quoted from Fan, *Huaji dashi*, 3–4.

33. See Xu Zhuodai, "Yishu shang de *Hongfen kulou* (yi)" [The Art of *Women Skeletons*, Part I], *Shenbao*, June 13, 1922, 18; Xu Zhuodai, "Yishu shang de *Hongfen kulou* (er)" [The Art of *Women Skeletons*, Part II], *Shenbao*, June 14, 1922, 18; Xu Zhuodai,

"Yishu shang de *Hongfen kulou* (san)" [The Art of *Women Skeletons*, Part III], *Shenbao*, June 15, 1922, 18; Xu Zhuodai, "Yishu shang de *Hongfen kulou* (si)" [The Art of *Women Skeletons*, Part IV], *Shenbao*, June 16, 1922, 18; Xu Zhuodai, "Yishu shang de *Hongfen kulou* (wu)" [The Art of *Women Skeletons*, Part V], *Shenbao*, June 17, 1922, 18.

34. Xu Zhuodai, "Yingxi zhe xi ye" [Film is Drama], *Minxin tekan* 3 (1926): 17.

35. Beside Happy Film, Xu and Wang also founded another small production house, Hezhong yingpian gongsi (Hezhong Film Company) in 1928. The company produced only one film, *Sanya qiwen* (*Three Deaf-Mutes*), starring Wang and directed by Xu.

36. Wang Youyou, "Guoqu de kaixin wanyi'er" [Little Toy in the Past], *Kaixin tekan* 3 (1926): 2.

37. For the full account of Kawatani Shohei's film related activity in China, see Yau Shuk-ting, "Cong Chuangu Chuangping kan ersanshi niandai Zhong Ri dianying jiaoliu" [Sino-Japanese Film Activity Exchanges in the 1920s and 1930s through the Case of Kawatani Shohei], *Dianying yishu* 341 (2011): 127–132.

38. A story told by Xu illustrates what he meant by "scavenger mode": one day he received a call from a friend, telling him that a kitchen set prepared for another film now was going to be demolished and asking him if he would like to use it for shooting. Xu and Wang then immediately made up a kitchen scene to make use of the leftover set for their *Guai yisheng* (*The Odd Doctor*, *Jialishi* [*The Fake Wrestler*], 1926). See Xu Zhuodai, "Shi xiangyan pigu zhuyi" [Scavenger Mode], *Kaixin tekan* 2 (1926): 4–8.

39. Xu Zhuodai, "Wo ban yingxi gongsi de shibai tan" [The Failure of My Film Company], *Dianying yuebao* 2 (1928): 92.

40. Yan Duhe, ed., *Mingxing yingpian gongsi tianzhao xingu jihuashu* [Proposal for Share Subscriptions for the Mingxing Film Company]. Also cf. Sun Lei, "Mingxing yingpian gongsi" [The Mingxing Film Company], in *Zhongguo dianying: miaoshu yu chanshi* [Chinese Cinema: Descriptions and Interpretations], ed. Lu Hongshi (Beijing: Zhonguo dianying, 2002), 149–151.

41. Yan Duhe, "Guochan yousheng dianying diyisheng" [The First Voice of Chinese-Produced Sound Film], *Genü Hongmudan tekan* (1931): 20.

42. Huang, *Shanghai Filmmaking*, 99.

43. Janet Wasko, *How Hollywood Works* (Padstow, Cornwall: Sage, 2003), 16.

44. Chen Jianhua regards Zhou Shoujuan as one of the greatest writers of the Butterflies school, calling him "da yuanyang" (the Leading Mandarin Duck) and "da hudie" (the Queen Butterfly). See Chen, "Zhongguo dianying piping de xianqu."

45. Lu Xun commented that the translation of *Series of Short Stories by Famous European and American Writers* "is a heartening attempt and does not only aim to entertain the populace. It is the pride of the recent translation works." See Lu Xun, "*Oumei mingjia duanpian xiao shuo congkan* pinglun" [Comments on *Series of Short Stories by Famous European and American Writers*], *Jiaoyu gongbao*, November 30, 1917, 4.

46. See Chen, "Zhongguo dianying piping de xianqu."

47. See Xue Feng, "'Fuxian lishi piping' yu Zhongguo chuantong de xiandai huixiang."

48. Zhou Shoujuan, "Axiong" [The Elder Brother], *Libai liu* 24 (1914): 11–28. The film *Le Petit Chose* (1912) is based on the novel of the same title by Alphonse Daudet; Zhou Shoujuan, "Waiting," *Libai liu* 25 (1914): 1–6; Zhou Shoujuan, "Hedeng yingxiong" [What a Hero], *Youxi zazhi* 9 (1914): 27–44; Zhou Shoujuan, "Pangbeicheng zhi mori" [The Last Days of Pompeii], *Libai liu* 32 (1915): 1–20. *The Last Days of Pompeii* (1913) is based on the novel of the same title by Edward Bulwer-Lytton; Zhou Shoujuan, "Wuhu . . . Zhan" [Alas . . . Fight], *Libai liu* 33 (1915): 7–19; Zhou Shoujuan, "Qi zhi xin" [The Heart of the Wife], *Zhonghua funü jie* 1, no. 2 (1915): 329–339; Zhou Shoujuan, "Bu bi zhi men" [The Open Gate], *Libai liu* 59 (1915): 14–28; Zhou Shoujuan, "Nü zhen hua" [Flower of Female Chastity], *Xiaoshuo daguan* 11 (1917): 1–12; Zhou Shoujuan, "Ai zhi fendou" [Strive for Love], *Libai liu* 153 (1922): 11–16. *The Woman Thou Gavest Me* (1919) is based on the novel of the same title by Hall Caine; Zhou Shoujuan, "Laba dao shang" [Trumpet Island 1], *Youxi shijie* 14 (1922): 1–7. *Trumpet Island* (1920) is based on Gouverneur Morris's "On Trumpet Island," published in *Pearson's Magazine* no. 25 (1911): 42–53.

49. Shan Dong, "Minchu yingxi xiaoshuo yanjiu" [A Study of Cine-Fiction in the Early Republican China] (MPhil thesis, University of Hong Kong, 2014), 5.

50. Chen Jianhua, "Wenren congying: Zhou Shoujuan yu Zhongguo zaoqi dianying" [From Literati to Film Practitioner: Zhou Shoujuan and Early Chinese Film], *Dianying yishu* 1 (2012): 134.

51. Zhou Shoujuan, "Xiao changzhu" [The Boy Heiress], *Xiao Changzhu tekan* (1925): 45–58.

52. For the synopsis of *The Boy Heiress*, see Zhou Shoujuan, "*Xia changzhu* benshi" [Synopsis of *The Boy Heiress*], *Xia chanzhu tekan* (1925): 17, 19, 21.

53. Lu Jie, *Lu Jie riji zhaicun* [Lu Jie Diaries: Selected Extracts] (Beijing: Zhongguo dianying ziliao guan, 1962), 16.

54. See Zhou Shoujuan, ed., *Xia chanzhu tekan* [*The Boy Heiress* Special Issue] (1925).

55. Zhou Shoujuan, *Zhou Shoujuan shuo ji xiace* [Collected Fiction of Zhou Shoujuan], vol. 2 (Shanghai: Dadong shuju, 1927). Fan Boqun, *Yuanyang hudie: Libai liu pai zuopin xuan shang* [Mandarin Ducks and Butterflies: Selected Works of the *Saturday* Part One] (Beijing: Renmin wenxue, 1991).

56. Advertisements on *Shenbao* indicated that *The Last Days of Pompeii* was shown in Shanghai's Tokyo Theatre March 13–16, 1914. See "Dongjing huodong yingxiyuan" [Tokyo Theatre], *Shenbao*, March 13, 1914, 12; "Dongjing huodong yingxiyuan" [Tokyo Theatre], *Shenbao*, March 14, 1914, 9; "Dongjing huodong yingxiyuan" [Tokyo Theatre], *Shenbao*, March 15, 1914, 9; "Dongjing huodong yingxiyuan" [Tokyo Theatre], *Shenbao*, March 16, 1914, 12.

57. Advertisements in the *North China Daily News* indicated that *The Last Days of Pompeii* was shown March 3–11, 1914. See "Victoria Theatre," *North China Daily News*, March 3, 1914, 4; "Victoria Theatre," *North China Daily News*, March 4, 1914, 4; "Victoria Theatre," *North China Daily News*, March 5, 1914, 4; "Victoria Theatre," *North China*

Daily News, March 6, 1914, 4; "Victoria Theatre," *North China Daily News*, March 7, 1914, 4; "Victoria Theatre," *North China Daily News*, March 8, 1914, 4; "Victoria Theatre," *North China Daily News*, March 10, 1914, 4; "Victoria Theatre," *North China Daily News*, March 11, 1914, 4.

58. Zhou, "Pangbeicheng zhi mori," 1.

59. See Miriam Hansen, *Babel and Babylon: Spectatorship in American Silent Film* (Cambridge, MA: Harvard University Press, 1991), 175.

60. Ian Christie, "Ancient Rome in London: Classical Subjects in the Forefront of Cinema's Expansion after 1910," in *The Ancient World in Silent Cinema*, ed. Pantelis Michelakis and Maria Wyke (Cambridge: Cambridge University Press, 2013), 117.

61. Kristin Thompson and David Bordwell, *Film History: An Introduction* (New York: McGraw-Hill, 1994), 58.

62. Thompson and Bordwell, *Film History*, 5.

63. Thompson and Bordwell, *Film History*, 11.

64. Thompson and Bordwell, *Film History*, 9.

65. Thompson and Bordwell, *Film History*, 9.

CHAPTER 11

Rhythmic Movement, Metaphoric Sound, and Transcultural Transmediality

Liu Na'ou and *The Man Who Has a Camera* (1933)

Ling Zhang

> Rhythm is the most supreme and sacred law of the universe; the wave phenomenon is the primal and universal phenomenon.
>
> —RUDOLPH LOTHAR, *THE TALKING MACHINE: A TECHNICAL-AESTHETIC ESSAY*, 1924.[1]

In his brief yet prolific creative life, Liu Na'ou (1905–1940) worked in Shanghai as a neosensationalist (*Xin ganjue pai*) writer, translator, publisher, editor, film critic and theorist, screenwriter, and filmmaker.[2] Born into an affluent family in Taiwan, Liu attended high school and college in Japan and studied French at a Catholic university in Shanghai.[3] Liu was proficient in Chinese, Japanese, French, and English, which facilitated his intellectual exploration of multiple cultures and media.[4] Liu's linguistic aptitude and peripatetic experiences contributed to his utopian cosmopolitanism, in particular his view that art, especially cinema, could transcend national, linguistic, racial, and ethnic boundaries. Raised in Taiwan while it was under Japanese colonial rule, and lived in semicolonial Shanghai, Liu embodied an urban cosmopolitanism that indexed the contradictions of colonial modernity.[5]

In this chapter, I examine how Liu Na'ou's literary, cinematic, and theoretical work was enriched through the cross-fertilization of his transcultural and transmedial aspirations. Furthermore, I investigate how camera movement and bodily kinesis, rhythm and musicality, communicate and become intertwined with the means of transcultural transmediality, creating a vivid sense of "metaphoric sound."[6] By "metaphoric sound" in cinema, I refer to the sense of rhythm and musicality suggested by camera movement, bodily kinesis, and editing. In this case, "sound" cannot be heard but can be imagined even through silence. In American sound designer Walter Murch's words, "Once you stray into metaphoric sound, which is simply sound that does not match what you are looking at, the human mind will look for deeper and deeper patterns . . . at the geographic level, the natural level, the psychological level . . . the ultimate metaphoric sound is silence." Moreover, I outline how these intermingled concepts and practices created the possibility for a new audiovisual aesthetic with multilayered remediations (across different media, art forms, and materials, and between life and art) in 1930s Shanghai and advanced—as well as constrained—a distinctively cosmopolitan vision.

While cosmopolitanism and travel film (Liu's *The Man Who Has a Camera*, on which I will elaborate later) denote border crossing and transculturality, metaphoric sound is intimately linked to transmediality. When conceptualizing the complex status of cinema as "pure" or "impure" and accounting for its "interbreeding with other arts and media," film and media scholars have adopted the terms "intermediality" and "transmediality."[7] Intermediality and transmediality point to "the 'in-between' of the forms," and "processes leaving traces that have to be reconstructed."[8] Such highly interactive procedures could include transposition, combination, coexistence, integration, and transformation between and among two or more art forms and media. In Liu Na'ou's case, we find cross-pollination among literature, music, translation, screenwriting, film criticism, and filmmaking, as well as between his dramatic life experiences and everyday activities (such as travel and dance). In addition, the temporality and movement characterizing the fluid circuit between forms are "used in the sense of transfer and processuality in medial exchanges that resist closure."[9]

Under certain circumstances, intermediality and transmediality can be discussed almost interchangeably; however, in this chapter, I specifically underline the separate but intimately related dimensions of transmediality and transculturality in Liu Na'ou's work and life. By emphasizing "trans" rather than "inter," I focus on the elements of process and mobility characterizing transfer, transposition, transformation, transgression, transcendence, and boundary traversing. As Nadja Gernalzick and Gabriele Pisarz-Ramirez state, "The terms 'transmediality' and 'transculturality,' by the ambiguity of the prefix, denote transcendence as well as processuality and provisionality." Furthermore, they point to "the ambiguity of 'trans' as denoting processes as between media-bound and non-media specific, or, as both at the same time."[10] Compared to other contemporary Chinese literary luminaries engaged in similarly "trans" practices—Hong Shen[11] and Tian Han[12]—Liu was less accomplished at screenwriting and filmmaking, but his work is notable for its profound contribution to Chinese modernist literature and Liu's understanding of film theory, rigorous attention to cinematic aesthetics, and ambiguous political and cultural position.[13]

Building upon and pushing beyond the existing perceptive scholarship on Liu Na'ou's literary work, dandyish lifestyle, and complex cultural identity[14] in semicolonial metropolitan Shanghai,[15] my research contributes to both cinema and East Asian studies in two respects: first, this chapter extensively discusses Liu's overlooked amateur travel film *The Man Who Has a Camera* (1933) and his kaleidoscopic film theories, to enrich our understanding of how early Chinese cinema and film history are in dialogue with European-American counterparts. Second, by linking "city symphony" film techniques, including camera and body movement, rhythm, and musicality, the chapter provides a nuanced treatise of "metaphoric sound" in relation to transmediality, thus complicating our perception of film sound and sound studies in general.

THE MAN WHO HAS A CAMERA: THE AMATEUR FILM, THE TRAVELOGUE, AND THE CITY SYMPHONY

In this section, I examine Liu Na'ou's amateur film *The Man Who Has a Camera* and explore how the "city symphony" as a modernist film mode intimately interacts with the multisensory experience of traversing urban space by conveying a strong sense of mobility and rhythmicity. *The Man Who Has a Camera* is primarily a venture in border crossing, as it traverses various film modes and travels through different regions and across national borders. In this way, Liu creates a flowing transmedial aesthetic that embraces the transcultural circulation of film texts, criticism, and culture.[16] The city symphony film is cited in the genealogy of the modernist avant-garde, imbricated with poetry, photography, music, dance, graphic design, and modernist literature, as well as the constructivist and futurist art movements of the 1920s.

The city symphony film mode possesses a vivid literal and metaphoric sound aesthetic (including movement, rhythm, and musicality) that incorporates sensory perceptions and urban soundscapes, even in its early silent incarnations.[17] Most of these films were screened with live musical accompaniment, which occasionally corresponded to the soundscape outside the exhibition space. For instance, the Austrian composer Edmund Meisel, who created the score for the prototypical city symphony film, *Berlin, Symphony of a Great City* (*Berlin: Die Sinfonie der Großstadt*, dir. Walter Ruttmann, 65 min., 1927), conceived of his work as an assemblage of noises that characterized a cosmopolitan center. The expectation was that the urban spectator would recognize the "symphony" of sounds that emanated from, and resonated with, the sonic environment of quotidian life in the metropolis.[18] Moreover, the intense sensations produced by the rhythm and speed of the metropolis and the spectacle of a "world in motion" are enhanced by a montage technique based on "visual rhythm."[19] The visual elements—the intensive tempo underlined by alternation between stasis and movement, variations in camera angles, intertitles,[20] and rapid montage—powerfully evoke musicality and a dynamic acoustic environment.

Analogously, the travel film is a diverse and porous form.[21] It is embedded in and reflects modern networks of transportation, communication, and colonialist values. In the silent era, travelogue exhibitions were usually accompanied by live illustrated lectures and imbued with pedagogical significance.[22] As a subset of travel film, the amateur travel film underwent technological transformations, shifting from the 9.5 mm format introduced in 1923 specifically for the amateur market to the popularization of 16 mm in the post–World War II era. As rare case of an amateur travel film made in 1930s China, *The Man Who Has a Camera* was shot in a 9.5 mm "Pathé Baby" amateur film system. It not only combines various styles of film (e.g., city, essay/diary, amateur, travel, sketch, and experimental/avant-garde) but also transcends dogmatic topographical, national, racial, linguistic, and media boundaries. This film had fallen into oblivion for more than half a century before Liu's grandson, the documentary filmmaker Lin Jianxiang, rediscovered the film rolls in 1986, in a rusty tin box in their family's attic in Xinying, Tainan.[23] The rediscovery and restoration of the film have inspired a few essays in Chinese, but a comprehensive, in-depth treatise on the work has yet to be produced.[24]

While most city films focus on a specific city, *The Man Who Has a Camera* presents the journey and experience of traveling as being as significant as the city itself.[25] The film documents Liu and his companions' peregrinations in and among four cities that traverse various political boundaries around 1933: Tainan, in colonial Taiwan; Canton (then under the control of the Nationalist government); Mukden (of ambiguous status); and Tokyo, Japan.[26] The film essentially unfolds as a private visual journal and souvenir or diary film, with Liu as its privileged agent.

The Man Who Has a Camera comprises five sections. The first is entitled "Human Life" (11 min.) and was shot in the Liu family mansion in Xinying, Tainan. It has the explicit characteristics of a home movie,[27] presenting Liu's family members and friends as they pose in front of the camera. The second segment, "Tokyo" (10 min.), unfolds as a travelogue about Liu and his companions' voyages, adopting certain patterns of the "city symphony" film. This is especially evident in the time-based structure, in the dynamic mobility of vehicles, and in the oblique camera movement and rhythmic editing. The third segment, "Scenery: Mukden" (10 min.), follows Liu's fellow travelers as they wander around Fengtian city.[28] The fourth section (10 min.) is shot in Canton, the only place among the four locations in which the Chinese Nationalist government had complete sovereignty in 1933.[29] The fifth and final segment (4 min.) portrays a street pageant in Tainan, on some unspecified special occasion.

The first section of the film highlights the subjects' keen affection and curiosity about the encounter with filming. The subjects inquisitively and intensely look into the camera, a recently invented "bizarre" mechanical gadget. Some shots are close-ups or even extreme close-ups, suggesting that the camera/cameraman came very close to the subjects, creating a sense of proximity and intimacy. The adults and older children seem to be taking instructions from the man behind the camera, taking a few steps, pausing, resuming their walk, shaking hands, and so forth. They pose ritualistically, as if being photographed, confused about being filmed since the practices with which they are familiar have previously been limited to photographic experiences. The experiential aspects of this section, and its images, fall into the interstices between still photography and the moving image, strongly evoking a transmedial implication. These scenes echo Alexandra Schneider's argument that the family film intersects with the travelogue, oscillating between spontaneous observation, playful staging, and photographic posing.[30]

Moments of "looking back at the camera" strongly raise the spectator's awareness of the film medium and the mediation of the image. This technique not only frequently appears in home movies, but also constitutes the self-reflexive convention in city symphony films. It draws attention to the filmic medium itself by disclosing the process of film production—utilizing unusual camera positions and rapid montage or simultaneously presenting different events to reconfigure the big city as a palimpsest.[31] *The Man Who Has a Camera* takes such practices further by illuminating a dramatic and transparent form of revelation as a man points his still camera at Liu's movie camera on a ship while on an excursion to Canton (in section 3): there is a moment of demystification and transmedial revelation as the two cameras and media encounter and grapple with each other, such that the ongoing manipulation and mediation of the photographic and cinematic apparatuses are suddenly illuminated for the viewer.

The vigorous intensity of movement in the city symphony and travel film and the way these forms thematize the accelerated pace of the urban experience can be traced to the representation of dynamic machines like modern transportation vehicles, entertainment apparatuses (including the swing, the carousel, Ferris wheel, and roller coaster) and cinematic devices. Most of these machine elements are abundant in *The Man Who Has a Camera*, conspiring to highlight the movement, speed, and thrill of trains, steamships, automobiles, and airplanes—and creating an extraordinary sensational audiovisual and visceral experience.[32] As a technological invention and industrial machine, the train embodies the novel attractions of mobility and speed.[33] In the "Tokyo" segment, the exhilarating sensations afforded by these new forms of transport for the rider/camera are highlighted throughout the film. Here, double or triple movements are captured and intensified by the camera. By "double or triple movements," I mean (1) the camera movement; (2) the camera mounted on a moving vehicle of some kind; and (3) the movement of a subject within the frame. When all three appear simultaneously, the sense of mobility is both multiplied and intensified. For instance, the audience is treated to aerial views from a plane and a train blazing past a haze of trees.[34] The built urban environment and landmarks of downtown Tokyo thus assume a kinetic presence within the film:[35] on one hand, the immobility of the buildings intensifies the sense of mobility by sharply contrasting with the moving vehicles and cameras; on the other hand, the movements of the vehicle and the camera animate these stationary constructions. The upbeat rhythm of urban life is externalized in this cinematic reconfiguration of urban space.

The Man Who Has a Camera can also be considered a work exemplary of the kinds of amateur and avant-garde filmmaking that took hold around the world.[36] In the 1920s and 1930s, with the advent of modern technology and entertainment, affluent people in Taiwan (as well as in other East Asian regions including Japan and mainland China) started to deploy novel audio and visual devices like cameras, phonographs, and films (in 8 mm or 9.5 mm).[37] Taiwanese film scholar Lee Daw-Ming considers Liu's *The Man Who Has a Camera* a home movie lacking thematic and artistic sophistication and coherence—a far cry from its model, Vertov's *Man with a Movie Camera* (1929).[38] While Lee's description draws attention to the composite nature and tentative experimentalism of Liu's aesthetic, his negative judgment of the work underestimates Liu's stylistic aspirations and the artistic sensitivities embedded in this film, as well as the film's historical significance within the context of 1930s East Asian amateur film practice and audiovisual culture. As an amateur film, *The Man Who Has a Camera* should not to be compared with *Man with a Movie Camera* in terms of scope and cinematic techniques like framing, camera movement, and rhythmic editing. Yet Liu's film is imbued with the vitality and spontaneity of amateur improvisation, playfully embracing and exploring the contingencies of the medium. For instance, two men mischievously make faces in front of the camera (section 3) and children frolic in the film (especially in the first section) with a sense of dynamism and vigor reminiscent of the moving train. Such seemingly insignificant yet whimsical details are juxtaposed with a high-angle panoramic view of the cityscape. The editing in the first section seems haphazard, yet the recurrence of a few shots and jump cuts indicates that Liu deliberately manipulated rhythm and refrain to produce a sense of temporal and spatial disorientation, which is further enriched by the rhythmic patterns of acceleration.

Liu's camera is fascinated by the flow of the crowd in a street parade (the final section), during which anonymous human faces metamorphose as they confront the mobile camera, turning the human face and body into a constantly changing landscape. This is the "noisiest" section in the silent film, which conveys a "silent musicality"[39] of movement and a sense of metaphoric sound within and between the frames. Even though the street sounds are inaudible in the silent film, energy and clamor are strongly evoked by visual references to trumpets and other musical instruments being played, costumed performers dancing, the enthusiastic crowds streaming past, and firecrackers exploding. Like the archetypal city symphony films, *The Man Who Has a Camera* connects urban masses, velocity, and technology with perceptual disorientation: "The crowd and speed of modernization cause a constituent, profound uncertainty in perception that disrupts clear subject-object distinctions."[40]

Although Shanghai itself is absent from *The Man Who Has a Camera*, its imprint is omnipresent, since it was the film's backstage and provided the stimulating cultural milieu that Liu immersed in, conceptualized, and wrote about in his literary work, screenwriting, film criticism, and production.[41] Traveling and travel film for Liu Na'ou represented a means and practice of transcultural exploration: the film begins in Tainan, Liu's hometown, and winds up in the same location, forming a symbolic temporal-spatial circuit. The cinematic itinerary echoes Liu's life trajectory: his struggle with his status as a Japanese colonial subject and a Chinese litterateur. In his concern with formal issues, Liu attempted to transcend various boundaries and establish a depoliticized cosmopolitan cinematic utopia, a pure cinema, and a fluid cultural identity.

RHYTHMICITY, MUSICALITY, AND TRANSMEDIALITY IN LIU NA'OU'S FILM THEORY

Academic interest in the kaleidoscopic urban cultures and cinema of Republican Shanghai has been revived since the late 1990s. The significance of Liu's status as a cosmopolitan figure and the cultural value of his literary and film work have been rediscovered. Although Liu's film theories and criticism have also become more recognized by film scholars, his perceptive treatise on cinematic aesthetics and his contributions to Chinese (and world) film theory call for still more reflection and elaboration. Liu Na'ou extensively and insightfully discussed ontological and stylistic concepts of cinema, especially with regard to movement, rhythm, and sound. From the late 1920s to 1933, Liu Na'ou published more than ten critical essays,[42] and proposed that cinema should be differentiated from other media, cultivate its own aesthetics, and achieve what literature and theater cannot, by developing its own specific techniques, such as camera work, montage, fading in and out, and newfangled components like sound and color.

Liu's film theory and criticism were inspired by various intellectual sources, including European and American directors and film theorists.[43] He also examined the works of French and German "pure cinema" and "absolute cinema" auteurs[44] and praised their experimental works for relinquishing anything explicitly literary, theatrical, or painterly (such as plot, acting, and composition), in order to create a pure absolute for those visual and musical elements that are essentially cinematic.[45] Liu Na'ou's understanding of cinema as a modern combination of artistic sensibility and mechanical innovation, and his sophisticated deliberations about the substantial components of cinematic art, produced a constructive comparison of Chinese and foreign films and engaged in fruitful dialogue with film criticism of the global 1930s. In this section, I will trace Liu's film theory in relation to movement, rhythmicity, and musicality, to delineate his theoretical and cultural contribution to studies of sound and transmediality.

Motion and Rhythm: Dance of Body, Landscape, and Image

In his everyday life, literary writing, cinematic work, and film criticism, Liu Na'ou accentuated the significance of kinetic bodily movement (like dance) and the intoxicating corporeal experience of a rhythmic modernity in cinema. As studies on dance and intermediality in film history and culture suggest, early cinema emerged in a world where interest in bodily movement straddled aesthetic and scientific preoccupations.[46] From Liu Na'ou's viewpoint, modern urban dwellers were eager for speed, movement, and thrills. Since city people had become accustomed to urban noise, harmonious symphonic music was no longer essential or popularly prized.[47] In cinema as in dance, motion became a universal language and an emblem of modernity.

Liu and his renowned neosensationalist writer friend, Mu Shiying, notoriously frequented dance halls and had liaisons with dance hostesses.[48] Liu was a devoted dancer and gained the nickname "the Dancing King."[49] Some of Liu's and Mu's short stories are set in nightclubs and dance halls, exploring their multisensual imagery and synesthetic potentials, as well as the intensity of the sensorial stimulation.[50] The "dance craze" in Shanghai corresponded to the global dance fad in the 1920s and 1930s.[51] Commercial dance halls were launched in the 1920s; newspapers and pictorials introduced social dancing and initiated exuberant discussions about the "craze."[52] Japanese writer Akutagawa Ryūnosuke (1892–1927) also kept an account of Shanghai's dance scene during his 1921 China tour.[53]

Physical performances such as dance (also sports and gymnastics) not only attracted early film spectators, they also served as the basis for public discourse about machine aesthetics, the synchronism of aural and visual rhythms, and the "dance of images" (the editing model for 1920s French avant-garde cinema).[54] French filmmaker and theorist Jean Epstein referred to dance as a general metaphor for the paradigm of mobility in *Bonjour Cinéma* (1921), where he qualified the "landscape's dance," taken from a train or from a car at full speed, as *photogénic*.[55] *Photogénie* was capable of multiplying and expanding movement, and this movement was what distinguished cinema from the plastic arts that were primarily considered a static means of expression.

This dance of landscape is widely highlighted in 1920s and 1930s city and travel films, including Liu Na'ou's *The Man Who Has a Camera*.[56] As a condition of cinema's true specificity, *photogénie*, or the "dance of images," as Jean Epstein noted, is organized in a manner analogous to the principles of musical composition. Dziga Vertov's theorization of film was also informed by music, most notably in the theory of intervals. He proclaimed that film was already a rhythmic and musical art, one that structured time and strove to find its specific rhythm.[57] In an article entitled "Film Theories of the Soviet Union and France," Liu Na'ou elaborated on the variations and rhythm of speed and energy espoused by "pure cinema," claiming that the films were "orchestral ensembles woven by light and shadow in connection with temporal duration."[58]

Liu Na'ou also summarized the interdependence of "interior" and "exterior" rhythm underlined by French film theorists and artists of the 1920s, including Fernand Divoire, René Clair, and Léon Moussinac. In Liu's discussion, the substance of cinema lies in movement, which epitomizes vitality and rhythm and whose qualities are determined by speed, direction, and force. He describes interior rhythm as the structuring principle within the cinematic frame, and it includes the movement of subjects and the camera; exterior rhythm instead is created by the succession of shots. On the one hand, film rhythm emanates from the actors' physical performances, for instance, the "serpentine dance" in early cinema; on the other hand, the cinematic rhythm enhanced by montage is an example of what sets cinema off from other arts. Liu Na'ou pointed out rhythmic components of film that escaped Clair's and Moussinac's attention and delineated their multisensory impact on cinematic style. For instance, he argued that interior rhythm could be achieved by a variation of light hues within the frame (which suggested the passage of time) or alternations of camera angles or changes of background induced by a tracking shot; all these elements helped constitute the interior rhythm. In Liu's view, exterior rhythm is more expressive than interior rhythm in developing a compelling cinematic style.[59]

Liu discussed Walter Ruttmann's city symphony film *Berlin, Symphony of a Great City* in the "pure/abstract cinema" category and praised it for four stylistic aspirations (first, orchestrating musical rhythm across the whole film through modern visual means; second, completely distinguishing itself from filmed theater; third, using no artificial settings; fourth, using no intertitles), particularly its "orchestrating musical rhythm across the whole film through modern visual means."[60] The French "pure cinema" advocates Léon Moussinac, Emile Vuillermoz, and Paul Ramain dreamed of an art based on mastering the rhythm of movement, purified of dramatic convention.[61] Liu claimed that the essence of cinema is a visual symphony (*symphonie visuelle*)[62] and a form of imaginary visual poetry generated by light and shadow, lines and angles; it is inseparable from musical rhythm but can be distant from plot.[63] In this sense, watching a film was analogous to attending a concert, with spectators perceiving the visual symphony as the mechanical dance of light.[64]

In his essay "On Cinematic Art," Liu claimed that montage (interweaving)[65] is the essential component of cinema, since it enlivens images from the *photographique* to the *cinegraphique*[66] and organizes them into an orderly, unified rhythm; this re-creates a new cinematic time-space that does not duplicate actual time-space. This type of effect is exemplified in Soviet filmmaker Vsevolod Pudovkin's *Mother* (1926) and *The End of St. Petersburg* (1927).[67] In their still silent films, Soviet directors became increasingly skilled in rhythmic editing and the use of images to evoke aural associations.[68] Liu contended that such montage was cinema-specific because of its transmedial analogies: montage is at once the verses of a poet, the form of an article, and the visual expression of a filmmaker.[69]

Liu described various rhythmic styles ("linear" or "curved" lines, in his words) in films of different genres and narrative structures. He praised the concordance of rhythm/cadence and songs/melody in film musicals, which visualized rhythm and created films that had "symphonic orchestration." As an example of a well-executed *interweaving/montage* in sound films, Liu acclaimed Viktor Tourjansky's *Le Chanteur Inconnu* (*The Unknown Singer*, 1931):

> The director Tourjansky is able to use silent images to emphasize musical effects. The unknown singer's enchanting voice is transmitted from a broadcast station, gliding over clouds and mountains, traversing various countries in Europe and entering different houses as well as the bosoms of affectionate lovebirds. This sequence is an exquisite example of montage that complements the musical score and imparts to the audience an intoxicating rhythm.[70]

Liu considered this film free of the trite "canned theater" conventions of early sound films. To him it introduced a truly innovative style that opened up a promising road for future sound films.

SOUNDS OF THE EVERYDAY, IN THE FILM THEATER AND ON THE SCREEN

In addition to writing about metaphoric sound elements, Liu Na'ou's acoustic sensitivity was equally captivated by sound culture and the variations of the human voice characterizing daily life, Chinese operatic performance, the film theater, and on screen. During his three-month sojourn in Beijing with his poet friend Dai Wangshu in 1927, Liu frequented the Beijing opera and Kun opera performances[71] and learned opera singing from his friend, as he had earlier learned to play the *huqin*.[72] Liu's diary from 1927 also documents his experience of listening to phonographs in Shanghai and Tokyo.[73] All of this suggests that listening to phonographic records was an important popular pastime and a method for cultural cultivation of urbanites in the 1920s and 1930s. Liu clearly had a strong penchant for music, whether in the form of live performance or personal practice, or mediated through sound technology.

These acoustic experiences inspired Liu Na'ou to assume a more sophisticated approach to sound aesthetics when he wrote the screenplay of *Eternal Smile* (*Yongyuan de weixiao*, dir. Wu Cun, 1936), whose protagonist is a singsong girl, thus rendering music and singing essential features in the film.[74] Liu invokes various sound elements in abundant detail in his screenplay, including sound effects (the clatter of horse hooves, skylarks singing, dogs barking, street clamor, and the sound of rain, wind, sirens, and bells), the human voice (peddlers shouting, the heroine singing, people laughing), and music (*huqin* performances and popular songs, both as diegetic and extradiegetic music). Through an elaborately interwoven acoustic texture and careful attention to sound scales,[75] Liu attempted to create acoustic realism and capture the urban aural atmosphere. When he expressed dissatisfaction after seeing the completed film, several of his criticisms were directed toward the film's sound techniques. For instance, Liu wrote, "If 'laughter' appears in inappropriate occasions, it is like jazz mingled into Beethoven's Ninth Symphony; this is a bad screen—Americanism!" He also argued that the "diction" (delivery of dialogues) is too slow and flat, making the film drag and lose its psychological tension.[76]

The chaotic soundscape in many Chinese film theaters[77] impelled Liu to write a section called "In Chinese Film Theaters" in a longer 1928 article titled "Random Thoughts on Cinema."[78] Liu sarcastically complained about the roar of the crowd, the vendors shouting, children clapping, people reading intertitles aloud or cracking sunflower seeds, and the incompatibility of musical accompaniment to the films being exhibited. All this discordance and disturbance made him dizzy and light-headed; he wrote that he had to leave before the film ended. Disciplining the audience and controlling the sound environment in theaters had been a concern for different cultures beginning in the early twentieth century.[79] In the Chinese case that concerned Liu, it was related to social class and cultural differences.[80]

Liu Na'ou offered insightful reflections on sound film aesthetics and pertinent theory and criticism. In his article "Pursuing the Formal Beauty of Cinema,"[81] Liu proclaimed that the two essential sensual factors creating cinematic beauty are the senses of vision and hearing. He believed that when the three aural components of sound films (music, sound effects, and dialogue) intertwined to create a symphonic audio texture, they contributed to the formal attraction of cinema.[82] Liu derided early American all-talkies for resembling the typewriter: the action and the sound were synchronized, becoming more like exhibitions of sound technology than artistic creations, since Liu argued that the expressive effects of sounds did not just depend on *synchronization*[83] but on whether the coordination of image and sound was able to create cinematic significance. Liu urged Chinese film professionals to catch up with the sound film trend; otherwise they would not be able to resist the invasion of foreign films.[84]

In his 1932 article "On Cinematic Art," Liu introduced the Soviet avant-garde filmmaker Dziga Vertov's first sound film, *Enthusiasm: The Symphony of the Don Basin* (1931) to Chinese readers. He identified the film as an embodiment of the transition between Vertov's cinematic concepts of "kino eye" and "radio ear."[85] Liu applauded the natural sounds present in *Enthusiasm*, which were recorded in industrial locations, including coal mines and steel plants, without artificial manipulation or embellishment. Nonetheless, Vertov's conception and editing were able to render these mechanical sounds musical.[86]

In another article that directly addressed film sound, Liu Na'ou drew comparisons between "light tone" and "acoustic tone" in relation to various cinematic genres and styles.[87] He argued that variations of volume and pitch in acoustic tone are comparable to those of light and shadow in "light tone." Liu outlined the affinities between different sound pitches (high, midregister, and low) and the various film genres and styles. Higher-pitched sounds should be employed for comedies, to match their faster dialogue and action and depict a brisk, jaunty atmosphere. In addition, high-pitched sound better pierces through the laughter and clamor made by the audiences in the theater. This sound, however, is not appropriate for serious dramas like tragedies or the German-style *Schauspiel*,[88] because it does not match the solemn emotion and atmosphere of such genres. A low-pitched tone is more suitable for expressing restraint and austerity, as well as the profound emotional force of dramas, whose audiences were inclined to be more serious and subdued. As an example, Liu praised Franklin H. Hansen for designing a low-pitched tone that was almost a whisper for *A Farewell to Arms* (dir. Frank Borzage, 80 min., 1932). Alternatively, the middle-pitched tone suits melodrama and its sentimental emotional fluctuations, since the flexibility of the midpitch tone can be employed to express and reinforce a sense of the vicissitudes of life and their alternation between joy and sorrow. In retrospect, Liu's insightful discussions about sound design are visionary and forward thinking, especially since sound would become a pivotal part of cinema's "medium specificity." His concepts seem especially prescient since "sound design" as a category and creative concept would not emerge in Hollywood until the 1970s.[89]

CONCLUSION

> When I knew such a genius with languages, it was like seeing a person who had lost his nationality and social belonging, a human being deprived of his shadow: one must often feel emptiness and trepidation.—Keiji Matsuzaki[90]

Liu Na'ou made a seemingly naive attempt to transcend the tensions surrounding his complex colonial and transcultural identity by devoting himself to the elusive values of itinerant cosmopolitanism. Given the political and cultural struggles complicated by the contesting forces of the era,[91] and Liu's lack of national allegiance and ideological commitment, it seems logical that he aspired to find opportunities for "pure art" and "free" cinematic creation and condemned leftist writers' works as being "contaminated by politics."[92] However, according to a memoir by Huang Gang, Liu worked with the Japanese closely after the latter fully occupied Shanghai[93] and directly profited from the collaboration.[94] Consequently, Liu's claim to being apolitical may be challenged. As Leslie Pincus observes, "Cosmopolitan concentration on values of an intangible and universal nature encouraged adherents to withdraw into an expanded and enriched realm of interiority while distancing themselves from more immediate and more material social realities."[95]

In Liu Na'ou's trajectory as a transcultural raconteur, Shanghai became a symbolic location, one with which he both identified and associated his "future."[96] Rather than in Tokyo or Taiwan, Liu chose to live and work in Shanghai, "a space of shifting struggles and alignments,"[97] where confrontations among various imperial powers both from the West and from Japan were being negotiated. This "intertwined colonization" illuminates China's multilayered colonial past and attends to the intersecting relationship of cosmopolitan Shanghai and colonial Taiwan.[98] There Liu's sense of alienation and rootlessness could be ameliorated or even alleviated, and he could reside there emancipated and anonymous and might easily assume any number of identities. By drifting among and immersing himself in different cultural identifications, Liu might be understood to have located himself in the dissolution of the essential self into "an endlessly fragmented subject in process," in an interstitial temporality, a "space-in-between."[99]

By framing Liu Na'ou's life experience, film career, literary and cinematic writings, and film *The Man Who Has a Camera* as transcultural and transmedial, I have accentuated issues related to mobility and border crossing. In a larger historical context, as modern technology made traveling across long distances and the resulting translation and transculturation increasingly possible, such boundary-traversing journeys gave rise to a metamovement—an aesthetic cosmopolitanism born of the flow of technology, knowledge, film production, and cinematic discourse. The center of gravity in Liu Na'ou's versatile creative life was Shanghai, with its uncertain subjectivity at the extraterritorial borders of the nation-state and the intersection of Chinese, European, American, and Japanese interests.[100] Shanghai was the epicenter of conflicts and tensions around sovereignty, the expansion of global capital, and the flourishing of entertainment and consumption. Liu Na'ou himself embodied many of these same tensions; and yet, his works on sound, movement, rhythm, and musicality in the transcultural and transmedial milieu can yield profound insights for how we envision metaphoric sound in relation to proliferating transcultural and transmedial cinematic practice.

Notes

1. Rudolph Lothar, *Der Andere: Schauspiel in vier Aufzugen* (Leipzig). Quote from Friedrich A. Kittler, *Gramophone, Film, Typewriter*, trans. Geoffrey Winthrop-Young and Michael Wutz (Stanford, CA: Stanford University Press, 1999), 71.

2. Neosensationalist literature is a modernist literary school that came into existence in Japan in the mid and late 1920s. As Yokomitsu Riichi, a representative neosensationalist writer, explained: "I believe that futurism, stereo-school, symbolism, structuralism, modernism and part of factualism—all of these belong to neo-sensationalism." The Japanese neosensationalist writers pursued "new sensations," new life modes, and new ways of perceiving objects. Their mental states, sentiments, nerves, and moods all boasted the most intense perceptibility. This form, introduced to China from Japan by Liu Na'ou, was influenced by French modernist writer Paul Morand (1888–1976). Represented by Liu Na'ou, Mu Shiying, and Shi Zhecun, Chinese neosensationalist literature remained active in the history of Chinese modern literature for six years, from the launch of the literary journal *Trackless Train* by Liu Na'ou in September 1920 to Shi Zhecun's departure from *Modern Times* at the end of 1934. Around 1935, novelists in this school changed direction, fell into decline, or converted to realism. For more information, see David Der-wei Wang, "Chinese Literature from 1841–1937," in *The Cambridge History of Chinese Literature*, vol. 2, *From 1375*, ed. Kang-I Sun Chang and Stephen Owen (Cambridge: Cambridge University Press, 2010), 413–564.

3. Liu received his bachelor's degree in English literature from Aoyama College in Tokyo in 1926 and soon thereafter registered for a French class at L'Université L'Aurore in Shanghai, establishing friendships and forming a collaboration with later literary luminaries Dai Wangshu, Shi Zhecun, and Mu Shiying.

4. In the "Chinese" category, he could converse in Mandarin, the Shanghai dialect, and Cantonese, in addition to speaking his mother tongue, the Minnan dialect.

5. Taiwan was ceded to Japan in 1895 by the Qing dynasty as a consequence of its defeat in the First Sino-Japanese War, in line with the Treaty of Shimonoseki. It was returned to the government of the Republic of China government in 1945, with the unconditional surrender of Japan at the end of World War II.

6. Walter Murch, "Touch of Silence," in *Soundscape: The School of Sound Lectures, 1998–2001*, ed. Larry Side, Jerry Side, and Diane Freeman (London: Wallflower Press, 2003), 100.

7. *Pure* refers to a medium specificity and is stressed by 1920s European, and especially French, avant-garde filmmakers and critics; *impure* refers to the cinematic hybrid-

ization accentuated by André Bazin in 1951. See André Bazin, "In Defense of Mixed Cinema," in *What Is Cinema?* vol. 1, ed. and trans. Hugh Gray (Berkeley: University of California Press), 53–75; Lúcia Nagib and Anne Jerslev, "Introduction," in *Impure Cinema: Intermedial and Intercultural Approaches to Film*, ed. Lúcia Nagib and Anne Jerslev (New York: I. B. Tauris, 2013), xix. For a brief history of the critical terms *intermediality* and *intermedia*, see Stephanie A. Glaser, "Introduction," *Media inter Media: Essays in Honor of Claus Clüver*, ed. Stephanie A. Glaser (Amsterdam, NY: Rodopi, 2009), 12–28. For the conceptual history of "transmediality" and "transculturality," see Nadja Gernalzick and Gabriele Pisarz-Ramirez, "Preface and Comparative Conceptual History," in *Transmediality and Transculturality*, ed. Nadja Gernalzick and Gabriele Pisarz-Ramirez (Heidelberg: Universitätsverlag Winter, 2013), xii–xxiii.

8. Jürgen E. Müller, "Media Encounters—an Introduction," in *Media Encounters and Media Theories*, ed. Jürgen E. Müller (Münster: Nodus Publikationen Munster, 2008), 10.

9. Gernalzick and Pisarz-Ramirez, *Transmediality and Transculturality*, xii.

10. Gernalzick and Pisarz-Ramirez, *Transmediality and Transculturality*, xiii. The authors also assert that "since the mid-20th century, transmediality and transculturality have been launched into debates about cultural and medial sectionalism when competing terms such as inter- or multiculturality and transmediality and transculturality entrenched virulent distinctions for the organization of privilege and hierarchy . . . [We] seek to describe experience with more comprehensive realism and greater temporary adequacy."

11. Hong Shen (1894–1955) was a pioneering Chinese dramatist and filmmaker. Educated in Beijing and at Harvard University, Hong taught dramatic arts and Western literature at various universities after his return to China in 1922. He directed plays by both Chinese and Western writers (e.g., Oscar Wilde's *Lady Windermere's Fan*) in the 1920s. Hong also worked as a film producer, screenwriter, and film director at Star Motion Picture Company in the 1930s. See *Encyclopedia Britannica*, "Hong Shen" (Chicago: Encyclopedia Britannica, 2014), http://www.britannica.com/EBchecked/topic/276606/Hong-Shen (last updated July 22, 2005).

12. Tian Han (1898–1968) was a Chinese playwright and poet known for his expressive and powerful one-act plays. He studied for several years in Japan, where he developed a lasting interest in modern drama. Tian experimented in and popularized modern vernacular drama and films in the 1920s. He also wrote a few successful screenplays with progressive inclinations. He composed librettos for traditional Chinese opera and is the author of the national anthem of the People's Republic of China, "March of the Volunteers." See *Encyclopedia Britannica*, "Tian Han," (Chicago: Encyclopedia Britannica, 2014), http://www.britannica.com/EBchecked/topic/594812/Tian-Han (last updated July 22, 2005). For a more comprehensive discussion of Tian Han's creative career and transmedial practice, see Liang Luo, *The Avant-Garde and the Popular in Modern China: Tian Han and the Intersection of Performance and Politics* (Ann Arbor: University of Michigan Press, 2014).

13. As previously mentioned (note 3), Liu experienced a complicated identity as a colonial subject of Japan living in semicolonial Shanghai.

14. In the words of his writer friend Shi Zhecun, "1/3 Shanghainese, 1/3 Taiwanese, and 1/3 Japanese."

15. Liu's film writings were largely neglected by official Chinese film historiography until the 1990s, due to their strong formalist tendencies (considered sign of the lack of a progressive social consciousness) and harsh criticism of 1930s Chinese left-wing films. There was also a stigma attached to Liu as a "cultural traitor." In recent years, a growing body of scholarship from mainland China, Taiwan, Japan, and the United States has taken up his literary creations and cultural identity in relation to modernity, modernism, and Shanghai urban culture. See Shu-mei Shih, *The Lure of the Modern: Writing Modernism in Semicolonial China, 1917–1937* (Berkeley: University of California Press, 2001); Lee Daw-ming, "Liu Na'ou de dianying meixueguan: Jiantan ta de jilu dianying 'Xiezhe sheyingji de nanren'" [Liu Na'ou's Concept of Film Aesthetic, and His Documentary *The Man Who Has a Camera*], in *Liu Na'ou guoji yantaohui lunwenji* [Proceedings of the International Conference on Liu Na'ou], ed. Department of Chinese Literature of National Central University (Tainan: National Museum of Taiwan Literature choubeichu, 2005), 145–159; Leo Ou-fan Lee, "Face, Body, and the City: The Fiction of Liu Na'ou and Mu Shiying," in *Shanghai Modern: The Flowering of a New Urban Culture in China, 1930–1945* (Cambridge, MA: Harvard University Press, 1999), 190–231; Leo Ou-fan Lee, "Shanghai Modern: Reflection on Urban Culture in China in the 1930s," *Public Culture* 11, no. 1 (1999): 75–107; Hsiao-yen Peng, *Dandyism and Transcultural Modernity: The Dandy, the Flaneur, and the Translator in 1930s Shanghai, Tokyo, and Paris* (New York: Routledge, 2010); Peng Hsiao-yen, *Haishang shuo qingyu: cong Zhang Ziping dao Liu Na'ou* [Shanghai Desire: From Zhang Ziping to Liu Na'ou] (Taipei: Zhongyanyuan wenzhesuo, 2001); Yomi Braester, "Shanghai's Economy of the Spectacle: The Shanghai Race Club in Liu Na'ou and Mu Shiying's Stories," *Modern Chinese Literature* 9, no. 1 (1995): 39–57; Li Jin, *Haipai xiaoshuo lun* [On Shanghai-Style Fiction] (Taipei: Xiuwei zixun, 2005); Li Jin, "Xin ganjuepai he ersanshi niandai haolaiwu dianying" [Neosensationalism and Hollywood Films in the 1920s and 1930s], *Modern Chinese Literature Studies* 3 (1997): 32–56; Hsu Chen-chin, "Chongdu Taiwanren Liu Na'ou (1905–1940): Lishi yu wenhua de hudong kaocha" [Rereading Taiwanese Liu Na'ou (1905–1940): A Study on History and Culture] (master's thesis, National Central University, 1998); Hsu Chen-chin and Kang Laixin, eds., *Liu Na'ou quanji* [The Complete Works of Liu Na'ou] (Tainan: Museum of Taiwan Literature and Tainan County Bureau of Culture, 2001); Hsu Chen-chin and Kang Laixin, eds., *Liu Na'ou quanji: zengbuji* [The Complete Works of Liu Na'ou: The Supplement] (Tainan: Museum of Taiwan Literature and Tainan County Bureau of Culture, 2010); Hsu Chen-chin, *Modeng, Shanghai, xin ganjue: Liu Na'ou, 1905–1940* [Modern, Shanghai, Neosensationalist: Liu Na'ou, 1905–1940] (Taipei: Xiuwei zixun keji gufen youxian gongsi, 2008); Mamie Misawa, *Zai "diguo" yu "zuguo" de jiafeng jian: Rizhi shiqi Taiwan dianyingren de jiaoshe yu kuajing*

[Between the "Empire" and the "Mother Country": Taiwanese Filmmakers' Transcultural Negotiations during the Japanese Occupation], trans. Li Wenqing and Xu Shijia (Taipei: Taiwan University Press, 2012).

16. See, for instance, works by Liu Na'ou and Mu Shiying, as well as Japanese writer Yokomitsu Riichi's modernist installment fiction *Shanghai* (1928–1929).

17. Early city films or city symphony films include Alberto Cavalcanti's *Rien que les Heures* (1926), Walter Ruttmann's *Berlin, Symphony of a Great City* (1927), Mikhail Kaufman and Ilja Kopalin's *Moskva* (*Moscow*, 1928), Dziga Vertov's *Man with a Movie Camera* (1929), Joris Ivens's *Rain* (1929), László Moholy-Nagy's *Impressionen vom alten Marseiller Hanfen* (*vieux port*) (1929), Corrado D'Erric's *Stramilano* (1929), Jean Vigo's *À Propos de Nice* (1930), Herman Weinberg's *City Symphony* (1930), as well as other early avant-garde films picturing New York City in the 1920s, such as Charles Sheeler and Paul Strand's *Manhatta* (1920), Jay Leyda's *A Bronx Morning* (1931), and so on.

18. Nora M. Alter, "*Berlin, Symphony of a Great City* (1927): City, Image, Sound," in *Weimar Cinema: An Essential Guide to Classic Films of the Era*, ed. Noah William Isenberg (New York: Columbia University Press, 2009), 196. Interestingly, *Berlin* was categorized as a "pure film" or an "absolute film" in Liu Na'ou's writing, since it was not a plot-oriented fictional film with an artificial setting (although it contains a couple of constructed dramatic scenes, such as a woman jumping from a bridge to commit suicide), and has an overall cinematic rhythm uninterrupted by verbose explanatory intertitles. See Liu Na'ou, "Yingpian yishu lun" [On Cinematic Art], in *Liu Na'ou quanji: dianying ji* [The Complete Works of Liu Na'ou: On Cinema] in Hsu and Kang, *Liu Na'ou quanji*, 274.

19. Alter, "*Berlin, Symphony of a Great City* (1927)," 199.

20. For instance, the shape, size, length, and frequency of the intertitles also influence the audience's perception of rhythm and speed. See Liu, "Yingpian yishu lun," 276–280.

21. Travel film dominated the early cinema period from 1895 to 1905 and is considered the "first chapter" in the history of the documentary by British documentary filmmaker John Grierson. The genre was later incorporated into mainstream Hollywood fiction films as spectacular attractions, showcasing exotic cultures and locales.

22. For books on amateur cinema, see Charles E. Tepperman, *Amateur Cinema: The Rise of North American Movie Making, 1923–1960* (Berkeley: University of California Press, 2015); Laura Rascaroli, Gwenda Young, and Barry Monahan, eds., *Amateur Filmmaking: The Home Movie, the Archive, the Web* (New York: Bloomsbury Academic, 2014); Jennifer Lynn Peterson, *Education in the School of Dreams: Travelogues and Early Nonfiction Film* (Durham, NC: Duke University Press, 2013); Patricia R. Zimmermann, *Reel Families: A Social History of Amateur Film* (Bloomington: Indiana University Press, 1995).

23. This is now called the Xinying District, a second administration center of the Tainan City Government. Sugar production was the most important industry in Xinying during the Japanese colonial period. The Liu family was prominent there, holding

large parcels of land, and the family sent many of its descendants to study abroad, either in mainland China, Japan, or Germany. After format conversion and restoration by NHK (Japan Broadcasting Corporation), Liu's film was released on DVD in 2006 as part of the fifteen-film collection, "Moving Images in Contemporary Taiwan: From Documentary to Experimental Films." These details were gathered from my several interviews with Lin, in 2010 and on September 26, 2015 respectively.

24. See Lee, "Liu Na'ou de dianying meixueguan," 145–159.

25. Vertov's *Man with a Movie Camera* is an exception, with footage shot in five different Soviet cities, including Moscow, Kiev, and Odessa.

26. The area, located in northeast China, was known as Manchuria and designated by the Qing dynasty as the homeland of the ruling family's ethnic group, the Manchus. In 1931, Japan seized Fengtian (Mukden) following the Mukden Incident and in 1932 installed a Japanese puppet state, Manchukuo, with Puyi, the last Qing emperor, as its ruler. Puyi was forced to abdicate in 1912, in response to the Republican revolution of the previous year, thus ending 267 years of Qing rule. During the Manchukuo era (1932–1945), the city was called Fengtian in Chinese and Mukden in English. Manchukuo's government was abolished in 1945 after the defeat of Japan at the end of World War II. Since then, the city has been called Shenyang.

27. For scholarship on "home movie," see Karen L. Ishizuka and Patricia R. Zimmermann, eds., *Mining the Home Movie: Excavations in Histories and Memories* (Berkeley: University of California Press, 2007).

28. They visit tourist destinations such as the Northern Mausoleum and Xinjing Park. Northern Mausoleum Park was established in 1927 and located in the northern part of Fengtian. It includes Zhaoling, the tomb of the second Qing emperor, Huang Taiji, which was constructed between 1643 and 1651.

29. In addition to Tokyo, Tainan and Fengtian were also under Japanese control.

30. Alexandra Schneider, "Homemade Travelogues: *Autosonntag*—a Film Safari in the Swiss Alps," in *Virtual Voyages: Cinema and Travel*, ed. Jeffrey Ruoff (Durham, NC: Duke University Press, 2006), 158.

31. Derek Hillard, "Walter Ruttmann's Janus-Faced View of Modernity: The Ambivalence of Description in *Berlin: Symphony of a Great City*," *Monatshefte* 96, no. 1 (2004): 88.

32. As Heiner Fruhauf points out, the large-scale steamship and its dense facsimile of modern society was a topic of universal interest during the 1920s and 1930s. On the one hand, it is a floating hotel equipped beyond the standard luxuries of its counterparts on land; to the beholder ashore, on the other hand, the ship moves from and to infinity, eventually merging with all-encompassing nature at the meeting point of sky and ocean. Most of all, this elaborate construction bears witness to the superhuman qualities of mankind. Heiner Fruhauf, "Urban Exoticism and Its Sino-Japanese Scenery, 1910–1923," *Asian and African Studies* 6 (1997): 145.

33. For trains and the cultural perception of speed and visuality, see Wolfgang Schivel-

busch, *The Railway Journey: The Industrialization of Time and Space in the 19th Century* (Berkeley: University of California Press, 1986); Lynn Kirby, *Parallel Tracks: The Railroad and Silent Cinema* (Durham, NC: Duke University Press, 1997).

34. This view of a "phantom ride" strongly evokes Jean Epstein's *La Glace à Trois Faces* (1927), with its sense of mysterious and compelling excitement engendered by speed.

35. Many urban landmarks in Tokyo appear in this film, including the Japan Theater and the Imperial Theatre in Ginza. Thanks to Michael Raine for pointing this out.

36. See Tepperman, *Amateur Cinema*, 2015; and Jan-Christopher Horak, ed., *Lovers of Cinema: The First American Film Avant-Garde, 1919–1945* (Madison: University of Wisconsin Press, 1995). There were also numerous advertisements for 8 and 9.5 mm equipment in Chinese film magazines in the 1930s. More substantive research on this issue in 1930s China has yet to be conducted.

37. Lee, "Liu Na'ou de dianying meixueguan," 152. Liu Na'ou's contemporary, Deng Nanguang, a Taiwanese photographer who also studied in Japan, likewise made a short amateur film in the 1930s: *Fishing Tour* (Yuyou, 1935, 8 mm).

38. Lee, "Liu Na'ou de dianying meixueguan," 153.

39. Yuri Tsivian, *Early Cinema in Russia and Its Cultural Reception* (New York: Routledge, 1994), 81.

40. Hillard, "Ruttmann's Janus-Faced View," 88.

41. Shanghai was where Liu Na'ou worked and lived; the life and scenery there for him was probably quotidian, lacking the splendor and excitement of faraway places and requiring more artistic effort to be defamiliarized. Another possibility is Shanghai's debris: the city had endured severe Japanese bombardment in 1932, and the Chinese section outside of the International Settlement was nearly reduced to ruins. Thanks to Kristine Harris for pointing this out.

42. Including Liu Na'ou, "Yingpian yishu lun" [On Cinematic Art], *Dianying zhoubao*, published as installments July 1–October 8, 1932; Liu Na'ou, "Dianying jiezou jianlun" [A Brief Discussion of Film Rhythm], *Modern Screen* 6 (1933): 1–2; Liu Na'ou, "Kaimaila jigou—weizhi jiaodu jinenglun" [On the Mechanism of the Camera—the Function of Camera Positions and Angles], *Modern Screen* 7 (1934): 1–2; Liu Na'ou, "Dianying xingshimei de tanqiu" [Pursuing a Formal Beauty in Cinema], *Wanxiang* 1, May, 1934; Liu Na'ou, "Guangdiao yu yindiao" [Light Tone and Acoustic Tone], *Shidai dianying*, November 5, 1934.

43. For example, Léon Moussinac, Rudolf Arnheim, Vsevolod Pudovkin, Sergei Eisenstein, Dziga Vertov, and Hugo Münsterberg.

44. Including Viking Eggeling, Hans Richter, Fernand Léger, Walter Ruttmann, René Clair, Alberto Cavalcanti, and Man Ray. Liu introduces Eggeling's two seminal abstract films, *Horizontal-Vertitak Messe* (*Horizontal-Vertical Orchestra*, 1921, now lost) and *Symphonie Diagonale* (*Diagonal Symphony*, 7 min., 1924), and mentions Richter's abstract films *Rhythmus 23* (1923) and *Rhythmus 25* (1925). He also introduces the use of close-ups on faces and objects as a means of constructing visual rhythms and psychological

effects in his *Inflation* (1927). Liu assesses Léger's *Ballet Mécanique* (1924) in terms of its employing images of ordinary objects and use of skillful cinematography to create "significance of movement" without scenario. More importantly, the harmony of speed, force, and rhythm in this film strongly evokes cinematic attraction. Liu differentiates Ruttmann's attitude and method of filmmaking from that of Eggeling and Richter, stating that the latter two place more emphasis on cinema's scientific and mathematical base. Ruttmann, however, concentrates more on empathy, ornamental beauty, and psychological effects, through multiplying modes of movement and employing sensational techniques. Clair's *Entr'acte* (1924), Cavalcanti's *Rien que les heures* (1926), and Man Ray's *Emak-Bakia* (1926) are also under discussion.

45. Liu, "Yingpian yishu lun."

46. For the Symbolists, the art of motion evoked the harmonious rhythm of dance. See Tom Gunning, "Loïe Fuller and the Art of Motion," in *The Tenth Muse: Cinema and Other Arts*, ed. Leonardo Quaresima and Laura Vichi (Udine: Forum, 2001), 25–53; Laurent Guido, "Rhythmic Bodies/Movies: Dance as Attraction in Early Film Culture," in *The Cinema of Attractions Reloaded*, ed. Wanda Strauven (Amsterdam: Amsterdam University Press, 2006), 139–152.

47. Liu, "Dianying jiezou jianlun."

48. Mu married the dance hostess Qiu Peipei in 1934. Liu Na'ou's diaries in 1927, as well as Shanghai tableau newspapers, described his infatuation with dance girls, both Japanese and Chinese, in Shanghai, Tokyo, and Nanjing. See Hsu Chen-chin and Kang Laixin, eds., *Liu Na'ou quanji: riji ji* [The Complete Works of Liu Na'ou: Diaries] in Hsu and Kang, *Liu Na'ou quanji*.

49. Peng, *Dandyism and Transcultural Modernity*, 27–35. Miaodou, "Zuojia yu wudao: Liu Na'ou shi huoshanshang de qianbei" [Author and Dance: Liu Na'ou Is a Veteran in the Dancing World], *Tiaowushijie* 2, no. 2, 1937, n.p.

50. For instance, Mu's famed short stories "Shanghai Foxtrot" ("Shanghai de hubuwu") (1932) and "Five People in the Nightclub" ("yezonghui li de wugeren") (1932) and Liu's short story collection, *Urban Scenery* (*dushi fengjingxian*, 1930).

51. The Soviet compilation/city film *Shanghai Document* (*Yakov Bliokh*, 1927) juxtaposes Western expatriates having a dance party in a lavish garden with impoverished Chinese children dragging heavy carts in the street, graphically matching the rotating phonograph with the cart's wheels, creating a trenchant social and racial critique. 1930s Chinese leftist films also portray characters' decadent dance hall lifestyles in a sarcastic tone; see, for instance, *New Woman* (*Xin nüxing*, dir. Cai Chusheng, 1935) and *City Scenes* (*Dushi fengguang*, dir. Yuan Muzhi, 1935), among others.

52. Many dance schools were founded by both Russian expatriates and the Chinese. They offered classes ranging from the tango, fox trot, and waltz to the Charleston. Instruction books on dancing were widely published and popularized among fashion-conscious business people and urbanites. In 1933, thirty-nine dance halls had official operating licenses. In 1946, there were 1,622 registered dance hostesses in Shanghai. Luo

Suwen and Song Zuanyou, *Minguo shehui* [Republican Society], vol. 9 of *Shanghai tongshi* [History of Shanghai], ed. Xiong Yuezhi (Shanghai: Shanghai renmin chubanshe, 1999), 177–178.

53. He observed people (including a cross-racial couple: a Filipino girl in red and a young American man in a suit) dancing in a café named "Paris" and noticed that the level of orchestral performance was much higher there than in the Asakusa-area cafés and dance halls of Tokyo. Akutagawa Ryūnosuke, *Zhongguo youji* [Travel Notes of China], trans. Chen Hao (Beijing: Xinshijie chubanshe, 2011), 10.

54. Guido, "Rhythmic Bodies/Movies," 139.

55. Guido, "Rhythmic Bodies/Movies," 150.

56. Liu's short story "Scenery" ("Fengjing") (1930) recounts the chance encounter and erotic adventures of a woman and a man on a train and in an open landscape. Liu describes the characters' experience in the train as "sitting on speed."

57. Jeremy Hicks, *Dziga Vertov: Defining Documentary Film* (London: I. B. Tauris, 2007), 79.

58. Liu Na'ou, "E'fa de yingxi lilun" [Film Theories of the Soviet Union and France], in *Liu Na'ou quanji: zengbuji*, 179.

59. Liu, "Dianying jiezou jianlun."

60. Liu, "Dianying jiezou jianlun."

61. Liu, "Dianying jiezou jianlun."

62. Originally in French in the text. Liu, "Yingpian yishu lun."

63. Liu, "Yingpian yishu lun." Originally in English.

64. Liu, "E'fa de yingxi lilun," 180.

65. A literal translation of the Chinese term *zhijie* would be "interweaving." To learn more about the theoretical permutations and cinematic practice of montage after it was translated and introduced to China in the early 1930s, see Jessica Ka-yee Chan, "Translating 'Montage': The Discreet Attractions of Soviet Montage for Chinese Revolutionary Cinema," *Journal of Chinese Cinemas* 5, no. 3 (2011): 197–218.

66. Liu's original text used the French words; Liu, "Yingpian yishu lun."

67. Liu, "Yingpian yishu lun."

68. Hicks, *Dziga Vertov*, 71.

69. Liu, "Yingpian yishu lun."

70. Liu, "Yingpian yishu lun." The Chinese films *Fate in Tears and Laughter* (*Tixiao yinyuan*, 1932) and *A Night of Glamour* (*Yiye haohua*, dir. Shao Zuiweng, 1932) were cited as negative examples for their primitive editing, which Liu Na'ou critiqued and compared to *The Volga Boatman* and *Le Chanteur Inconnu*.

71. Hsu and Kang, *Liu Na'ou quanji: riji ji*, 688, 702, 708, 734, 740.

72. "Gen Laopang xuele jiju Ma Lianliang de *Zhulianzhai*" [Learn a Few Lines of Ma Lianliang's Zhulianzhai from Laopang], in *Liu Na'ou quanji: riji ji*, 662; The *huqin* belongs to a family of bowed string instruments; *jinghu* is used primarily for Beijing opera accompaniment.

73. See Hsu and Kang, *Liu Na'ou quanji: riji ji*, 176, 186, 328, 346, 370, 476, 550, 594.

74. For the complete screen script, see "'Yongyuan de weixiao' jiben (zi di 1 mu zhi 566 mu)" [Script of *Eternal Smile* (Scene 1 to Scene 566)], in *Liu Na'ou quanji: dianying ji*, 46–219.

75. Sound in "close-up" or in "long shot"; the scale refers to the distance between the sound source and the camera.

76. Liu, "Yingpian yishu lun," 40–45.

77. In Republican Shanghai, the most luxurious first-run film theaters were mostly owned by foreign exhibitors and usually showed foreign films (mainly from Hollywood). Chinese films were primarily shown in the second- or third-tier film theaters, whose equipment was relatively humble and which catered to a lower-class demographic by offering more affordable ticket prices.

78. Published in the journal *Trackless Train* (*Wugui lieche*), which was funded by Liu Na'ou. "Yingxi manxiang" [Random Thoughts on Cinema], *Wugui lieche* 5 (1928): 281–284.

79. For audience discipline related to gender issues in early American film culture, see Shelly Stamp, *Movie-Struck Girls: Women and Motion Picture Culture after the Nickelodeon* (Princeton, NJ: Princeton University Press, 2000), particularly chapter 1, 1–40.

80. Most Chinese theaters screened films in addition to presenting other kinds of performance, such as Chinese operas; in the latter, the audiences were used to eating, drinking, and chatting during the performance. This habit continued during film exhibitions.

81. In Liu, "Dianying xingshimei de tanqiu."

82. Words in italics are originally in English.

83. Originally in English.

84. Liu Na'ou, "Ecranesque," *Modern Screen* 2 (1933): 1.

85. See Liu, "Yingpian yishu lun," 267–269.

86. This is reminiscent of a note that Charlie Chaplin wrote Vertov after watching *Enthusiasm*: "Never had I known that these mechanical sounds could be arranged to sound so beautiful. I regard it as one of the most exhilarating symphonies I have heard. Mr. Dziga Vertov is a musician. The professor should learn from him, not quarrel with him. Congratulations." See Hicks, *Dziga Vertov*, 126.

87. Liu, "Guangdiao yu yindiao."

88. Originally in German. *Schauspiel* refers to any spectacle or public performance. In late eighteenth-century German literature, the word took on the more specific meaning of a play with the characteristics of both tragedy and a comedy, meaning a serious play with a happy ending and in which the hero does not die. See *Encyclopedia Britannica*, "Schauspiel" (Chicago: Encyclopedia Britannica, 2014), https://global.britannica.com/art/Schauspiel (last updated September 17, 1999).

89. The term "sound designer" gained wider currency in connection with the work of film editor and sound designer Walter Murch, for his significant contributions to Fran-

cis Ford Coppola's *The Conversation* (1974) and *Apocalypse Now* (1979); Murch, "Touch of Silence."

90. Referring to Liu Na'ou's death. Keiji Matsuzaki, "Liu Canbo qiangji" [Liu Canbo Was Shot], in *Liu Na'ou quanji: zengbuji*, 258.

91. For example, the Western colonial powers, Japanese military invasion, the Nationalist regime, and the underground Communist activities.

92. Huang Gang, "Liu Na'ou zhilu (baogao): huiyi yige 'gaogui' de ren, ta de dijiande xunshen" [The Road of Liu Na'ou (Report): Recalling A "Noble" Man, and His Contemptible Death], *Ta Kung Pao*, January 27–February 7, 1941.

93. After the outbreak of the Pacific War on December 7, 1941.

94. See Huang, "Liu Na'ou zhilu (baogao)." Japanese film writer and producer Keiji Matsuzaki (1905–1974) also recalls that Liu worked as an "emissary" for the Japanese to approach Chinese film professionals and intellectuals. In Matsuzaki, "Liu Canbo qiangji," 273.

95. Leslie Pincus, *Authenticating Culture in Imperial Japan: Kuki Shuzo and the Rise of National Aesthetics* (University of California Press, 1996), 39.

96. Hsu and Kang, *Liu Na'ou quanji: riji ji*, 446.

97. Seiji M. Lippit, *Topographies of Japanese Modernism* (New York: Columbia University Press, 2002), 86.

98. Ying Xiong, "Ethno Literary Identity and Geographical Displacement: Liu Na'ou's Chinese Modernist Writing in the East Asian Context," *Asian Culture and History* 3, no. 1 (2011): 5.

99. Jessica Berman, *Modernist Fiction, Cosmopolitanism, and the Politics of Community* (Cambridge University Press, 2001), 17.

100. Lippit, *Topographies of Japanese Modernism*, 77.

Chinese and Japanese Glossary

Ai zhi hua 愛之花
Aihe chao 愛河潮
Aikoku fujinkai 愛国婦人会
Aiqing daili ren 愛情代理人
aiqing dianying 哀情電影
Aishen zhi feiliao 愛神之肥料
Akashi Motojirō 明石元二郎
Baihe yingpian gongsi 百合影片公司
Baijinlong 白金龍
Baiyue 百粵
banjin 蕃人
banjin kankō 蕃人観光
Bao Qingjia 鮑慶甲
Bao Tianxiao 包天笑
Bao'an 寶安
benshi 弁士
Bijou 比照
Bu Wancang 卜萬蒼
bungei 文艺
bunmei kaika 文明開化
Butokuden 武徳殿
buzhong buxi 不中不西
Cai Chusheng 蔡楚生
Cao Xuegeng 曹雪賡
chayuan 茶園
Chen Jiongming 陳炯明
Chen Junchao (Chan Kwan-chiu) 陳君超
Chen Zhiqing 陳趾青
Cheng Bugao 程步高
Cheng Xiaoqing 程小青
chi'an iji hō 治安維持法
chō 庁
Chongqing (Chung Hing) 重慶
Congjun meng 從軍夢
cuzhi lanzao 粗製濫造
Dazhonghua yingpian gongsi 大中華影片公司
Daguan 大觀
Dahan (Dai Hon) 大漢
Dai Wangshu 戴望舒
Dailao baishou 呆佬拜壽
Dalai (Dai Lo) 大來
dan 旦
Dan Duyu 但杜宇
Dao minjian qu 到民間去
Daya 大亞
Dazhonghua baihe yingpain gongsi 大中華百合影片公司
Den Kenjirō 田健治郎

diandeng yingxi 電燈影戲
dianhua 電畫
dianying wenren 電影文人
Dingjunshan 定軍山
Ersun fu 兒孫福
Fei Mu 費穆
Feifei 非非
feijin feigu 非今非古
Feng shen bang 封神榜
Fengyu zhi ye 風雨之夜
Gakuso zaidan 学租財団
Gao Lihen (Ko Lei-hen) 高梨痕
Gaosheng (Ko Shing) 高陞
gentō 幻燈
gentō-kai 幻燈会
Genü Hongmudan 歌女紅牡丹
Gotō Shimpei 後藤新平
Gongpingbao 公評報
Gu Kenfu 顧肯夫
Gu Mingdao 顧明道
Gu'er jiuzu ji 孤兒救祖記
Gu'er tuoxian ji 孤兒脫險記
Guan Wenqing (Kwan Man-ching, Moon Kwan) 關文清
Guaming fuqi 掛名夫妻
Guangya (Kwong Ah) 光亞
Guangzhou minguo ribao 廣州民國日報
Guangzhou nanyue 廣州南粵
Gujing chongbo ji 古井重波記
guofang dianying 國防電影
Hagiya Kenzō 萩屋堅藏
Haijiao shiren 海角詩人
haipai 海派
Haishang shuomengren 海上說夢人
Haishi 海誓
Hara Takashi 原敬
He Tingran 何挺然
Hei ji yuanhun 黑籍冤魂
Hongfen kulou 紅粉骷髏
Hong Shen 洪深
hontō-jin 本島人
Hou Yao 侯曜
Hsun Huan Jih Pao 循環日報
Huan jin ji 還金記
Huang Manli (Wong Man-lei) 黃曼梨
Huang Xiulan 黃秀蘭
huatu yingxi 畫圖影戲
Huayuan xiangma 花園相罵
Huoshao hongliansi 火燒紅蓮寺
Itō Hirobumi 伊藤博文
Jinghuatai 鏡花台
Jinqian nie 金錢孽
Jinsheng 金聲
Kaixin tekan 開心特刊
Kaixin yingpian gongsi 開心影片公司
Kan'in-no-miya Kotohito Shin'nō 閑院宮載仁親王
Khoojin Whatchay 苦力人發財
Kodama Gentarō 児玉源太郎
kō-gakkō 公学校
kokumin seishin 国民精神
Kong'gu lan 空谷蘭
Kote Shō 古亭庄
Ku'er liulang ji 苦兒流浪記
Kuaihuo lin 快活林
Kumon no shocho (Kumen de xiangzeng) 苦悶の象徵（苦悶的象徵）
kunrei 訓令
Kurihara Kisaburô 栗原喜三郎
Kuriyagawa Hakuson 廚川白村
Kyōiku ni kansuru chokugo 教育ニ関スル勅語
Lang die 浪蝶

Li Beihai (Lai Buk-hoi) 黎北海
Li Donghai (Lai Dong-hoi) 黎東海
Li Haishan (Lai Hoi-shan) 黎海山
Li Minwei (Lai Man-wai) 黎民偉
Lianai yu yiwu 戀愛與義務
Liang Shaopo (Leung Siu-bo) 梁少坡
Liangyi (Leung Yee) 兩儀
Lianhua 聯華
Liao Huashen 廖華燊
Libai liu 禮拜六
Lin Jianxiang 林建享
Lin Meimei (Lam Mui-mui) 林妹妹
Linshi gongguan 臨時公館
Liu Na'ou 劉吶鷗
Liu Jintao 劉錦濤
Lo Kan (Lo Gun, Lu Gen) 盧根
Lu Dun 盧敦
Lu Jie (Lok Key) 陸潔
Lu Juefei (Lo Kok-fei) 盧覺非
Lu Mengshu 盧夢殊
Luo Mingyou (Lo Ming-yau) 羅明佑
Ma Jiefu 馬介甫
Ma Shizeng 馬師曾
Meihua luo 梅花落
Meiren guan 美人關
Mingda (Ming Tat) 明達
Mingyuan 名園
Mingjiao zuiren 名教罪人
Mingxing yingpian gongsi 明星影片公司
Minxin 民新
Minzhi 民智
Mingzhu 明珠
Mo Gansheng (Mok Kon-sang) 莫幹生
Mu Shiying 穆時英
naichi 内地
naichi enchō shugi 内地延長主義
naichi kankō 内地観光
Naimukyoku 内務局
Nanyang 南洋
Nanyue 南粵
Ōtsu Rinpei 大津麟平
Peng Nian (Pang Nin) 彭年
Pichong 丕崇
qiqiao yanghua 奇巧洋畫
qingjie yundong 清潔運動
rakugo 落語
Rendao 人道
Rouji 柔濟
Sakuma Samata 佐久間左馬太
Sawamura Kunitaro 沢村国太郎
Shanghai huabao 上海畫報
Shanghai yingxi gongsi 上海影戲公司
Shanghai yingxi yanjiu hui 上海影戲研究會
Shao Zuiweng (Runje Shaw) 邵醉翁
Shenbao 申報
Shenxian bang 神仙棒
shi xiangyan pigu zhuyi 拾香烟屁股主義
Shi Dongshan 史東山
Shishi 石室
Shokusankyoku 殖產局
shū 州
Shui shi zhenai 誰是真愛
Shuihuo yuanyang 水火鴛鴦
Sishi (Sei Si) 四匙
Sun Fo 孫科
Sun Shiyi 孫師毅
Taipingyang 太平洋
Taiwan Dōjinsha 台湾同仁社
Taiwan jijō shōkai 台湾事情紹介
Taiwan jikkyō shōkai 台湾実況紹介
Taiwan kyōiku-kai 台湾教育会

Taiwan kyokai 台湾协会
Taiwan nichinichi shimpō 台湾日日新報
Taiwan no tabi 台湾の旅
Takamatsu Toyojirō 高松豊次（治）郎
Tang Xiaodan 湯曉丹
Tang Xueqing 唐雪卿
Tanizaki Jun'ichirō 谷崎潤一郎
teikoku gikai 帝国議会
Tian Han 田漢
Tian'nan 天南
Tianyi 天一
Taohua qixue ji 桃花泣血記
Tixiao yinyuan 啼笑因緣
Toda Seizō 戸田清三
Tonglingtai 通靈台
Toyo Kyokai 東洋協会
Tsuchiya Tsunekichi 土屋常吉
Uchida Kakichi 内田嘉吉
Umi no gōzoku 海の豪族
utsushi-e 写し絵
Wah Tsz Yat Po 華字日報
Wang Dungen 王鈍根
Wang Hanlun 王漢倫
Wang Youyou 汪優游
wanneng laoguan 萬能老倌
wansei 湾生
wenmingxi 文明戲
wenyi jupian 文藝巨片
Wu Jianren 吳趼人
Wu Mali (Mary) 吳瑪麗
Xiaocheng zhi chun 小城之春
Xiao changzhu 小廠主
Xiao pengyou 小朋友
Xiao xunhuan 小循環
Xiepu chao 歇浦潮
Xiguan 西關
Xilai (Hei Loi) 喜來
Xin Baijinlong 新白金龍
Xin ganjue pai 新感覺派
Xin nüxing 新女性
Xin'er jiuxue ji 馨兒就學記
Xinren tekan 新人特刊
Xinwenbao 新聞報
xiyang yingxi 西洋影戲
xizhuang yueju 西裝粵劇
Xu Baijinlong 續白金龍
Xu Bibo 徐碧波
Xu Yuan 徐園
Xu Zhenya 徐枕亞
Xu Zhuodai (Xu Fulin; Xu Banmei) 徐卓呆（徐傅霖；徐半梅）
Xuangong yanshi 璇宮艷史
Xuanyuan 璇源
Xue Juexian (Sit Gok-sin; Zhang Fei) 薛覺先（章非）
Yan Duhe (Yan Zhen) 嚴獨鶴（嚴楨）
Yan Ruisheng 閻瑞生
Yang Gongliang (Yeung Kung-leong) 楊工良
Yang Naimei 楊耐梅
Yanzhi 胭脂
Yi lü ma 一縷麻
Yihua yingye gongsi 藝華影業公司
Yijing 一景
Yin Mingzhu 殷明珠
Ying Hei Ho (Yingxihao) 影戲號
yinghua 影畫
Yinguang 銀光
Yingxi hua 影戲話
yingxi xiaoshuo 影戲小說
Yingxi zazhi 影戲雜誌

Yingxi xue 影戲學
Yinshen yi 隱身衣
Yinxing 銀星
Yonghan 永漢
Yongyuan de weixiao 永遠的微笑
youxichang 遊戲場
Yu Fungshun (Yu Feng-shun) 余豐順
Yu li hun 玉梨魂
Yuchan 玉蟬
Yuet Wa Po 越華報
Yuzhang 豫章
Zai jiaceng li 在夾層裡
Zhang Henshui 張恨水
Zhang Rougu 張若谷
Zhang Shichuan 張石川
Zhang Yuniang (Cheung Yuk-neung) 張玉娘
Zhang Zhiyun 張織雲
Zhao Shushen (Chiu Shu-sun, Joseph Sunn) 趙樹燊
Zheng Zhengqiu 鄭正秋
Zheng Mengxia (Cheng Mang-ha) 鄭孟霞
Zhenye (Chun Yip) 振業
Zhongguo dianying yishu yanjiuhui 中國電影藝術研究會
Zhongguo yingxi daguan 中國影戲大觀
Zhonghua dianying xuexiao 中華電影學校
Zhou Jianyun 周劍雲
Zhou Shixun 周世勳
Zhou Shoujuan (Zhou Zufu) 周瘦鵑 (周祖福)
Zhou Shoujuan shuoji 周瘦鵑說集
Zhu Shouju 朱瘦菊
Zhuangzi shi qi 莊子試妻
Ziluolan 紫羅蘭
Zimei hua 姊妹花
Ziyou tan 自由談
Zuozei bucheng 做賊不成

Contributors

Shi-Yan Chao is Research Assistant Professor in the Academy of Film, Hong Kong Baptist University. He holds a PhD in cinema studies from New York University, and taught at NYU and Columbia University. Chao has published articles on Chinese-language film and media in a number of anthologies and academic journals.

Ting-yan Cheung holds a master of philosophy degree from the Department of Comparative Literature at the University of Hong Kong. She was Research Associate at the Centre for Media and Communication Research, Hong Kong Baptist University.

Yongchun Fu is Associate Professor in the School of Media and Design, Ningbo Institute of Technology, Zhejiang University. He has published in the *Journal of Chinese Cinemas* and *Sungkyun Journal of East Asian Studies*. Fu is currently completing a manuscript on foreign filmmakers in the Chinese film industry before 1937.

Daw-Ming Lee is Professor and Chair of the Department of Filmmaking at the Taipei National University of the Arts. A renowned documentary filmmaker as well as an expert on Taiwan cinema, Lee's many publications include *Historical Dictionary of Taiwan Cinema* (Scarecrow, 2013).

Hui Liu is Associate Professor at the School of Communication, Shenzhen University. He was a visiting scholar at UCLA in 2015–16. His research interests include the commerce and aesthetics of early Chinese film, the Chinese film industry under the Japanese occupation between 1941 and 1945, and the Shaw studio. He is now working on a book on how Western cinema influenced early Chinese film production.

Kenny K. K. Ng is Associate Professor in the Academy of Film, Hong Kong Baptist University. He is author of *Li Jieren, Geopoetic Memory, and the Crisis of Writing Chengdu in Revolutionary China* (Brill, 2015). His ongoing book projects include the study of censorship and visual cultural politics in Cold War China and Asia, and the history of Cantonese cinema.

Yoshino Sugawara is Professor of Letters at Kansai University. She has published widely on early Chinese film history. Her latest publication includes *Modernity inside the Movie House: A History of Movie Spectatorship in Shanghai* (Japanese, forthcoming in 2018).

Enoch Yee-lok Tam is Program Director of Creative Writing for Film, Television and Creative Media at Hong Kong Baptist University. He is recipient of the Best Young Artist Award (Arts Criticism Category) in 2015 by Hong Kong Arts Development Council. His doctoral thesis focuses on film and literature in early Chinese cinema.

Pablo Sze-pang Tsoi received his doctoral degree from the Department of Comparative Literature at the University of Hong Kong. He teaches cultural studies at the College of International Education, Hong Kong Baptist University.

Laura Jo-Han Wen is Assistant Professor in the Asian Studies Program at Randolph-Macon College. She received her doctoral degree in East Asian literature and visual culture from the University of Wisconsin-Madison in August 2016. Her research primarily focuses on the media culture in colonial East Asia.

Richard Xiaying Xu is Assistant Professor in the Public Relations and Advertising Program, Division of Humanities and Social Sciences, Beijing Normal University–Hong Kong Baptist University United International College. His research interests include cultural and creative industries and Chinese animation.

Emilie Yueh-yu Yeh is Lam Wong Yiu Wah Chair Professor of Visual Studies at the Lingnan University in Hong Kong. She has published nine books and more than sixty articles on Chinese film and Asian media.

Ling Zhang is Assistant Professor of Cinema Studies at SUNY Purchase. She received her PhD from the Department of Cinema and Media Studies at the University of Chicago. She has published academic articles on 1930s Chinese cinema and film theory, contemporary Chinese independent documentary, Taiwan New Cinema, socialist road movies, and Chinese opera films in *Journal of Chinese Cinemas*, *CLCWeb: Comparative Literature and Culture*, *Film Quarterly*, *New Zealand Journal of Asian Studies*, *Asian Cinema*, *Film Art* (mainland China), and *Film Appreciation* (Taiwan), among others. She is also translating Chinese film theory into English for the forthcoming anthology *Chinese Film Theory and Criticism*.

Bibliography

English translations of the Chinese and Japanese references are provided by authors, except those that already have English renditions.

Sources with No Author Listed

"10 Lots Sold in Topanga." *Daily Outlook*, July 19, 1915.
1915 North China Desk-Hong List. Shanghai: North China Daily News Publishing House, 1915.
1916 North China Desk-Hong List. Shanghai: North China Daily News Publishing House, 1916.
"A Crowded Cinema: Proprietor Fined." *South China Morning Post*, April 6, 1918.
""Beijing daxiyuan kaimu guanggao" [Ad for the Opening of the Peking Theatre]. *Shenbao*, November 7, 1926.
"Bijou Scenic Theatre." *Hong Kong Telegraph*, December 3, 1910.
"Bijou Scenic Theatre." *South China Morning Post*, November 26, 1910.
"The Bijou Scenic Theatre." *South China Morning Post*, November 1, 1910.
"Bijou." *Hong Kong Telegraph*, June 2, 1913.
"Bu jingqi niantou: Guangzhou shi jinsui yulejie gaikuang" [The Rainy Days: An Overview of This Year's Guangzhou Entertainment Industry]. *Youyou zazhi* 7 (1935): 2.
"Chalei minghua da jihui" [Famous Pictures of Charlie]. *Chinese Mail*, November 20, 1924.
The China Factor in Hong Kong Cinema. Hong Kong: Urban Council, 1990.
Cinema of Two Cities, Hong Kong–Shanghai. Hong Kong: Urban Council, 1994.
"Chongqing yuan huaji yan shidi fenchen yingxu" [Stevenson's Pictures at Chung Hing]. Supplements of *Chinese Mail*, 1903, January 19.
"City Hall–Music Room: For the First Time in Hongkong." *Hong Kong Daily Press, April 26, 1897.*
"Consolidated Rubber Estates Limited." *North-China Herald*, December 13, 1913.
"Dahan yingye gongsi gaobai" [Advertisements by Dai Hon Film Company]. *Chinese Mail*, February 20, 1924.

"Dai go ka" [Lesson 5]. In *Shotokubun kyōjusho: Taiwan tekiyō* [Instruction for Writing Letters and Documents: Applicable to Taiwan]. Tokyo: Taiwan Sōtokufu Minseikyoku Gakumubu, 1897.

Dai ni nen ni okeru kōmin hōkō undō no jisseki [Imperial People Public Service Movement: Second-Year Report]. Taipei: Imperial People Public Service Association, 1943.

"Dakai huandenghui" [Grand Scale Magic Lantern Shows]. *Kanbun Taiwan nichinichi shinpō*, September 12, 1905.

"Datong jiaoyisuo chuangli huiji" [Minutes of the Commencement of the Mutual Stock & Produce Company]. *Shenbao*, November 28, 1921.

"Diandeng yingxi" [Electric Lantern Pictures]. *Taiwan nichinichi shimpō* (Taihoku), September 5, 1899.

"Dianying de ticai" [Topics of Films]. *Guangzhou minguo ribao*, October 30, 1935.

"Dianying zatan (er)" [A Sequel to Miscellaneous Impressions about Movies]. *Shenbao*, January 14, 1925.

"Dianying zatan" [Miscellaneous Impressions about Movies]. *Shenbao*, January 13, 1925.

"Dongjing huodong yingxiyuan" [Tokyo Theatre]. *Shenbao*, March 13-16, 1914.

Early Images of Hong Kong and China. Hong Kong: Urban Council, 1995.

"Edison's Latest: The Wonderful Animatoscope." *Hong Kong Daily Press*, January 20, 1898.

"Eisha gijutsu kōshūkai" [Projection Techniques Training Sessions]. *Monthly Report of Taiwan Taxation* 245 (1930): 46.

"The Empire—New Cinematograph Theatre." *South China Morning Post*, April 4, 1910.

"Engei: Zenshin-tai katsudō shashin" [Entertainment: Advance Corps' Motion Pictures]. *Taiwan nichinichi shimpō* (Taihoku), April 3, 1912.

"Fang lao yanjiang dianyinghui canguan hou zhongzhong ganxiang" [Film Screening for Tuberculosis Prevention at the YMCA]. *Yuet Wa Po*, November 25, 1947.

"Fanren zhi neidi guanguang" [Aborigines' Mainland Sightseeing]. *Taiwan nichinichi shimpō* (Chinese edition), December 26, 1907.

"Gaoxing yuan rongji yan hedingcai ban" [Performances by Ho Ting Choi Troupe at Ko Shing Theatre]. Supplements of *Chinese Mail*, January 1, 1903.

"Gekisen katsudōshashinkai" [Fierce Battle Motion Pictures Screening]. *Taiwan nichinichi shimpō* (Taihoku), October 23, 1901.

"General Ledgers and Producers Account." Series 5C: Foreign General Ledgers and Journals, Reel 3, China. United Artists Corporation Archive. Madison: Wisconsin Historical Society.

"General Report for Two Months Ending 20 June 1928." Series 2A: O'Brien Legal File, 1919–1951, Folder 95, Box 4, United Artists Corporation Archive. Madison: Wisconsin Historical Society.

"Gentō no riyō ga saigen" [Use of Magic Lantern Resurged]. *Taiwan nichinichi shinpō*, March 12, 1941.

"Gongjie qingnianhui zhi chengji" [The Activities of the Young Men Association in the Laborers' Society]. *Shenbao*, September 15, 1914.

"Guan kexue yingpian hou" [On Science Film]. *Gongpingbao*, October 14, 1930.

"Guan Meiguo shiye yingpian ji" [A Record of Watching American Industrial Movies]. *Shenbao*, December 19, 1918.

"Guan yinghua you zengpin" [Gifts for Moviegoers]. Supplements of *Chinese Mail*, December 24, 1921.

"Gudu yi tan xin zuzhi" [New Art Organization]. *Guangzhou minguo ribao*, February 1, 1934.

"Guochan yingpian zai nanyang zhi jinkuang" [The Current Situation of Chinese Films in Nanyang]. *Gongpingbao*, November 9, 1927.

"Guochan yingpian zhi jianglai" [The Future of Domestic Film]. *Guangzhou minguo ribao*, December 20, 1926.

"H. Wellby-Cook's Animatoscope." *Hong Kong Daily Press*, August 19, 1897.

"Home from Orient." *Daily Outlook*, June 29, 1914.

Hong Kong Cinema in the Eighties: A Comparative Study with Western Cinema. Hong Kong: Urban Council, 1991.

"Hongkong Cinematograph—under New Management." *China Mail*, April 13, 1908.

"Honkai sendentai no katsudōshashin Tomiya denka kaku ōji denka no tairan wo tamaharu" [HRH Tomiya and Other Princes Did TES the Favor of Watching Films Screened by Our Propaganda Team]. *Taiwan Education* 217 (1920): 46.

"Huashang bu tai xi tebie tongtian yinghua chang" [Outdoor Film Screening by Chinese Merchants]. *Chinese Mail*, August 25, 1916.

"Huashang Xin shijie yinghua xiyuan guangao" [Advertisement by Chinese Merchants' New World Theatre]. Supplements of *Chinese Mail*, October 12, 1921.

"Huaxi chudai" [Pictures for Rent]. *Chinese Mail*, March 8, 1904.

"Huodong huandeng" [Moving Magic Lantern]. *Taiwan nichinichi shimpō* (Taihoku), November 21, 1901.

Images of the Overseas Chinese in Cinema. Hong Kong: Urban Council, 1992.

"The Imperial Bioscope." *Hong Kong Daily Press*, January 8, 1903.

"The Imperial Bioscope Co." *Hong Kong Daily Press*, January 7, 1903.

"The Imperial Bioscope Co." *Hong Kong Daily Press*, January 9, 1903.

"Ippan kyōka" [General Education]. *Taiwan Education* 351 (1931): 137–138.

"Jiangyou zhicao yingpian gongsi chuxian" [New Film Production Company]. Supplements of *Chinese Mail*, December 13, 1922.

"Jiaoyu ju jin ying 'Wan wang zhi wang' qingnianhui qing reng zhunyu fangying jiao ju chi reng zun qian ling banli" [Education Bureau Banned *The King of Kings*; YMCA Pleaded; Education Bureau Overruled]. *Guangzhou minguo ribao*, October 28, 1929.

"Jin ying ru guo huapian fang zhi wenhua qinlue" [Racist Films Banned to Thwart Cultural Invasion]. *Guangzhou minguo ribao*, May 2, 1930.

"Jinji issoku" [Personnel Notice]. *Taiwan Education* 288 (1926): 65.

"Jinnian dianying tan" [On Films of the Year]. *Guangzhou minguo ribao*, February 2, 1928.

"Jūjikan no katsudōshashin" [Motion Pictures at Jūjikan]. *Taiwan nichinichi shimpō* (Taihoku), September 8, 1899.

"Kaihō: Dai jūyokai sōkai" [Bulletin: The Fourteenth General Assembly]. *Taiwan Education* 186 (1917): 90.

"Kaihō: Katsudōshashin fuirumu kizō" [Bulletin: Motion Pictures Films Donation]. *Taiwan Education* 176 (1917): 84.

"Kaihō: Katsudōshashin satsuei" [Bulletin: Motion Pictures Photographing]. *Taiwan Education* 185 (1917): 66.

"Kan le 'Huan jin ji' yihou" [On *Returning the Money*]. *Guangzhou minguo ribao*, February 6, 1928.

"Katsudōshashin satsuei no shūryō" [Photographing of Motion Pictures Ends]. *Taiwan nichinichi shimpō*, April 12, 1907.

"Katsudōshashin" [Motion Pictures]. *Taiwan nichinichi shimpō* (Taihoku), June 19, 1900.

"'Kong gu lan' yu ye zhi ji qita" [*Orchid of the Valley* and Other Films]. *Guangzhou minguo ribao*, August 22, 1931.

"Kyōikukai katsudōshashin koteisō suieijō satsuei" [TES Motion Pictures: Photographing in Kote Shō Swimming Site]. *Taiwan nichinichi shimpō* (Taihoku), August 16, 1917.

"Kyōshinkai fuirumu kyōikukai nite eisha" [Exhibition Film: Screening by TES]. *Taiwan nichinichi shimpō* (Taihoku), April 29, 1907.

"Laou Kung Mow Cotton S. & W. Co." *North-China Herald*, February 19, 1915.

"Life Condition of Guangzhou." *Guangzhou minguo ribao*, July 20, 1935.

"Look out! Look out!." *South China Morning Post*, October 24, 1910.

"'Lou dong yuan' yuxi ji" [Site Visit of Lou dong yuan]. *Guangzhou minguo ribao*, April 15, 1927.

"Lyceum Theatre." *Peking and Tientsin Times*, June 26, 1897.

"Lynch Writes to the Outlook." *Daily Outlook*, April 9, 1913.

"Maitian faxian nushi sizhi" [The Fourth Report on Finding a Woman's Body in a Wheat Field]. *Xinwenbao*, June 19, 1920.

Mandarin Films and Popular Songs: 40's-60's. Hong Kong: Urban Council, 1993.

"Meeting, Shanghai Life Insurance Co." *North-China Herald*, June 12, 1914.

"Meiguo dianying nuzi qingxin dianying de tongji" [Statistics on American Women's Interest in Film Acting]. *Guangzhou minguo ribao*, May 28, 1933.

"Mingda Yingpian chuanyuan huigang" [Ming Tat Representatives Return to Hong Kong]. *Chinese Mail*, July 12, 1932.

"Motion Picture Theatre Permitted within the Walls of Changsha, Letter from C.D. Meinhardt to American Consulate, January 30, 1923." Record of the Department of State Relating to Internal Affairs of China, 1910–1929. Washington, DC: National Archives and Records Service, 1923.

"Moving Picture Exhibition." *China Mail*, July 17, 1907.

"Moving Pictures of the Fire." *Daily Outlook*, September 5, 1912.

"The Municipal Gazette." *North-China Herald*, March 14, 1918.

"Nama-ban to gentō-kai" [Mountain Savages and Magic Lantern Show]. *Taiwan nichinichi shinpō*, November 5, 1904.

"The New Theatre—Opened Last Night." *South China Morning Post*, May 27, 1911.

"Nichirosensō gentō" [Magic Lantern Show on the Russo-Japanese War]. *Taiwan nichinichi shinpō*, April 15, 1904.

"Ontairei katsudōshashin haikan" [Have the Honor of Seeing the Film about the Accession Ceremony]. *Taiwan Education* 167 (1916): inside front cover.

"Passengers." *North-China Herald*, March 28, 1914.

"Passengers." *North-China Herald*, November 15, 1913.

"Passengers." *North-China Herald*, October 26, 1912.

"Ping 'Xinren de jiating'" [On *The Newlyweds*]. *Guangzhou minguo ribao*, November 9, 1926.

"Qimiao yingxi" [Amazing Pictures]. *Chinese Mail*, September 4, 1907.

"Qingnianhui ershinian lai zhi xiaoshi" [A Short History of the YMCA's Last Twenty Years]. *Shenbao*, April 20, 1918.

"Qingnianhui fayin *dianying* gongkai yanjiu" [A Public Talk on Sound Film at the YMCA]. *Guangzhou minguo ribao*, March 4, 1929.

"Qingnianhui guan ju ji" [On a Film Show at the YMCA]. *Guangzhou minguo ribao,* February 9, 1928.
"Qingnianhui jinwan zhi lequ" [Tonight's Entertainments at YMCA]. *Shenbao,* April 13, 1918.
"Qingnianhui jinwan zhi yingxi" [Tonight's Movies at the YMCA]. *Shenbao,* April 20, 1918.
"Qingnianhui shen pian ying chang jin xun" [Latest Sound Films at the YMCA]. *Yuet Wa Po,* September 18, 1933.
"Qingnianhui sheng pian ying chang que xun" [An Exact Account of Sound Films at the YMCA]. *Yuet Wa Po,* July 16, 1933.
"Qingnianhui xuyan dianguang yingxi" [The Sequel Movie Exhibition by the YMCA]. *Shenbao,* September 27, 1907.
"Qingnianhui yinghua" [YMCA Film Screening]. *Chinese Mail,* February 2, 1925.
"Queshenyuan yinghua" [Kok San Yun Screening]. *Chinese Mail,* December 3, 1902.
"Santan taru riban no jikkyō" [Difficult State of Ruling the Aborigines]. *Yomiuri Shimbun,* February 12, 1912.
"Seiban tsuitachi no yūran" [One Day Sightseeing of Raw Aborigines]. *Yomiuri Shimbun,* May 6, 1912.
"Seiban ikkō kaeru" [The Raw Aborigines Group Returns Home]. *Yomiuri Shimbun,* May 13, 1912.
"Shanghai dianying ye yu Guangdong ren" [Shanghai Film Industry and the Cantonese]. *Guangzhou minguo ribao,* August 31, 1926.
"Shanghai shangye chuxu yinhang youguan yingxiyuan de diaocha baogao" [On the Theater Houses Industries, a Survey Conducted by the Shanghai Commercial & Saving Bank]. n.d. Q275–1-1949. Shanghai Municipal Archive.
"Shanghai shangye chuxu yinhang youguan yingxiyuan de diaocha baogao" [On the Theater Houses Industries, a Survey Conducted by the Shanghai Commercial & Saving Bank]. n.d. Q275–1-2041. Shanghai Municipal Archive.
"Shangwu yinshuguan huodongbu jinkuang" [The Recent Situation of the Film Division of Commercial Press]. *Shenbao,* June 11, 1921.
"Shangwu yinshuguan suochu yingpian zhi tongji" [Statistics about the Movies Produced by Commercial Press]. *Shenbao,* May 10, 1923.
"Shi nian qian zhi yousheng dianying" [A Decade of Sound Films]. *Gongpingbao,* November 26, 1929.
"Shina to kinsei teki kōgyō (shita)" [The Sequel of New China, and Modern Commerce and Industry]. *Taiwan nichinichi shimpō,* February 22, 1918.
"Shinchiku Shū shusai katsudōshashin eishajutsu kōshūkai" [Training Sessions of Motion Picture Projection Techniques Conducted by Shinchiku Shū]. *Taiwan Education* 260 (1924): 135–137.
"Shōgakusen no enei: dakuryū wo sagaru sanriyo" [Primary School Students' Long-Distance Swimming: Down the Muddy Stream for More Than Three Miles]. *Taiwan nichinichi shimpō,* August 25, 1917.
"Shokuminchi to katsudō shashin" [Colony and Motion Pictures]. *Tokyo Asahi Shimbun,* October 4, 1912.
Shōwa jūnen jūgatsu Taiwan shakai kyōiku gaiyō [Summary of Taiwan Social Education—October of Showa Year 10]. Taihoku: Government-General of Taiwan, 1935.
Shōwa kyūnen nigatsu Taiwan shakai kyōiku gaiyō [Summary of Taiwan Social

Education—February of Showa Year 9]. Taihoku: Department of Social Education, Taiwan Education Society, 1934.

"Shuo yingxi" [On Photoplay]. *Guangzhou minguo ribao*, September 25, 1923.

"Sishi huapian gongsi guanggao" [Advertisement by the Sei Si Film Company]. *Chinese Mail*, September 12, 1924.

"Sport, Baseball." *North-China Herald*, March 21, 1914.

"Start on Trip." *Daily Outlook*, September 5, 1912.

"Taiping xiyuan yan yinghua xi" [Film Screening at Tai Ping Theatre]. *Chinese Mail*, March 16, 1905.

"Taishō jūyonnen Taiwan kyōikukai jūyō kiji" [Important Accounts of Taiwan Education Circle in Taishō Year 14]. *Taiwan Education* 283 (1926): 95.

Taiwan gakuji yōran—Taishō yonnen [Taiwan Educational Affairs Handbook, Taishō Year 4]. Taihoku: Ministry of Educational Affairs, Government-General of Taiwan, 1915.

Taiwan gakuji yōran—Taishō yoūnen [Taiwan Educational Affairs Handbook, Taishō Year 10]. Taihoku: Ministry of Educational Affairs, Government-General of Taiwan, 1921.

"Taiwan kyōikukai dai nijū kai sōkai" [The Twentieth General Assembly]. *Taiwan Education* 300 (1927): 146–159.

"Taiwan kyōikukai shusai Taiwan jijō shōkai kōenkai nami katsudōshashinkai jōkyō hōkoku" [A Report on the Situation of TES-Sponsored Lectures and Film Screenings Introducing Current Situations in Taiwan]. *Taiwan Education* 218 (1920): 51–54.

"Taiwan kyōikukai sōkai" [General Assembly of Taiwan Education Society]. *Taiwan Education* 270 (1924): 85–90.

"Tansui-kan getsurei-kai" [Monthly Meeting at Tansui Hall]. *Taiwan nichinichi shinpō*, July 28, 1903.

"Tansuikan getsurei kai yokyōhyō" [A Criticism on the Entertainment Program of Monthly Meeting at Tansui-kan] and "Katsudoushashin" [Motion Pictures]. *Taiwan nichinichi shimpō* (Taihoku), June 19, 1900.

"Theatre Royal." *Hong Kong Daily Press*, April 16, 1900.

"Theatre Royal: City Hall." *Hong Kong Daily Press*, March 28, 1898.

"Theatre Royal: City Hall." *Hong Kong Daily Press*, October 16, 1897.

"To-night: Grand Opening of the Victoria Cinematograph." *China Mail*, October 31, 1907.

"Tōban to aikoku fujinkai" [Subjugating the Aborigines and Patriotic Women's Association]. *Taiwan nichinichi shimpō* (Taihoku), February 10, 1912.

"Tong Qing Tea Garden." *Xinwenbao*, October 3, 1897.

"To-night." *China Mail*, November 1, 1907.

"The Triumph of Moving Pictures." *China Mail*, July 19, 1907.

"Tsūshin ihō: Taihoku tsūshin" [Communication Bulletin: Taipei Correspondence]. *Taiwan Education* 258 (1923): 78–82.

"U.S. Consular Registration Certificates of Arthur Israel (1914)." U.S. Consular Registration Certificates, 1907–1918, General Records of the Department of State, 1763–2002, Record Group 59. Washington, DC: National Archives and Records Administration.

"U.S. Passport Application of Arthur Israel (1917)." Emergency Passport Applications,

Argentina thru Venezuela, 1906–1925. ARC Identifier 1244183/MLR Number A1544, Box 4485, Volume 2. Washington, DC: National Archives and Records Administration.

"U.S. Passport Application of Arthur Israel (1918)." Passport Applications, January 2, 1906-March 31, 1925. ARC Identifier 583830/MLR Number A1534, NARA Series: M1490, Roll 626. Washington, DC: National Archives and Records Administration.

"U.S. Passport Application of Thomas Suffert (1916)." Passport Applications for Travel to China, 1906–1925. ARC Identifier 1244180/MLR Number A1540, NARA Series: M4419, Volume 7. Washington, DC: National Archives and Records Administration.

"Victoria Theatre." *North China Daily News*, March 3-8, 10-11, 1914.

"Viloudaki to Canning." June 5, 1918. U1-2-548. Shanghai Municipal Archives.

"Weichunyuan guanyingxi ji xuqiangao" [Sequel Article about Watching Movies in Weichunyuan]. *Xinwenbao*, June 13, 1897.

"Wo ping '*Kong gu lan*'" [On *Orchid of the Valley*]. *Guangzhou minguo ribao*, November 18, 1926.

"Wo ping '*kong gu lan*' xu" [Second Take on *Orchid of the Valley*]. *Guangzhou minguo ribao*, November 19, 1926.

"Women's World." *Daily Outlook*, January 27, 1913.

"Xianggang dianying da xiezhen" [Snapshots of Hong Kong Cinema]. *Yuet Wa Pao*, August 14, 1935.

"Xiamen zhi dianyingyuan" [Theaters in Xiamen]. *Gongpingbao*, April 19, 1929.

"Xianggang huapian gongsi zhidiaocha" [A Survey of Film Production Companies in Hong Kong]. *Chinese Mail*, August 1, 1927.

"Xianggang min xin zhizao yinghua pian youxian gongsi" [Minxin Film Company]. *Chinese Mail*, April 9, 1925.

"Xiangshan mofan xiang zhi yingpian" [A Film about Xiangshan]. *Chinese Mail*, May 24, 1924.

"Xilai yuan yan huaqi shengdong huaxi" [Lively Moving Pictures from the United States at Hei Loi Garden]. Supplements of *Chinese Mail*, October 28, 1902.

"Xin bizhao yinghua xiyuan" [Coronet Theatre]. *Chinese Mail*, June 27, 1919.

"Xin bizhao yingxi yuan guanggao" [Advertisement by Coronet Theatre]. *Chinese Mail*, January 19, 1923.

"Xin bizhao yingxi yuan zhi ba da teshe" [Eight Highlights of the Coronet Theatre]. *Chinese Mail*, May 31, 1924.

"Xinshe yinghua zhang" [The New Film Screen]. Supplements of *Chinese Mail*, May 15, 1922.

"Xin shijie xiyua shengdan ri teshe zengpin guanggao" [Advertisement by New World Theatre: Special Gifts on Birthday of Confucius]. *Chinese Mail*, September 28, 1921.

"Xin shijie yingxi yuan zhi jiu gudong" [Ex-Shareholders of the New World Theatre]. *Chinese Mail*, August 3, 1927.

"Xinxilai shengdong huaxi" [New Hei Loi Theatre Life-like Picture Photoplay]. *Chinese Mail*, December 27, 1902.

"Xuanchuan Taiwan shiqing" [Publicize Situations of Taiwan]. *Taiwan nichinichi shimpō* (Taihoku), May 4, 1920.

"'Xuanya zhi lian' jijiang shangyan" [Cliff Love Coming Soon]. *Gongpingbao*, October 9, 1947.

"Xue Juexian chongpai *Xu Baijinlong*: Xiwang ta xian cha yi cha jiancha ling" [Xue Juexian remakes *The Platinum Dragon: Part Two*: He Better Check the Censorship Order Beforehand]. *Ying yu xi* 1 no. 4 (1936): 6.

"Xue Juexian zai Xianggang zuzhi gongsi: Pai yueyu shengpian busong Nanjing jiancha" [Xue Juexian has established his own company in Hong Kong to make sound films, which he will not submit to Nanjing for inspection]. *Yule* 1 (Inauguration issue) (1935): 25.

"Xylophone & Kinematograph Entertainment." Hong Kong Daily Press, December 23, 1899.

"Yanying Zhongguo minghua (haishi)" [Showing a Famous Chinese Film, *A Fisherman's Honor*]. *Chinese Mail*, December 1, 1925.

"Ying haijun yan mei shuibing" [British Navy Receiving the U.S. Navy]. *Chinese Mail*, October 31, 1922.

"Yingxi chang zhi mao" [Hat off in the Cinema]. *Guangzhou minguo ribao*, July 12, 1927.

"You '*Fushide*' shuo dao '*Wan wang zhi wang*'" [Review of *Faust* and *The King of Kings*]. *Gongpingbao*, October 26, 1929.

"Yousheng yingpian suo ji" [On Sound Film]. *Gongpingbao*. April 20, 1929.

"Yu duo li yingxi yuan teping yingyue chuanjia" [Music Talents at Victoria Cinematograph]. *Chinese Mail*, November 1, 1915.

"Yueyu shengpian kaishi moluo, Shao Zuiweng deng dashou shenchi" [Cantonese Films in Decline: Shao Zuiweng Gets Reprimanded]. *Yule* 1, no. 24 (1935): 593.

"Yueyupian jiangqu juejing" [Cantonese Films Soon to Be extinct]. *Qingqing Dianying* 32 (1948): n.p.

"Zappō: honkai sakusei no kyōzai eiga nit suite" [Miscellaneous Report: About the Educational Films produced by the TES]. *Taiwan Education* 357 (1932): 150–152.

"Zappō: Taichū eisei tenrankai" [Miscellaneous Report: Taichū Hygiene Exhibition]. *Taiwan Police Association Journal* 4 (1917): 72–73.

"Zhang Garden." *Xinwenbao*, June 8–13, 1897.

"Zhenye zhipian chang canquan ji" [A Visit to the Chun Yip Studio]. *Chinese Mail*, April 1, 1935.

"Zhongguo xin zhi yingpian da mingxing" [A New Star in Film Production]. *Chinese Mail*, August 2, 1924.

"Zuixin yingpian jiang chushi" [Latest Films to Be Released]. *Chinese Mail*, November 12, 1924.

Other Sources

A'na. "Shanghai dianyingyuan de jinxi" [Old and New Stories about Film Theaters in Shanghai: Part I]. *Shenbao*, November 2, 1938.

A-kwok. "Tongxun" [Newsletter]. Film Corner, *Chinese Mail*, July 12, 1924.

Alter, Nora M. "*Berlin, Symphony of a Great City* (1927): City, Image, Sound." In *Weimar Cinema: An Essential Guide to Classic Films of the Era*, edited by Noah William Isenberg, 193–216. New York: Columbia University Press, 2009.

Altman, Rick. *Silent Film Sound*. New York: Columbia University Press, 2007.

Bai, He. "Xiwang Zhongguo diba yishu zhi jianglai" [Hoping for the Future of the Eighth Art of China]. *Yinxing* 14 (1927): 28–29.

Bao, Chun Tsing. "Riben Guanxi cuoying shuo fangwen ji" [A Visit to the Kansai Studio in Japan]. Film Corner, *Chinese Mail*, August 9, 1924.
Bao, Tianxiao. *Chuanying lou huiyi lu* [Chuanying lou Memoirs]. Taipei: Longwen chuban gongsi, 1990.
Bao, Weihong. "Baptism by Fire: Aesthetic Affect and Spectatorship in Chinese Cinema from Shanghai to Chongqing." PhD diss., University of Illinois, Chicago, 2006.
Bao, Weihong. "Diary of a Homecoming: (Dis-)Inhabiting the Theatrical in Postwar Shanghai Cinema." In *The Blackwell Handbook on Chinese Cinema*, edited by Yingjin Zhang, 377–399. London: Blackwell, 2012.
Bao, Weihong. *Fiery Cinema: The Emergence of an Affective Medium in China, 1915–1945*. Minneapolis: University of Minnesota Press, 2015.
Ba-shi. "Zhipian zuoyi zhi zhongzhong" [Popular Tricks in Film Production]. Film Corner, *Chinese Mail*, June 21, 1924.
Baskett, Michael. *The Attractive Empire: Transnational Film Culture in Imperial Japan*. Honolulu: University of Hawai'i Press, 2008.
Bazin, André. "In Defense of Mixed Cinema." In *What Is Cinema?*, vol. 1, edited and translated by Hugh Gray, 53–75. Berkeley: University of California Press, 1967.
Berman, Jessica. *Modernist Fiction, Cosmopolitanism, and the Politics of Community*. New York: Cambridge University Press, 2001.
Berry, Chris. "Sino-Korean Screen Connections: Towards a History of Fragments." *Journal of Chinese Cinemas* 10, no. 3 (2016): 247–264.
Berry, Chris. "Transnational Chinese Cinema Studies." In *Chinese Cinema Book*, edited by Song Hwee Lim and Julian Ward, 9–16. London: British Film Institute, 2011.
Berry, Chris, and Mary Farquhar. *China on Screen: Cinema and Nation*. New York: Columbia University Press, 2006.
Bourdieu, Pierre. *Distinction: A Social Critique of the Judgment of Taste*. Translated by Richard Nice. Cambridge, MA: Harvard University Press, 1987.
Bourdieu, Pierre. *The Field of Cultural Production: Essays on Art and Literature*. Edited by Randal Johnson. New York: Columbia University Press, 1993.
Braester, Yomi. "Shanghai's Economy of the Spectacle: The Shanghai Race Club in Liu Na'ou and Mu Shiying's Stories." *Modern Chinese Literature* 9, no. 1 (1995): 39–57.
Braun, Marta, Charles Keil, Rob King, Paul Moore, and Louis Pelletier, eds. *Beyond the Screen: Institutions, Networks and Publics of Early Cinema*. New Barnet, UK: John Libbey, 2012.
Butrick, Richard P. "The Motion Picture Industry in China." 893.4061/69. Confidential U.S. State Department Central Files, China, Internal Affairs, 1930–1939. Washington, DC: National Archives and Records Administration, 1932.
Cai, Guorong. *Zhongguo jindai wenyi dianying yanjiu* [Studies on Contemporary Chinese *Wenyi* Film]. Taipei: Zhonghunminguo dianying tushuguan chubanbu, 1985.
Cavell, Stanley. *Pursuits of Happiness: The Hollywood Comedy of Remarriage*. Cambridge, MA: Harvard University Press, 1981.
Chan, Him. *Xianggang jiushi jianwen lu* [Stories from Old Hong Kong]. Hong Kong: Zhongyuan Publishing, 1987.
Chan, Jessica Ka-yee. "Translating 'Montage': The Discreet Attractions of Soviet Montage for Chinese Revolutionary Cinema." *Journal of Chinese Cinemas* 5, no. 3 (2011): 197–218.
Chan, Nadine. "Making 'Ahmad Problem Conscious': Educational Film and the Rural Lecture Caravan in 1930s British Malaya." *Cinema Journal* 55, no. 4 (2016): 84–107.

Chan-shek. "Wei duiyu Zhongguo huapian shuoming wen de yijian" [My Views on Language in Chinese Films]. Film Corner, *Chinese Mail*, August 30, 1924.

Chen, Jianhua. "Cong yingmi dao yinmu qingyuan: Dan Duyu, Ying Mingzhu yu zaoqi Zhongguo dianying de shenti zhengzhi" [From Cinephile to Lovers on the Silver Screen: Dan Duyu, Yin Mingzhu, and Body Politic in Early Chinese Cinema]. *Zhongguo bijiao wenxue* 1 (2015): 9–24.

Chen, Jianhua. "Wenren congying: Zhou Shoujuan yu Zhongguo zaoqi dianying" [From Literati to Film Practitioner: Zhou Shoujuan and Early Chinese Film]. *Dianying yishu* 1 (2012): 133–139.

Chen, Jianhua. "Zhongguo dianying piping de xianqu: Zhou Shoujuan 'Yingxi hua' dujie" [Pioneer of Chinese Film Criticism: A Reading of Zhou Shoujuan's "Shadow Play" Discourses]. *Xiandai zhongguo* 9 (2007): 53–76.

Chen, Mingqiu, and Rao Meijiao, eds. *Lingnan jindai shi lun: Guangdong yu yuegang guanxi, 1900–1938* [Modern History of Lingnan: The Relationship between Guangdong and the Hong Kong–Guangdong Region, 1900–1938]. Hong Kong: Commercial Press, 2010.

Chen, Pingyuan. *Ershi shiji Zhongguo xiaoshuo shi* [History of Chinese Novels in the Twentieth Century]. Beijing: Beijing University Press, 1989.

Chen, Su, Dagmar Getz, and David Klaassen, eds. *The Archives of the Young Men's Christian Association in China at the University of Minnesota Libraries: The Annual Reports 1896–1949*. Vol. 2, 3, 7, 11. Guilin, Guangxi: Guangxi Normal University Press, 2012.

Chen, Xihe. "Zhongguo dianying meixue de zairengshi—ping yingxi jubeng zuofa." [Rethinking Chinese Film Aesthetics: On the Writing of Filmscripts]. *Dangdai dianying* 1 (1986): 82–90.

Chen, Zhiqing. "Lun shezhi guzhuang yingju" [On Producing Costume Film]. *Shenzhou tekan* 6 (1927): 24–34.

Chen, Zhiqing. "Zailun xinyingxiong zhuyi de yingju" [Revisiting New Heroic Film]. *Yinxing* 8 (1927): 10–13.

Chen, Zhiqing. "Zhongguo yingju zhong jige zhongyao de wenti, shang" [Some Important Issues of Chinese Cinema, Part 1]. *Yinxing* 3 (1926): 6–12.

Chen, Zhiqing. "Zhongguo yingju zhong jige zhongyao de wenti, zhong" [Some Important Issues of Chinese Cinema, Part 2]. *Yinxing* 4 (1926): 6–11.

Cheng, Bugao. *Yingtan yijiu* [Reminiscences of the Film World]. Beijing: Zhongguo dianying chubanshe, 1983.

Cheng, Jihua, Li Shaobai, and Xing Zuwen. *Zhongguo dianying fazhan shi* [A History of the Development of Chinese Film]. Beijing: China Film Press, 1963, 1980.

Cheng, Po-hung. *Entertainment for the Chinese in Hong Kong over a Century*. Hong Kong: iGlobe Publishing, 2013.

Cheng, Shuren, ed. *Zhonghua yingye nianjian* [China Cinema Yearbook]. Shanghai: Zhonghua yingye nianjian she, 1927.

Ching, May-bo. "Where Guangdong Meets Shanghai: Hong Kong Culture in a Trans-regional Context." In *Hong Kong Mobile: Making a Global Population*, edited by Helen F. Siu and Agnes S. Ku, 45–62. Hong Kong: Hong Kong University Press, 2008.

Chou, Wan-yao. *Taiwan lishi tushuo: Shiqian zhi yijiusiwu nian* [Illustrated History of Taiwan: From Prehistory to 1945]. Taipei: Linking Publishing, 1997.

Chow, Rey. *Woman and Chinese Modernity: The Politics of Reading between West and East*. Minneapolis: University of Minnesota Press, 1991.

Christie, Ian. "Ancient Rome in London: Classical Subjects in the Forefront of Cinema's Expansion after 1910." In *The Ancient World in Silent Cinema*, edited by Pantelis Michelakis and Maria Wyke, 109–124. Cambridge: Cambridge University Press, 2013.

Chung, Stephanie Po-yin. *Xianggang yingshiye bainian* [One Hundred Years of Hong Kong Film and Television Industry]. Hong Kong: Joint Publishing, 2011.

Chung, Stephanie Po-yin. "Xinlian gushi: Zhengzhi wenyi he yueyu yingye" [Sun Luen Story: Politics, *Wenyi*, and the Cantonese Film Industry]. In *Wenyi renwu, Xinlian qiusuo* [The Mission of *Wenyi*, the Searching of Sun Luen], edited by Sam Ho, 35–52. Hong Kong: Hong Kong Film Archive, 2011.

Corbin, Alain, dir. *Rejā no tanjō* [The Birth of Recreation]. Translated by Watanabe Kyōko. Tokyo: Hujiwara shoten, 2010. Original work published as *L'avènement des loisirs, 1850–1960*. Paris: Aubier, 1995.

Cui, Songming, ed. *Tushuo Xue Juexian yishu rensheng* [Pictorial Illustration of Xue Juexian's Artistic Life]. Guangzhou: Guangdong Bahe huiguan, 2013.

Deocampo, Nick. *Cine: Spanish Influences on Early Cinema in the Philippines*. Manila: National Commission for Culture and the Arts, 2003.

Dianying ziliaoguan koushu dianying shi xiaozu (The Oral History Unit of the Film Archive). *Taiyupian shidai* [The Era of the Taiwanese Dialect Film]. Taipei: Taiwan Film Archive, 1994.

Diawara, Manthia. *African Cinema: Politics and Culture*. Bloomington: Indiana University of Press, 1992.

Dirlik, Arif. *Marxism in the Chinese Revolution*. Lanham, MD: Rowman & Littlefield, 2005.

Doane, Mary Ann. "The Location of the Image: Cinematic Projection and Scale in Modernity." In *Art of Projection*, edited by Stan Douglas and Christopher Eamon, 151–166. Berlin: Verlag, 2009.

Escudero, Juan Ignacio Toro. "España y los españoles en el Shanghai de entreguerras (1918–1939)" [Spain and Spaniards in Shanghai between the Wars]. Master's thesis, East China Normal University, 2012.

Fan, Boqun, ed. *Huaji dashi: Xu Zhuodai* [The Master of Comedy: Xu Zhuodai]. Taipei: Yeqiang, 1993.

Fan, Boqun. *Minguo tongsu xiaoshuo yuanyang hudie pai* [Mandarin Ducks and Butterfly School: The Popular Fiction in Republican China]. Taipei: Guowen tiandi zazhi she, 1990.

Fan, Boqun. *Yuanyang hudie: Libai liu pai zuopin xuan shang* [Mandarin Ducks and Butterflies: Selected Works of the *Saturday* Part One]. Beijing: Renmin wenxue, 1991.

Fan, Boqun. "Zhu Shouju lun" [On Zhu Shouju]. *Xin wenxue shiliao* 1 (2013): 103–124.

Fan, Victor. *Cinema Approaching Reality: Locating Chinese Film Theory*. Minneapolis: University of Minnesota Press, 2015.

Fan, Victor. "The Cinema of Sun Yu: Ice Cream for the Eye . . . but with a Homo Sacer." *Journal of Chinese Cinemas* 5, no. 3 (2001): 219–251.

Farquhar, Mary Ann, and Chris Berry. "Shadow Opera: Toward a New Archaeology of the Chinese Cinema." *Post Script* 20, nos. 2–3 (2000): 27–42.

Feng, Min. "Bao Tianxiao yu Zhongguo dianying" [Bao Tianxiao and Chinese Cinema]. *Dangdai dianying* 1 (1997): 46–49.

Foucault, Michel. "Nietzsche, Genealogy, History." In *Language, Counter-Memory, Practice: Selected Essays and Interviews*, edited by Donald F. Bouchard, 76–120. Ithaca, NY: Cornell University Press, 1977.

Fruhauf, Heiner. "Urban Exoticism and Its Sino-Japanese Scenery, 1910–1923." *Asian and African Studies* 6 (1997): 126–169.

Fu, Poshek. *Between Shanghai and Hong Kong: The Politics of Chinese Cinemas*. Stanford, CA: Stanford University Press, 2003.

Fu, Poshek. *Passivity, Resistance, and Collaboration: Intellectual Choices in Occupied Shanghai, 1937–1945*. Stanford, CA: Stanford University Press, 1993.

Fu, Yongchun. "Movie Matchmakers: The Intermediaries between Hollywood and China in the Early Twentieth Century." *Journal of Chinese Cinemas* 9, no. 1 (2015): 8–22.

Fujii, Shizue. *Lifan: Riben zhili Taiwan de jice* [Administrating Aborigines: The Strategy of Japanese Rule]. Taipei: Wenyingtang, 1997.

Fujiki, Hideaki. "Benshi as Stars: The Irony of the Popularity and Respectability of Voice Performers in Japanese Cinema." *Cinema Journal* 40, no. 2 (2006): 68–84.

Fujiki, Hideaki. *Making Personas: Transnational Film Stardom in Modern Japan*. Cambridge, MA: Harvard University Asian Center, 2013.

Fujisaki, Seinosuke. *Taiwan no banzoku* [Aboriginal Tribes of Taiwan]. Tokyo: Kokushi kankōkai, 1936.

Garret, Shirley S. *Social Reformers in Urban China: The Chinese Y.M.C.A., 1895–1926*. Cambridge, MA: Harvard University Press, 1970.

Gernalzick, Nadja, and Gabriele Pisarz-Ramirez, eds. *Transmediality and Transculturality*. Heidelberg: Universitätsverlag Winter, 2013.

Gerow, Aaron Andrew. *Visions of Japanese Modernity: Articulations of Cinema, Nation, and Spectatorship, 1895–1925*. Berkeley: University of California Press, 2010.

Glaser, Stephanie A., ed. *Media inter Media: Essays in Honor of Claus Clüver*. Amsterdam, New York: Rodopi, 2009.

Goldstein, Joshua. *Drama Kings: Players and Publics in the Re-creation of Peking Opera, 1970–1937*. Berkeley: University of California Press, 2007.

Gongsu. "Xinju tuibian ji" [A Record of New Play's Degradation]. *Xinju zazhi* 1 (1922): 9.

Greis, Peter Hays. *China's New Nationalism: Pride, Politics, and Diplomacy*. Berkeley: University of California Press, 2004.

Gu, Jianchen. "Zhongguo dianying fadashi" [The Development of Chinese Film]. In *Zhongguo dianying nianjian 1934* [Chinese Film Yearbook 1934], edited by Zhongguo jiaoyu dianying xiehui, 321–346. Beijing: Zhongguo guangbo dianshi chubanshe, 2008.

Gu, Kenfu. "Fakan ci" [Inaugurating Preface]. *Yingxi zazhi* 1, no. 1 (1920): 7–13.

Guan, Ji'an. "Naimei nushi" [Miss Anna May Yang]. *Dianying zazhi* 1, no. 1 (1924): 46.

Guan, Wenqing. *Zhongguo yintan waishi* [Unofficial History of the Chinese Screen Industry]. Hong Kong: Wide Angle Press, 1976.

Guangdong sheng defangzhi bianzhuan weiyuanhui, ed. *Guangzhou shi zhi* [Guangzhou Municipal History]. Vol. 18. Guangzhou: Guangzhou chubanshe, 1996.

Guangzhou Film Company. *Guangzhou dianyingzhi* [Documentation of Guangzhou Films]. Guangzhou: Guangzhou Film Company, 1993.

Guido, Laurent. "Rhythmic Bodies/Movies: Dance as Attraction in Early Film Culture." In *The Cinema of Attractions Reloaded*, Wanda Strauven, 139–151. Amsterdam: Amsterdam University Press, 2006.

Gunning, Tom. "An Aesthetic of Astonishment: Early Film and the (In)Credulous Spectator." *Art and Text* 34 (1989): 114–133.

Gunning, Tom. "The Cinema of Attractions: Early Film, Its Spectator and the Avant-Garde." In *Early Cinema: Space, Frame, Narrative*, edited by Thomas Elsaesser, 56–62. London: BFI Publishing, 1990.

Gunning, Tom. "Landscape and the Fantasy of Moving Pictures: Early Cinema's Phantom Rides." In *Cinema and Landscape*, edited by Graeme Harper and Jonathan Rayner, 31–70. Bristol: Intellect, 2010.

Gunning, Tom. "Loïe Fuller and the Art of Motion." In *The Tenth Muse: Cinema and Other Arts*, edited by Leonardo Quaresima and Laura Vichi, 25–53. Udine: Forum, 2001.

Habermas, Jürgen. *The Structural Transformation of Public Sphere: An Inquiry into a Category of Bourgeois Society*. Transated by Thomas Burger. Cambridge, MA: MIT Press, 1989.

Han, Yanli. "Butan zhengzhi de zhengzhixue: Gangchan lunli qinqing pian shixi" [Political Discourse without Politics: An Analysis of Hong Kong–Produced Familial Ethic Film]. In *Lengzhan yu Xiangang dianyin* [The Cold War and Hong Kong Cinema], edited by Wong Ain-ling and Lee Pui-tak, 209–219. Hong Kong: Hong Kong Film Archive, 2009.

Hansen, Miriam. *Babel and Babylon: Spectatorship in American Silent Film*. Cambridge, MA: Harvard University Press, 1991.

Hansen, Miriam. "Early Cinema, Late Cinema: Permutations of the Public Sphere." *Screen* 34, no. 3 (1993): 197–210.

Hansen, Miriam. "Fallen Women, Rising Stars, New Horizons: Shanghai Silent Film as Vernacular Modernism." *Film Quarterly* 54, no. 1 (2000): 10–22.

Hansen, Miriam. "The Mass Production of the Senses." In *Reinventing Film Studies*, edited by Christine Gledhill and Linda Williams, 332–350. New York: Oxford University Press, 2000.

Hao, Yen-p'ing. *The Comprador in Nineteenth Century China: Bridge between East and West*. Cambridge, MA: Harvard University Press, 1970.

He, Xiujun. "Zhang Shichuan he Mingxing yingpian gongsi" [Zhang Shichuan and His Star Motion Picture Company]. In *Wenshi ziliao xuanji* [Anthology of Literature and History Materials], vol. 67, edited by Quanguo zhengxie wenshi he xuexi weiyuanhui, 182–257. Beijing: China Literature and History Press, 1980.

Hicks, Jeremy. *Dziga Vertov: Defining Documentary Film*. London: I. B. Tauris, 2007.

High, Peter B. *The Imperial Screen: Japanese Film Culture in the Fifteen Years' War, 1931–1945*. Madison: University of Wisconsin Press, 2003.

Hillard, Derek. "Walter Ruttmann's Janus-Faced View of Modernity: The Ambivalence of Description in Berlin: Symphony of a Great City." *Monatshefte* 96, no. 1 (2004): 78–92.

Hiratsuka, Yoshinori. *Hiratsuka Yoshinori chosaku shū II: Chūgoku kindai kyōikushi* [Selected Works by Hiratsuka Yoshinori II: The Modern History of Education in China]. Tokyo: Kyōiku kaihatsu kenkyūsyo, 1985. Original work published 1924.

Hisazumi, Eiichi. "Taiwan jijō shōkai zakkan" [Miscellaneous Thoughts about the "Introducing Current Situations in Taiwan" Project]. *Taiwan Education* 234 (1921): 33–37.

Hockx, Michel. *Questions of Style: Literary Societies and Literary Journals in Modern China, 1911–1937*. Leiden: Brill, 2003.

Hong, Guo-Juin. *Taiwan Cinema: A Contested Nation on Screen*. New York: Palgrave Macmillan, 2011.

Horak, Jan-Christopher, ed. *Lovers of Cinema: The First American Film Avant-Garde, 1919–1945*. Madison: University of Wisconsin Press, 1995.

Hsu, Chen-chin, and Kang Laixin, eds. *Liu Na'ou quanji* [The Complete Works of Liu Na'ou]. Tainan: Museum of Taiwan Literature and Tainan Country Bureau of Culture, 2001.

Hsu, Chen-chin, and Kang Laixin, eds. *Liu Na'ou quanji: zengbuji* [The Complete Works of Liu Na'ou: The Supplement]. Tainan: Museum of Taiwan Literature and Tainan Country Bureau of Culture, 2010.

Hsu, Chen-chin. "Chongdu Taiwanren Liu Na'ou (1905–1940): Lishi yu wenhua de hudong kaocha" [Rereading Taiwanese Liu Na'ou (1905–1940): A Study on History and Culture]. Master's thesis, National Central University, 1998.

Hsu, Chen-chin. *Modeng, Shanghai, xin ganjue: Liu Na'ou, 1905–1940* [Modern, Shanghai, Neosensationist: Liu Na'ou, 1905–1940]. Taipei: Xiuwei zixun keji gufen youxian gongsi, 2008.

Hu, Chia-yu. "Bolanhui yu Taiwan yuanzhumin: zhimin shiqi de zhanshi zhengzhi yu 'tazhe' yixiang" [Great Exhibitions and the Taiwan Indigenous Peoples: The Politics of Representation and the Images of "Others" in the Colonial Period]. *Journal of Archaeology and Anthropology* 62 (2004): 3–39.

Hu, Jubin. *Projecting a Nation: Chinese National Cinema before 1949*. Hong Kong: Hong Kong University Press, 2003.

Hu, Yongqi. "Qingnianhui yu qingnian zhi guanxi" [The Relation between the YMCA and Young Men]. *Shanghai qingnian* 17, no. 1 (1918): n.p.

Huang, Boli. "Dushi wenhua de xiandaixing xiangxiang—yi xiguan xiaojie wei ge'an de kaocha" [An Imagination of Modernity through Urban Culture—a Case Study of Miss Xiguan]. *Jiangxi shehui kexue* 4 (2010): 235–240.

Huang, Dequan. "Dianying chudao Shanghai kao" [On the Arrival of Cinema in Shanghai]. *Film Art* 314 (2007): 102–109.

Huang, Dequan. "Dianying gujin ciyi kao" [The Meaning of Film in Ancient Times and Now]. *Contemporary Cinema* 6 (2009): 59–64.

Huang, Dequan. "Shanghai shangwu yinshuguan chuchuang huodong yingpian kao" [Study of Early Filmmaking by Commercial Press in Shanghai]. *Contemporary Cinema* 170 (2010): 56–63.

Huang, Dequan. "Xiqu dianying *Dingjunshan* zhi youlai yu yanbian" [The Origin and Development of *Dingjun Mountain*]. *Contemporary Cinema* 2 (2008): 104–111.

Huang, Dequan. *Zhongguo zaoqi dianying shishi kaozheng* [A Textual Critique of Early Chinese Film History]. Beijing: China Film Press, 2012.

Huang, Gang. "Liu Na'ou zhilu (baogao): huiyi yige 'gaogui' de ren, ta de dijiande xunshen" [The Road of Liu Na'ou (Report): Recalling a "Noble" Man, and His Contemptible Death]. *Ta Kung Pao*, January 27–February 7, 1941.

Huang, Jen, and Wang Wei, eds., *Taiwan dianying bainian shihua* [One Hundred Years of Taiwan Cinema]. Vol. 1. Taipei: Zhonghua yingpingren xiehui, 2004.

Huang, Nicole. *Women, War, Domesticity: Shanghai Literature and Popular Culture of the 1940s*. Leiden: Brill, 2005.

Huang, Xuelei. *Shanghai Filmmaking: Crossing Borders, Connecting to the Globe, 1922–1938*. Leiden: Brill, 2014.

Huang, Yikuan. "Taiwan yanqing xushi yu dianying gaibian zhi kongjian zaxian: Yi liuling zhi baling niandai wenhua changyu wei zhu" [Space Representations in Taiwan Love Narratives and Their Film Adaptations: From the 1960s–1980s Literary Field]. *Zhongxzheng daxue zhongwen xueshu niankan* 14 (2009): 135–164.

Huang, Yikuan. "Yanqing xushi yu *wenyipian*: Qiong Yao xiaoshuo gaibian dianying zhi kongjian xinggou yu xiandai lianai xiangxiang" [Love Narrative and *Wenyi* Film: Space Construction and Modern Love Imagination in Film Adaptations of Qiong Yao's Novels]. *Dong Hwa Journal of Chinese Studies* 19 (2014): 329–372.

Huang, Zhen. "Dongxi liangfang de wenyi" [The *Wenyi* of the East and the West]. *Yinxing* 12 (1927): 28–31.

Huters, Theodore. *Bringing the World Home: Appropriating the West in Late Qing and Early Republican China*. Honolulu: University of Hawai'i Press, 2005.

Ichikawa, Sai. "Taiwan eiga jigyō hatsutatsu shikō" [A Preliminary History of the Taiwan Film Industry]. In *Ajia eiga no sōzō oyobi kensetsu* [Creating and Developing an Asian Cinema], edited by Ichikawa Sai, 86–98. Tokyo: Kokusai Eiga Tsūshinsha Shuppanbu, 1941.

Irvine, Clarke. "Chinese Photoplays." *Moving Picture World* 19, no. 8 (1914): 935.

Irvine, Clarke. "Doings at Los Angeles." *Moving Picture World* 21, no. 10 (1914): 1360.

Ishizuka, Karen L., and Patricia R. Zimmermann, eds. *Mining the Home Movie: Excavations in Histories and Memories*. Berkeley: University of California Press, 2007.

Iwamoto, Kenji. *Gentō no seiki: eiga zenya no shikaku bunkashi* [Centuries of Magic Lantern in Japan: A History of Visual Culture on the Eve of Cinema]. Tokyo: Shinwasha, 2002.

Jacobs, Lea. *The Decline of Sentiment: American Film in the 1920s*. Berkeley: University of California Press, 2008.

Jacobs, Lewis. *The Rise of the American Film*. New York: Harcourt, Brace & Co., 1939.

Jiang, Jianguo. "Wanqing Guangzhou chengshi xiaofei wenhua yanjiu" [A Study of Guangzhou Urban Consumption Culture in the Late Qing Dynasty]. PhD diss., Jinan University, 2005.

Ji-chen. "Guanyu jinying yueyupian zhi mianmianguan" [A Look at the Ban on Cantonese Films in Different Aspects]. *Yilin*, no. 3 (1937).

Jing-tsz. "Yingpian de guancha (xu)" [Film Observations (Continued)]. Film Corner, *Chinese Mail*, July 19 and July 26, 1924.

Jing-tsz. "Yingpian de guancha" [Film Observations]. Film Corner, *Chinese Mail*, July 12, 1924.

Johnson, Matthew D. "Journey to the Seat of War: The International Exhibition of China in Early Cinema." *Journal of Chinese Cinemas* 3, no. 2 (2009): 109–122.

Jones, Andrew F. *Yellow Music: Media Culture and Colonial Modernity in Chinese Jazz Age*. Durham, NC: Duke University Press, 2001.

Kaihase-sei. "Tongxin: Longtan tongxin" [Correspondence: Ryūtan]. *Taiwan Education* (Chinese-language edition) no. 256 (1923): 8.

Katō-sei. "Tsūshin ihō: Taihoku tsūshin" [Communication Bulletin: Taipei Correspondence]. *Taiwan Education* 209 (1919): 50–51.

Katō-sei. "Tsūshin ihō: Taihoku tsūshin" [Communication Bulletin: Taipei Correspondence]. *Taiwan Education* 215 (1920): 51–52.

Katō-sei. "Tsūshin ihō: Taihoku tsūshin" [Communication Bulletin: Taipei Correspondence]. *Taiwan Education* 241 (1922): 69–73.

Katō-sei. "Tsūshin ihō: Taihoku tsūshin" [Communication Bulletin: Taipei Correspondence]. *Taiwan Education* 246 (1922): 65–67.

Kaufman, George. "Bret Harte Said It: The Heathen Chinese Is Peculiar." *New York Tribune*, August 27, 1916.

Keifū-sei. "Jidō no suiren jikkyō wo mite" [Watching the Actual Scenes of Children Practicing Swimming Skills]. *Undō to shumi* 2, no. 9 (1917): 37–39.

Ken. "Yingxi guanzhong zhi shijie" [Ten Prohibitions of Moviegoers]. *Film Magazine* 1, no. 3 (1922): 202. Reprint, Jiang Yasha, Jing Li and Chen Zhanqi, eds. *Zhongguo zaoqi dianying huakan* [Chinese Early Movie Magazines]. Vol. 1. Beijing: Quanguo tushuguan wenxian suowei fuzhi zhongxin, 2004.

King-ming. "Wei gangzhong yingxi jie jing yiyan" [A Few Suggestions for the Hong Kong and Chinese Film Industry]. Film Corner, *Chinese Mail*, December 29, 1924.

King-ming. "Wo de Zhongguo xiying tan" [My Views on Chinese Films]. Film Corner, *Chinese Mail*, August 23, 1924.

Kirby, Lynn. *Parallel Tracks: The Railroad and Silent Cinema*. Durham, NC: Duke University Press, 1997.

Kittler, Friedrich A. *Gramophone, Film, Typewriter*. Translated by Geoffrey Winthrop-Young and Michael Wutz. Stanford, CA: Stanford University Press, 1999.

Kok. "Yingxi xue de fanwei he dingyi (xu)" [Definition and Scope of Film Studies (Continued)]. Film Corner, *Chinese Mail*, October 4, 1924.

Kok. "Yingxi xue de fanwei he dingyi" [Definition and Scope of Film Studies]. Film Corner, *Chinese Mail*, September 20, 1924.

Kok-fei. "Mingxing zhengming" [Correct Translation of Names of Movie Stars]. Film Corner, *Chinese Mail*, May 31, 1924.

Kok-fei. "Xiaoyan" [A Few Words]. Film Corner, *Chinese Mail*, April 19, 1924.

Kok-fei. "Yingxi jinghua shi (yi)" [The Evolution of Film (Part 1)]. Film Corner, *Chinese Mail*, July 12, 1924.

Kowner, Rotem. "Between a Colonial Clash and World War Zero: The Impact of the Russo-Japanese War in a Global Perspective." In *The Impact of the Russo-Japanese War*, edited by Rotem Kowner, 1–25. London: Routledge, 2007.

Kuo, Jason C. ed. *Visual Culture in Shanghai, 1850s–1930s*. Washington, DC: New Academic Publishing, 2007.

Kurita-sei. "Tsūshin ihō: Taihoku tsūshin" [Communication Bulletin: Taipei Correspondence]. *Taiwan Education* 166 (1916): 52–53.

Kwok, Ching-ling, ed. *Hong Kong Here I Come*. Hong Kong: Hong Kong Film Archive, 2000.

Kwok, Ching-ling, and Grace Ng, eds. *Director Chor Yuen*. Hong Kong: Hong Kong Film Archive, 2006.

Lam, Agnes, Maggie Lee, and Wong Kee-chee, eds. *The Glorious Modernity of Kong Ngee*. Hong Kong: Hong Kong Film Archive, 2006.

Lam, King-fei. "Yingxi yu jiaoyu zhi guanxi (xu)" [Film and Education (Continued)]. Film Corner, *Chinese Mail*, February 14, 1925.

LaMarre, Thomas. "Magic Lantern, Dark Precursor of Animation." *Animation* 6, no. 2 (2011): 127–48.

Langman-sheng. "Yi pie *Aihe chao*" [A Glance at *Tidal Wave of Love*]. *Guangzhou minguo ribao*, February 26, 1926.

Latham, Kevin. "Consuming Fantasies: Mediated Stardom in Hong Kong Cantonese Opera and Cinema." *Modern China* 26, no. 3 (2000): 329–30.

Latourette, Kenneth. *A History of Christian Missions in China*. New York: Macmillan, 1929; Piscataway, NJ: Gorgias Press, 2009.

Law, Kar, and Frank Bren. *From Artform to Platform: Hong Kong Plays and Performances, 1900–1941*. Honk Kong: International Association of Theatre Critics, 1999.

Law, Kar, and Frank Bren. *Hong Kong Cinema: A Cross-Cultural View*. Lanham, MD: Scarecrow Press, 2004.

Law, Kar, and Frank Bren. *Xianggang dianying kua wenhua guan* [Hong Kong Cinema: A Cross-Cultural View]. Translated by Liu Hui. Beijing: Beijing University Press, 2012.

Law, Kar, and Lai Shek. *Li Minwei: ren, shidai, dianying* [Lai Man-wai: The Man, the Time, and the Cinema]. Hong Kong: Mingchuang Publishing, 1999.

Law, Kar. "Archetypes and Variations: Observation on Six Cantonese Films." In *Cantonese Melodrama, 1950–1969*, edited by Li Cheuk-to, 15–20. Hong Kong: Urban Council, 1986.

Law, Kar. "Jiekai Xianggang dianying qiyuan de mituan" [Doubts and Suspicions about Hong Kong Movie's Origin]. *Contemporary Cinema* 4 (2010): 78–85.

Lee, Daw-Ming. "Liu Na'ou de dianying meixueguan: Jiantan ta de jilu dianying '*Xiezhe sheyingji de nanren*'" [Liu Na'ou's Concept of Film Aesthetic, and His Documentary *The Man Who Has a Camera*]. In *Liu Na'ou guoji yantaohui lunwenji* [Proceedings of the International Conference on Liu Na'ou], edited by Department of Chinese Literature of National Central University, 145–159. Tainan: National Museum of Taiwan Literature choubeichu, 2005.

Lee, Leo Ou-fan. "Literary Trends: The Quest for Modernity, 1895–1927." In *An Intellectual History of Modern China*, edited by Merle Goldman and Leo Ou-fan Lee, 142–195. Cambridge: Cambridge University Press, 2002.

Lee, Leo Ou-fan. "Shanghai Modern: Reflection on Urban Culture in China in the 1930s." *Public Culture* 11, no. 1 (1999): 75–107.

Lee, Leo Ou-fan. *Shanghai Modern: The Flowering of a New Urban Culture in China, 1930–1945*. Cambridge, MA: Harvard University Press, 1999.

Lei-gong. "Yingpian zhong de Zhongguo wushu" [Chinese Kung Fu in Films]. Film Corner, *Chinese Mail*, October 4, 1924.

Leung, Ping-kwan. "Cong guozu dao siqing: Huayu tongsu qingjieyu de bianhua, Lanyuhei de lizi" [From Nation-Building to Private Passion: The Changes in Chinese Melodrama]. In *Shaoshi yingshi digou: Wenhuua Zhongguo de xiangxiang* [Shaw Bros. Enterprise: Cultural China Imaginary], edited by Liao Jinfeng, Cheuk Pak-tong, and Yung Saishing, 295–306. Taipei: Rye Field Publishing, 2003.

Lewis, Robert E. *Search of Far Horizons*. West Conshohocken, PA: Infinity Publishing, 2003.

Leyda, Jay. *Dianying/Electric Shadows: An Account of Films and the Film Audience in China*. Cambridge, MA: MIT Press, 1972.

Li, Baijin. "Lun dianyin yu jiaoyu" [On Film and Education]. *Yinxing* 12 (1927): 36–39.

Li, Bin. "Yuanyang hudie pai wenren: Di yi dai Zhongguo dianying ren" [Literati of the Mandarin Ducks and Butterflies School: Pioneers of Chinese Cinema]. *Suzhou keji xueyuan xuebao (shehui kexue ban)* 28, no. 3 (2011): 96–102.

Li, Gucheng. *Xianggang baoye bainian cangsang* [One Hundred Years of Hong Kong Newspapers]. Hong Kong: Ming Pao Publications, 2000.

Li, Gucheng. *Xianggang zhongwen baoye fazhang shi* [A History of the Chinese-Language Newspaper Industry in Hong Kong]. Shanghai: Shanghai Classics Publishing House, 2005.

Li, Jin. *Haipai xiaoshuo lun* [On Shanghai-Style Fiction]. Taipei: Xiuwei zixun, 2005.

Li, Jin. *Haipai xiaoshuo yu xiandai dushi wenhua* [Shanghai-Style Fiction and Modern Urban Culture]. Hefei: Anhui jiaoyu chubanshe, 2001.

Li, Jin. "Xin ganjuepai he ersanshi niandai haolaiwu dianying" [Neosensationalism and Hollywood Films in the 1920s and 1930s]. *Modern Chinese Literature Studies* 3 (1997): 32–56.

Li, Suyuan, and Hu Jubin. *Zhongguo wusheng dianyingshi* [A History of Chinese Silent Film]. Beijing: China Film Press, 1996.

Li, Yi. "Xue Juexian yu yueju *Baijinlong*" [Xue Juexian and the Cantonese Opera *The Platinum Dragon*]. *Nanguo hongdou* 3 (2009): 16–19.

Liang, Jiwen. "Wo duiyu guochan yingpian zhi leguan" [My Optimistic View on Domestic Films]. *Guangzhou minguo ribao*, June 7, 1926.

Liang, Liang. "Zhongguo wenyi dianying yu dangdia xiaoshuo, shang" [Chinese *Wenyi* Film and the Contemporary Novel, Part 1]. *Wenhsun* 26 (1986): 257–262.

Liang, Liang. "Zhongguo wenyi dianying yu dangdia xiaoshuo, xia" [Chinese *Wenyi* Film and the Contemporary Novel, Part 2], *Wenhsun* 27 (1986): 266–277.

Lin, Youlan. *Xianggang shihua* [Historical Anecdotes of Hong Kong]. Hong Kong: Shanghai Book Store, 1985.

Lindvall, Terry. *Sanctuary Cinema: Origins of Christian Film Industry*. New York: New York University Press, 2007.

Link, Perry. *Mandarin Ducks and Butterflies: Popular Fiction in Early Twentieth-Century Chinese Cities*. Berkeley: University of California Press, 1981.

Lippit, Seiji M. *Topographies of Japanese Modernism*. New York: Columbia University Press, 2002.

Liu, Jintao. "Guangzhou zaoqi zhipian ye" [The Early Film Production Industry in Guangzhou]. *Guangzhou cultural history website*, last modified September 17, 2008, http://www.gzzxws.gov.cn/gzws/gzws/ml/28/200809/t20080917_9128_1.htm

Liu, Lydia H. *Translingual Practice: Literature, National Culture, and Translated Modernity-China, 1900–1937*. Stanford, CA: Stanford University Press, 1995.

Liu, Na'ou. "Dianying jiezou jianlun" [A Brief Discussion of Film Rhythm]. *Modern Screen* 6 (1933): 1–2.

Liu, Na'ou. "Dianying xingshimei de tanqiu" [Pursuing a Formal Beauty in Cinema]. *Wanxiang* 1, May, 1934.

Liu, Na'ou. "Ecranesque." *Modern Screen* 2 (1933): 1.

Liu, Na'ou. "Guangdiao yu yindiao" [Light Tone and Acoustic Tone]. *Shidai dianying*, November 5, 1934.

Liu, Na'ou. "Kaimaila jigou—weizhi jiaodu jinenglun" [On the Mechanism of the Camera—the Function of Camera Positions and Angles]. *Modern Screen* 7 (1934): 1–2.

Liu, Na'ou. "Yingxi manxiang" [Random Thoughts on Cinema]. *Wugui lieche* 5 (1928): 281–284.

Liu, Shuyong. *Jianming xianggang shi* [A Brief History of Hong Kong]. Hong Kong: Joint Publishing, 2009.

Liu, Xiancheng. "Zhongguo yixu: Li Xing dianying tanyuan" [Chinese Remnant: The Origin of Li Xing's Films]. *Journal of Beijing Film Academy* 4 (1998): 50–62.

Liu, Zhenggang. *Huashuo Yueshang* [On Cantonese Merchants]. Beijing: Zhonghua gongshang lianhe chubanshe, 2008.

Lo, Ming-cheng M. *Doctors within Borders: Profession, Ethnicity, and Modernity in Colonial Taiwan*. Berkeley: University of California Press, 2002.

Lobingier, Charles. "Toeg & Read v. Suffert, Sept. 3, 1907." In *Extraterritorial Cases*, ed. Charles Lobingier, 112–120. Manila: Bureau of Printing, 1920.

Longmen, Jianke. "*Mingjiao zuiren* zhi wo guan" [My View of *The Law Breaker*]. *Guangzhou minguo ribao*, September 10, 1926.

Lu, Dun. "Yuepian jidi heyi bu she zai Guangzhou?" [Why Wasn't the Base of Cantonese Films Set in Guangzhou?)]. In *Fengzi shengya ban shiji* [The Life of a Mad Man over Half a century]. Hong Kong: Xiangjiang publication company limited, 1992.

Lu, Jie. *Lu Jie riji zhaicun* [Lu Jie Diaries: Selected Extracts]. Beijing: Zhongguo dianying ziliao guan, 1962.

Lu, Mengshu. "Dianying yu geming" [Film and Revolution]. *Yinxing* 9 (1927): 36–42.

Lu, Mengshu. *Dianying yu wenyi* [Film and *Wenyi*]. Shanghai: Liangyou tushu, 1928.

Lu, Mengshu. "Guochan dianying jinhou yingyou de xinqushi" [The Expected Tendency of Local Film]. *Yinxing* 3 (1926): 24–25.

Lu, Mengshu. "Juantouyu" [Editorial]. *Yinxing* 1 (1926): 4.

Lu, Mengshu. *Xinghuo* [A Little Sparkle]. Shanghai: Liangyou tushu, 1927.

Lu, Mengshu. "Xin yingxiong zhuyi" [New Heroism]. *Yinxing* 4 (1926): 16–18.

Lu, Mengshu. "Zai heian de yingjuchang zhong" [In a Dark Motion Picture Theater]. *Yinxing* 13 (1927): 20–24.

Lu, Mengshu. "Zai heian de yingjuchang zhong 2" [In a Dark Motion Picture Theater 2]. *Yinxing* 14 (1927): 30–33.

Lu, Sheldon Hsiao-peng, ed. *Transnational Chinese Cinemas: Identity, Nationhood, Gender*. Honolulu: University of Hawai'i Press, 1997.

Lu, Xun. *Lu Xun quanji di shisan juan* [Collection of Lu Xun, Book 13]. Beijing: Renmin wenxue chubanshe, 1973.

Lu, Xun. "*Oumei mingjia duanpian xiao shuo congkan* pinglun" [Comments on *Series of Short Stories by Famous European and American Writers*]. *Jiaoyu gongbao*, November 30, 1917.

Lubinsheng. "Jiating zhi heimu" [Gossips about Families]. In *Zhongguo heimu daguan* [Collections of Gossips in China], the first issue of vol. 1, 5–6. Shanghai: Zhonghua tushu jicheng gongsi, 1918.

Luo, Liang. *The Avant-Garde and the Popular in Modern China: Tian Han and the Intersection of Performance and Politics*. Ann Arbor: University of Michigan Press, 2014.

Luo, Suwen, and Song Zuanyou. *Minguo shehui* [Republican Society]. Vol. 9 of *Shanghai tongshi* [History of Shanghai], edited by Xiong Yuezhi (Shanghai renmin chubanshe, 1999.

L. Y. "Yingxi de yanjiu (xu)" [A Study of Film (Continued)]. Film Corner, *Chinese Mail*, November 15, 1924.

Matsuda, Kyoko. *Teikoku no shikō: nihon "teikoku" to Taiwan genjūmin* [The Thinking of the Empire: The "Empire" of Japan and Taiwan Indigenous Peoples]. Tokyo: Yūshisha, 2014.

Matsui-sei. "Tsūshin ihō: Taihoku tsūshin" [Communication Bulletin: Taipei Correspondence]. *Taiwan Education* 240 (1922): 81–84.

Matsumoto, Kappei. *Nihon shakai shugi engekishi: Meiji Taishō hen* [History of Japanese Socialist Theater: Meiji Taishō Part]. Tokyo: Chikuma Shobō, 1975.

McGrath, Jason. "Acting Real: Cinema, Stage and the Modernity of Performance in

Chinese Silent Film." In *The Oxford Handbook of Chinese Cinemas*, edited by Carlos Rojas and Eileen Cheng-ying Chow, 401–420. New York: Oxford University Press, 2013.

Mei, Chia-ling. *Cong shaonian Zhongguo dao shaonian Taiwan: ershi shiji Zhongwen xiaoshuo de qingchun xiangxiang yu guozu lunshu* [From Young China to Young Taiwan: Youth Imagination and National Discourse in Chinese Novels in the Twentieth Century]. Taipei: Maitian chuban, 2013.

Mei, Wen. *Posui de yingxiang yu shiyi de lishi: Cong jiupai yuanhu dianying de shuailuo kan Zhongguo zhishi fanxing de zhuanbian* [Broken Images and Forgotten History: The Shift in the Chinese Intellectual Paradigm through the Lens of Mandarin Ducks and Butterflies Films]. Beijing: China Film Press, 2007.

Miaodou. "Zuojia yu wudao: Liu Na'ou shi huoshanshang de qianbei" [Author and Dance: Liu Na'ou Is a Veteran in the Dancing World]. *Tiaowushijie* 2, no. 2, 1937.

Mingming. "Xianggang yingyuan de canghai sangtian" [The Vicissitudes of Hong Kong Movie Theaters]. *Youyou zazhi* 2 (1935): 13.

Misawa, Mamie. *Zai "diguo" yu "zuguo" de jiafeng jian: Rizhi shiqi Taiwan dianyingren de jiaoshe yu kuajing* [Sandwiched between the "Empire" and the "Motherland": Taiwan Film Workers' Negotiation and Border-Crossing during Japanese Occupation]. Translated by Li Wenqing and Hsu Shijia. Taipei: National Taiwan University Press, 2012.

Misawa, Mamie. *Zhimindi xia de yinmu: Taiwan zongdufu dianying zhengcezhi yanjiu (1895 Occupa* [The "Screen" under Colonial Rule: The Film Policy in Taiwan in the Japanese Colonial Period (1895–1942)]. Taipei: Avanguard Publishing, 2002.

Mittler, Barbara. *A Newspaper for China: Power, Identity, and Change in Shanghai's News Media, 1872–1912*. Cambridge, MA: Harvard University Asia Center, 2004.

Miyao, Daisuke. *Sessue Hayakawa: Silent Cinema and Transnational Stardom*. Durham, NC: Duke University Press, 2007.

Morris, Gouverneur. "On Trumpet Island." *Pearson's Magazine* 25 (1911): 42–53.

Müller, Jürgen E. *Media Encounters and Media Theories*. Münster, Germany: Nodus Publikationen Munster, 2008.

Municipal Administrative Council. *Compte Rendu De La Gestion Pour L'exercice 1913* [Account Management of 1913]. Shanghai: Imprimerie Muncipale, 1913.

Murch, Walter. "Touch of Silence." In *Soundscape: The School of Sound Lectures, 1998–2001*, edited by Larry Side, Jerry Side and Diane Freeman, 83–102. London: Wallflower Press, 2003.

Musser, Charles. *The Emergence of Cinema: The American Screen to 1907*. Berkeley: University of California Press, 1990.

Musser, Charles. *High-class Moving Pictures: Lyman H. Howe and the Forgotten Era of Traveling Exhibition, 1880–1920*. Princeton: Princeton University Press, 1991.

Musser, Charles. "Toward a History of Screen Practice." *Quarterly Review of Film Studies* 9, no. 1 (1984): 59–69.

Nagib, Lúcia, and Anne Jerslev, eds. *Impure Cinema: Intermedial and Intercultural Approaches to Film*. New York: I. B. Tauris, 2014.

Nakagawa, Yoichi. "Shina no eiga" [Movies in China]. *Eiga jidai* (1926): 34–35.

Nakamura, Tsurayuki. "Taiwan ni okeru eiga kyōiku" [Film Education in Taiwan]. *Taiwan Education* 360 (1932): 47–53.

Ng, Grace, ed. *One for All: The Union Film Spirit*. Hong Kong: Hong Kong Film Archive, 2011.

Ng, May Gwan-yuk, ed. *Xianggang Chaoyu dianying xunji* [The Chaozhou-dialect Films of Hong Kong]. Hong Kong: Hong Kong Film Archive, 2013.

Ng, May Gwan-yuk, ed. *Xianggang Xiayu dianying fangzong* [The Amoy-dialect Films of Hong Kong]. Hong Kong: Hong Kong Film Archive, 2012.

Ng, May Gwan-yuk. "*Xu Baijinlong* de qingchang, shangchang, yangchang" [The Love Battlefield, Business World and Foreign Influence in *The White Gold Dragon, Part Two*]. In *Early Cinematic Treasures Rediscovered*, edited by Winnie Fu and May Gwan-yuk Ng. Hong Kong: Hong Kong Film Archive, 2015. Exhibition program brochure.

Ng, Wing-chung. *The Rise of Cantonese Opera*. Urbana: University of Illinois Press, 2015.

Nishimura, Hiroshi. "Jōshiki butsuri" [The Essential Knowledge of Physics]. *Taiwan keisatsu kyōkai zasshi* (1929): 151–162.

Ōhashi, Sutesaburō. *Aikoku Fujinkai Taiwan Honbu enkakushi* [History of the Development of the Patriotic Women's Association Taiwan Main Office]. Taihoku: Aikoku Fujinkai Taiwan Honbu, 1941.

Okabe, Ryū, ed. *Shiryō: Takamatsu Toyojirō to Okasawara Meihō no gyōseki (Nihon eigashi sukō 9)* [Documents: The Business Traces of Takamatsu Toyojirō and Okasawara Meihō (Unedited Manuscripts of Japanese Film History 9)]. Tokyo: Film Library Council, 1974.

Okubo, Ryo. "The Magic Lantern Show and Its Spectators during Late Nineteenth-Century Japan: Control of Perception in Lantern Shows for Education and News Report of Sino-Japanese War." *Iconics* 11 (2014): 7–26.

Pan, Anzhu. *Shangdu wangshi: Guangzhou chengshi lishi yanjiu shouji* [History of a Commercial City: Manuscripts of the Historical Research on Guangzhou City]. Beijing: Chinese Architectural Industry Press, 2010.

Pang, Laikwan. *The Distorting Mirror: Visual Modernity in China*. Honolulu: University of Hawaiʻi Press, 2007.

Pang, Laikwan. "Walking into and out of the Spectacle: China's Earliest Film Scene." *Screen* 47, no. 1 (2006): 66–80.

Peng, Hsiao-yen. *Dandyism and Transcultural Modernity: The Dandy, the Flaneur, and the Translator in 1930s Shanghai, Tokyo, and Paris*. New York: Routledge, 2010.

Peng, Hsiao-yen. *Haishang shuo qingyu: cong Zhang Ziping dao Liu Na'ou* [Shanghai Desire: From Zhang Ziping to Liu Na'ou]. Taipei: Zhongyanyuan wenzhesuo, 2001.

Peterson, Jennifer Lynn. *Education in the School of Dreams: Travelogues and Early Nonfiction Film*. Durham, NC: Duke University Press, 2013.

Pickowicz, Paul, Kuiyi Shen, and Yingjin Zhang, eds., *Liangyou: Kaleidoscopic Modernity and the Shanghai Global Metropolis, 1926–1945*. Leiden: Brill, 2013.

Pincus, Leslie. *Authenticating Culture in Imperial Japan: Kuki Shuzo and the Rise of National Aesthetics*. Berkeley: University of California Press, 1996.

Piredda, Maria Francesca. "Cinema and Popular Preaching: The Italian Missionary Film and *Fiamm*". In *Italian Popular Cinema*, edited by Louis Bayman and Sergio Rigoletto, 214–225. London: Palgrave Macmillan, 2013.

Qilang. "Kai pai nu chao zhi bo ling" [The Booming of the Local Film Industry]. *Yuet Wa Pao*, September 20, 1933.

Qin, Xiqing. "1920 niandai: minzu rentong yu Zhongguo zaoqi dianying de queli" [The 1920s: National Identity and Establishment of the Early Chinese Cinemas]. PhD diss., Film Art Research Center of China, 2006.

Qing, Xiqin. *Oumei dianying yu Zhongguo zaoqi dianying, 1920–1930* [European Film and Chinese Early Cinema, 1920–1930]. Beijing: China Film Press, 2008.

Qing, Zhi. "Tianyi gongsi de yueyu yousheng pian wenti" [Questions Concerning Tianyi's Cantonese Sound Films]. *Diansheng zhoukan* l.3, no. 17 (1934): n.p.

Qingjuan. "Tantan yinghua xiyuan de weisheng" [Remarks on the Hygiene Conditions of Movie Theaters]. *Guangzhou minguo ribao*, November 6, 1926.

Rapp, Dean. "The British Salvation Army, the Early Film Industry and Urban Working-Class Adolescents, 1897–1918." *Twentieth Century British History* 7, no. 2 (1996): 157–188.

Rascaroli, Laura, Gwenda Young, and Barry Monahan, eds. *Amateur Filmmaking: The Home Movie, the Archive, the Web*. New York: Bloomsbury Academic, 2014.

Rea, Christopher. "Enter the Cultural Entrepreneur." In *The Business of Culture: Cultural Entrepreneurs in China and Southeast Asia, 1900–65*, edited by Christopher Rea and Nicolai Volland, 9–34. Vancouver: UBC Press, 2015.

Reed, Christopher A. *Gutenberg in Shanghai: Chinese Print Capitalism, 1876–1937*. Vancouver: UBC Press, 2004.

Richie, Donald. *A Hundred Years of Japanese Cinema*. Tokyo: Kodansha, 2001.

Rojas, Carlos, and Eileen Chow, eds. *Rethinking Chinese Popular Culture: Cannibalizations of the Canon*. New York: Routledge, 2009.

Ryūnosuke, Akutagawa. *Zhongguo youji* [Travel Notes of China]. Translated by Chen Hao. Beijing: Xinshijie chubanshe, 2011.

Sang, Tze-lan. "The State of the Field in Taiwan Film Studies." Presentation at the Second World Congress of Taiwan Studies, London, June 18–20, 2015.

Sato, Akinari. "Zhu Shouju yu tade dianying zuopin *Fengyu zhi ye*: Zhongguo wusheng dianying Dongjing jianding shouji" [Zhu Shouju and His Film *Stormy Night*: Notes on Authentication of Chinese Silent Film from Tokyo]. *Ming Pao Weekly*, June 1, 2011.

Schivelbusch, Wolfgang. *The Railway Journey: The Industrialization of Time and Space in the 19th Century*. Berkeley: University of California Press, 1986.

Schneider, Alexandra. "Homemade Travelogues: *Autosonntag*—a Film Safari in the Swiss Alps." In *Virtual Voyages: Cinema and Travel*, edited by Jeffrey Ruoff, 157–176. Durham, NC: Duke University Press, 2006.

Shan, Dong. "Minchu yingxi xiaoshuo yanjiu" [A Study of Cine-Fiction of the Early Republican China]. MPhil thesis, University of Hong Kong, 2014.

Shanghai YMCA. "Minguo qinian ji yiqian jiubai shiba nian Shanghai jidujiao qingnainhui baogao—deyu bu baogao" [Report of Lecture Department, in the Annual Report for 1918 by Shanghai YMCA]. *Shanghai qingnian* 18, no. 4 (1919): n.p.

Shanghai YMCA. "Annual Report for 1917." *Shanghai qingnian* 17, no. 11 (1918): 3–29.

Shanghai YMCA. Ad of Shanghai YMCA Movie Exhibition. *Shenbao*, September 24–26, 1913.

Shanghai YMCA. Ad of Shanghai YMCA. *Yingxi zazhi* 1, no. 2 (1922). Reprint, Jiang Yasha, Jing Li and Chen Zhanqi, eds. *Zhongguo zaoqi dianying kuakan* [Chinese Early Movie Magazines]. Vol. 1. Beijing: Quanguo tushuguan wenxian wuowei fuzhi zhongxin, 2004.

Shanghai YMCA. "Annual Report for Year 1915." *Shanghai qingnian*, n.d.: 1–21.

Shanghai YMCA. "Annual Report for Year 1916." *Shanghai qingnian* 16, no. 8 (1917): 1–21.

Shanghai YMCA. "Annual Report for Year 1919." *Shanghai qingnian* 19, no. 8 (1920): 11–34.

Shanghai YMCA. "Benhui huiwu baogao jilue" [A Brief Report of the Association]. *Shanghai qingnian* 18, no. 43 (1919): n.p.

Shanghai YMCA. "Cangshushi tonggao" [An Announcement from the Library]. *Shanghai qingnian* 16, no. 32 (1917): n.p.

Shanghai YMCA. "Huiyuan timing" [List of Members]. *Shanghai qingnian* 16, no. 31 (1917): n.p.

Shanghai YMCA. "Jiaoji bu" [Department of Friendship and Entertainment]. *Shanghai qingnian* 14, no. 24 (1915): 6.

Shanghai YMCA. "Jiaoyi dahui zhi sheng" [The Success of the Member's Entertainment]. *Shanghai qingnian* 16, no. 27 (1917): n.p.

Shanghai YMCA. "Minguo wunian ji yujiuyiliunian Shanghai jidujiao qingnianhui baogao" [Social Department, Annual Report for 1916 by the Shanghai YMCA]. *Shanghai qingnian* 16, no. 8 (1917): n.p.

Shanghai YMCA. "Qing kan yingxi" [Watch the Movies]. *Shanghai qingnian* 16, no. 48 (1917): n.p.

Shanghai YMCA. "Qingnianhui cangshushi qishi" [Information from the YMCA Library]. *Shanghai qingnian* 14, no. 15 (1915): 8.

Shanghai YMCA. "Qingnianhui lifachu" [The Barber of the YMCA]. *Shanghai qingnian* 14, no. 15 (1915): 14.

Shanghai YMCA. "Tonglehui zhaochang kaihui" [Grand Entertainment Is Opening as Announced]. *Shanghai qingnian* 16, no. 37 (1917): n.p.

Sheng, Hua, and Huang Yuqi. "*Ming jiao zuiren* shipianji" [Preview of *The Law Breaker*]. *Guangzhou minguo ribao*, September 9, 1926.

Shih, Shu-mei. *The Lure of the Modern: Writing Modernism in Semicolonial China, 1917–1937*. Berkeley: University of California Press, 2001.

Shimo-sei. "Tsūshin ihō: Taihoku tsūshin" [Communication Bulletin: Taipei Correspondence]. *Taiwan Education* 168 (1916): 73.

Shu, Jing. "Chan: yefang Zhang Ailing" [Cicadas: Evening Chat with Eileen Chang]. In *Zhang Ailing pingshuo liushi nian* [Sixty-Year Criticisms of Eileen Chang], edited by Zi Tong and Yi Qing, 146–158. Beijing: Zhongguo huaqiao, 2001.

Sing-co. "Huaming de yanjiu (xu)" [A Study of the Film Titles (Continued)]. Film Corner, *Chinese Mail*, August 9, 1924.

Stamp, Shelly. *Movie-Struck Girls: Women and Motion Picture Culture after the Nickelodeon*. Princeton, NJ: Princeton University Press, 2000.

Standish, Isolde. *A New History of Japanese Cinema: A Century of Narrative Film*. New York: Continuum, 2006.

Strauven, Wanda. *The Cinema of Attractions Reloaded*. Amsterdam: Amsterdam University Press, 2006.

Sugawara, Yoshino. "Beyond the Boundary between China and the West: Changing Identities of Foreign-registered Film Theatre Companies in Republican Shanghai." *Journal of Chinese Cinemas* 9, no. 1 (2015): 23–41.

Sugawara, Yoshino. "Minkokuki Shanghai no eigakan ni tsuite: kokusan eiga jōeikan to eigakan no keiei jōkyo o chūshin ni" [Film Theaters in Shanghai in the Republic of China: Research on the Business Operations of Theaters Showing Chinese Films]. *Yaso* 81 (2008): 94–111.

Sugawara, Yoshino. "'Waizatsu' no higan e: 'Kenzen naru goraku' toshite no eiga no tanjō to Shanghai Y.M.C.A." [Toward the Opposite Side of "Vulgarity": The Birth of Cinema as a "Healthful Entertainment"]. *Japanese Journal of Image Arts and Sciences* 90 (2013): 41–56.

Sugawara, Yoshino. "Zouxiang 'Weiza' de bian: Zuowei 'jiankang yule' de dianying zhi dansheng yu Shanghai jidujiao qingnianhui" [Toward the Opposite side of "Vulgarity": The Birth of Cinema as a "Healthful Entertainment"]. *Communication and Society* 29 (2014): 147–172.

Sun, Lei. "Mingxing yingpian gongsi" [The Mingxing Film Company]. In *Zhongguo dianying: miaoshu yu chanshi* [Chinese Cinema: Descriptions and Interpretations], edited by Lu Hongshi, 115–173. Beijing: Zhonguo dianying, 2002.

Sun, Lianggong. *Wenyi cidian* [*Wenyi* Dictionary]. Shanghai: Minzhi shuju, 1928.

Sun, Shiyi. "Wan xiaceng de yingju" [Motion Picture for the Underclass]. *Yinxing* 1 (1926): 6–8.

Takamatsu, Toyojirō. *Taiwan dōkakai sōsai Itagaki hakusha kukakka kangei no ji* [A Welcome to Count Itagaki, President of the Taiwan Assimilation Society]. Taihoku: Taiwan Dōjinsha, 1914.

Takekoshi, Yosaburō. *Japanese Rule in Formosa*, translated by George Braithwaite. London, New York, Bombay and Calcutta: Longmans, Green and Co., 1907.

Tam, Enoch Yee-lok. "The Silver Star Group: A First Attempt at Theorizing *Wenyi* in the 1920s." *Journal of Chinese Cinemas* 9, no. 1 (2015): 62–75.

Tanaka, Jun'ichirō. *Nihoneiga hattatsushi I: katsudōshashin jidai* [A History of the Development of Japanese Cinema I: The Katsudo Shashin Era]. Tokyo: Chūō kōronsha, 1961.

Tanaka, Jun'ichirō. *Nihon kyōiku eiga hattatsushi* [History of the Development of Japanese Educational Film]. Tokyo: Kagyūsha, 1979.

Tang, Weimin. "Youyi wenyi zhandou fusheng, dianying zhengjing jiankong qifei, xushiwenben meixue zaixian: Liushi niandai Taiwan jiankangxieshi dianying de jueqi" [Recurring Right-Wing *Wenyi* Discursive Tactics, Policing the Political Economy of Cinematic Production, and Representing Narrative Aesthetic: The Rise of Healthy Realistic Cinema in Taiwan]. PhD diss., Fu Jen Catholic University, 2008.

Taylor, Jeremy E. *Rethinking Transnational Chinese Cinemas: The Amoy-Dialect Film Industry in Cold War Asia*. London: Routledge, 2011.

Teo, Stephen. "Chinese Melodrama: The *Wenyi* Genre." In *Traditions in World Cinema*, edited by Linda Badley, R. Barton Palmer, and Steven Jay Schneider, 203–213. Edinburgh: Edinburgh University Press, 2006.

Teo, Stephen. "The Hong Kong Cantonese Cinema: Emergence, Development and Decline." In *The Chinese Cinema Book*, edited by Song Hwee Lim and J. Ward, 103–110. London: British Film Institute, 2011.

Teo, Stephen. *Hong Kong Cinema: The Extra Dimension*. London: BFI Publishing, 1997.

Teo, Stephen. *Wong Kar-wai*. London: BFI Publishing, 2005.

Tepperman, Charles E. *Amateur Cinema: The Rise of North American Movie Making, 1923–1960*. Berkeley: University of California Press, 2015.

Thompson, Kristin, and David Bordwell. *Film History: An Introduction*. New York: McGraw-Hill, 1994.

Tian, Han. "Yinse de meng xu" [The Silver Dream Continued]. *Yinxing* 6 (1927): 8–15.

Toda, Seizō. "Katsudōshashin ni tsuite" [About Motion Pictures]. *Taiwan Education* 261 (1924): 68–77.

Ts'ai, Caroline Hui-yu. *Taiwan in Japan's Empire Building: An Institutional Approach to Colonial Engineering*. London: Routledge, 2009.

Tsai, Chin-tang. "Jiaoyu chiyu, yuzhenying yu xiushen jiaokeshu" [The Imperial Rescript on Education, the Imperial Portrait, and Teaching Morals Education]. *Journal of Taiwan History* 2 (2006): 133–166.

Tsau, Shu-ying. "They Learn in Suffering What They Teach in Song: Lu Xun and Kuriyagawa Hakuson's Symbols of Anguish." In *Symbols of Anguish: In Search of Melancholy in China*, edited by Wolfgang Kubin, 441–469. Bern: Peter Lang, 2001.

Tsing-po. "Yingpian wenti de taolun" [A Discussion on Film]. Film Corner, *Chinese Mail*, May 31, 1924.

Tsivian, Yuri. *Early Cinema in Russia and its Cultural Reception*. New York: Routledge, 1994.

Tsurumi, E. Patricia. *Japanese Colonial Education in Taiwan, 1895–1945*. Cambridge, MA: Harvard University Press, 1977.

Tsz-suet. "Shezhi yingpian de shouxu (xu)" [How to Shoot a Film (Continued)]. Film Corner, *Chinese Mail*, November 8, 1924.

Tsz-suet. "Yingmu tanpian" [About the Silver Screen]. Film Corner, *Chinese Mail*, August 23, 1924.

Tudor, J. M. *Sound and Sense Music and Musical Metaphor in the Thought and Writing of Goethe and His Age*. New York: Peter Lang, 2011.

U.S. Department of Commerce. *Motion Pictures in China*. Washington, DC: U.S. Government Printing Office, 1930.

Wa. "Yingpian de timing" [The Naming of Films]. Film Corner, *Chinese Mail*, November 15, 1924.

Wang, Chaoguang. *Yingyi de zhengzhi: Minguo dianying jiancha zhidu yanjiu* [The Politics of Film Art: A Study of the Institution of Film Censorship in the Republican Era]. Beijing: Zhongguo renmin daxue chubanshe, 2013.

Wang, Chunchi. "Xiandai lianai yu chuantong jiating de lunli chongtu: Cong Taiyu dianying jiating lunli wenyi aiqing leix- ing kan 1950–1960 niandai aiqing, hunting, jianting de daode xiangxiang" [Ethical Conflicts between Modern Romance Relationships and Traditional Family: An Investigation of the Moral Imagination of Romance, Marriage, and Family in the 1950s and 1960s through the Lens of Tai-Language Familial Ethic and Romantic *Wenyi* Film]. *Applied Ethics Review* 53 (2012): 57–81.

Wang, David Der-wei. "Chinese Literature from 1841–1937." In *The Cambridge History of Chinese Literature*, vol. 2, *From 1375*, edited by Kang-I Sun Chang and Stephen Owen, 413–564. Cambridge: Cambridge University Press, 2010.

Wang, David Der-wei. *Fin-de-siecle Splendor: Repressed Modernities of Late Qing Fiction, 1849–1911*. Stanford, CA: Stanford University Press, 1997.

Wang, Di. *The Teahouse: Small Business, Everyday Culture, and Public Politics in Chengdu, 1900–1950*. Stanford, CA: Stanford University Press, 2008.

Wang, Gang. *An Illustrated Story of Wyndham Street, Hong Kong 1840s–1960s*. Hong Kong: Chung Hwa Book Co., 2008.

Wang, Molin. *Daoyan yu zuopin* [Directors and Their Works]. Taipei: Lianya chubanshe, 1978.

Wang, Molin. *Zhongguo dianying yu xiju* [Chinese Film and Drama]. Taipei: Lianya chubanshe, 1981.

Wang, Yiman. "*The Love Parade* Goes On: 'Western-Costume Cantonese Opera Film' and the Foreignizing Remake." In *Remaking Chinese Cinema: Through the Prism of Shanghai, Hong Kong, and Hollywood*. Honolulu: University of Hawai'i Press, 2013.

Wang, Yiman. "The 'Transnational' as Methodology: Transnationalizing Chinese Film Studies through the Example of *The Love Parade* and Its Chinese Remakes." *Journal of Chinese Cinemas* 2, no. 1 (2008): 10.

Wang, Youyou. "Guoqu de kaixin wanyi'er" [Little Toy in the Past]. *Kaixin tekan* 3 (1926): 2.

Washitani, Hana. "The Revival of '*Gentou*' (magic lantern, filmstrips, slides) in Showa Period Japan: Focusing on Its Developments in the Media of Post-war Social Movements." *Iconics* 11 (2014): 27–46.

Wasko, Janet. *How Hollywood Works*. Padstow, Cornwall: SAGE, 2003.

Wei, Shaochang. *Wo kan yuanyang hudie pai* [My View of the Mandarin Ducks and Butterflies School]. Hong Kong: Chung Hwa, 1990.

Wong, Ain-ling. "The Black-and-White *Wenyi* Films of Shaws." In *China Forever: The Shaw Brothers and Diasporic Cinema*, edited by Poshek Fu, 115–132. Urbana: University of Illinois Press, 2008.

Wong, Ain-ling, ed. *The Cinema of Lee Sun-fung*. Hong Kong: Hong Kong Film Archive, 2004.

Wong, Ain-ling, ed. *The Hong Kong-Guangdong Film Connection*. Hong Kong: Hong Kong Film Archive, 2005.

Wong Ain-ling, ed., *An Age of Idealism: Great Wall & Feng Huang Days*. Hong Kong: Hong Kong Film Archive, 2001.

Wong, Ain-ling, ed. *Li Han-hsiang, Storyteller*. Hong Kong: Hong Kong Film Archive, 2007.

Wong, Ain-ling, ed. *Zhongguo dianying suyuan* [Chinese Cinema: Tracing the Origins]. Hong Kong: Hong Kong Film Achieve, 2011.

Wong Ain-ling, ed., *Zhu Shilin: A Filmmaker of His Times*. Hong Kong: Hong Kong Film Archive, 2008.

Wong, Ain-ling, and Angel Shing, eds. *Wang Tianlin [Director Wong Tin-lam]*. Hong Kong: Hong Kong Film Archive, 2007.

Wong, Lai-ming, ed. *Bujing moshushi: Chen Qirui, Chen Jingsen fuzi de bujing meixue* [A Touch of Magic: Veteran Set Designers Chan Ki-yui & Chan King-sam]. Hong Kong: Hong Kong Film Archive, 2013.

Xiao, Zhiwei. "Movie House Etiquette Reform in Early-Twentieth-Century China." *Modern China* 32, no. 4 (2006): 513–536.

Xiao, Zhiwei. "Translating American Films into Chinese Audiences." In *Transnational Asian Identities in Pan-Pacific Cinemas: The Reel Asian Exchange*, edited by Philippa Gates and Lisa Funnell, 88–100. New York: Routledge, 2012.

Xin, Min. "Yingpian yu xiaoshuo zhi butong" [The Differences between Film and Literature]. *Yinxing* 3 (1926): 37.

Xiong, Ying. "Ethno Literary Identity and Geographical Displacement: Liu Na'ou's Chinese Modernist Writing in the East Asian Context." *Asian Culture and History* 3, no. 1 (2011): 3–13.

Xu, Jianxiong. *Jingju yu Shanghai dushi shehui (1867–1949)* [Peking Opera and Urban Society in Shanghai]. Shanghai: Shanghai sanlian shudian, 2012.

Xu, Zhuodai. "Shi xiangyan pigu zhuyi" [Scavenger Mode]. *Kaixin tekan* 2 (1926): 4–8.
Xu, Zhuodai. "Wo ban yingxi gongsi de shibai tan" [The Failure of My Film Company]. *Dianying yuebao* 2 (1928): 92.
Xu, Zhuodai. "Yingxi zhe xi ye" [Film Is Drama]. *Minxin tekan* 3 (1926): 17.
Xu, Zhuodai. "Yishu shang de *Hongfen kulou* (yi)" [The Art of *Women Skeletons*, Part I]. *Shenbao*, June 13, 1922.
Xu, Zhuodai. "Yishu shang de *Hongfen kulou* (er)" [The Art of *Women Skeletons*, Part II]. *Shenbao*, June 14, 1922.
Xu, Zhuodai. "Yishu shang de *Hongfen kulou* (san)" [The Art of *Women Skeletons*, Part III]. *Shenbao*, June 15, 1922.
Xu, Zhuodai. "Yishu shang de *Hongfen kulou* (si)" [The Art of *Women Skeletons*, Part IV]. *Shenbao*, June 16, 1922.
Xu, Zhuodai. "Yishu shang de *Hongfen kulou* (wu)" [The Art of *Women Skeletons*, Part V]. *Shenbao*, June 17, 1922.
Xue, Feng. "'Fuxian lishi piping' yu Zhongguo chuantong de xiandai huixiang: yi ershi shiji er san shi niandai 'yuanyang hudie pai' wenren de dianying piping wei zhongxin" ["Bifurcated Historic Review" and Modern Echo of Chinese Tradition: Using Mandarin Ducks and Butterflies Literati's Film Criticisms in the 1920s and 1930s as Examples]. *Dangdai dianying* 5 (2010): 101–107.
Xue, Feng. "'Richang wenhua piping': xiandai Zhongguo chenshi pingmin shenghuo de zhinan yu xiangxiang—yi ershi shiji er san shiniandai 'yuanyang hudie pai' wenren de yingping shuxie wei zhongxin" ["Everyday Cultural Criticism": Guidance and Imagination of the Everyday Life in Modern Chinese Cities—from the Perspective of Film Criticism of Mandarin Ducks and Butterflies Literati in the 1920s and 1930s]. *Dangdai dianying* 10 (2012): 101–106.
Yan, Duhe. "Guochan yousheng dianying diyisheng" [The First Voice of Chinese-Produced Sound Film]. *Genü Hongmudan tekan* (1931): 20.
Yan, Duhe, ed., *Mingxing yingpian gongsi tianzhao xingu jihuashu* [Proposal for Share Subscriptions for the Mingxing Film Company]. 1926.
Yanaihara, Tadao. *Teikoku shugika no Taiwan* [Taiwan under Japanese Imperialism]. Tokyo: Iwanami Shoten, 1929.
Yang, Yingyu. "Jindai Guangzhou changti de xingzhu yu Guangzhou chengshi fazhan de guanxi" [The Relationship between the Construction of the Long Bund of Guangzhou and the Urban Development of Guangzhou in Modern History]. *Guangdong shizhi* 4 (2002): 12–17.
Yasuyama-sei. "Tsūshin ihō: Taihoku tsūshin" [Communication Bulletin: Taipei Correspondence]. *Taiwan Education* 322 (1929): 133–134.
Yat-man. "Lun wuguo dianying nüjue zhi fuzhuang" [About the Costume for Chinese Actresses]. Film Corner, *Chinese Mail*, December 20, 1924.
Yat-shi. "Pingju zuidi xiandu zhi tiaojian" [The Least Quality That a Film Critic Should Possess]. Film Corner, *Chinese Mail*, August 9, 1924.
Yat-shi. "Yingmu tanpian" [About the Silver Screen]. Film Corner, *Chinese Mail*, June 28, 1924.
Yau, Shuk-ting. "Cong Chuangu Chuangping kan ersanshi niandai Zhong Ri dianying jiaoliu" [Sino-Japanese Film Activity Exchanges in the 1920s and 1930s through the Case of Kawatani Shohei]. *Dianying yishu* 341 (2011): 127–132.

Yeh, Emilie Yueh-yu. "A Small History of *Wenyi*." In *Oxford Handbook of Chinese Cinema*, edited by Carlos Rojas and Eileen Chow, 225–249. New York: Oxford University Press, 2013.

Yeh, Emilie Yueh-yu. "Between Shanghai and Hong Kong: The Politics of Chinese Cinemas." Review of *Between Shanghai and Hong Kong: The Politics of Chinese Cinemas*, by Poshek Fu. *Film Quarterly* 59, no. 3 (2006): 64–65.

Yeh, Emilie Yueh-yu, ed. *Huayu dianying gongye: Fangfa yu lishi de xin tansuo* [Rethinking the Chinese Film Industry: New Histories, Mew Methods]. Beijing: Beijing University Press, 2011.

Yeh, Emilie Yueh-yu. "New Takes on Film Historiography: Republican Cinema Redux, An Introduction." *Journal of Chinese Cinemas* 9, no. 1 (2015): 1–7.

Yeh, Emilie Yueh-yu. "Pitfalls of Cross-Cultural Analysis: Chinese *Wenyi* Film and Melodrama." *Asian Journal of Communication* 19, no. 4 (2009): 438–452.

Yeh, Emilie Yueh-yu. "The Road Home: Stylistic Renovations of Chinese Mandarin Classics." In *Cinema Taiwan: Politics, Popularity and State of Arts*, edited by Darrell William Davis and Ru-shou Robert Chen, 203–216. Oxford: Routledge, 2007.

Yeh, Emilie Yueh-yu. "Translating *Yingxi*: Chinese Film Genealogy and Early Cinema in Hong Kong." *Journal of Chinese Cinemas* 9, no. 1 (2015): 76–109.

Yeh, Emilie Yueh-yu. "*Wenyi* and the Branding of Early Chinese Film." *Journal of Chinese Cinemas* 6, no. 1 (2012): 65–94.

Yeh, Emilie Yueh-yu, Feng Xiaocai, and Liu Hui, eds. *Zouchu Shanghai: Zaoqi dianying de linglei jingguan* [Beyond Shanghai: New Perspectives on Early Chinese Cinema]. Beijing: Beijing University Press, 2016.

Yeh, Emilie Yueh-yu, Feng Xiaocai, Liu Hui, and Poshek Fu, eds. *Early Chinese Film Database*, Hong Kong: Hong Kong Baptist University Library, 2015. http://digital.lib.hkbu.edu.hk/chinesefilms/

Yeh, Lung-yen. *Rizhi shiqi Taiwan dianying shi* [The History of Taiwanese Movies during the Japanese Colonization]. Taipei: Yushan, 1998.

Yeh, Lung-yen. *Taipei Ximenting dianying shi, 1896–1997* [The Film History of Ximenting in Taipei, 1896–1997]. Taipei: Xingzhengyuan wenhua jianshe weiyuanhui: Guojia dianying ziliaoguan, 1997.

Yeh, Wen-hsin. "Shanghai Modernity: Commerce and Culture in a Republican City." *China Quarterly* 150 (1997): 378.

Yeh, Wen-hsin. *Shanghai Splendor: A Cultural History, 1843–1949*. Berkeley: University of California Press, 2008.

Yeh, Yueh-yu. "Historiography and Sinification: Music in Chinese Cinema of the 1930s." *Cinema Journal* 40, no. 3 (2002): 78–97.

Ying, Dou. "Zhipian gongsi ying jiqi zhuyi zhege wenti, shang" [The Urgent Issues Concerning Production Companies, Part 1]. *Yinxing* 16 (1928): 10–13.

Yu, Dafu. "Dianying yu *wenyi*" [Film and *Wenyi*]. *Yinxing* 12 (1927): 12–17.

Yu, Mo-wan. *Xianggang dianying shihua (juan yi)-mopian niandai: 1896–1929* [Notes on Hong Kong Film History I: The Silent Era, 1896–1929]. Hong Kong: Subculture Press, 1996.

Yu, Mo-wan. "Xianggang yueju dianying fazhan shihua" [Words on the History of Development of the Hong Kong Cantonese Opera Film]. In *The 11th Hong Kong Film Festival: Cantonese Opera Film Retrospective*. Hong Kong: Hong Kong Urban Council, 1987.

Yu, Mo-wan. "Xue Juexian yu dianying" [Xue Juexian and Cinema]. In *Zhen shan mei:*

Xue Juexian yishu rensheng [The Authentic, the Good, and the Beautiful: Xue Juexian's Artistic Life], edited by Guangdong Bihe huiguan and Hong Kong University Art Museum. Hong Kong: Hong Kong University Art Museum, 2009.

Yu, Shengwu, and Liu Cunkuan. *Shijiu shiji de xianggang* [Hong Kong in the Nineteenth Century]. Hong Kong: Qilun, 1994.

Yung, Sai-shing. *Xunmi Yueju shengying: Cong Hongchuan dao Shuiyindeng* [Tracing Cantonese Opera: From Red Boat to Silver Light]. Hong Kong: Oxford University Press, 2012.

Yung, Sai-shing. *Yueyun Liusheng: Changpian gongye yu Guangdong quyi 1903–1953* [Recording Cantonese Tunes: The Gramophone Industry and Cantonese Folk Arts, 1903–1953]. Hong Kong: Cosmic Books, 2006.

Zhan, Jinni. "Minguo Guangzhou Zhongyang gongyuan yu shimin shenghuo de gonggong xing" [Guangzhou Central Park and the Public Nature of Civilian Lives during the Period of the Republic of China]. *Heilongjiang shizhi* 17 (2009): 117–118.

Zhang, Fangwei. "Sanshi niandai Guangdong yueju gaikuang" [An Overview of Cantonese Opera of the 1930s]. *Chinese opera website*, last modified January 14, 2014, http://www.yuejuopera.org.cn/yjjs2/yjgs/zjlwkzyd/20140114/26.html

Zhang, Huiyu. "Yingxilun de xingcheng: chongti shangshiji bashi niandai de yici dianying shixue yanjiu" [The Formation of *Yingxi*: Reaffirming a Study on Cinematic History in the 1980s]. *Film Art* 350 (2013): 103–111.

Zhang, Ling. "Rhythmic Movement: The City Symphony and Transcultural Transmediality: Liu Na'ou and *The Man Who Has a Camera* (1933)." *Journal of Chinese Cinemas* 9, no. 1 (2015): 42–61.

Zhang, Qian. "From Hollywood to Shanghai, American Silent Films in China." PhD diss., University of Pittsburgh, 2009.

Zhang, Rougu. "Dianying yu shengjing" [Film and the Bible]. *Yingxin* 5 (1927): 20–24.

Zhang, Rougu. "Diba yishu" [The Eighth Art]. *Yingxin* 8 (1927): 20–24.

Zhang, Shichuan. "Zi wo daoyan yilai" [Since My Director Career Commenced]. *Minxin* 3 (1935): 10–14.

Zhang, Wei. *Yuanyang hudie pai wenxue yu zaoqi Zhongguo dianying de chuangzuo* [Mandarin Ducks and Butterflies Literature and Early Chinese Film Production]. Beijing: China Film Press, 2004.

Zhang, Xiaohui. *Minguo shiqi Guangdong de duiwai jingji guanxi* [The Foreign Economic Relations of Guangzhou during the Period of the Republic of China]. Beijing: Shehui kexue wenxian chubanshe, 2011.

Zhang, Yingjin, ed. *Cinema and Urban Culture in Shanghai, 1922–1943*. Stanford, CA: Stanford University Press, 1999.

Zhang, Yingjin. *Chinese National Cinema*. New York: Routledge, 2004.

Zhang, Yingjin. *Screening China: Critical Interventions, Cinematic Reconfigurations and the Transnational Imaginary in Contemporary Chinese Cinema*. Ann Arbor, MI: Center for Chinese Studies, 2002.

Zhang, Yingjin, and Zhiwei Xiao. *Encyclopaedia of Chinese Cinema*. London: Routledge, 1998.

Zhang, Zhen. *An Amorous History of the Silver Screen: Shanghai Cinema, 1896–1937*. Chicago: University of Chicago Press, 2005.

Zhang, Zhen. "Transplanting Melodrama: Observations on the Emergence of Early Chinese Narrative Film." In *A Companion to Chinese Cinema*, edited by Yingjin Zhang, 25–41. Malden, MA: Wiley-Blackwell, 2012.

Zhang, Zhiwei. *Jiduhua yu shisuhua de zhengzha: Shanghai jidujiao qingnianhui yanjiu 1900–1922* [The Struggle between Christianity and Secularization: Research on the Shanghai YMCA, 1900–1922]. Taipei: Taiwan daxue chubanshe, 2010.

Zhao, Weifang. *Xianggang dianying shi (1897–2006)* [A History of Hong Kong Cinema (1897–2006)]. Beijing: China Broadcast Television Press, 2007.

Zhao, Weiqing. *Shanghai gonggong zujie dianying shencha (1927–1937)* [The Film Censorship of the Shanghai International Settlement: 1927–1937]. Shanghai: Shanghai jiaotong daxue chubanshe, 2012.

Zhao, Xiaoxuan. *Yuanyang hudie pai xinlun* [The New Discussion and Evaluation of the Mandarin Ducks and Butterflies School]. Lanzhou: Lanzhou University Press, 2004.

Zheng, Junli. *Xiandai Zhongguo dianying shi lue* [A Brief History of Modern Chinese Cinema]. Shanghai: Shanghai liangyou, 1936.

Zheng, Zhengcheng. *Renshi tazhe de tiankong: Rizhi shiqi Taiwan yuanzhumin de guanguang xinglü* [The Sky of the Other: Indigenous People's Sightseeing Tours in Colonial Taiwan]. Taipei: Boyang wenhua shiye youxian gongsi, 2005.

Zhong, Dafeng. "Lun 'yingxi'" [On "Shadow Play"]. *Beijing dianying xuebao* 2 (1985): 54–92.

Zhong, Dafeng. "'Yingxi' lilun lishi suoyuan" [Tracing the History of the "Shadow Play" Theory]. *Dangdai dianying* 3 (1986): 75–80.

Zhong, Ru. "Huanan di yi jian dianyingyuan tao youshengpian shi shemo?" [Which Was the First Sound Film Shown in Southern China?]. *Huanan dianying* 5 (1944): 8.

Zhou, Chengren, and Li Yizhuang. *Zaoqi Xianggang dianying shi, 1897–1945* [A History of Early Hong Kong Film, 1897–1945]. Hong Kong: Joint Publishing, 2005.

Zhou, Chengren. "Shanghai's Unique Film Productions and Hong Kong's Early Cinema." In *The Shaw Screen: A Preliminary Study*, edited by Ain-ling Wong, 19–36. Hong Kong: Hong Kong Film Archive, 2003.

Zhou, Haibin. "Jiaguo guangying kaiguo yuanxun houren koushu (11)" [Light and Shadow of Family and State: Oral Histories by the Heirs of the Founding Fathers of the Country (11)]. *Beijing wanbao*, June 15, 2011. Retrieved from http://blog.sina.com.cn/s/blog_55dde65f0102eej6.html?tj=1

Zhou, Jianyun, Chen Zuiyun, Wang Xuchang, and Cheng Bugao. *Dianying jiangyi* [Syllabus on Introduction to Motion Pictures]. Shanghai: Dadong Book Store, 1924.

Zhou, Jianyun. "Benkan Zhi Shiming" [The Mission of the Journal]. *Mingxing tekan* 1 (1925): 1–8.

Zhou, Jianyun. "Zhongguo yingpian zhi qiantu (1)" [The Future of Chinese Films (1)]. In *Dianying yuebao (April 1928—September 1929)*, edited by Feng Pei-ling, 9–11. Shanghai: Shanghai Academy of Social Sciences Press.

Zhou, Shoujuan. "Ai zhi fendou" [Strive for Love]. *Libai liu* 153 (1922): 11–16.

Zhou, Shoujuan. "Axiong" [The Elder Brother]. *Libai liu* 24 (1914): 11–28.

Zhou, Shoujuan. "Bu bi zhi men" [The Open Gate]. *Libai liu* 59 (1915): 14–28.

Zhou, Shoujuan. "Hedeng yingxiong" [What a Hero]. *Youxi zazhi* 9 (1914): 27–44.

Zhou, Shoujuan. "Laba dao sheng" [Trumpet Island 1]. *Youxi shijie* 14 (1922): 1–7.

Zhou, Shoujuan. "Nü zhen hua" [Flower of Female Chastity]. *Xiaoshuo daguan* 11 (1917): 1–12.

Zhou, Shoujuan. "Pangbeicheng zhi mori" [The Last Days of Pompeii]. *Libai liu* 32 (1915): 1–20.

Zhou, Shoujuan. "Qi zhi xin" [The Heart of the Wife]. *Zhonghua funü jie* 1, no. 2 (1915): 329–339.

Zhou, Shoujuan. "Waiting." *Libai liu* 25 (1914): 1–6.

Zhou, Shoujuan. "Wuhu . . . Zhan" [Alas . . . Fight]. *Libai liu* 33 (1915): 7–19.

Zhou, Shoujuan, ed. *Xia chanzhu tekan* [*The Boy Heiress* Special Issue]. October 4, 1925.

Zhou, Shoujuan. "*Xia changzhu* benshi" [Synopsis of *The Boy Heiress*]. *Xia chanzhu tekan*, October 4, 1925.

Zhou, Shoujuan. "Xiao changzhu" [The Boy Heiress]. *Xiao Changzhu tekan* (1925): 45–58.

Zhou, Shoujuan. *Zhou Shoujuan shuo ji xiace* [Collected Fiction of Zhou Shoujuan]. Vol. 2. Shanghai: Dadong shuju, 1927.

Zhou, Wan-yao. *Haiyang yu zhimindi Taiwan lunji* (Essays on Maritime and Colonial Taiwan). Taipei: Lianjing chuban shiye gufen youxian gongsi, 2012.

Zhu, Shouju. "Shu Shanghai Yingxi Gongsi chungli jingguo" [On the Establishment of the Shanghai Film Company]. *Yue du MOOK* 33 (2013): 88–95.

Zimmermann, Patricia R. *Reel Families: A Social History of Amateur Film*. Bloomington: Indiana University Press, 1995.

Index

Note: Page numbers in italics refer to the tables.

absolute cinema, 284
Administrating Aborigines Plan, 105–7
affiliation, 5, 23, 31, 62, 206, 229
Akashi, Motojirō, 109
An Amorous History in the Jade Palace (*Xuangong yanshi*, 1934), 158. *See also The Love Parade*
An Amorous Man (*Duoqing de gege*, 1928), *262*, *265*
An Amorous Wife (*Fengliu shaonainai*, 1927), *262*, *265*
Another Village (Youyicun), 24–25
Apocalypse Now (1979), 301n89
Apollo Theatre, *193*, 195n5, 198n35
Army Dream (*Congjun meng*, 1926), 84–85, 143, *144*
Artland (*Yilin*), 167, 174n20
Asiatic Film Company, 204–8, 210–12, 218n18, 220n30, 220n33
assimilation policy, 55, 58–60, 109, 116
avant-garde, 13, 279, 280, 282, 285, 289, 292n7, 295n17

Baiyue Film Company, 143, *144*, 145
Ballet Mécanique (1924), 298n44
Báng-kah, 51–53
banjin, 63, 108
Bao, Qingjia, 11, 192, 197n24
Bao, Tianxiao, 246–47, 250–52, 258–59, *262*, *265*
Bao, Weihong, 4, 45n10
Baudelaire, Charles, 233, 236
A Beauty Remembered (*Renmian taohua*, 1925), *265*
A Beauty's Seduction (*Meiren guan*, 1928), 250, *266*
A Beauty's Trap (*Meiren ji*, 1927), *263*
benshi (*benzi*), 7, 54, 57–58, 65–66
Berlin, Symphony of a Great City (*Berlin: Die Sinfonie der Großstadt*, 1927), 280, 286, 295n17
Berry, Chris, 31
Big Asia Film Company (Daya), 148
Bijou Scenic Theatre, 39, 49n75, 76–81. *See also* Coronet Theatre
Biweekly (*Banyue*), 253
Blind Love (*Mangmu de aiqing*, 1929), *262*
Blood of the Beauty (*Meiren xue*, 1948), 274n29
Bonjour Cinéma (1921), 285
Bourdieu, Pierre, 248–49
bourgeois public sphere, 72, 88, 93
The Boy Heiress (*Xiao changzhu*, 1925), 258–59
Brodsky, Benjamin, 206, 208, 218n18, 219n28, 220n40
A Bronx Morning (1931), 295n17
Bryant, Charles, 233
Bu, Wancang, 224–25, 250–51, *262*, *266*
bungei 225, 227. *See also wenyi* film
The Burning of Red Lotus Temple (*Huoshao hongliansi*, 1928), 215

Burning of the Nine-Dragon Mountain (*Huoshao Jiulongshan*, 1930), 263

Cabiria (1914), 261
Cai, Chusheng, 233, 298n51
Cai, Guorong, 224
The Calamity of Money (*Jinqian nie*, 1924), 84–85
Canton–Hong Kong strike, 142, 150
Cantonese film (cinema), 9–10, 137, 139, 143, 145, 148–51, 156–60, 162–64, 166–67, 169, 171–72, 173n7, 174n13, 175n24, 175n30
Cantonese opera, 156–58, 161–62, 170–71, 173n9, 174–75n22; film, 158–60, 165; Western-costume Cantonese opera (*xizhuang yueju*), 158, 163, 165, 176n42
Cantophone cinema, 3, 9–10. *See also* Cantonese film
Cao, Xuegeng, 182
Carlton Theatre, 198n35, 213
Cathay Theatre, 213
censorship, 4, 53, 102, 122, 156–57, 166–67, 169, 171, 175n30, 245
Chains of Debt (*Lianhuan zhai*, 1926), 263
Chan, Ming K., 148
charity, 7, 37, 40, 64
Charvet, Maurice, 24, 74, 96n12
Chen, Baoqi, 265
Chen, Duxiou, 247
Chen, Jianhua, 245, 249, 257–58, 275n44
Chen, Jiongming, 140, 154n20
Chen, Junchao (Chan Kwan-chiu), 81, 84–85, 143
Chen, Shouyin, 265
Chen, Tian, 266
Chen, Xihe, 28–30, 33
Chen, Zhiqing, 228–29, 233–35
Cheng, Bugao, 196n7, 250, 253, 257, 265–66
Cheng, Jihua, 19, 25, 153n15, 204, 214
Cheng, Xiaoqing, 246
China Cinema Company, 206
China Film School (Zhonghua dianying xuexiao), 256
The China Mail, 34–35, 74, 76–77
China Sun Motion Picture Company (Minxin), 42, 83–85, 142, 144
The Chinese Mail (*Wah Tsz Yat Po*), 26, 35–36, 75–76, 79–81, 83–87, 94
Chongqing Theatre (Chung Hing), 38, 79–80
Chow, Eileen Cheng-ying, 245
Chow, Rey, 270n3
cine-fiction (*yingxi xiaoshuo*), 3, 5, 12, 246–47, 250–52, 256–60, 263, 267, 270
cinema of reassurance, 43–44
cinematograph, 15, 27, 34–35, 39, 74–78, 124n3, 249. *See also* Lumière
City Scenes (*Dushi fengguang*, 1935), 298n51
City Symphony (1930), 295n17
city symphony, 279–83, 286
civilization, 5, 57, 63, 89, 104, 112, 141, 179
civilized drama (*wenmingxi*), 179, 210, 225, 229
Clair, René, 286, 298n44
Clan of the Sea (*Umi no gōzoku*, 1942), 121
colonial, 1, 3, 5, 13, 15nn13–14, 203, 212, 280, 290–91, 301n91; Hong Kong, 6–7, 34, 40–41, 72–73, 77–78; in Guangzhou, 9, 135, 140, 148, 151; in Shanghai, 181, 279, 294n13; Japanese's governance in Taiwan, 60–64, 101–5, 107–11, 114–16, 118, 120–23, 127nn35–36m 128n41; Taiwan, 4, 7–8, 51–55, 58, 65–68, 106, 112–13, 124nn2–3, 126n30, 128n44, 277, 281, 284, 295n23
Commercial Press, 11, 82, 181, 189, 191–193, 196n11, 197n24, 199n37, 200n49, 201n57, 201n61
Conscienceless (*Rendao*, 1932), 225
The Conversation (1974), 301n89
Coronet Theatre, 78, 81, 83–85, 146
cosmopolitanism, 2, 277–78, 290–91
A Couple in Name Only (*Guaming fuqi*, 1927), 251, 262
Cross Theater, 52–53
Crystal Palace, 213
cultural capital, 248–49, 253, 255
Cupid's Feed (*Aishen zhi feiliao*, 1925), 254, 264

Dadaocheng, 51–53
Daffodil Fairies (*Lingbo xianzi*, 1926), 264
Dai, Wangshu, 288, 292n3
Dalai Theatre (Dai Loi), 73
Dan, Duyu, 85, 226, 250, 252, 263, 266
Danhan Company (Dai Hon), 84–85, 142
The Daughter of a Wealthy Family (*Furen zhi nü*, 1926), 262
Den, Kenjirō, 109, 116
Diagonal Symphony (*Symphonie Diagonale*, 1924), 297n44
Diamond Film Company (Zuanshi), 142, 144

diandeng yingxi, 51, 69n1. *See also* magic lantern shows
Dingjun Mountain (*Dingjunshan*, 1905), 32–33
Dirlik, Arif, 204
Divoire, Fernand, 286
Doane, Mary Ann, 25–27

Eastern Association (Toyo Kyokai), 120, 126n30
Edison, Thomas, 52–53, 74–75, 124nn2–3
education, 6, 33–34, 44, 57, 60, 63, 87–88, 90, 93, 104, 110–14, 117–18, 120–21, 128n42, 130n65, 133n102, 180, 182–83, 189–91, 192, 201n57, 227, 232, 234, 238
egoism (*liji zhuyi*), 234–35
electric pictures (*dianhua*), 37, 39
Emak-Bakia (1926), 298n44
Embassy Theatre, 193, 15n13, 198n35
Empire Cinematograph, 77, 80
The End of St. Petersburg (1927), 287
enlightenment, 8, 43, 57, 66, 93, 105, 109, 113, 123
Enthusiasm: The Symphony of the Don Basin (1931), 289
Entr'acte (1924), 298n44
Epstein, Jean, 285–86
Eternal Smile (*Yongyuan de weixiao*, 1936), 288

Fake Mask (*Jia mianju*, 1927), 144
Fallen Plum Blossoms (*Meihua luo*, 1927), 251, 262
Fan, Boqun, 259, 270n3, 274n31
Fan, Victor, 175n26, 232
Fantômas series (1913–14), 187
A Farewell to Arms (1932), 290
Farquhar, Mary Ann, 31
Fate in Tears and Laughter (*Tixiao yinyuan*, 1932), 225–26, 255, 265
Fei, Mu, 225
Feifei Movie Production Company, 162
Feuillade, Louis, 187
field, 1, 5, 12–13, 30–33, 81, 89, 107, 118–19, 159, 172, 183, 189, 207, 223, 225–26, 229, 237, 246–50, 253, 256, 258, 270. *See also* movie field
Fighting for Life (*Pinming*, 1933), 265
Film and Wenyi (*Dianying yu wenyi*), 223, 226, 230–31
Film Corner (*Ying Hei Ho, Yingxihao*), 84; content of, 89–93; introduction of, 86–88. *See also The Chinese Mail*
film exhibition, 1, 3–4, 6, 11, 15nn13–14, 19–20, 21, 25–28, 31, 42–44, 50n82, 159–60, 211, 213–14, 229, 245, 280, 300n80; in Guangzhou, 49n76, 134; in Hong Kong, 7, 33–37, 40–42, 29n75, 71, 74–75, 77–78, 80–81, 83, 85–86, 92, 212; in Shanghai, 10–11, 39, 179–82, 184–88, 190–94, 198n30, 198n37, 199nn42–43, 200n56, 201n57; in Taiwan, 54, 57, 60, 61, 102–6, 114–15, 120, 125n17, 127n35, 129n65, 130n70. *See also* garden; tea house; travelogue
film literati (*dianying wenren*), 3, 10, 12, 244, 246–50, 270; examples of, 251, 253–55, 257
Film Magazine (*Yingxi zazhi*), 226, 228
Film Monthly (*Dianying Yuebao*), 258
Film Pictorial (*Dianying huabao*), 256
Flesh Soup (*Xiaofu geng*, 1922), 199n16
Flower of Love (*Ai zhi hua*), 256
The Fool Pays Respect (*Dailao baishou*, 1933), 149, 216
For My Country (*Man jiang hong*, 1933), 272n11
For the Defense (1916), 187
Fox, 212
Fule Theater, 65
fund-raising, 5, 37, 40, 42, 44, 106

Gao, Jilin, 265–66
Gaosheng Theatre (Ko Shing), 38, 79–80
garden, 19–20, 23–25, 27, 34, 44, 194
gentō-kai, 7, 57–60, 62–63, 67–68
Gernalzick, Nadja, and Gabriele Pisarz-Ramirez, 278–79
Gong, Lusu, 265–66
Gongpingbao (*The Public Comment*), 39, 139
A Good Guy (*Hao nan'er*, 1926), 262
Gotō, Shimpei, 103–4, 107, 119, 125n9
Governor General of Taiwan (GGT), 60–63
Graft (1916), 187
The Grand Duchess and the Waiter (1926), 158, 161, 163
Grand Theatre, 213
Grandview Film Company (Daguan), 147, 149–50
Great China Film Company (Dazonghua), 253. *See also* Great China Lilium Pictures

Great China Lilium Pictures Company (Dazhonghua baihe), 82, 253, 257–59
Great Wall Film Company (Changcheng), 148
Green Poplar, Red Tears (*Lüyang honglei*, 1926), 266
Gu, Jianchen, 204
Gu, Kenfu, 228, 253, 257
Gu, Mingdao, 246
Guan, Wenqing (Kwan Man-ching, Moon Kwan), 138, 147, 153n12
Guan Yu Fooled Cao Cao (*Guangong ci Cao*, 1928), 265
Guangya Company (Kwong Ah), 84–85, 142–43
Guangzhou, 2–6, 8, 10, 20, 49n76, 134, 153n12, 156, 159–62, 171–72, 174n12; history of, 9, 135–138; film companies, 139, 147, 151, 154n22; Lo Kan's role, 81, 143, 149; relationship with Hong Kong 38–39, 142, 145, 148, 150–51, 175n23; theaters in, 145–47. *See also* Guangzhou film
Guangzhou film, 3, 9, 134, 137–40; demise of, 149–50; rise of, 140–43, 144, 145
Guangzhou Nanyue Film Company, 143, 144
Gunning, Tom, 40, 43, 102, 124n4
Guomin Theater, 144, 146

habitus, 248–50
Hagiya, Kenzō, 114, 119, 130n66
Hansen, Franklin H., 290
Hansen, Miriam, 22–23, 93, 260
Hao, Yen-p'ing, 203
Happy Film Company (Kaixin), 254–55, 274n35. *See also Happy Special Issue*
Happy Forest (*Kuaihuo lin*), 255. *See also Xinwenbao*
Happy Special Issue (*Kaixin tekan*), 254
Hara, Takashi, 116
He, Tingran, 11, 192, 194, 197n24, 201n64
healthful entertainment, 10, 39, 179–81, 183–86, 188, 194, 196n9
Her Sorrows (*Ta de tongku*, 1926), 262
Here I am (*Jiushi wo*, 1928), 263
The Heroic Wife (*Xiong xifu*, 1926), 264
Hisazumi, Eiichi, 119
historiography, 1–3, 5–7, 9, 11, 13, 23, 38–30, 33, 42, 55, 67–68, 134, 152, 157, 172, 202, 215, 238, 244–45, 294n15
Hockx, Michel, 227
Hong, Guo-Juin, 54, 101, 123n1
Hong, Shen, 203, 265, 279, 293n11
Hongkew Cinema, 15n13, 195n3, 198n35
Hong Kong, 1–5, 7–8, 11, 15n13, 19–20, 25, 30, 37–38, 43, 71, 94–95, 152n20, 156–57, 159–61, 166–67, 169–72, 173n4, 175n24, 194, 207, 223–25, 245; film companies, 84–85, 175n32, 212; "Film Corner" and *The Chinese Mail*, 86–89, 92–94; film scene of, 38–42, 76–80; history of, 6, 72–73; Lo Kan's role, 81–83, 148–49, 212–13, 216; motion pictures' arrival in, 34–36, 74–75; news in, 33–34; relationship with Guangzhou film, 140–43, 145–48, 153n12; relationship with Guangzhou, 9, 134–35, 137–40, 150–51, 152n2; relationship with Xue Juexian, 162–64, 171. *See also* Cantonese cinema; Cantonese film; Cantophone cinema
Hong Kong Amusements Limited, 212, 215
Hong Kong Cinematograph, 77
Hong Kong Daily Press, 34–35, 74, 78–79
Horizontal-Vertical Orchestra (*Horizontal-Vertitak Messe*, 1921), 297n44
Hou, Yao, 149, 216, 226, 228
How Heroes are Made (1912), 257
Howe, Lyman Hakes, 43
Hu, Jubin, 30, 205, 214, 229
Huanan Film Association, 149
Huang, Gang, 291
Huang, Jen, 52–53
Huang, Kuaisheng, 265
Huang, Nicole, 2
Huang, Zhen, 236
Huygens, Christiaan, 57
hygiene, 7, 37, 40, 115, 118, 130nn69–70, 180, 183, 193, 195, 199n46

An Ill-Fated Couple (*Shuihuo yuanyang*, 1924), 250, 266
Imperial Bioscope and Animated Picture Company, 79
Imperial People Public Service Association, 67
Impressionen vom alten Marseiller Hanfen (vieux port) (1929), 295n17
indigenization of cinema, 3, 7–8, 10; in Hong Kong, 72, 76, 80–81, 86, 94; in Taiwan, 63
Inflation (1927), 298n44
intermediaries, 11, 202–4, 211–13, 215–17

Into the People (*Dao minjian qu*), 232
Intolerance (1916), 261
An Introduction to the Actual Conditions in Taiwan (*Taiwan jikkyō shōkai*, 1907), 108–9, 122, 126n30
The Invisible Cloak (*Yinshen yi*, 1925), 254, 264
Irvine, Clarke, 210
Isis Theatre, 192, 193, 194, 198n35, 213, 260
Israel, Arthur Julius, 206–8, 219n28, 220n30, 220n40
itinerant, 3, 5, 168, 290
Itō, Hirobumi, 103, 125n9

Jade Pear Spirit (*Yu li hun*, 1924), 244
Jenkins, C. Francis, 56, 69n9
Jiang, Qifeng, 263
Jinsheng Theater, 146–47
Jones, Andrew F., 2
Julius Caesar (1916), 187

kaleidoscope, 5, 10, 13, 279, 284
Karma of Love (*Qingyu baojian*, 1929), 263
Kawatani, Shohei, 254, 274n37
kinetoscope, 34, 74, 124n2. *See also* Edison, Thomas
Kircher, Athanasius, 56–57
Kurihara, Kisaburô (Thomas Kurihara), 233
Kuriyagawa, Hakuson, 12, 223, 227, 229–31, 235, 238

Lai, Wing-kee, 80
Lai Brothers, 81, 83
LaMarre, Thomas, 67–68
Lan, Sum-ng, 80
The Last Days of Pompeii (1913), 257, 260–61, 263, 269–70, 275n48, 276nn56–57
The Last Love (*Zhihou zhi ai*, 1932), 265–66
Law, Kar, 224
The Law Breaker (*Mingjiao zuiren*, 1926), 142–43, 144, 45
Lee, Daw-Ming, 8, 53, 283
Lee, Leo Ou-fan, 2
Le Petit Chose (1912), 257, 275n48
Les Misérables (1912), 187
Lewis, Robert E., 182
Li, Baijin, 232
Li, Beihai (Lai Buk-hoi), 32, 81–82, 85, 142
Li, Dazhao, 247
Li, Donghai (Lai Dong-hoi), 81
Li, Haishan (Lai Hoi-shan), 81–82
Li, Minwei (Lai Man-wai), 42, 81–83, 85
Li, Pingqian, 263, 265–66
Liang, Chi-chao, 231, 237
Liang, Liang, 224, 226
Liang, Shaopo (Leung Siu-bo), 85, 142
Liangyi Company (Leung Yee), 84–85, 142
Lilium Pictures (Baihe), 252–53. *See also* Great China Lilium Pictures
Lin, Jianxiang, 280
Lin, Meimei (Lam Mui-mui), 169
Link, Perry, 270n3
Little Friends (*Xiao pengyou*, 1925), 251, 262
Little Lord Fauntleroy (1921), 258
Liu, Chungshan, 265
Liu, Jintao, 145, 154n28
Liu, Na'ou, 12–13, 277–79, 288–92, 292n3, 294nn14–15, 297nn41, 297–98n44, 298n48; amateur film of, 279–81, 283–84; film theory of, 284–88
A Living Billboard (*Huo zhaopai*, 1926), 264
Living Buddha Ji Gong 1–3 (*Jigong huofo 1–3*, 1926–27), 264
Lo, Kan (Lo Gun, Lu Gen), 11, 49n75, 76–78, 81, 83–84, 143, 145, 149, 203, 212–16
Lothar, Rudolph, 277
Love and Duty (*Lianai yu yiwu*, 1931), 225
Love Is Dangerous (*Rouge*, *Yanzhi*, 1925), 85, 142–43, 144
Love Letters (*Aiqing daili ren*), 259
The Love Parade (1929), 158–59, 173n7, 174n10
A Lovelorn Actress (*Duoqing de nüling*, 1926), 262
Lu, Dun, 150–51
Lu, Jie (Lok Key), 197n24, 257–59, 263
Lu, Juefei (Lo Kok-fei), 81, 84–85, 88–89, 91
Lu, Mengshu, 226, 229–30, 233–35
Lu, Sheldon, 4
Lu, Xun, 12, 229–30, 238, 247, 256, 275n45
Lubitsch, Ernst, 158–59, 163, 173n7
The Lucky Man (*Dai zhong fu*, 1925), 263
Lumière, 15, 64, 74, 96n12, 124n3
Luo, Mingyou (Lo Ming-yau), 148–49
Luo, Yongxiang (Law Wing-cheung), 82
Lynch, William Henry, 11, 203–5, 207–8, 210–12, 218n18, 220n36, 220n38, 221n49

Ma, Shizeng, 158–59
Ma Jiefu (1926), 250, 263, 266
Ma Zhenhua (1928), 263
Madam Lü Si (*Lüsi niang*, 1948), 274n29

Madam Nine Flowers (*Jiuhua niang*, 1929), 263
The Magic Club (*Shenxian bang*, 1926), 254, 264
The Magic Eyes (*Qianli yan*, 1927), 265
magic lantern shows, 3, 5, 7, 25–27; as education, 62–64; history of, in Taiwan, 51–55; in Hong Kong, 31, 38, 42, 44; Japanese colonial cultural assimilation in Taiwan, 58–61; screen modernity of, 56–58; Shanghai YMCA and, 184–85, 188–90, 192–93, 200n49, 201n61; war-themed, 65–68. *See also gentō-kai*
The Man Who Has a Camera (1933), 13–14, 277–79, 280, 284, 286, 291; "Human Life," segment of, 281; "Tokyo," segment of, 282; other segments of, 283
Man with a Movie Camera (1929), 283, 295n17, 195n25
Mandarin Ducks and Butterflies (*yuangyang hudie pai*), 12, 226, 244–47, 249–50, 252–54, 256–59, 268–70
Manhatta (1920), 295n17
Mao, Zedong, 204, 238
Matsuzaki, Keiji, 290, 301n94
Metro-Goldwyn-Mayer, 212
Mingda Company (Ming Tat), 81, 83, 143, 146
Mingxing Special (*Mingxian tekan*), 228, 250
Mingyuan Studio, 149
Mingzhu Theater, 144, 146–47
Misawa, Mamie, 102, 112, 118–19, 124, 119
missionary, 5, 15n11, 39, 149, 182, 188–89
Mittler, Barbara, 2
Mo, Gansheng (Mok Kon-sang), 84
modernity, 1–2, 7, 13, 14n4, 23, 51–55, 63, 66–68, 93, 113, 171, 237, 245, 259, 277, 285, 294n15; screen, 56–58
Money Returned (*Huan jin ji*, 1926), 250, 266
Moscow (*Moskva*, 1928), 295n17
Mother (1926), 287
Mother's Happiness (*Ersun fu*, 1926), 253, 263
Moussinac, Léon, 286–87, 297n43
movie field, 12, 246–48, 253–57, 270
The Moving Picture World, 210, 218n18
The Moving Safe (*Huodong yinxiang*, 1926), 264
Mu, Shiying, 285, 292nn2–3, 295n16
Multiply and Make a Fortune (*Tianding facai*, 1928), 144
Murch, Walter, 278, 300n89
Musser, Charles, 22, 43, 56–57
My Kingdom for a Honeymoon (*Xuangong yanshi*, 1958), 173n7
My Kingdom for a Husband (*Xuangong yanshi*, 1957), 173n7
My Pitiful Daughter (*Kelian de guinü*, 1925), 262

Nanguan Theater, 144
Nanyang, 138, 170
Nanyang Brothers Tobacco Company, 160–61
Nanyang Studio, 168
nationalism, 6, 93, 102, 113–14, 118, 123, 202, 204–5, 211, 217
Nationalist Party (Kuomintang, KMT), 1, 136, 148, 156, 204, 244
neosensationalist (*xin ganjue pai*), 277, 285, 292n2
New Helen Theatre, 193, 198n35
New Heroism (*xin yingxiong zhuyi*), 223, 227, 234–38
New Life Movement (*xin shenghuo yundong*), 238
The New Platinum Dragon (*Xin Bajinlong*, 1947), 158, 163–66, 175n26
New Shenbao (*Xin Shenbao*), 252. *See also Shenbao*
New Woman (*Xin nüxing*, 1935), 233, 298n51
The Newlyweds (*Xinren de jiating*, 1925), 262
A Night of Glamour (*Yiye haohua*, 1932), 265–66, 299n70
Nishimura, Hiroshi, 60–61
Nothing But Time (*Rien que les Heures*, 1926), 295n17, 298n44
novelty, 22, 27, 41, 43, 104, 191; as imported, 5, 871–72, 78, 94

Obscenity of the Viper (*Jasei no Midara*, 1921), 233
The Odd Doctor (*Guai yisheng*, 1926), 264, 274n38
Ōhashi, Sutesaburō, 106–7
Okubo, Ryo, 57
An Old Affair (*Qianqing*, 1925), 263
On a Stormy Night (*Fengyuzhi ye*, 1925), 253, 263
On the Cinematograph (*Yingxi hua*), 249
One True Love (*Shui shi zhen ai*), 85
The Open Gate (1909), 257
Orchid of the Valley (*Kong'gu lan*, 1925), 251, 262

An Orphan Rescues His Grandpa (*Gu'er jiuzu ji*, 1923), 85, 93, 226, 265
An Orphan's Escape (*Gu'er tuoxian ji*, 1926), 143, 144, 145
Out of the Hell (*Jie hou yan*, 1925), 272n12

Pacific Film Company (Taipingyang), 148
Pang, Laikwan, 23–25, 27
Paramount, 82, 212
Paris Theatre, 213
Pathé, 77, 82, 127n36, 130n66, 280
The Peach Girl (*Taohua qixue ji*, 1931), 225
Peacock Motion Pictures Company, 214
The Pearl Crown (*Zhenzhu guan*, 1929), 263
Pearl River Film Studio, 151
Pearl Theatre, 213
Peng, Nian (Pang Nin), 81, 83–85
phantasmagoria, 5, 57
photo pictures (*yinghua*), 2, 7, 20, 37–39, 43–44, 92. *See also* photoplay; shadow play
photogénie, 286
photography, 5, 21, 29, 32, 44, 64–65, 82, 120, 122, 279, 281
photoplay (*yingxi*), 7, 27, 38, 42–45. *See also* photo picture; shadow play
Pincus, Leslie, 291
The Platinum Dragon (*Bajinlong*, 1933), 9–10, 150, 156–158, 160–61, 163, 165–68, 171–72, 175nn23–24, 176n42. *See also The New Platinum Dragon*; *The Platinum Dragon: Part Two*
The Platinum Dragon: Part Two (*Xu Bajinlong*, 1937), 167–69, 176n39
A Poet from the Sea (*Haijiao shiren*, 1927), 226
A Poor Man Wins a Lottery (*Khoojin Whatchay*, 1913), 211
projected imagery, 5, 22, 35, 40, 51, 54, 56, 60, 63, 65, 75
propaganda, 6–8, 62, 65–68, 102, 105–8, 117, 119, 122–23; Takamatsu's films as, 103–4, 109
À Propos de Nice (1930), 295n17
public health, 6, 40, 186, 188–89
Pudovkin, Vsevolod, 287, 297n43
pure cinema, 284, 286–87
Purity (1916), 257

Qin, Jian (Chin Chien, Kim Chun), 224
Qiong, Yao, 234
Queen of the Silver Screen (*Yinmu zhi hua*, 1929), 263
Quo Vadis? (1913), 261

Rain (1927), 295n17
Ramain, Paul, 287
Ramos, Antonio, 6, 15n13, 77–78
Ray, H. W., 49n75, 76–78, 81
The Red Rose (*Hong meigui*, 1926), 264
Redress a Grievance (*Wupen ji*, 1927), 263
The Regret of the Songstress (*Genühen*, 1931), 265
Ren, Jinping, 262, 265
Republic Theatre, 193
Republican, 1–5, 8–10, 12–13, 20–21, 37–38, 93, 134–35, 137–38, 147–48, 151–52, 157, 159, 224–25, 238, 244–48, 258, 270, 284, 296n26, 300n77
Resurrection (*Liangxin fuhuo*, 1926), 262
The Revival of an Old Well (*Gujing chongbo ji*, 1923), 85, 252, 263
rhythm, 277–80, 284–86, 292, 295n18, 295n20, 297–98n44; rhythmic editing, 281–83, 287
Rhythmus 23 (1923), 297n44
Rhythmus 25 (1925), 297n44
Ritz Theatre, 213
Robertson, Clarence H., 188
Rojas, Carlos, 245
Rolland, Romain, 12, 223, 234, 236
The Romance of the Opera (*Gechang chunse*, 1931), 265–66
Romance of the Songsters (*Gelu qingchao*, 1934), 150
The Room Next to the Staircase (*Zai jiaceng li*), 259
Runaway Lovers (*Luoxia guwu*, 1932), 272n11
The Russo-Japanese War, 40, 43, 65–66, 103–5
Ruttmann, Walter, 280, 286, 295n17, 297–98n44
Ryūnosuke, Akutagawa, 285

Sakuma, Samata, 105
Salome (1922), 233
Saturday (*Libai Liu*), 256–57, 259–60
Schauspiel, 290, 300n88
Schneider, Alexandra, 281
The Schooling of Xin'er (*Xin'er jiuxue ji*), 251

science, 37, 40, 55, 60–61, 89, 91, 167, 186–88, 190–91, 228, 250
shadow play (*yingxi*), 3, 6–7, 11, 20, 23, 25,33–34, 37–40, 44; as puppet show (*piyingxi*), 28–31; problem of using the term, 31–33. *See also* photo pictures; photoplay
Shadows in the Old Palace (*Gugong moying*, 1928), 263
The Shameless Girl (*Lang die*, 1926), 162, 176n41
Shanghai Battles (1913), 211
"Shanghai cinema," 1–3, 12, 134, 139–40, 152, 174n13
Shanghai Document (*Yakov Bliokh, 1927*), 298n51
Shanghai Film Company, 85, 252
Shanghai Film Study Society (Shanghai yingxi yanjiu hui), 252
Shanghai huabao (*Shanghai Pictorial*), 256
Shanghai YMCA, 3, 10–11, 179–81, 191–92, 194, 196n9, 197n22, 198n29, 198n37, 199n33, 200n49; as a cultural salon, 182–84; movie exhibitions as entertainment, 185–88; movie exhibitions for lectures, 188–91, 201n61
Shao, Zuiweng (Runje Shaw), 149, 156, 159, 167, 168, 265–66, 299n70
Shaw Brothers, 139, 163, 240n11
The Second Spring (*Erdu mei*, 1928), 263
Shenbao, 225, 249–50, 254–57, 276n56
Shenzhou Special (*Shenzhou tekan*), 233
Shi, Dongshan, 253, 263, 272n11
Silver Light (*Yinguang*), 256
Silver Star (*Yinxing*), 223, 225–26, 230, 237. *See also* Silver Star group
Silver Star group, 12, 227–31; compare *wenyi* film to literature, 231–34, 236–37
Sino-Japanese War, 4, 57, 59, 148, 167, 292n5
Sishi Company (Sei Si), 84–85, 142
A Small Circle (*Xiao xunhuan*, 1926), 142, 144
Social Puck Motion Pictures Association, 103
Society of Chinese Film Art Studies (Zhongguo dianying yishu yanjiuhui), 256
Son Abandoned (*Qi er*, 1923), 263
The Songstress Red Peony (*Genü Hongmudan*, 1930), 255, 265
South China Morning Post, 77, 80
Soviet, 13, 286–87, 289, 296n25, 298n51
The Spanish-American War (1898), 52
Spring in a Small Town (*Xiaocheng zhi chun*, 1948), 225
Spring Willow in the Wind (*Chunfeng yangliu*, 1933), 265–66
Star Motion Picture Company (Mingxing), 85, 197n24, 205–6, 211, 251–52, 255, 257, 293. *See also Mingxing Special*
Stephenson, R. H., 77, 79
The Story of a Poor Vagrant Boy (*Ku'er liulang ji*), 251, 262
Stramilano (1929), 295n17
A Strange Girl (*Guai nülang*, 1928), 265
Su, Yi, 265–66
Suffert, Thomas Henry, 206–9, 219n28, 220n30, 220n40
Sun, Fo, 136
Sun, Lianggong, 227
Sun, Shiyi, 231, 233
Sun, Yat-sen, 84, 135–36, 140, 149, 152n2, 154n20
Supreme Motion Picture Company (Tian'nan), 142, 144
Swear and Oath (*Haishi*, 1921), 226, 252–53
Swordsmen Legends 1–2 (*Jianxia qizhongqi 1–2*, 1927), 264
symbolic capital. *See* cultural capital
Symbols of Anguish (*Kumon no shocho, Kumen de xiangzeng*), 229

Taiwan Association (Taiwan Kyokai), 120
Taiwan Bureau of Police Affairs, 110, 128n41
Taiwan Daily News (*Taiwan nichinichi shimpō*), 51–54, 63–64, 67, 70n17, 103, 127n32, 130
Taiwan Dōjinsha, 106, 114–15, 127n35
Taiwan Education Society (Taiwan kyōiku-kai, TES), 8, 102, 110, 126n26, 127n35, 128nn44–45, 130n66; promoting modern images of Taiwan, 118–22; use of film in social education in the 1910s, 111–15; use of film in social education in the 1920s, 113, 116–18
Taiwan Ministry of Educational Affairs, 110–11, 114, 117, 128n41
Taiwan Patriotic Women's Association (Aikoku fujinkai, PWA), 8, 105–7, 110, 118, 125n17, 127n35
Takamatsu, Toyojirō, 102–4, 106, 108–10, 114–15, 124n6, 125n9, 126n30, 127n35, 129n65

Talking Freely (*Ziyou tan*), 249, 256–57. *See also Shenbao*
Tang, Xiaodan, 156
Tang, Xueqing, 162–63, 168, 175n22
Tanizaki, Jun'ichirō, 233
Tansui Hall, 64
Tao, Qin (Doe Ching), 224
Taylor, Jeremy, 4
teahouse (*chayuan*), 6, 19–20, 24, 27, 30–31, 44, 140, 179; setting of, 21–23
The Tea Picking Girl (*Caicha nü*, 1924), 263
technology, 5–7, 9, 13, 22–23, 32, 43, 56, 75, 87, 89–91, 102, 135, 150–51, 159–61, 171, 174, 191, 228, 245, 269, 280, 282–83, 288–89, 291
Temporary Residence (*Linshi gongguan*, 1925), 254, 264
Ten Thousand Taels of Gold (*Huangjin wanliang*, 1937), 265
Teo, Stephen, 4, 225
Terada, Torahiko, 68
Theatre Royal (City Hall), 19, 35, 73–74, 79
theory, 4, 12, 22–24, 28–30, 44, 53, 89, 91–92, 102, 159, 204–5, 223, 226–27, 231–32, 238, 248–49, 254, 257, 277, 279, 284–86, 289
A Thief Comes Unstuck (*Zuozei bucheng*, 1924), 84
A Thread of Hemp (*Yi lü ma*), 251, 262
Three Deaf-Mutes (*Sanya qiwen*, 1928), 265, 274n35
Tian, Han, 232, 236, 279, 193n12
Tidal Wave of Love (*Aihe chao*, 1926), 142–43, 144
Tides of Huangpu (*Xiepu chao*), 252, 273n24
Toda, Seizō, 113, 119, 132n102
Tonglingtoi, 140, 154n22
Tourjansky, Viktor, 287
tragic love genre (*aiqing dianying*), 252
transmedial, 13, 277–79, 281–82, 284–85, 287, 291–92, 293n7, 293n10, 293n12
Traveling Taiwan (*Taiwan no tabi*, 1929), 120
travelogue, 13, 37, 187, 192, 199n44, 200n52, 279–81
A Trip to the Moon (1902)
True Love (*Zhen'ai*, 1925), 266
Trumpet Island (1920), 257, 275n48
Tsuchiya, Tsunekichi, 106
Twin Sisters (*Zimei hua*, 1933), 225
Two Stars (*Yinhan shuangxing*, 1931), 272n11

Uchida, Kakichi, 106
Unique Film Productions (Tianyi), 139, 147, 149, 156, 163, 256–57
Unique Studio, 168–69
United Film Company (Lianhua), 148, 215
United Theatre, 213
United Theatres Corporation, 213
Universal Circulating Herald (*Hsun Huan Jih Pao*), 35
The Unknown Singer (*La Chanteur Inconnu*, 1931), 287
urban space, 2, 9, 279, 282
utsushi-e, 57–58

Variety Film Exchange, 206
vernacular modernism, 21–23, 27
Vertov, Dziga, 283, 286, 289, 295n17, 296n25, 297n43, 300n86
Victoria Cinematograph, 39, 49n75, 77–80
Victory at Gaotangzhou (*Dapo Gaotangzhou*, 1926), 263
Victory at the Nine-Dragon Mountain (*Dapo Jiulongshan*, 1930), 263
A Virtuous Daughter-in-law (*Kongmen xianxi*, 1926), 265
Vitascope, 52–53, 124n3. *See also* Edison, Thomas
Vuillermoz, Emile, 287
vulgarity, 10, 180, 188–89, 194, 199n46, 201n65

Waiting (1911), 257
Wang, Bei'er, 263
Wang, David Der-wei, 245, 292n2
Wang, Dungen, 246
Wang, Fuqing, 265–66
Wang, Hanlun, 148
Wang, Molin, 224, 238n1
Wang, Yiman, 159
Wang, Youyou, 254, 264–65
Wang, Yuanlong, 263
War is Hell (1914), 257
Ward Theatre, 213
Warner Bros., 82–83
wartime, 3, 7, 55, 62, 67, 116
Washitani, Hana, 67
wenyi film, 12, 223, 237–38, 238n1; contemporary discussions on, 224–27; as art, 227–31; literature and, 231–34, 236–37
When a Lovely Girl Bestows her Favors (*Meiren en*, 1935), 272n11

The Wife of a Worker (*Gongren zhi qi*, 1926), 272n12
A Woman's Sacrifice (1906), 257
The Woman Thou Gavest Me (1919), 257
Women Skeletons (*Hongfen kulou*, 1922), 93, 254
Wordsworth, William, 233
World Theatre, 81–85, *144*
Wretched Spirit (*Hei ji yuanhun*, 1916), 244
Wu, Cun, 288
Wu, Jianren, 244
Wu Song Makes Havoc in the Lion Building (*Qu Song danao shizilou*, 1928), *265*

Xiao, Zhiwei, 194, 203
Xilai Theatre (Hei Loi), 26, 36, 50, 75
Xin, Min, 232
Xin Guomin Theater, *144*, 147
Xinren Sepcial Issue (*Xinren tekan*), 255
Xinwenbao, 255
Xu, Bibo, 246
Xu, Hu, *263*
Xu, Zhuodai (Xu Fulin, Xu Banmei), 225–26, 246, 250, 253–55, 259, *264–65*
Xue, Juexian (Sit Gok-sin, Zhang Fei), 9, 150, 156–60, 171–72, 174n20, 174–75nn22–23, 176n41; career of, 161–63; as Platinum Dragon, 164–66, 168–70
Xu Garden (Xu Yuan), 3, 21, 24–25

Yan, Duhe (Yan Zhen), 246, 250, 255–56, *265*, 273n24
Yang, Gongliang (Yeung Kung-leong), 158
Yang, Naimei, 148
Yan Ruisheng (1921), 180
Yao, Sufeng, 256, *265–66*
Yeh, Wen-hsin, 2
Yeh, Yueh-yu Emilie, 93, 225, 227, 246
Yihua Film Company, 255
Yin, Mingzhu, 253
yingxi. *See* photoplay; shadow play
YMCA: in Guangzhou, 49n76; in Hong Kong, 36–37, 39–40, 42–44. *See also* Shanghai YMCA
Yonghan Theater, *144*, 146–47
Yu, Dafu, 228, 230, 233, 236
Yu, Fengshun (Yu Fung-shun), 80
Yu, Mo-wan, 84, 158, 175n24, 176n39, 176n41

Zhang, Henshui, 226, 246, 255
Zhang, Huichong, 148, 272n12
Zhang, Rougu, 228, 230
Zhang, Shichuan, 11, 202, 205–6, 210–12, 215, 225–26, 244, 251, 255, *262*, *265*
Zhang, Yingjin, 2, 4, 28, 101
Zhang, Zhen, 2, 20–22, 24, 33
Zhang, Zhiyun, 148
Zhao, Chen, *265*
Zhao, Shushen (Joseph Sunn, Chiu Shu-sun), 147, 149–50
Zhao, Xiaoxuan, 245
Zheng, Jiduo, *263*
Zheng, Junli, 212, 229
Zheng, Mengxia (Cheng Mang-ha), 164
Zheng, Zhengqiu, 11, 205, 210–11, 225–26, 251, *262*, *265–66*
Zhenye Film Company (Chun Yip), 83–84, 149
Zhong, Dafeng, 23, 28–29, 33
Zhonghua Theater, 146–47
Zhongyang Theater, *144*
Zhou, Jianyun, 142, 228
Zhou, Shixun, *266*
Zhou, Shoujuan, 246–47, 249–50, 253, 255–59, *266*, 275n43; adaption of *The Last Day of Pompeii*, 260–61, 263, 267–70
Zhou, Wan-Yao, 60
Zhu, Shouju, 246, 250, 252–54, *263*, *266*
Zhu, Shuangyun, *264*
Zhuang Zi Tests His Wife (*Zhuangzi shi qi*, 1913), 32
Zigomar (1911), 187
Ziluolan (*The Violet*), 256